The Literary Lacan

The Literary Lacan

From Literature to Lituraterre and Beyond

EDITED BY

SANTANU BISWAS

LONDON NEW YORK CALCUTTA

Seagull Books, 2024

First published by Seagull Books in 2012

© Santanu Biswas, 2012

ISBN 978 1 8030 9 453 3

British Library Cataloguing-in-Publication Data
A catalogue record for this book is available from the British Library

Typeset by Seagull Books, Calcutta, India
Printed and bound by WordsWorth India, New Delhi, India

Dedicated to
Professor Harjeet Singh Gill
who introduced me to Lacan

Contents

Foreword to the Second Edition

The first edition of *The Literary Lacan*, pubished in 2012, was not formally launched at any event, although Seagull Books had graciously offered me a venue and other logistical support to organise one at the time of its release. No review of the book was ever published anywhere, though there was no dearth of friends, especially overseas colleagues, who strongly wished to review it for psychoanalytic journals or for newspapers. And the volume was never formally promoted in any form anywhere, even though that would not have been a difficult thing to do. I had deliberately decided against all forms of publicity.

The fact that the first edition has sold out nevertheless, and the publication of a second edition considered necessary, proves that even in this day and age the sale of a book does not depend too much on events, reviews, and promotions, which is so heartening.

Santanu Biswas
Kolkata, 12 January 2024

Acknowledgements

Many people have helped this collection become a reality. First and foremost, I am greatly indebted to my colleague Supriya Chaudhuri on several counts. She had approved the proposal for the conference on Jacques Lacan, titled 'The Literary Lacan: From Literature to Lituraterre', provided the funds for it, assisted me in organizing the conference, suggested that we publish the proceedings, liaised with Seagull Books and paid them a subvention, all in the capacity of the coordinator of the Centre of Advanced Study in English. I am deeply grateful to Jean-Pierre Klotz, Ellie Ragland, Nancy Blake, Christopher Lane, Patricia Gherovici and others for presenting papers at the conference and making it an exceptionally stimulating event, as well as for contributing their papers to this collection. I express my gratitude to Slavoj Žižek, Jean-Michel Rabaté, Russell Grigg, Geoff Boucher, Matthew Sharpe and Gautam Basu Thakur for their contributions to this collection. My special thanks go to my students, Samya Seth, Anik Samanta, Arka Chattopadhyay and Dipanjan Maitra, all members of the Lacan Study Circle of Calcutta, for assisting me at different stages of the work. Above all, I owe a special debt of gratitude to Jacques-Alain Miller for generously granting me the permission to reprint his 'Préface' in Jacques Aubert's *Joyce avec Lacan* (1987) as the foreword to this collection, and to Russell Grigg for his fine English translation of it. Finally, a special word of thanks to Seagull Books for publishing the collection with diligence and care.

Santanu Biswas
Kolkata, 2012

Joyce with Lacan[1]

JACQUES-ALAIN MILLER

'Joyce with Lacan' does not mean James Joyce and Jacques Lacan walking arm in arm, as I have often observed Jacques Lacan and Jacques Aubert doing on their way down rue de Lille, whenever the latter brought the former the latest book about the third. No, 'Joyce with Lacan' echoes the singular title of one of Lacan's articles, his 'Kant with Sade' [1963; here 2006b],[2] in which the by-now-many readers of *The Seminar of Jacques Lacan. Book VII. The Ethics of Psychoanalysis, 1959–60* [1986; here 1992] can find, if they care to make the effort to refer to it, this seminar's major theme elaborated or, rather, incandescently illuminated.

'Kant with Sade' for Lacan means that *Philosophy in the Bedroom* [1795; here 1994] harmonizes with *The Critique of Practical Reason* [1788; here 2008], that it completes it, that it reveals its truth. Or more precisely, it uncovers the object that is missing from the experience of the moral law, namely, that in formulating [Marquis de] Sade's principle 'in the manner of Kant' (that is, the right to jouissance in the form of a universal law) one verifies that the will to the law for the law's sake, is homologous to the will to jouissance. Both divide the subject, ($), into his well-being (morality) and a good that gives him no pleasure (jouissance).

---

1 The essay was first published as 'Préface' in Jacques Aubert (ed.), *Joyce avec Lacan* (Paris: Navarin, 1987), pp. 9–12. An English translation of the essay by Josefina Ayerza and Cory Reynolds, entitled 'Joyce avec Lacan', was published in 1996 in *Lacanian Ink* 11: 7–11. This translation by Russell Grigg has been published with the permission of the author. Some of the expressions in the essay, such as, 'the essays gathered here' or 'the lecture, "Joyce le Symptôme", reproduced here' refer to the contents of Aubert's collection. All the notes and references in this essay are mine.—Ed.

2 With regard to Lacan's works: here and henceforth in this volume, the first date refers to the publication of the text in French and the second to that of the English translation cited from in the essay.

1

This impeccable demonstration is not carried out, as one would expect, without humour—as happens whenever the rational is pushed to its extreme consequences with no regard for the reasonable. Everything is here in its place, since it is a question of the superego, whose presence [Sigmund] Freud explicitly indicates in every bit of humour, and since the clinical thesis that he unveils can be articulated in the simplest of terms: the post-Oedipal superego that Freud isolates is the inheritor of the pre-Oedipal superego that Melanie Klein discovers. In other words, 'Kant with Sade' cloaks a more secret 'Freud with Klein'.

But it is no less true that a certain procedure has been uncovered that is generalizable to 'X with Y'. This way of reading via interference would not be unworthy, perhaps, of the critical paranoiac method, of illustrious memory.

I will not say whether the essays gathered here address the finesse of this title, since I whispered it to Jacques Aubert before having read them and since it is to him that I defer concerning its pertinence. No doubt Joyce is here spoken about in Lacan's terms, rather than Lacan in the manner of Joyce. And myself, even when I make a special effort, what do I do in my course in the Department of Psychoanalysis [Département de Psychanalyse, Université de Paris VIII, Saint-Denis] if not speak about Lacan in Lacan's terms? This would not be very promising if it were not the case that there is more than one Lacan . . .

Pursuing this line of approach, I take this opportunity to comment on how Joyce came to enter Lacan's considerations. I will therefore say, as preface to this collection, what it was that Lacan wanted to do with Joyce.

I will go straight to 'a letter, a litter' [Lacan 2006d: 18] that he first invokes in 1956 in the 'Seminar on "The Purloined Letter"' to emphasize that a letter is not merely a signifier. A letter is a message; it is also an object.

What is a signifier, in fact? This is the word with which we designate a sign in so far as it has a signified effect. But this is not all that a sign is. It is possible to think it is when one speaks (since the sound dissipates, or so we think, despite the evidence of the Freudian unconscious), but not when one writes: a letter, once read, remains. Will it end up in the rubbish bin? Will it be torn up, archived, displayed, lost, sold, purloined? In each case, the destiny of the letter is disjoined from its function as a signifier; the addressee of one is not the addressee of the other. What, then, shall we call a letter as such? A sign; but a sign that is defined, not by its signified effect but by its nature as an object.

This is where Lacan's [Edgar Allan] Poe has to be read with his [André] Gide—'The Youth of Gide, or the Letter and Desire' [1958; here 2006e]—when Madeleine, burning André's letters, of which there were no copies, revealed their meaning as jouissance, their fetish nature. It is not the signified effect that is at issue here, but, beyond that, what jouissance, always extracted from the sender, the sign as written bears within it—and this is why, whatever becomes of a letter's support, it always comes back to him to close the account.

To restate: the function of speech does not exhaust the field of language. Why not rewrite the title with which Lacan inaugurates his teaching, making it consistent with the complement that he adds to it four years later: 'Function, Instance and Field of Speech, Letter and Language in Psychoanalysis'?[3]

Take note of the fact that it is clinical experience that requires this complement. For how are symptoms to be explained without implying letters in the structure of language? Psychoanalyzable symptoms are interpretable: a symptom is therefore, undoubtedly, a message; but its consistence is not only semantic, it includes this jouissance that Freud discovered as the limit of the power of interpretation, in what he called the 'negative therapeutic reaction'. It is in this respect that symptoms, if they are supported by a structure that is identical to the structure of language, are not articulated in a process of speech, but are 'inscribed in a writing process' [Lacan 2006c: 371]. This is explicitly formulated by Lacan in 1957.

How are jouissance and meaning conjugated in the writing of symptoms? This question is everywhere present in his teaching; the large graph offers a Freudian solution, through the interference of fantasy ($\$<>a$) in the signification of needs, $s(A)$; Lacan re-formulates this interference *de novo* in *Television* [1974; here1990] as the *sens joui* or *jouis-sens*, 'enjoy-meant', and this leads

---

3 The essay being referred to here is 'The Function and Field of Speech and Language in Psychoanalysis' [1956; here 2006a], more popularly known as 'The Discourse of Rome', as it was presented in 1953 at the Rome Congress at the Institute of Psychology at the University of Rome and then published in 1956.

him to 'Joyce le Symptôme' [Joyce-the-Symptom, delivered in 1975; here 1987a and b][4]; that is, to question psychoanalysis in the field of language on the basis of writing.

For this reason, the schema of communication loses its prevalence; while the unconscious is structured like a *language*, it is not initially the Other's *discourse*. It only becomes so by means of the artifice of psychoanalytic experience. Where jouissance, always autistic, was, analysis shall bring signified effects to be; it operates on symptoms by introducing a special effect of signification into them, called the 'subject supposed to know'; but in themselves symptoms say nothing to anyone. A symptom is encipherment and it is jouissance; it is the pure jouissance of writing.

This year, I have thus commented at length on the definition of a symptom that Lacan commenced his later teaching with: 'the manner in which each person enjoys the unconscious, in so far as the unconscious determines him'. This seminar, 'Le Séminaire. Livre XXII. R. S. I., 1974–75' [1975], would culminate with the lecture, 'Joyce le Symptôme', reproduced here, in which he announced the seminar for the following year, *Le Séminaire. Livre XXIII. Le Sinthome, 1975–76* [2005] a lesson from which can be read below.

It was a matter at that time for Lacan—who grasped this?—of the most radical questioning ever formulated of the very foundation of psychoanalysis, conducted on the basis that symptoms are outside discourse.

Hence the abandonment of previous constructions that were diversely established on the structure of discourse, and the recourse to a topology in which the symbolic, as the locus of the Other, does not hover over the imaginary, nor encompass the real as impossible, but returns to the ranks as one of the three. Hence the reference to the insignia of Joyce, handling the letter outside of signified effects, for the purpose of pure jouissance. Evoking psychosis was in no way applied psychoanalysis; on the contrary, it was *with* the Joyce-symptom held to be unanalyzable, calling the analyst's discourse into question, in so far

---

4 'Joyce le Symptôme I' was delivered in Paris on 16 June 1975 at the opening of the Fifth International James Joyce Symposium, and 'Joyce le Symptôme II' on 20 June.

as a subject who is identified with his or her symptom is closed off to the artifice of analysis. And perhaps an analysis has no better end . . .

With these few lines I hope to have made you sufficiently aware that there is not one of Lacan's sentences, as opaque as they can initially seem to the reader, that cannot be explained by a veritable 'order of reasons', throwing light in return on questions that are still unperceived—and in the first instance, on the analytic experience.

Inspiring no contempt for artists. Inviting analysts, rather, to learn from the example.

30 March 1987

Translated from the French by Russell Grigg

References

ENGLISH SOURCES

KANT, Immanuel. 2008. *The Critique of Practical Reason* (Thomas Kingsmill Abott trans.). Virginia: Wilder Publications.

LACAN, Jacques. 1990. *Television: A Challenge to the Psychoanalytic Establishment* (Joan Copjec ed., Denis Hollier, Rosalind Krauss and Annette Michelson trans). New York and London: W. W. Norton.

————. 1992. *The Seminar of Jacques Lacan. Book VII. The Ethics of Psychoanalysis, 1959–60* (Jacques-Alain Miller ed.). New York and London: W. W. Norton.

————. 2006a. 'The Function and Field of Speech and Language in Psycho-analysis' in *Écrits: The First Complete Edition in English* (Bruce Fink trans.). New York and London: W. W. Norton, pp. 31–106.

————. 2006b. 'Kant with Sade' in *Écrits: The First Complete Edition in English* (Bruce Fink trans.). New York and London: W. W. Norton, pp. 645–68.

————. 2006c. 'Psychoanalysis and Its Teaching' in *Écrits: The First Complete Edition in English* (Bruce Fink trans.). New York and London: W. W. Norton, pp. 364–83.

———. 2006d. 'Seminar on "The Purloined Letter"' in *Écrits: The First Complete Edition in English* (Bruce Fink trans.). New York and London: W. W. Norton, pp. 6–48.

———. 2006e. 'The Youth of Gide, or the Letter and Desire' in *Écrits: The First Complete Edition in English* (Bruce Fink trans.). New York and London: W. W. Norton, pp. 623–44.

SADE, Marquis de. 1994. 'Philosophy in the Bedroom' in *Justine, Philosophy in the Bedroom, and Other Writings* (Richard Seaver and Austryn Wainhouse trans). New York: Grove Press, pp. 177–370.

FRENCH SOURCES

LACAN, Jacques. 1956. 'Fonction et champ de la parole et du langage en psychanalyse'. *La Psychanalyse* 1: 81–166. Subsequently published in *Écrits* (1966).

———. 1957a. 'La psychanalyse et son enseignement'. *Bulletin de la société Française de philosophie* 49: 65–85. Subsequently published in *Écrits* (1966).

———. 1957b. 'Le séminaire sur "La Lettre Volée"'. *La Psychanalyse* 2: 1–44. Subsequently published in *Écrits* (1966).

———. 1958. 'Jeunesse de Gide ou la lettre et désir'. *Critique* 131: 291–315. Subsequently published in *Écrits* (1966).

———. 1963. 'Kant avec Sade'. *Critique* 191: 291–313. Subsequently published in *Écrits* (1966).

———. 1966. *Écrits*. Paris: Éditions du Seuil.

———. 1974. *Télévision*. Paris: Éditions du Seuil.

———. 1975. 'Le Séminaire. Livre XXII. R. S. I., 1974–75'. *Ornicar? Bulletin périodique du champ freudien* 2: 87–105; 3: 96–110; 4: 92–106); 5: 17–66).

———. 1986. *Le Séminaire. Livre VII. L'éthique de la psychoanalyse, 1959–60* (Jacques-Alain Miller ed.). Paris: Éditions du Seuil.

———. 1987a. 'Joyce le Symptôme I' in Jacques Aubert (ed.), *Joyce Avec Lacan*. Paris: Navarin, pp. 21–9.

———. 1987b. 'Joyce le Symptôme II' in Jacques Aubert (ed.), *Joyce Avec Lacan*. Paris: Navarin, pp. 31–6.

———. 2005. *Le Séminaire. Livre XXIII. Le Sinthome, 1975–76* (Jacques-Alain Miller ed.). Paris: Éditions du Seuil.

Introduction

SANTANU BISWAS

This collection of essays entitled *The Literary Lacan: From Literature to Lituraterre and Beyond* evolved largely from the papers presented at the first international conference on Jacques Lacan in India, held under the aegis of the Centre of Advanced Study in English and the Department of English, Jadavpur University, Calcutta, on 3 and 4 December 2007. The title of the collection is derived from the title of the conference.

At several important moments in his teaching, Lacan read psychoanalysis with literature, primarily European, by invoking, usually, a set of literary works. Among the *littérateurs* he spoke or wrote about, Sophocles, Dante Alighieri, William Shakespeare, Molière, Marquis de Sade, Johann Wolfgang von Goethe, Ernst Theodor Wilhelm Hoffmann, Edgar Allan Poe, Lewis Carroll, Anton Chekhov, Benjamin Franklin Wedekind, Paul Claudel, André Gide, James Joyce, Jean Genet, Maurice Blanchot and Marguerite Duras are, in varying degrees, the important ones. In addition, he spoke or wrote fairly extensively on tragedy, comedy, rhetoric and what he termed *lituraterre* in contexts of great importance to psychoanalysis. In the course of doing so, Lacan also commented on literary criticism—especially of *Hamlet* and Joyce—and, in the essay 'Lituraterre' (written in 1971; here 2001a), designated literary criticism in general as a university discourse that could be brought closer to the psychoanalyst's discourse. There are other brief but significant remarks on literature and literary criticism in some of his well-known and not-so-well-known non-literary texts, such as the following comment made in course of his conversation with the students of Yale University in 1975: 'Explaining art by the unconscious appears to me very suspect; however, it is what analysts do. Explaining art by the symptom appears to me more serious' (1976a: 4). Despite the magnitude of Lacan's 'literary' output, no book-length study has been devoted to it in English yet, barring Jean-Michel Rabaté's *Jacques Lacan: Psychoanalysis and the Subject of Literature* (2001). The present collection addresses this and other gaps in the interface between Lacan and literature in terms of a threefold aim: First, to study some of the literature-related works of Lacan from clinical, philosophical and literary points of view so as to begin to assess the nature and extent of his contribution to literary studies and, through literature, to psychoanalysis itself, which is addressed in the close readings of several seminal works of Lacan not yet formally available in English, such as, the complete seminar on *Hamlet* (1958–59), the homages to Duras (1965) and Carroll (1966), 'Lituraterre' (written in 1971) and the seminar and lectures on Joyce (1975–76).

Second, to read works of literature in conjunction with Lacan's teachings so as to explicate one another, to extend Lacan's reading of a set of literary works to areas of the works not addressed by him and to extend his reading of a work to another work by the same author. These exercises have been carried out on Samuel Beckett's 1972 play *Not I* (here 2003), Lewis Carroll's/Charles Dodgson's writings and Marguerite Duras's 1958 novel *Moderato Cantabile* (here 1965) respectively.

Third, to address various broad questions pertaining to 'literature and psychoanalysis' following Lacan, such as, the trajectory of the 'literary' letter in Lacan's works; the crucial lessons on 'literature and psychoanalysis' in 'Lituraterre'; the applicability or non-applicability of literature on psychoanalysis; transsexual memoirs as *sinthome*; and interpretation of the colonizer's anxiety.

The collection comprises an essay by Jacques-Alain Miller which serves as the foreword, 11 essays distributed in four parts and an afterword. I will briefly introduce them here in the words of their respective authors.

In his essay entitled 'Joyce with Lacan', Miller first explains the title by clarifying that it is an echo of the phrase 'Kant with Sade' used in *The Seminar of Jacques Lacan. Book VII. The Ethics of Psychoanalysis, 1959–60* (1986; here 1992) and later in *Écrits* (1966), by which Lacan meant that, on the question of the superego and its imperatives, Sade's *Philosophy in the Bedroom* (1795; here 1994; arguably, a literary work) completes and renders truthful *The Critique of Practical Reason* (1788; here 2008) by Immanuel Kant. By stating it thus, Miller argues, Lacan added a new phrase to the original 'Freud with Klein', because 'the post-Oedipal superego that Freud isolates is the inheritor of the pre-Oedipal superego that Melanie Klein discovers.' This feature, Miller writes, can in fact be generalized to an 'X with Y', as a way of reading through interference that he practised in his own course in the Department of Psychoanalysis [Département de Psych-analyse, Université de Paris VIII, Saint-Denis] by reading one Lacan with an-other Lacan. Miller then asks: how did Lacan come to consider Joyce? He begins his answer, as well as a demonstration of reading one Lacan with another, with 'a letter, a litter' that Lacan invoked in his 1956 'Seminar on "The Purloined Letter"' (1957b; here 2006d) to emphasize that there is nothing but the signifier in a letter, although a letter as such—that is, a letter disjoined from the function of the signifier—is a sign defining its nature as an object and not as a message. Miller suggests that reading Lacan's Poe with Lacan's Gide ('The Youth of Gide, or the Letter and Desire', 1958; here 2006e) on the question of the letter and rewriting the title of the essay, 'The Function and Field of Speech and Language in Psychoanalysis' (1956; here 2006a), as 'Function, Instance and Field of Speech, Letter and Language in Psychoanalysis'—by taking into account its counterpart in *Écrits*, 'The Instance of the Letter in the Unconscious, or Reason since Freud' (1957a; here 2006b)—explicates that the question for Lacan was: how does one render the symptom without implicating the letter in the structure of language? The psychoanalyzable symptom is a message that can be inter-preted, but its consistency is not only semantic but also includes the jouissance discovered by Sigmund Freud as a limit to interpretation. More pertinently, with reference to his formulation since 1957 that the symptom is 'inscribed in a process of writing' and not articulated in a process of speech, Lacan's question was: how do jouissance and sense conjoin in the writing of the symptom? Miller explains that Lacan first proposed a Freudian answer to it in the graph of desire, in the form of 'the interference of fantasy ($S \Diamond a$) in the signification of needs, $s(A)$', then re-formulated this interference in *Television* (1974; here 1990) as *sens joui*, or *jouis-sens*, and from there, in order to 'question psychoanalysis in the field of language on the basis of writing', he turned to Joyce and produced his 1975 'Joyce le Symptôme' (Joyce-the-Symptom; here 1987a and b), stressing therein that 'the unconscious [that] is structured like a language' becomes 'the Other's discourse' due to the artifice of the psychoanalytic experience. The an-alytic experience, while operating on the symptom, enables the effects of the signified to arise at the place of an autistic jouissance by introducing 'the subject supposed to know' as a special effect of signification, an effect that stands not for a message addressed to the Other but for an 'encipherment and [. . .] jouissance', a 'pure jouissance of writing'. At about the same time, Miller points out, in 'Le Séminaire. Livre XXII. R. S. I., 1974–75' (1975b) that was to be followed by *Le Séminaire. Livre XXIII. Le Sinthome, 1975–76* (2005), Lacan defined the symptom as 'the manner in which each person enjoys the unconscious, in so far as the unconscious determines him', which was, for him at that time, the most radical question ever formulated in psychoanalysis, and following which he moved from the structure of discourse to topology, in which the symbolic 'returns to the ranks as one of the three [orders]', and from there, with reference to 'the insignia of Joyce', to the letter of pure jouissance, outside the effects of the signifier. Lacan evoked 'psychosis' in this context, argues Miller, primarily to put the discourse of the analyst into question, given that Joyce's symptom was unanalyzable, for 'a subject who is identified with his or her symptom is closed off to the artifice of analysis,' which Miller considers possibly the best end of an analysis. He concludes by stressing that Lacan's phrases can thus be explained, always, in the 'order of reasons', and that the analyst can learn from the examples offered by the artist.

The nature of Lacan's engagement with literature bears at the broadest level the 'X with Y' pattern mentioned by Miller in the form of its 'early with later' structure. Briefly put, setting aside Lacan's sonnet, 'Panta Rei' (1929)[1], and the chapter of his 1932 doctoral thesis in psychiatry, devoted to one of his first patients who was a writer, whom he named 'Aimée' (Beloved) after the heroine of her autobiographical romance, as his pre-psychoanalytic engagement with literature, and focusing instead on what Lacan the psychoanalyst and teacher of psychoanalysis had to say about literature, he can be found devoting large parts of several early seminars to reading the Coufontaine trilogy (1911–16)[2], 'The Purloined Letter' (1844; here 1983), *Hamlet* (here 2003) and

---

1 A slightly different version titled 'Hiatus Irrationalis' was published in 1933 in the journal *Le Phare de Neuilly* 3/4.

2 The Coufontaine trilogy by Paul Claudel comprises the three plays *L'Otage* [*The Hostage*, 1911], *Le Pain dur* [*Crusts*, 1914] and *Le Père humilié* [*The Humiliation of the Father*, 1916].

Antigone in order to shed light on the concepts of the letter, desire, between two deaths and transference in psychoanalysis, which constitute his early teachings on literature. This is followed by a break of almost a decade during which Lacan spoke on Carroll and wrote on Duras and others but did not engage with literature in the same serious and sustained manner as before. He resumed his serious engagement with literature with 'Lituraterre', which marked a radical shift of focus from the signifier in the symbolic to the letter in the real. Following 'Lituraterre' as the pivot, he spoke on Joyce at the Fifth International James Joyce Symposium in Paris in 1975 and devoted a good part of *Le Sinthome* to the Irish writer. These constitute Lacan's later teachings on literature. These two sets of teachings offer, very broadly speaking, an '*Atè*'-based conceptualization of tragedy and a litter-based conceptualization of literature.[3] Evidently therefore, the two cannot be reduced to one and must be read with or against one another.

The first part of the collection entitled 'The Literary Lacan' comprises two essays that, in course of dealing with Lacan's literary metaphors and the question of the applicability of literature on psychoanalysis respectively, highlight the important signposts of Lacan's long and meaningful engagement with literature. In the first of these, 'From the Letter to the *Objet petit a*: The Evolution of Lacan's Literary Metaphors', Nancy Blake focuses on four points concerning the letter and writing in Lacan: First, she examines the figuration of the letter in the 'Seminar on "The Purloined Letter"' with respect to reading, language, truth, power, owner, sender, holder and above all, the subject or subjects, to

---

3 *Atè* (Ath) is the name of the ancient Greek goddess of criminal recklessness or fatal blindness and consequent punishment. The word '*Atè*', therefore, variously stands for the spirit of recklessness; divine punishment for recklessness, especially in the form of bewilderment caused by delusion or blindness, or ruin brought about by such recklessness or blindness; and destiny. Accordingly, it is often translated as the spirit of delusion, infatuation, blind folly, rash action and reckless impulse leading to ruin. In Lacan's reading, too, *Atè* broadly stands for criminal recklessness and self-destruction; but more precisely, it stands for the limit between life and death. He took the word from Sophocles's *Antigone* in which it is repeated 20 times, and explained *Hamlet*, *Antigone* and the Coufontaine trilogy in terms of this concept.

explain how 'all identifications, even sexual identifications, can be seen as related to the sway of the letter'. Second, she examines the relation between the letter and desire, and the hole caused by Gide's lost love letters as discussed by Lacan in 'The Youth of Gide, or the Letter and Desire', to explain why the letter is an 'illustration of the fact that the speaking subject elects a fetish to hide the lack he experiences in the field of desire'. Third, she briefly touches upon the *a* of the *objet petit a* as a letter, pointing to its function with respect to the hole in the locus of the A (*Autre*), and its relation to the Thing (*la Chose*). Fourth, with reference to *Le Sinthome*, she examines the relation of writing to truth and the real, as well as the mission of art to 'bypass the impact of the symptom'. She concludes that in 'the case of Joyce, Lacan comes to the function of art, per se, as the *sinthome* as that which binds together the registers of symbolic, imaginary and real and thus prevents the subject from falling into psychosis'.

In the second essay entitled 'Psychoanalysis Applicable and Inapplicable: The Case of Literature', Jean-Michel Rabaté raises, problematizes and replies to a set of extremely pertinent questions, such as: if '[p]sychoanalysis can be applied in a strict sense only as treatment and therefore to a speaking and hearing subject', as Lacan had claimed, then can psychoanalysis be applied to literature? Is it more appropriate to apply literature to psychoanalysis? What are the problems of canonical psychoanalytic literary criticism, especially in terms of the limits of its conclusion that literature anticipates or parallels the findings of psychology? How does one account for Lacan's seeming vacillation between psychobiographical and structuralist literary criticism? How did Lacan manage to offer a centrality to the letter and literature in psychoanalysis without ceasing to eschew application as exemplification? How far was Jacques Derrida justified in critiquing Lacan's 'illustration' of psychoanalysis with literary 'examples'? In reply to these and other questions, Rabaté explains that Lacan was opposed to Freud's non-dialectical reading of literature and his strategy of 'verifying' psychoanalysis by 'applying' it to literature, as well as to a reductive structuralism that limited itself to the logic of the signifier, and was interested in criticism that illuminated the textual processes. He was *contre* psychobiographical literary criticism not in the sense of 'against' but in the sense of 'leaning against' it. He variously avoided the reduction of textual singularity to dogmatic schemes by using his theory of the *sinthome* while reading Joyce, by constantly reopening

SANTANU BISWAS

Freud's texts and reading them *literally* as well as *literarily*, and by producing readings of literature that were themselves literary. Rabaté maintains that a distinction should be made between application and exemplification and Lacan's literary criticism should be viewed more as the 'textual experiments of a quester' than the 'definitive statement of a founder'. In the concluding section of his essay, he suggests that Lacanian literary criticism should entail reading literature *with* psychoanalysis and not applying psychoanalysis to literature, and demonstrates this with a brief reading of Vladimir Nabokov's *Lolita* (1955; here 1974) with Lacan's notion of perversion.

The second part of the collection entitled 'From Literature' consists of three essays dealing with Lacan's works on *Hamlet*, Carroll and Joyce respectively, produced at three very different moments of his teaching. In the first of these, '"To Be or Not . . .": Lacan and the Meaning of Being in Shakespeare's *Hamlet*', Matthew Sharpe, focusing on the centrality of the *Seinsfrage* (question of the meaning of Being) to Hamlet in Lacan's reading of the play, extracts lessons from the eight sessions of 'The Seminar of Jacques Lacan. Book VI. Desire and its Interpretation, 1958–59' (1958–59a)[4] devoted to Shakespeare's masterpiece. First, the 'horror of femininity' that characterizes Hamlet's relation to Ophelia between the two moments of his proclamation of love for her suggests that if *Hamlet* is the drama of Hamlet's failing desire then Ophelia is the very symbol of this repudiation of desire. Second, Lacan's emphasis is on the Hamlet-Gertrude axis and not on Hamlet's relations to Claudius. More specifically, the desire of the mother is responsible for putting Hamlet's time out of joint, which Hamlet himself speaks of candidly from the very beginning. It is only after this that his father's ghost instructs him to end Gertrude's 'luxury' with Claudius, which he fails to do because he cannot comprehend her desire or what shaped it. This explains Lacan's *matheme* S(Ø) that stands for the signifier of the

---

4 Here and henceforth in this volume, with regard to the citation of unpublished translations of Lacan's works, unless otherwise stated, the date in the parenthesis refers to the year of publication (or delivery of the seminar in some cases; here, for example) of the version of the French text translated and the page numbers correspond to the web version of the English translation used.

final inconsistency of the Other; in this case the incomprehensible aspect of Gertrude's desire. This S(Ø) is the abyss into which Hamlet had stared; and, by being 'fixed' in his mother's desire due to his inability to fathom this S(Ø), he is turned into the 'reverse side of a message that is not even his own' (Lacan 1958–59a: Session 17, p. 265). Third, *Hamlet* is about what persists when the symbolic order fails, of which there are extraordinary indicators from its very first lines. It is, moreover, a play about the failure to mourn, and more specifically, about the consequences of Hamlet's failure to mourn the loss of the phallus. Fourth, when the opportunity of killing Claudius arises, as he sits praying, Hamlet's worry about 'the eternal "to be" of Claudius' stays his hand. Besides, the phallus, which is with Claudius in this case, is completely outside its usual Oedipal position because it is 'well and truly real here', which makes it extraordinarily difficult to strike at. Moreover, the phallus is a 'shade'. It is something which 'always slips through your fingers', like a 'Thing of Nothing'. Fifth, what is at stake in the play is an inability to fully engage in the symbolic order except by the repetition which a humorist portrayed with the famous 'to be or not'. He scratched his head in order to be able to continue: 'to be or not . . .', 'to be or not . . .', and in the repetition he found the end of the sentence. Sixth, in the episode involving Hamlet and Laertes inside Ophelia's grave, Hamlet's imaginary identification with Laertes can be seen, which will play itself out in the final encounter, as well as his symbolic identification with himself in his concluding remark: the one who is crying 'is I, Hamlet the Dane'. Seventh, in Hamlet's duel with Laertes framed by the symbolic register, there is a pun on 'foil' in Hamlet's expression, 'I'll be your foil, Laertes.' It suggests how he will set off his rival's brilliance and also be his nemesis in the duel, without knowing that the tip of Laertes' foil has been laced with poison and that he will shortly come to wield it fatally against both Laertes and the king. But he had to be mortally wounded by this death-dealing phallus, and know himself to be dying, in order to assume the capacity to act.

In the next essay, 'Lewis Carroll and Psychoanalytic Criticism: Why Nothing Adds Up in Wonderland', Christopher Lane separates Carroll's novellas from psychobiography and reductive quasi-Freudian readings by William Empson, Phyllis Greenacre and Paul Schilder. He focuses instead on Lacan's and Carroll's respective interests in nonsense and adaptation to demonstrate how fiction can alter our understanding of crises in the symbolic order. Lane goes on to argue along the following, overlapping lines. First, the relationship between nonsense and joy that Lacan revealed in Carroll's fiction points to 'discordances of personality' that highlight the ordeal of Alice's (and, by extension, our) adaptation to a contingent, often-senseless symbolic order. Second, the ontological question that concludes *Through the Looking-Glass and What Alice Found There* (1872; here 1998)—'Which dreamed it?'—invites us to wonder whether Carroll, the Oxford don Charles Dodgson, or even Alice herself should claim authorship of the madcap fantasy. Third, according to Lacan, Carroll wanted to 'prepare' Alice for the lesson that 'one only ever passes through a door one's own size' (Lacan 2002a: 11), which suggests that an answer can emerge only after one has discovered how to ask its corresponding question. Consequently, much happens in Wonderland the wrong way round, playing havoc with cause and effect, and with meaning and intention. 'Is interpretation a key that unlocks secrets,' asks Lane, 'or are secrets the enigmatic signifiers that taunt and seduce us into a world of symbols which, as readers and children, we are not quite equipped to understand?' The provocation of enigmatic signifiers and the task of deciphering them extend to Wonderland's legal apparatus, too, as it is governed by a presumption that guilt long precedes any state of innocence, a key reason accusations of wrongdoing predate even the fantasy to act. Sir John Tenniel's illustrations capture this ontological crisis, Lane argues, by emphasizing not just the difficulty but also the *price* of Alice's attempt to conform and adapt to circumstances. She is either too small or too big for the world; she is unprepared for it yet finds herself in it long after the rules and laws have been established. In this understanding, Carroll anticipates the radical Freudian idea that one arrives too quickly into a symbolic order that one fathoms and comprehends, if at all, only quizzically and belatedly. Fourth, Carroll's fiction often focuses on the play and limits of meaning across numerous semantic and ontological registers, the resulting 'vertigo' dramatizing the difficulty for Alice (as for us) of adapting to the world of language and symbols. The rules and rituals governing everything in Wonderland and Outerland (the imaginary realm of Carroll's proto-Joycean novel *Sylvie and Bruno*, 1889; here 1991) seem whimsical and arbitrarily enforced, which casts the adult world as undesirable, authoritarian and perverse. One instance of this in *Looking-Glass* is when Alice tries to progress from the third to the fourth square on the chessboard by train, a surreal idea in itself. She cannot fulfil the demands made of her—she cannot buy a ticket for the journey, because a ticket office does not exist. The asymmetry between Wonderland and the adult world seems to indicate to Alice that the symbolic order does not and cannot add up. Fifth, Carroll's novellas complicate 'the notion of a lucid, unidirectional ontogenesis'. But what is truly 'Lacanian' about them is that the young girl's bizarre, unpredictable experiences work themselves out without tragedy, teleology or recourse to a preordained fate. At other times, Alice tries to fathom whether the symbolic order is hiding an enigma or, indeed, hiding that it does not have one. Red King's engagement with automatic writing implies that language speaks us, revealing truths one might wish to veil, especially the truth that there often is not much to veil. The drama of symbolization instead plays itself out on the surface of Carroll's fiction. Sixth, Carroll's ontology makes unexpected patterns of meaning and resemblance collide in Wonderland. Its many creatures miraculously share the same language yet rarely communicate straightforwardly. Moreover, these creatures, for the most part insistently singular, do not easily coexist. Seventh, Carroll viewed the symbolic order of the Victorians as equally nonsensical, for in *Sylvie and Bruno*, Fairyland and Outerland are largely interchangeable. Relatedly, according to Lacan, one reason Carroll's fiction could produce a *joie singulière* is that the novelist made the stubborn refusal of children to adapt to the world look almost ethical. Eighth, the consequence of adaptation to the symbolic order in Carroll is a jarring melancholy in the gaps between the games. White Knight and especially his song 'I'll tell thee everything I can: / There's little to relate,' and the surreal, quasi-cannibalism of 'The Walrus and the Carpenter' interlude are two instances of it in *Looking-Glass*, both of which indicate that adaptation to the world of adults is risky and not without costs. In Lacanian terms, one receives some meaning in exchange for being, which is not a fair exchange. And those witnessing the loss cannot symbolize it completely, because their recognition of the loss comes too late: they are already on the side of language. From this Lane concludes that the *Alice* stories subtly reveal the deceits and falsehoods of the symbolic order. To use his words, 'In refusing to imitate the comic pretensions of a system bound by the contingency of signifiers,

Carroll gives us that world aslant and askew. His oblique perspective under-scores the drives and psychical effects that exceed symbolization—drives that in his fiction come to assume an ardent, impossible meaning.'

In the next essay, 'Joyce: Lacan's Sphinx', Geoff Boucher examines *Le Sinthome*, especially the ideas of 'nomination', the *sinthome*, *LOM*, the Joycean ego as an alternative to psychosis, the character of the unconscious and the replacement of *linguistrickery* by a new *faunetics*, and claims that this seminar which constitutes Lacan's last revision of his entire corpus, gives rise to two main unresolved problems: did Lacan regard Joyce as a psychotic? And, to what degree does the seminar represent a belated *rapprochement* with Derrida on the question of 'generalized writing'? On the second problem, Boucher states that Lacan's question in this seminar, indicative of his involvement in a theoretical confrontation with Derrida is: given that the identity of the speaking subject is generated in the anonymity of the signifying chain, how can the style of the subject and its idiosyncratic adoption of language that is expressive of a unique subjectivity be accounted for? Boucher thinks that although Lacan stated otherwise, he was highly sceptical of the deconstructive effort that sought to demonstrate that the dissemination of the textual infrastructures explained the Joycean text. Boucher thinks that whereas deconstruction grinds out the same threnody on every author, Joyce, for Lacan, is a signature; and that Lacan—because he proposed that the *objet petit a* is a non-specular double for the subject—could, unlike Derrida, explain the emergence of meaning without reverting to the fiction of the self-present intentionality of the speaking subject.

Boucher then questions Lacan's strategy of interpreting not the uncon-scious in the text but the activity of writing as a symptom. That Lacan's question is not regarding the meaning of these texts but regarding the function of his art for Joyce, Boucher thinks, commits Lacan to a biographical approach that eventually forced him to regard the Joycean text as unreadable. He then argues that Lacan interpreted both *A Portrait of the Artist as a Young Man* (1916) and *Ulysses* (1922) as autobiographical novels because the crucial issue for him was the failure of the paternal function, by way of the failure of John Joyce, as that to which Joyce responded by making his writing act a supplement to this fail-ure. The *sinthome* as this supplement knotted together the real, symbolic and imaginary and thus helped Joyce retain his sanity. Joyce-the-Symptom therefore

18

signifies that Joyce the literary name is the symptom of Joyce the man. This also implies that Joyce made a Name (of the Father) for himself through his endless writing, thus fathering himself, which, Boucher thinks, led Lacan to interpret Bloom and Stephen as sons rather than as a father–son duo, and rendered Joyce's literary fathers, Homer, Dante and, especially, Shakespeare, problematic for Lacan. Lacan did not fully follow up this insight in *Portrait*, *Ulysses* and *Finnegans Wake* (1939) possibly in order to be able to interpret art as symptom.

Regarding the first problem, Boucher points to four symptoms of the psychotic process, identified by Lacan, in Joyce: hallucinations in the form of imposed voices and a redeemer delusion; disintegration of language into letters and the irruption of the real in the form of epiphany; aetiological indications of a schizophrenic situation in the family and Joyce's daughter Lucia's schizophrenic breakdown; in his reading of the transition from *Portrait* to *Ulysses*, Lacan demonstrated that the lack of the Name-of-the Father is a correlate of the existence of a sexual relation, in so far as Joyce lacked the Name-of-the-Father until he forged one for himself, and at the same time shared a sexual relation with Nora Joyce (née Barnacle). Nora, as the Woman, fitted him like a glove; that is to say, there was nothing contingent about their encounter. And yet, argues Boucher, instead of declaring the Joycean text psychotic, Lacan regarded it as unreadable and a mimicry of schizophrenic discourse.

Boucher then moves to a question that he thinks the readers of *Le Sinthome* are likely to encounter; namely, does the *sinthome* appear when the Name-of-the-Father fails, or does every person have a *sinthome*? He suggests in reply that although Lacan preferred the second option, his propositions that Joyce was 'disinvested from the unconscious', that is to say he was not a divided subject, and that Joyce was not analyzable because he believed in his symptom, are perfectly reasonable with Joyce but hard to apply to everyone. Finally, Boucher suggests that Lacan's thesis is really a Joycean anti-psychoanalysis in so far as it echoes the following well-known positions of Joyce: 'the suspicion towards both Jung and Freud, the rejection of the unconscious as operating at any level other than the collective/mythical, the radical individual ability to transcend linguistic determinations, the insistence on the possibility of a harmonious sexual relation, [and] the belief that it is possible after all to fabricate a paternal signifier and thereby choose one's own destiny'. Based on his study,

Boucher concludes that readers of *Le Sinthome* should be 'careful' before ascribing to it the status of a wholly new psychoanalytic theory.

The third part of the collection called 'To Lituraterre' comprises two essays written from literary and clinical perspectives respectively on 'Lituraterre'. In my essay, 'A Literary Introduction to "Lituraterre"', I have concentrated on the following four fundamental questions concerning literary studies and psychoanalysis raised and addressed by Lacan in this essay. First, how might literature turn towards *lituraterre* in search of a discourse that might not be a semblance? Second, is the literature of the littoral a discourse that is not a semblance? Third, what should be the concern of psychoanalytic literary criticism that is not a university discourse? Fourth, how might writers try to instal the sexual relationship? I have closely referred to the translation of 'Lituraterre' in *Autres écrits* (2001), and 'The Seminar of Jacques Lacan. Book XVIII. On a Discourse that Might not be a Semblance, 1971' (1971), especially the session dated 12 May 1971 on *lituraterre*, in order to comprehend Lacan's answers to these questions. First, there are several instances of this in the essay, from the title to the 'writing effect' in the Japanese tongue, but the most revealing instance is the apologue on the *sibériétique*. Second, the literature of the littoral comes closest to but, in the final analysis, is not really a discourse that is not a semblance. Third, psychoanalytic literary criticism should concentrate on how the letter makes holes in writing, and compare the holes made by the letter in literary and psychoanalytic works. Fourth, writers trying to instal the sexual relationship should enable an 'asceticism of writing' to rejoin an impossible 'it is written.'

In the next essay, 'The Littoral Condition of the Letter', Jean-Pierre Klotz regards 'Lituraterre' as the starting point of Lacan's later teachings in which the *objet petit a* and the Borromean knots became increasingly important. Klotz explains that like literature and other aspects of culture, psychoanalysis is interested in the limit and in the 'impossible to say' that lies beyond the limit, which leads to the problem of the 'letter', especially in so far as in Joyce and French avant-garde literature there is no meaning of the letter beyond a point, and the accent is increasingly put on the letter itself as material. Klotz further clarifies that in his early teachings, Lacan's emphasis was on language, the signifier and the signifying chain, which subsumed the ideas of the letter and of writing, while in his later teachings, beginning in 1963–64, Lacan began to make a distinction between the letter and the signifier—as well as between transference and repetition—so as to highlight the specificity of the real, which led him to the problem of the paradoxical *link of separation* that characterized, among other things, his famous formula, 'there is no sexual relation', as a paradigm of the real. Having thus outlined the significance of the real order in Lacan's later teachings and his final clinic, Klotz proposes that the littoral condition of the letter in 'Lituraterre' is precisely a form of link of separation, and delineates it in terms of the following: First, that in 'Lituraterre' the letter is not primary but, rather, an *effect* of the language or of the signifier even if as a letter it does not belong to that language. In other words, it is 'something that is outside but not without'. Second, that the littoral as the shore is equivalent to litter. Third, that a river on the ground can be seen from an aeroplane because of its edge or shore, where the letter stands not for the water of the river but the shores without the water; that is to say, the letter, as real, is hollowed by the water. Its hollowness indicates that the materiality or the real of the letter is a gap and though it can be and often is filled by language, signifiers, meaning, etc., when the water is removed it is the hollowed letter that remains. Thus, whenever there is a littoral, there is always something that is hollowed, which is akin to Lacan's definition of the *objet petit a* as real in so far as he sometimes depicted it as a hollowed object similar to a frame. Fourth, the littoral condition is not a border or a frontier, which is a symbolic trait and is indicated by an Other and by way of discourse. The littoral, unlike a letter, is not a line that is written or inscribed, for the limit of the shore of the river that can change with the change of seasons and at other times too, cannot be traced on a map. Besides, a true border separates two equivalent domains, while the littoral separates the earth from the water. Fifth, since the littoral is not a writing but something situated at the limit of what is written, Lacan used it as a concept to explain a number of significant things, such as, Japanese calligraphy, etc.

The fourth part, entitled 'And Beyond', comprises four essays in which aspects of Lacan's teachings have been read in conjunction with a play (*Not I*), a novel

(*Moderato Cantabile*), a literary theory (postcolonialism) and a literary genre (transsexual memoirs and the clinic of transgender) not addressed by Lacan, though he had mentioned Beckett, written on Duras's 1964 novel *The Ravishing of Lol Stein* (here 1986), spoken on the 'empire', and interviewed the transsexual Michel H.

In the first of these, '*Cogito* in Literature: Descartes with Beckett', Slavoj Žižek, examining the *cogito* in Beckett's *Not I*, argues that Beckett is a kenotic writer who emptied the subject of subjectivity to a minimal difference, reducing the subject as the Cartesian *cogito* to its most radical. This subject, reduced to the 'barred S' ($), has even its innermost self-experience taken away, which exemplifies Lacan's claim that the subject is always 'decentred'. The very gap that bars the subject from its own 'inner life' is the primordial trauma constitutive of the subject. This inner and constitutive link between trauma and subject is the topic of *Not I*, an exercise in theatric minimalism, where intersubjectivity is reduced to its most elementary skeleton in the form of the speaker who is but a partial object, a faceless Mouth speaking, and an Auditor or a witness who says nothing. The logorrheic Mouth utters a barrage of fragmented, jumbled sentences which obliquely tells the story of a woman who appears to have suffered an unspecified traumatic experience. The woman has been virtually mute since childhood barring her occasional outbursts, in which she relates four incidents from her life: lying face down in the grass on a field in April; standing in a supermarket; sitting on a mound in Croker's Acre; and an incident at a court. The last three incidents relate to the repressed first 'scene' that is likened to an epiphany. Her initial reaction to this paralyzing event is to assume that she is being punished by God. She thinks she has something to tell, and though she does not know what, she believes that if she goes over the events of her life for long enough she will stumble upon that thing for which she needs to seek forgiveness; however, an abstract non-linguistic buzzing in her skull always intervenes whenever she gets too close to the core of her traumatic experience. A close reading of the text will show that there is a crucial break just before the play's end, a shift in the mode of subjectivity, signalled by the detail that in the last moment of pause in the text, Auditor does not intervene with his usual mute gesture. It is characterized by three crucial changes: first, the identical set of words which precedes in the previous four cases is supplemented here by a repeated capitalized 'SHE'; second, the pause is without the Auditor's movement; and third, it is not followed by the confused rumbling as in the previous four cases, but by the variation of the Beckettian ethical motto of perseverance.

Žižek thinks that the key to the entire play is provided by the way this shift is read. At the level of content, it can be read as the ultimate failure both of Mouth and Auditor in the sense that, when Mouth loses even the minimal thread of the content and is reduced to the minimalist injunction that the meaningless babble must go on, Auditor despairs and renounces even the empty gesture of helpless compassion. There is, however, the opposite reading that imposes itself at the level of form: Mouth emerges as a pure form of the subject, deprived of all substantial content, and, pending on this reduction, the Other is also de-psychologized, reduced to an empty receiver. This shift should be approached via its counterpart, the traumatic 'x' round which Mouth's log-orrhea circulates. So, in that fateful April, the woman suffered some kind of collapse, possibly even her death, not as a real-life event but as an unbearably intense 'inner experience'. The *sinful* character of the trauma is indicated by the fact that the speaker feels punished by God. In the final shift of the play, the speaker accepts the trauma in its meaninglessness, ceases to search for its meaning, restores its extra-symbolic dignity and thus, gets rid of the entire topic of sin and punishment. This is why Auditor no longer reacts with the gesture of impotent compassion for there is no longer any despair in Mouth's voice, for the standard Beckettian formula of the drive's persistence is asserted in the form of God as Love itself that makes things going. This does not mean that the trauma is finally subjectivized and therefore the speaker is no longer 'not I' but 'SHE'. Rather, the speaker is the detachable 'dead' organ, the partial object which is effectively alive, and whose dead dummy the 'real' person is, whereby the 'real' person is merely alive, a survival machine, a 'human animal', while the apparently 'dead' supplement is the focus of excessive Life.

In the next essay, 'The Practice of the Letter and Topological Structure', Ellie Ragland begins by explaining the expression 'the practice of the letter'—Lacan had used it for the first time in his 1965 'Hommage fait à Marguerite Duras du ravissement de Lol. V. Stein' (here 1985) when he said that the un-conscious touches on the practice of the letter—in terms of its convergence with the unconscious, its link with the void created by the loss of things, its appearance in literary art 'when the unconscious speaks at the juncture where *jouissance* bends itself to the signifier' (cited in Miller 1987: 41), and its emergence as a dimension of the reality of unconscious truth despite the real denoting its foreclosure. Ragland then reads Marguerite Duras's novel *Moderato Cantabile* and aspects of Lacanian psychoanalysis in terms of one another, and in the course of doing so, invokes several crucial lectures of Jacques-Alain Miller that are unknown to many English readers. She focuses on the idea that Duras organized the novel round the voice as a part object and the invocatory drive as a partial drive to narrate a story round a principal object that causes desire. She develops on this by explaining how the voice unveils a link to jouissance that owes little to the sounds of words uttered; how Duras's characters use a minimalist language to hollow out a meaning of the object they desire; and how the words that pass between Anne Desbaresdes and Chauvin seek to construct a love castle via the invocatory drive. Ragland then draws our attention to the following Lacanian ideas that Duras had raised at different levels of her novel: that the topological function of the letter is characteristic of literary language; that being is connected to language in a point of overlap between the real and a void located within language itself; that language cannot symbolize or say the beyond in itself; that jouissance materializes language; that speaking, like thought, is a jouissance; that jouissance which circles round the *objet petit a* resides between the lines of a fiction; that there is a gap in the heart of the fiction of one's identity; that there is an equation of the repetitions beyond the pleasure principle with the negative jouissance of the death drive; that ur-objects that cause desire can never correspond to the imaginary objects of fantasy sought at the level of lure objects; that there is a point at which 'the *jouis-sens* of meaning is a ciphering of the unconscious that seeks to ascertain what death weight the voice carries of the real' (Ragland 1995: 190); that the failures arising out of the impasses in the imaginary order point to a beyond in the imaginary that covers the 'grimace of the real' as it enters the symbolic; that 'jouissance cannot speak itself', while 'the truth of the real speaks loudly behind the images and words it shadows'; and that there is no rapport of sexual Oneness.

In the next essay entitled 'Reading Bhabha, Reading Lacan: Preliminary Notes on Colonial Anxiety', Gautam Basu Thakur argues that the colonizer's anxieties about the colonized are inextricably bound to the colonizer's *discourses* that aim to construct an imaginary and singular entity of the colonized as the Other by at once abstracting the latter from the pluralized reality of his space and culture, and rendering him as an inverse of the colonizer. Basu Thakur points to Homi Bhabha's figuration of anxiety as that which results either from the disruption of the constitutive metaphors of colonial discourse, most importantly signifiers of difference, or from the limits of discourse where discourse fails to adequately explain experiences in the colony due to the impossibility of univocally describing the variable and heterogeneous cultures, habits and idiosyncrasies of the colonized as singular. In other words, while colonial discourse constructs stereotypical 'fixities' to consolidate signs of otherness so as to differentiate the self from the Other, the Other escapes this fixity and produces a repetition of anxiety in the discourse of the self. Here anxiety is situated in the fissure arising between discourse as authority and discourse as failing to authorize the Other as authentic. Bhabha's figuration is then read in the light of the following Lacanian ideas: the alienation of the self from its inverse specular image and the dependence of the excentric identity thus formed on the misrecognition of the small other for the big Other, as developed by Lacan in 'The Mirror Stage as Formative of the *I* Function as Revealed in Psychoanalytic Experience' (1949; here 2006c); the *objet petit a* as defining the radical otherness of the Other that allows the subject to identify the other as Other and grasp the identity of the self as different from the Other, as developed by Lacan in 'The Seminar of Jacques Lacan. Book X. Anxiety, 1962–63' (1962–63) and the operations of alienation and separation and the passage of the *objet petit a* from being the signifier of the other's Otherness to becoming the phantasmatic object of the subject's desire, in *The Seminar of Jacques Lacan. Book XI. The Four Fundamental Concepts of Psychoanalysis, 1964* (1973b; here 1981). Colonial anxiety is then viewed, first, as that which is produced at the instance of the forced metaphorization of the colonial space, which exists as a nascent fault threatening the collapse of imperial identity, whereby every time the colonized announces its desire or breaks out of its objectified positions, such as in the times of armed anti-colonial resistance, the colonial imaginary breaks up round this fault. Second, that which is produced by the intrusion of the real order in the symbolic order of the subject—an intrusion that breaks

25

down the subject's fantasmatic relationship with the Other qua the *objet petit a* and involves a sudden transformation of the imaginary object of fantasy to an object revealing the real to the subject. This is exemplified with the help of John William Kaye's discourse on the panic caused by the false idea that the *lotah* (a metal vessel used for storing and drinking water out of) was a dangerous weapon. Third, the signal of the sudden appearance of the Other's jouissance as an 'insoluble' remainder in discourse, exemplified by Mahasweta Devi's short story 'Strange Children' (1987; here 1990). Fourth, the repetition and shift in the ideological positions of the colonizers across two phases of European territorial aspirations, read in terms of Lacan's concepts of the master's discourse and the university discourse. Fifth, that which is produced by the unrepresentable in the locus of the Other, explained with the help of Bhabha's examples of the nonsensical ambivalence of the 'Ou-boum' of the Marabar Caves in *A Passage to India* (1924) by E. M. Forster as something beyond all possibility of discursive reconstruction; and of the grim anxious space opened up between the colonizer and the colonized, as well as between the colonial military and native civil lines, by the chapatti during the 1857 Sepoy Mutiny that is indicative of the limits of the colonial symbolic system. Basu Thakur concludes by stating that, '[t]his "extinction" of the object shreds the imaginary masks of imperial identity and authority, and the subject is left stripped, negated and looking back at his abject self. It is in this looking back that the anxiety of the real is situated.'

In the final essay of this part, 'The Transsexual Body Written: Writing as *Sinthome*', Patricia Gherovici asserts that '[s]ince transgenderism cannot be systematically defined as pathology, sex change should not be considered either as treatment or as cure.' She assesses the phenomenon of transgenderism with the help of three sets of Lacanian concepts: the paternal metaphor and the formulae of sexuation with reference to the mythical father of the primal horde and the myth of the Woman; the logical instead of the biological notion of the phallus, the *pousse-à-la-femme* (thrust-towards-the-Woman), the *objet petit a* with regard to desire and the asexual nature of human sexuality, and phallic jouissance and the Other jouissance; and finally, the Borromean knot and, in particular, the *sinthome* as a way of writing, reparation and rethinking sexual difference. With reference to a large number of texts, including those by

Mario Martino, Jan Morris, Renée Richards, Nancy Hunt, Dhillon Khosla, Wayne/Jayne County and others, she then claims that the transsexual body is not only a matter of reading, in terms of 'passing' and 'interpretation', but a matter of writing in several important senses. First, the transsexual subject has to produce an appropriate autobiography in order to obtain the necessary medical treatment, where the sex-change autobiographies often consist of the three chronological stages of gender-dysphoria childhood, the move to a big city and the beginning of the transformation, and sex change. Nevertheless, these autobiographies are more of the nature of a 'novel of the artist' or a *Künstlerroman* than a 'novel of formation' or *Bildungsroman*. Second, memoirs of sex change often have a profoundly illuminating and a life-transforming effect on readers who are future transsexuals. Third, sex-change requests are literalization in the flesh of the psychoanalytic notion of castration. Fourth, transsexual memoirs may not be great literature but they aspire to the most essential function of literature in so far as they constitute a form of writing that, like literary writing, deals with castration and the real. Fifth, 'Memoirs of sex change offer for their authors the effect of a reparation.' As such, writing is an attempt to make the body and the spirit cohere, as well as to regulate excess jouissance. This is often achieved in terms of an artifice or a supplement by way of changing one's sex and writing about it, which allows for an incarnation of what was till then only experienced in the real.

Of all the concepts dealt with in the essay, the one that is central to Gherovici's argument is the concept of the *sinthome*, which she variously regards as 'the singularity of a creation compensating for a defect in the body image and its knotting with the main elements of a subject's structure'; the function of Joyce's literary works as a whole that Lacan stressed on by treating the works as a memoir; the basis of transsexual artificiality 'in the form of an answer that may help reclaim the body and regulate jouissance'; and the means to achieving the One through the necessary transformative power of writing, as in the case of Morris where it does not cease to be written.

In the afterword entitled 'The Enigma of Jouissance', Russell Grigg explains why Lacan's substantive claims about jouissance change not due to the attribution of different meanings to the term on different occasions, but due

27

to an internal criticism of his views. This essay evidently does not have a direct relation to literature barring a few significant remarks on Lacan's seminar on *Antigone*, and its 'literary' mode of composition. Just as writers of fiction rarely complete the book they begin to write, for in the very act of writing things shift, change and evolve, so did the original thesis of Grigg's essay change into a new one in course of its writing. Nevertheless, jouissance is a concept of utmost importance in all stages of Lacan's work, albeit for different reasons, as the numerous references to it in the essays in this collection itself would amply testify; and Grigg's essay offers several fresh insights into it. Grigg makes a distinction between what the concept of jouissance means and what Lacan thinks is true of it, and points to three general obscurities with the concept. First, that the source of jouissance is not the body, for there is jouissance in thinking, jouissance of meaning or *jouis-sens*, jouissance of the letter and so on, due to which Lacan described it as 'of the real'. But how clear is the concept that the source of jouissance is not the body but the real? Second, that the profound distinction that Lacan made between jouissance and language or the signifier is difficult to maintain because his references to the 'jouissance of the idiot' and the jouissance concerning Little Hans' *Wiwimacher* locate it in the field of meaning. Third, that by thinking of jouissance as a concept that makes sense only with reference to meaning, the distinction between phallic jouissance or the idiot's jouissance and jouissance of the Other can be understood.

Grigg then points out that despite all the changes in the figuration of jouissance in Lacan, there is nevertheless one constant; namely that its source is a symptom. He then goes on to describe the three important ways in which Lacan used the term. First, that jouissance is fixated and regulated by signifiers that 'encipher' the unconscious in the form of symptoms. In other words, a symptom *insignifies* jouissance. Second, that jouissance as impossible, or as real, is accessible only through 'transgression', as Antigone apparently did. This redefinition of jouissance offered in *The Ethics of Psychoanalysis* however is problematic for several reasons:

> (a) If there is an un-bridgeable gap between the signifier and jouissance, how could a cure that involves talking operate and produce any effect upon a subject's jouissance?

(b) If jouissance is accessible only through transgression, then what happens to symptoms that are a form of jouissance? Is not a symptom that results from repression, the opposite of transgression?

(c) Since enjoyment is inescapable for speaking beings, what is the relationship between jouissance and transgression? Although Lacan himself justly abandoned this thesis in *The Seminar of Jacques Lacan. Book XVII. The Other Side of Psychoanalysis, 1969–70* (1991; here 2007a), Grigg reminds us to retain the distinction between jouissance and desire—which are distinct but not completely independent—that Lacan made in *The Ethics of Psychoanalysis*.

Third, in *Le Séminaire. Livre XX. Encore, 1972–73* (1975a) and 'L'Etourdit' (1973a), Lacan introduced the idea of a specifically feminine jouissance that Grigg clarifies with the help of two remarks of Lacan, which he translates as: 'Jouissance of the Other, of the Other's body that symbolizes it, is not a sign of love' (Lacan 1975a: 11); and 'phallic enjoyment is the obstacle preventing a man from enjoying a woman's body because what he enjoys is enjoyment of the organ' (ibid.: 13). These two remarks appear contradictory when the subjective and objective senses of the genitive *de* in the expression '*jouissance de l'Autre*' are not recognized. In the subjective sense, the expression stands for the Other's jouissance or feminine jouissance, while in the objective sense it stands for [one's] jouissance of the Other or phallic jouissance. The Other's jouissance is in a sense the mystic's jouissance as a form of bodily jouissance that escapes the phallic economy. This offers in a nutshell Lacan's thesis that there is no sexual relation, for phallic jouissance is an obstacle that prevents access to the Other's jouissance. Moreover, these two forms of jouissance show the two forms of the failed relationship between the signifier and the real. Furthermore, both these jouissances are enigmatic, in so far as the Other's jouissance is an enigma that calls incessantly to be rendered and regulated, while phallic jouissance, as in the case of the psychotic, tends to find expression in forms that escape regulation.

Melbourne, 2011

References

ENGLISH SOURCES

BECKETT, Samuel. 2003. *Not I* in *The Complete Dramatic Works*. London: Faber and Faber, pp. 373–83.

CARROLL, Lewis. 1991. *The Complete Sylvie and Bruno* (Thomas Christensen ed.). San Francisco: Mercury House.

—. 1998. *Through the Looking-Glass and What Alice Found There* in Hugh Haughton (ed.), *Alice's Adventures in Wonderland and Through the Looking-Glass and What Alice Found There* (The Centenary Edition). London: Penguin Classics, pp. 111–241.

DEVI, Mahasweta. 1990. 'Strange Children' in *Of Women, Outcastes, Peasants, and Rebels* (Kalpana Bardhan trans.). Berkeley, LA and Oxford: University of California Press, pp. 229–41.

DURAS, Marguerite. 1965. *Moderato Cantabile* in *Four Novels: The Square; Moderato Cantabile; 10:30 on a Summer Night; The Afternoon of Mr. Andesmas* (Richard Seaver trans.). New York: Grove Press, pp. 61–118.

—. 1986. *The Ravishing of Lol Stein* (Richard Seaver trans.). New York: Pantheon Books.

FORSTER, E. M. 1924. *A Passage to India*. New York: Harcourt, Brace and Company.

JOYCE, James. 1960 [1916]. *A Portrait of the Artist as a Young Man*. Harmondsworth: Penguin Classics.

—. 1964 [1939]. *Finnegans Wake* (3rd edn). London: Faber and Faber

—. 2000 [1922]. *Ulysses*. London: Penguin Classics.

KANT, Immanuel. 2008. *The Critique of Practical Reason* (Thomas Kingsmill Abott trans.). Virginia: Wilder Publications.

LACAN, Jacques. 1932. *De la psychose paranoïaque dans ses rapports avec la personnalité*. Paris: Le Français.

—. 1958–59a. The Seminar of Jacques Lacan. Book VI. Desire and its Interpretation, 1958–59. Unofficially translated by Cormac Gallagher from the unedited and unpublished French typescripts of Le Séminaire. Livre VI. Le désir et son interprétation, 1958–59. The translation is available at http://www.lacaninireland.com/web/wp-content/uploads/2010/06/THE-SEMINAR-OF-JACQUES-LACAN-VI.pdf (Last accessed on 22 August 2012.)

———. 1962–63. The Seminar of Jacques Lacan. Book X. Anxiety, 1962–63. Unofficially translated by Cormac Gallagher from the unedited French typescripts of the seminar officially published in 2004. The translation is available at http://www.valas.fr/IMG/pdf/THE-SEMINAR-OF-JACQUES-LACAN-X_1_angoisse.pdf (Last accessed on 21 August 2012.)

———. 1971. The Seminar of Jacques Lacan. Book XVIII. On a Discourse that Might not be a Semblance, 1971. Unofficially translated by Cormac Gallagher from the unedited French typescripts of the seminar officially published in 2007. The translation is available at http://www.valas.fr/IMG/pdf/THE-SEMINAR-OF-JACQUES-LACAN-XVIII_d_un_discours.pdf (Last accessed on 22 August 2012.)

———. 1976a. '11-24-1975 Yale University. Conversation with Students' (Jack W. Stone trans.). Columbia, MO: University of Missouri. Available at http://web.missouri.edu/~stonej/1975-11-24a_Yale.pdf' (Last accessed on 21 August 2012). It is a part of 'Conferences in North American Universities'. *Scilicet* 6/7: 7–63.

———. 1981. *The Seminar of Jacques Lacan. Book XI. The Four Fundamental Concepts of Psychoanalysis, 1964* (Jacques-Alain Miller ed., Alan Sheridan trans.). New York and London: W. W. Norton.

———. 1990. *Television: A Challenge to the Psychoanalytic Establishment* (Joan Copjec ed., Denis Hollier, Rosalind Krauss and Annette Michelson trans). New York and London. W. W. Norton.

———. 1992. *The Seminar of Jacques Lacan. Book VII. The Ethics of Psychoanalysis, 1959–60* (Jacques-Alain Miller ed.). New York and London: W. W. Norton.

———. 2001a. 'Lituraterre' (Jack W. Stone trans.). Columbia, MO: University of Missouri. Available at http://web.missouri.edu/~stonej/Lituraterre.-pdf (Last accessed on 22 August 2012.)

———. 2002a. Homage to Lewis Carroll. Unpublished translation by Russell Grigg of 'Hommage rendu à Lewis Carroll'.

————. 2006a. 'The Function and Field of Speech and Language in Psychoanalysis' in *Écrits: The First Complete Edition in English* (Bruce Fink trans.). New York and London: W. W. Norton, pp. 31–106.

————. 2006b. 'The Instance of the Letter in the Unconscious, or Reason since Freud' in *Écrits: The First Complete Edition in English* (Bruce Fink trans.). New York and London: W. W. Norton, pp. 412–41.

————. 2006c. 'The Mirror Stage as Formative of the *I* Function as Revealed in Psychoanalytic Experience' in *Écrits: The First Complete Edition in English* (Bruce Fink trans.). New York and London: W. W. Norton, pp. 75–81.

————. 2006d. 'Seminar on "The Purloined Letter"' in *Écrits: The First Complete Edition in English* (Bruce Fink trans.). New York and London: W. W. Norton, pp. 6–48.

————. 2006e. 'The Youth of Gide, or the Letter and Desire' in *Écrits: The First Complete Edition in English* (Bruce Fink trans.). New York and London: W. W. Norton, pp. 623–44.

————. 2007a. *The Seminar of Jacques Lacan. Book XVII. The Other Side of Psychoanalysis, 1969–70* (Jacques-Alain Miller ed., Russell Grigg trans.). New York and London: W. W. Norton.

MILLER, John. 1987. 'Jacques Lacan's Télévision'. *Artscribe International* 66 (November–December): 40–1.

NABOKOV, Vladimir. 1974 [1955]. *Lolita*. New York: Crest Books.

POE, Edgar Allan. 1983. 'The Purloined Letter' in *The Complete Tales and Poems of Edgar Allan Poe*. Harmondsworth: Penguin Books, pp. 208–22.

RABATÉ, Jean-Michel. 2001. *Jacques Lacan: Psychoanalysis and the Subject of Literature*. Hampshire and New York: Palgrave.

RAGLAND, Ellie. 1995. *Essays on the Pleasures of Death*. New York and London: Routledge.

SADE, Marquis de. 1994. *Philosophy in the Bedroom* in *Justine, Philosophy in the Bedroom, and Other Writings* (Richard Seaver and Austryn Wainhouse trans). New York: Grove Press, pp. 177–370.

SHAKESPEARE, William. 2003. Philip Edwards (ed.), *Hamlet: The Prince of Denmark* (2nd edn). Cambridge: Cambridge University Press.

FRENCH SOURCES

LACAN, Jacques. 1932. *De la psychose paranoïaque dans ses rapports avec la personnalité*. Paris: Le Français.

———. 1949. 'Le stade du miroir comme formateur de la fonction du Je telle quelle nous est revelee dans l'experience psychanalytique'. *Revue Française de Psychanalyse* 13(4): 449–55. Subsequently published in *Écrits* (1966).

———. 1956. 'Fonction et champ de la parole et du langage en psychanalyse'. *La Psychanalyse* 1: 81–166. Subsequently published in *Écrits* (1966).

———. 1957a. 'L'Instance de la lettre dans l'inconscient ou la raison depuis Freud'. *La Psychanalyse* 3 (Psychoanalysis and the Sciences of Man): 47–81. Subsequently published in *Écrits* (1966).

———. 1957b. 'Le séminaire sur "La Lettre Volée"'. *La Psychanalyse* 2: 1–44. Subsequently published in *Écrits* (1966).

———. 1958. 'Jeunesse de Gide ou la lettre et désir'. *Critique* 131: 291–315. Subsequently published in *Écrits* (1966).

———. 1958–59b. Le Séminaire. Livre VI. Le désir et son interprétation, 1958–59. Some sessions published in 1982.

———. 1966. *Écrits*. Paris: Éditions du Seuil.

———. 1973a. 'L'Etourdit'. *Scilicet* 4: 5–52.

———. 1973b. *Le Séminaire. Livre XI. Les quatre concepts fondamentaux de la psychanalyse, 1964* (Jacques-Alain Miller ed.). Paris: Éditions du Seuil.

———. 1974. *Télévision*. Paris: Éditions du Seuil.

———. 1975a. *Le Séminaire. Livre XX. Encore, 1972–73* (Jacques-Alain Miller ed.). Paris: Éditions du Seuil.

———. 1975b. 'Le Séminaire. Livre XXII. R. S. I., 1974–75'. *Ornicar? Bulletin périodique du champ freudien* 2: 87–105; 3: 96–110; 4: 92–106; 5: 17–66.

———. 1976b. '1975-11-24. Yale University. Entretien avec des etudiants'. *Scilicet* 6/7: 32–7. Available as part of 'Conférences et Entretiens dans des universités nord-américaines'. *Scilicet* 6/7: 7–63.

———. 1982. 'Le désir et son interprétation'. *Ornicar? Bulletin périodique du champ freudien* 25: 13–36.

———. 1985. 'Hommage fait à Marguerite Duras, du ravissement de Lol V. Stein'. *Ornicar? Bulletin périodique du champ freudien* 34: 7–13.

———. 1986. *Le Séminaire. Livre VII. L'éthique de la psychoanalyse, 1959–60* (Jacques-Alain Miller ed.). Paris: Éditions du Seuil.

———. 1987a. 'Joyce le Symptôme I' in Jacques Aubert (ed.), *Joyce Avec Lacan*. Paris: Navarin, pp. 21–9.

———. 1987b. 'Joyce le Symptôme II' in Jacques Aubert (ed.), *Joyce Avec Lacan*. Paris: Navarin, pp. 31–6.

———. 1991. *Le Séminaire. Livre XVII. L'envers de la psychanalyse, 1969–70* (Jacques-Alain Miller ed.). Paris: Éditions du Seuil.

———. 2001b. 'Lituraterre' in Jacques-Alain Miller (ed.), *Autres écrits*. Paris: Éditions du Seuil, pp. 11–22.

———. 2002b. 'Hommage rendu à Lewis Carroll'. *Ornicar? Revue du champ freudien* 50: 9–12.

———. 2004. *Le Séminaire. Livre X. L'angoisse, 1962–63* (Jacques-Alain Miller ed.). Paris: Éditions du Seuil.

———. 2005. *Le Séminaire. Livre XXIII. Le Sinthome, 1975–76* (Jacques-Alain Miller ed.). Paris: Éditions du Seuil.

———. 2007b. *Le Séminaire. Livre XVIII. D'un discours qui ne serait pas du semblant, 1971* (Jacques-Alain Miller ed.). Paris: Éditions du Seuil.

PART 1

The Literary Lacan

From the Letter to the Objet petit a:
The Evolution of Lacan's Literary Metaphors

NANCY BLAKE

In 1966 when he published a collection of his essays on psychoanalysis entitled *Écrits*,[1] Jacques Lacan violated the chronological order that would have led him to initiate the volume with the 'Mirror Stage' article. Instead, he opened the book with the 1956 'Seminar on "The Purloined Letter"' (1957; here 2006a), an essay which had originally been part of his 1954-55 seminar (*The Seminar of Jacques Lacan. Book II. The Ego in Freud's Theory and in the Technique of Psychoanalysis, 1954–55*; published in 1978; here 1988). Edgar Allan Poe's short story 'The Purloined Letter' (1844; here 1983) is a fable that is also an example of literary production. For Lacan, it is also an occasion to demonstrate that 'the symbolic order [. . .] is constitutive for the subject'; that is to say, 'the subject receives [his major determination] from the itinerary of a signifier' (Lacan 2006a: 7).

What is this major determination? When we get to the end of Lacan's demonstration we will see that it is nothing less than gender identity itself.

A letter is something that is read or a letter is something that can be read or a letter is something one reads. '*La lettre, ça se lit*'—seven years after the publication of *Écrits*, Lacan opens his 9 January 1973 session of *The Seminar of Jacques Lacan. Book XX. Encore: On Feminine Sexuality, The Limits of Love and Knowledge, 1972–73* (1975; here 1998) with these words (1998: 26). In this paper, we will attempt to outline the evolution of the weight of the letter and thus of the literary, perhaps of the written, in Lacan's theory.

---

1 Lacan's *Écrits* was first published in 1966 (Paris: Éditions du Seuil). A selection was translated by Bruce Fink in collaboration with Héloïse Fink and Russell Grigg in 2004, and then *Écrits: The First Complete Edition in English* (New York and London: W. W. Norton) was published in 2006. All citations from *Écrits* in this essay are from the latter.

NANCY BLAKE

In an oft-quoted quip Lacan noted that if he called his collected essays *Écrits*—that is 'written'—it was especially to underline his opinion that they were not meant to be read. Yet, he immediately continues, '*La lettre, ça se lit.*' It is evident that it is not the same thing to read a letter as it is to read. The experience of psychoanalysis is expressed in that very difference—what is involved is the practice of reading beyond what the subject has to say, whence the equally frequently quoted axiom: 'A letter always returns to the sender, in inverted form' (Lacan 2006a: 30). This paradoxical formula is a nutshell definition of what happens in psychoanalysis as a practice.

That there is, for Lacan, some sort of essential relationship between the human subject and the letter becomes patent when he dismisses the 'supposed' language of bees. He writes that it is not a language in his sense but, rather, 'an imaginary function that is simply more differentiated than the others' (ibid.: 13).

The 'Seminar on "The Purloined Letter"' is one part of a widespread movement in linguistics that interrogates the notion of language as something other than the means of communication. Lacan will show us, after Poe, that what is transmitted—in this case the narration of the scene during which the letter is taken, through the very fact that this narrative is passed through multiple subjective filters (the queen tells the prefect of police, who tells Detective Dupin in the presence of his friend, the narrator, who tells us)—'truly belongs to the dimension of language' (ibid.: 12). Bees, on the other hand, while amazingly proficient at signalling the location of a food source to other members of their hive, never seem to have thought of creating an oral tradition in which, for example, they would impress upon their young that in past times honey was also available in places that have disappeared today.

In order to underline the fundamental difference that has been pointed out here, Lacan reminds us of the Jewish joke told by Freud which stages the relationship of truth and falsehood with its need to invent a natural language: '"Why are you lying to me?" one of Freud's characters exclaims exasperatedly, "Yes, why are you lying to me by saying you're going to Cracow in order to make me believe you're going to Lemberg, when in reality you *are* going to Cracow?"' (quoted in ibid.: 13).

38

Characteristically, although he has been demonstrating the great extent to which he faithfully follows Freud here, Lacan suddenly alludes to Martin Heidegger and his etymology for the word *alethes* in which Lacan sees the 'play of truth': 'it is in hiding that she offers herself [. . .] *most truly*' (ibid.: 15). The category of truth is an issue that will continue to preoccupy us throughout this study of Lacan's use of the letter.

Lacan then goes into a development on the relationship between the letter and location (*le lieu*) which, he says, Poe qualifies as 'odd'. Lacan notes that he has not confused the letter with the spirit, yet he comes out with this: 'the signifier [. . .] materializes the instance of death' (ibid.: 16). This materiality, according to Lacan, is singular in that it does not allow partition. This development in turn allows him to proceed to the next step: 'For the signifier is a unique unit of being which, by its very nature, is the symbol of but an absence' (ibid.: 17).

If the letter is hidden, it is simply because the letter is not in its place, as the library tells us when a book we have requested cannot be found; 'For it can *literally* be said that something is not in its place only of what can change places—that is of the symbolic' (ibid.: 17). The real, on the other hand, is always and in every case in its place.

The first category we have introduced is that of truth, the second that of the real, with the very special supplementary layers of meaning that Lacan attaches to that signifier.

So far, the argument has ignored the angle according to which a letter can be considered a message. Lacan notes, however, that the message has already reached the queen who had been reading the letter when the minister interrupted her and then stole the object from the table. If the communication of a message were all that is involved in a letter, 'the ceremony of returning letters would be a less commonly accepted way to bring to a close the extinguishing of the fires of Cupid's festivities' (ibid.: 18). '*Scripta manent verba volant*,' quotes Lacan, only to insist that, in fact, it is exactly the opposite. Spoken words are indelible, and we continue to repeat them unconsciously, as our transference activities prove only too well. Writings, on the other hand, scatter to the four winds like the blank cheques that so much wild interpretation has made of Lacan's attempts at writing.

It is also pertinent to ask, to whom a letter belongs, for if the sender retains certain rights then it cannot wholly belong to the addressee. Or perhaps, the person to whom the letter is addressed was never the true addressee. This dilemma is central to Lacan's essay on André Gide, subtitled 'The Letter and Desire' (1958; here 2006b)

Be this as it may, Poe's text tells us next to nothing about the sender or the content of the letter in question: love letter or conspiratorial letter, informant's letter or letter of distress or proof of debt. The only thing we know is that the queen cannot let her lord and master know of it, for what is at stake is the issue of legitimacy itself.

Then Lacan points out what is perhaps the most curious aspect of Poe's fiction: whoever 'holds' the letter is contaminated by its power. For Lacan, this illustrates the fact that the signifier sustains itself only in a displacement along a circular path. This is repetition compulsion. What Freud says of the subject's tendency to repeat, Lacan finds generalized, through the fable of Poe's story, to subjects caught in the play of intersubjectivity, who tend to model their very being on the signifying chain that runs through them: 'If what Freud discovered, and rediscovers ever more abruptly, has a meaning, it is that the signifier's displacement determines subjects' acts, destiny, refusals, blindnesses, success, and fate, regardless of their innate gifts and instruction, and irregardless of their character or sex; and that everything pertaining to the psychological pre-given follows willy-nilly the signifier's train, like weapons and baggage' (ibid.: 21). By coming into possession of the letter, each subject is possessed by it.

When the minister has stolen the letter from the queen, he is obliged to play her role, 'including even the attributes of woman and shadow, so propitious for the act of concealment' (ibid.: 22). That the minister has the courage to assume this risk is suggested already when the prefect of police qualifies him as someone 'who dares all things, those unbecoming as well as those becoming a man' (cited in ibid.: 23), which, Lacan tells us, is an appraisal 'far more appropriate to what concerns a woman' (ibid.: 24).

When the minister is in possession of the letter he is in the feminine position; that is, he is assigned passivity. In order to conceal the letter, he apes the queen's gesture and turns it over—though not precisely as she did, for he turns the letter inside out. He ascribes on the letter a new address, his own. And the writing appears in a diminutive feminine script, while the seal becomes that of the minister himself. The oddity of a letter marked with the cipher of its addressee is especially poignant if we assume that, ultimately, the minister addresses to himself a letter from a woman.

Lacan pokes gentle, subtle and obscure fun at Marie Bonaparte's interpretation of the letter as the penis of the mother from the symbolism of its hiding place beneath the jambs of the fireplace in Poe's story. Yet for his analysis, the meaning of the letter is really not so very different. For what is the exchange that Poe's detective Dupin is willing to effect of the letter for an enormous sum of money, if it is not a sure sign of the signifier of absolute value with which we are dealing here?

When Dupin succeeds in stealing the letter from the minister, he too comes under its power, occupying the position previously assigned to the queen and then to the minister. Why does Lacan say: 'This is why Dupin, *from the place where he is*, cannot help but feel rage of a manifestly feminine nature at he who questions in this manner' (ibid.: 29)? Asked what he got out of the whole adventure, Dupin replies that he 'acts in this matter as partisan of the lady'. Lacan adds: 'ladies, as we know, detest it when principles are called into question, for their charms owe much to the mystery of the signifier' (ibid.). This is still somewhat vague. The clue must be found in the lines that Dupin wrote as message in the facsimile letter that he left in its place when he purloined the original from the minister. These lines, says Dupin, will reveal to the minister the identity of the one who has robbed him. The couplet is a quotation from a play by the eighteenth-century libertine writer Claude Prosper Jolyot de Crébillon:

'*Un dessein si funeste,*

S'il n'est digne d'Atrée; est digne de Thyeste' (quoted in Poe 1983: 222).

These lines form the final words of Poe's text. However, Lacan misquotes: '*Un destin si funeste,/ S'il n'est digne d'Atrée; est digne de Thyeste*' (2006a: 29) for Poe wrote '*Un dessein si funeste*' (a plan so sinister), not '*Un destin si funeste*' (a destiny so sinister).

How does this slip accommodate Lacan's remark that he and his followers had made a joke, when they were in Zurich the previous year, incorporating the 'local password' 'Eat your *Dasein*' (ibid.)? Lacan needs to read *dessein* as *destin* since he needs to present what will happen to the minister as his fate. However, as psychoanalysts know only too well, fate is another name for unconscious desire.

Therefore, Lacan has been able to illustrate the maxims that he presented at the outset of this lesson: first, the sender receives from the receiver his own message in an inverted form; and second, the meaning of 'purloined letter' is that a letter always arrives at its destination.

The power, in this case the influence, that the possession of the letter allows its possessor to wield, is only potential, for it disappears the minute it is called upon to act. Minister D. and Detective Dupin are certainly for Poe— who had used this structure before—brothers, even doubles, like Atreus and Thyestes. In an act of revenge against the brother who betrayed him with his wife, Atreus served Thyestes a meal consisting of the latter's children. And D., should he ever attempt to use the queen's letter which he believes he still holds, will be obliged to 'eat his words', a fitting punishment in Poe's realm of the letter where the signifier holds ultimate sway.

GIDE'S LOVE LETTERS

The essay entitled 'The Youth of Gide, or the Letter and Desire' opens the sixth part of *Écrits* (1966) and dates from 1958 when it was first published in the journal *Critique*. On the occasion of the publication of a book by Jean Delay on the youth of writer André Gide, *La Jeunesse d'André Gide* (1956–57), Lacan announced his intention to consider the problem of 'man's relationship to the letter'. In this case, as he already had occasion to note in the 'Seminar on "The Purloined Letter"', the various meanings of the word letter—a typographical element, an epistle or what constitutes a man of letters—are evoked and are pertinent.

Delay's book is a psychobiography and Lacan claims it is a masterpiece of the genre. For Lacan, this review is also an opportunity, an occasion to demonstrate the *raison d'être* behind the psychoanalytic theorist's interest in literature, namely, that 'truth shows itself in a fictional structure' (Lacan 2006b: 625).

That Delay wrote a biography of Gide was not an accident. Lacan notes that Gide lived a life that he knew would one day be a biography. When Gide explained, in a letter to his mother, his loan of capital to a friend in need, he expressly indicated that he was 'looking after [his] biography' (ibid.: 626); there, Gide underlined his loyalty to the letter.

Gide chose the eminent psychiatrist Delay as his biographer to ensure that his life would become a psychobiography. However, Lacan insists that Delay's study is not applied psychoanalysis since, strictly speaking, analysis is applied only as treatment to a subject who speaks and hears. What Delay's work shows is the extent to which the proper method for reading literary material 'encounters the very structure of the subject that psychoanalysis sketches out in the organization of its own exposition' (ibid.: 630).

Gide was interested in psychoanalysis and even attempted to undergo the process with Mrs Eugénie Sokolnicka. He made good use of the experiment in his 1926 novel *The Counterfeiters* (here 1973), where his character Boris shares the author's experience of feeling smothered by the love that his mother lavishes upon him after the death of his father. Lacan goes on to outline the considerations that Gide and Delay, after him, have already laid bare concerning the history of the writer's awakening homosexual eroticism, as well as his grand and unique experience of love for his cousin Madeleine who would become his wife, 'unable to conceive that existence could have any other object than to shelter this child from fear, from evil, from life' (cited in Lacan 2006b: 634). As Delay rightly emphasizes, to Lacan's delight, everything here is supported by a very old tradition, that of the mystical bonds of courtly love. This is how Lacan sums the situation up: 'In fact, Gide's feeling for his cousin was truly the height of love, if love means giving what one does not have and if he gave her immortality' (ibid.: 635).

When he wrote about her to the poet Paul Valéry, Gide said of his cousin: 'She is Morella' (quoted in ibid.). Poe's heroine Morella is a woman who could not die even though a horrible illness was wreaking unspeakable suffering and deterioration on her body. Poe's narrator, her husband, wishes she would die, whereupon she does, giving birth to a daughter who is her reincarnation. When we know from Gide's autobiographical writing that his love for Madeleine had everything to do with his ambivalent attraction to her mother; that Madeleine's mother made her husband suffer because of her many infidelities and even seduced the 13-year-old Gide, we may well be authorized to wonder at this identification to Poe's Morella. So that if Gide decided to marry Madeleine, it was to save her from her painful proximity to her mother's guilt and to preserve her, through a white marriage, from the dangers of sexuality. The sexuality of the mother is lethal; ideal love, courtly love, is an attempt to circumvent it. Delay's biography leaves no doubt that Madeleine herself wanted an unconsummated marriage, yet, Lacan adds that her desire no doubt had unconscious motivations that happened to be very appropriate for leaving her husband's problems intact.

All of Gide's writing, crystal clear as it always attempts to be, is thus a cipher which becomes a hieroglyph, according to Lacan's metaphor (ibid.: 636). That is to say, it may be transferred from one text to another, but the meaning of the metaphor always remains inexhaustible because it has none, since it is simply the mark with which death brands the flesh when the Word has separated the flesh from love. Simply put, like so many others, where his flesh desired, Gide could not love, and where he loved, he could not desire.

After his wife's death, Gide wrote a text in 1947 with a Latin title, *Et nunc manet in te* (translated as *Madeleine*, 1952). A reference that continues to dwell on the ambiguous attachment of husband and wife, this title indicates the punishment that weighs upon Orpheus from beyond the grave. Gide imagines that Orpheus feels the resentment of Eurydice for the fact that, by turning round to look at her as they were climbing out of the underworld, her husband condemned her to return there. What remains in Orpheus (*manet in te*) is not the beloved object living beyond the grave but, rather, the eternal punishment of her resentment.

As Lacan sums it up: 'I would like this book by Gide to keep its cutting edge for those whose destiny in life is to pass on the furrow of a lack, in other words, all men, and for those who lament it, in other words, many of them' (Lacan 2006b: 638).

On the last page of *Et nunc manet in te*, which wraps up the relations between Gide and Madeleine, we find this: 'which offers nothing more, in the ardent place of the heart, than a hole' (quoted in ibid.: 641). The hole is not, however, the loss of the beloved being; it is, rather, the loss of the love letters that Gide had written to Madeleine throughout his life until 1918 when she burnt them. She burnt her collection of love letters, as a possession that was most precious to her, in order to 'do something' faced with the betrayal by her husband who had taken his young lover, Marc Allégret, on an escapade to London. These letters, as Madeleine well knew, were destined by Gide to form the centre of his biography, to consecrate his legend and their joint immortality.

These letters in which he placed his soul . . . had no double. They were lost forever. André Gide's groan, wailing over the loss of the letters that were a mirror, 'a doubling of himself, which is why he calls them his child—can but seem precisely to fill the very gap that the woman's act wished to open up in his being' (ibid.: 640). For Gide it was the loss of the most precious legacy that he had intended to bequeath to posterity. Or, as Lacan puts it: 'In other words, I am not aiming here at humanity's loss, or the humanities' loss, of Gide's correspondence, but rather at the fateful exchange by which the letter comes to take the very place from which desire has withdrawn' (ibid.: 641). If the 'Seminar on "The Purloined Letter"' did not suffice to convince us, this essay clearly demonstrates that according to Lacan, the letter is a fetish and it can be lost.

The Letter as *Objet petit a*

Lacan's writing of psychoanalytic theory comes to employ a set of algebraic symbols, the first of which is, of course, a, which Lacan named in order to stress the fact that it is only the first in a series: a, b, c, etc. In addition, he reminds us that a is the 'object', but, nevertheless, it is still only a letter. It functions in a relationship with A, which designates a place, a locus, called the 'locus of the Other'. Yet, Lacan continues, as such A does not quite hold up, for it is only encountered in so far as it is barred; that is, it is faulty—there is a hole, a gap, a lack involved. *Objet petit a* then comes to function with respect to that loss. That is essential to the function of language. This can easily be seen retrospectively if we reread Freud's chapter on '*fort!/da!*' in *Beyond the Pleasure Principle* (1920; here 1955: 7–64).

In psychoanalysis, the rhetorical character of the working of the unconscious has been explicitly recognized for a long time now. The concept of 'condensation' in Freud's description of the dream logic has been assimilated to metaphor and 'displacement' to metonymy. The logic of Lacan's *objet petit a* involves precisely an investment by which an ordinary object becomes a substitute for the unreachable Thing. In Lacan's terms, sublimation is the elevation of an object to the dignity of the Thing (*la Chose*).

As Lacan's *Encore* informs us, 'The letter is, radically speaking, an effect of discourse' (1998: 36).

THE PLACE OF LITERATURE

Lacan recommends that we read James Joyce. Why? Because in doing so we will see how the signifier stuffs the signified. The play of signifiers produces something close to what analysts can observe in a slip of the tongue, for example. What is at stake here is unconscious knowledge.

> I think you must have an inkling now of the function I grant the letter in relation to knowledge. I beg you not to too quickly associate this function with so-called messages, for it makes the letter analogous to a germ cell, which, in the realm of molecular physiology, must be strictly separated from the bodies with respect to which it transmits (véhicule) life and death together (ibid.: 97).

Lacan opens the Joyce seminar, *Le Séminaire. Livre XXIII. Le Sinthome, 1975–76* (2005) with a by-now-familiar mantra: 'Man stands apart from what seems to be the law of nature in so far as there is not, for him, any natural sexual relationship' (2005: 12; my translation).

Just as in the 'Seminar on "The Purloined Letter"', Lacan found that the letter consecrated gender identity, in the Joyce seminar, he returns to the question of phallic identification. He quips that Socrates did not want his wife to talk. That might mean that the use of language is a masculine prerogative. Then, a few pages later, Lacan supposes that Joyce's gender identification was weak but his use of language helped bolster it. 'And that is how his art is the real stand-in for his phallus' (ibid.: 15; my translation).

In his opening lecture of *Le Sinthome*, Lacan returns to the question of the definition of the category of perversion. Here he notes that while psychosis is recognizable in that the three registers of the symbolic, the imaginary and the real are disjointed, freed from the Borromean knot, in perversion that is far from being the case.

'It is not that the symbolic, the imaginary and the real are broken apart which is the distinguishing mark of perversion; it is that they are already distinct so that it becomes necessary to posit a fourth term, which happens to be the *sinthome*' (ibid.: 19; my translation).

Lacan then emphasizes that if he has spoken of perversion as *version vers le père*, it is because the father is in fact a symptom, or *sinthome*. From this point on, he explains that the Name-of-the-Father is the concept that will be essential to his development during the coming year of his interrogation on art.

Art, which is also artifice, has a mission to bypass the impact of the symptom, which is its truth. The *objet petit a* is the product of the artisan. It is striking that in this seminar, Lacan oscillates between the extremely abstract language of the knots and mathematical speculations, and the almost crude, staccato phrases that call upon the body and the Lacanian understanding of jouissance—for example, the phrase, 'Language eats the real' (ibid.: 31; my translation). We remember the joke 'Eat your *Dasein*.'

Here, Lacan feels the need to distance himself from Heidegger once more and does so by evoking the philosopher's use of the term *echt*, which can be translated variously as true, real, genuine, pure. This is yet another instance of the opposition that Lacan sets up between truth and the real that I have been emphasizing throughout this essay. For Lacan, with this one word *echt*, Heidegger confesses his failure. Admittedly, what Lacan is driving at here is far from evident. I would like to suggest that, when he accuses Heidegger of being 'metaphysical', Lacan is returning to his familiar argument. Heidegger is interested in the problem of 'being' (the *Dasein* mentioned in the 'Seminar on "The Purloined Letter"' with the joke 'Eat your *Dasein*') while Lacan is interested in the hole, the gap, the lack that signals the existence of the 'real'.

Perhaps, the session entitled 'Was Joyce Insane?' is the crux of this seminar. Lacan asks himself why he seems to be spending all of his time studying Joyce, critical editions, scholarly texts, etc. What is in it for him? He then passes on to the distinction between truth and the real, which he feels are easy to distinguish because the truth gives pleasure and the real is what gives just the opposite. In fact, the jouissance of the real is pure masochism. Then, when he goes back to Joyce, Lacan notes that if certain things puzzle us, we should see what Joyce says about them, but then he corrects himself: 'Joyce did not say it, he wrote it and that makes all the difference. When one writes, one can touch the real, but not the truth' (ibid.: 80; my translation). Here we have the core of the interest Lacan finds in Joyce, and in literature in general.

The notion that literature is the symptom, or *sinthome*, which allows one to avoid psychosis by introducing a fourth term which binds together the registers of the symbolic, the imaginary and the real, is perhaps not so hard to understand. So literature is the symptom. But you will notice that Lacan had said earlier that the father was a symptom and soon he will insist that woman is a symptom for man. So, what is at stake here? When it was a question of the father, it was Joyce's father in that he was deficient, defective, lacking for his son. As a result of which, Joyce felt obliged to have recourse to something else in that place—the place of A—the Church or literature and he finally chose the latter.

It is a bit more difficult to follow what all of this has to do with gender identity. Woman is a symptom for man but the reverse cannot be the case, simply because Lacan will not admit reciprocity between the genders. So what is man for a woman? Whatever you want, writes Lacan, perhaps *un ravage*, havoc (ibid.: 101).

To recapitulate what we have covered rather rapidly here: first, we have seen that the human subject, as subjected to language, receives his major determination from the symbolic order. That is to say, all identifications, even sexual, can be seen as related to the sway of the letter. Second, with the example of Gide's lost love letters, we see the letter as the illustration of the fact that the speaking subject elects a fetish to hide the lack he experiences in the field of desire. Finally, with the case of Joyce, Lacan comes to the function of art, per se, as the *sinthome*, as that which binds together the registers of symbolic, imaginary and real and thus prevents the subject from falling into psychosis—that was the fate of Joyce's daughter Lucia, for example. In this way, Lacan may well have been pointing to art as another possibility to be set alongside psychoanalysis.

One last point that we should not forget to mention is: Lacan quotes Joyce's play on words, 'letter–litter'. The letter is trash. This quote is mentioned in the conference of 16 June 1975 for the opening of the Fifth International James Joyce Symposium. As we reread this conference paper, we may get the idea that what Lacan has pointed out is, in fact, all too obvious, but what can be done about it?

References

ENGLISH SOURCES

GIDE, André. 1952. *Madeleine (Et nunc manet in te)* (Justin O'Brien trans.). New York: Alfred A. Knopf,

———. 1973. *The Counterfeiters* (Dorothy Bussy trans.). Reprint, New York: Vintage Books.

FREUD, Sigmund. 1955. *Beyond the Pleasure Principle* in *The Standard Edition of the Complete Psychological Works of Sigmund Freud*, VOL. 18 (James Strachey ed., and trans.). London: Hogarth Press and the Institute of Psycho-Analysis, pp. 7–64.

LACAN, Jacques. 1988. *The Seminar of Jacques Lacan. Book II. The Ego in Freud's Theory and in the Technique of Psychoanalysis, 1954–55* (Jacques-Alain Miller ed., Silvana Tomaselli trans., with notes by John Forrester). Cambridge: Cambridge University Press.

———. 1998. *The Seminar of Jacques Lacan. Book XX. Encore: On Feminine Sexuality, The Limits of Love and Knowledge, 1972–73* (Jacques-Alain Miller ed., Bruce Fink trans.). New York and London: W. W. Norton.

———. 2006a. 'Seminar on "The Purloined Letter"' in *Écrits: The First Complete Edition in English* (Bruce Fink trans.). New York and London: W. W. Norton, pp. 6–48.

———. 2006b. 'The Youth of Gide, or the Letter and Desire' in *Écrits: The First Complete Edition in English* (Bruce Fink trans.). New York and London: W. W. Norton, pp. 623–44.

Poe, Edgar Allan. 1983. 'The Purloined Letter' in *The Complete Tales and Poems of Edgar Allan Poe*. Harmondsworth: Penguin, pp. 208–22.

FRENCH SOURCES

Gide, André. *La Jeunesse d'André Gide*. 2 vols. Paris: Éditions Gallimard.

Lacan, Jacques. 1957. 'Le séminaire sur "La Lettre Volée"'. *La Psychanalyse* 2: 1–44. Subsequently published in *Écrits* (1966).

————. 1958. 'Jeunesse de Gide ou la lettre et désir'. *Critique* 131: 291–315. Subsequently published in *Écrits* (1966).

————. 1966. *Écrits*. Paris: Éditions du Seuil.

————. 1975. *Le Séminaire. Livre XX. Encore, 1972–73* (Jacques-Alain Miller ed.). Paris: Éditions du Seuil.

————. 1978. *Le Séminaire. Livre II. Le moi dans la théorie de Freud et dans la technique de la psychanalyse, 1954–55* (Jacques-Alain Miller ed.). Paris: Éditions du Seuil.

————. 2005. *Le Séminaire. Livre XXIII. Le Sinthome, 1975–76* (Jacques-Alain Miller ed.). Paris: Éditions du Seuil.

Psychoanalysis Applicable and Inapplicable:
The Case of Literature[1]

JEAN-MICHEL RABATÉ

My central insight was brought to me when I took a second look at Pierre Bayard's 2004 book whose challenging title posed a crucial question: can one apply literature to psychoanalysis? To such a question, I was tempted at first to give a very simple, monosyllabic and enthusiastically positive answer: 'Yes!' Yes, of course, one can and should apply literature to psychoanalysis. More precisely, it seemed to me, this is what Sigmund Freud, Jacques Lacan and a few others (Jacques Derrida, perhaps) always wanted to do. After all, was not Freud pleading for a similar notion when he pointed to literature as one of the fields that a psychoanalyst is expected to be conversant with in order to be fully prepared? You will find this stated in several places, and most explicitly in *The Question of Lay Analysis* (1926; here 1950), in the passage where he opposes the notion of a purely medical training for psychoanalysts:

> If a psychoanalytical faculty were to be set up [. . .] much would have to be taught in it which is also taught in a medical faculty. Besides depth-psychology, that is, the psychology of the unconscious, which will always be the main subject, some biology would be required; [. . .] and some knowledge of the clinical pictures dealt with in psychiatry. On the other hand, the analytical curriculum would include subjects which are far removed from medicine and which a doctor would never require in his practice: the history of civilization, mythology, the psychology of religion, and literature. Unless he is well oriented

---

1 The essay is based on an unpublished lecture given by the author at Leuven in February 2008.—Ed.

in these fields, the analyst will be unable to bring understanding to bear upon much of his material (1950: 118).

In the original, Freud does not simply allude to a knowledge of literature that might be accumulated via assiduous readings of poems, novels and plays. He uses the term *Literaturwissenschaft* (1926: 116), a term that combines literary expertise and literary criticism, the latter figuring as a plausible 'science of literature'. Literature, in so far as it is essential to the training of a competent analyst, defines a field that goes beyond his habitual peppering of psychoanalytic essays with quotes from Johann Wolfgang von Goethe, William Shakespeare and Heinrich Heine. It is to include a 'science of interpretation', which should not be limited to the literary field but can be appropriated to refine individual diagnoses, probe the complexities of patients' psychologies more deeply, attest to the power of transgenerational dramas. In Freud's view, *Literaturwissenschaft* is not merely a sign of one's good education in the humanities, not simply a token of cultural distinction but a training in itself: it condenses an entire knowledge that one will 'apply' with the greatest benefit.

This, however, does not seem to be what Bayard has in mind when he gives us this provocative title. By this question, which he means as an ironical or paradoxical inversion of the usual pattern, he wants to question the usual way in which psychoanalysis is applied to literature. Bayard aims at overturning the assumptions of standard psychoanalytic criticism. Even though he begins by stating that his attempt to launch a new critical school to consistently apply literature to psychoanalysis has been a failure, he assesses more seriously a current consensus about the failure of psychoanalytic literary criticism. Most of us would agree that schools of psychoanalytic criticism tend to seem like things of the past, at least in competitive academic circles. It would be hard for a candidate to a good American graduate programme to be accepted with a plan to study Hamlet's unconscious inhibitions or to assess the consequences of the castration complex in Fyodor Dostoyevsky. Vladimir Nabokov was the first among several visible novelists and critics in the 1950s to rail against 'the Viennese quack'; he would often dismiss Freud's medievalism, his alleged oeniromancy and mythogeny. I will return to Nabokov in conclusion, and take him now as only typical of this wholesale rejection. Indeed, if we hear the phrase philosophically, with Henri-Louis Bergson's ears let's say, 'applied' always carries an ironical ring—Bergson's definition of the comic as a mechanical element *plaqué* (that is, mechanically applied) to the human rings true in such a context. Laughter will thus generally greet any 'application' of psychoanalysis to literature. This ironical or sarcastic turn of mind is obviously not dominant in Bayard's case, since he is both a professor of French literature and a psychoanalyst in Paris. Like him, I would like to refrain from laughing so as to probe new directions, even if the zeitgeist may look inauspicious.

Accordingly, Bayard rings if not sarcastic at least critical when he examines how psychoanalysis has been applied to literature. Going back to carefully chosen canonical explorations such as Sarah Kofman's *L'enfance de l'art* (1970; here 1985) and Jean Bellemin-Noël's *Vers l'inconscient du texte* (1979), he points out that Freud's theory implies a dubious pre-eminence for creative writers: since they are credited with having hit upon Freud's concepts before he did, any awareness of the process is refused since they did not know what they had found or why. In fact, creative writers still need psychoanalytic discourse to make sense of their brilliant but opaque intuitions. Bayard rightly distinguishes between classical psychobiography as practised by Marie Bonaparte or Charles Mauron and Bellemin-Noël's psychoanalytic readings; that is, approaches deployed without any anchoring in the writer's subjectivity or biography. He does not spare Lacan in this general review: 'And Lacan does not seem to innovate on that issue, alternating critical texts in which the author is taken into account—as for Gide or Joyce—and texts in which the readings are not founded in any privileged manner on the life of the author, as with *Hamlet*' (2004: 37; my translation). However, Bayard adds in a footnote that the manner in which Lacan has invented concepts from his readings of literary works should bring him closer to 'applied literature' (ibid.: 37, 1n). Indeed, one cannot deny that Lacan was a 'structuralist' with Edgar Allan Poe, William Shakespeare, Paul Claudel and Marguerite Duras, and somewhat disconcertingly ventured towards psychobiography when dealing with André Gide and James Joyce. I will return to this hesitation to assess whether Lacan was inconsistent—as Élisabeth Roudinesco and others believe—or whether his indifference to the inclusion or exclusion of the author's life may not send us on a different path.

For Bayard, the main point is to acknowledge that both schools (psychobi-ographical or textualist) are united by a common belief in the anteriority and superiority of psychoanalysis facing literature (ibid.: 37). Both schools rely therefore on hermeneutics; they believe that all one has to do is disentangle meanings hidden or simply lurking latently in the works. As this meaning is, by definition, partly unconscious, the author cannot know nor control the dark forces that made the work happen. For Bayard, the problem is that these read-ings will only produce results that conform to an initial theory and thus will remain within the category of finalist readings. They deploy themselves exactly like religious readings since what is found in the texts will be less a product of the investigation than of its origins and presuppositions. This is a point made vehemently by Tzvetan Todorov about Biblical interpretations: in most of these, the Bible will have, first of all, to confirm Christian doctrine. In the same way, canonical psychoanalytical readings will merely confirm the truth of psy-choanalysis about the Oedipus complex, unconscious fantasies, primal scenes and the determining role of childhood memories. This does not entail, in fact, that the results will be false or the method wrong, but simply—and more dam-agingly perhaps—that they are entirely predictable. It was such repetitiveness and predictability that generated boredom and finally, theoretical sterility.

Bayard's choice, on the other hand, will be to opt for a literature that can be applied to psychoanalysis; thus he wants to meditate on the way in which texts reflect on psychological phenomena (ibid.: 48). Applied literature would focus on moments of emergence, on a new knowledge that would be shared by the reader. Bayard however readily admits that his strategy risks not con-vincing anyone. It will sway neither the psychoanalysts who will feel contested by it, nor the critics who come from other schools that have no patience with psychoanalysis as such. True to his misgivings, I have to confess that I have not been convinced in the least by his examples. All the plays or novels that he adduces (one can recognize a canon that he has explored earlier, with Pierre Laclos, Marcel Proust, Guy de Maupassant, Agatha Christie and William Shakespeare) tend to show that literature 'thinks' by itself, unaided, and that it can stage the most complex psychological problems. This is hardly news for any teacher of literature! The last part of his book, which follows a historical recapitulation of the predecessors and successors of Freud (especially those who have not read him but 'know' him somehow), is entitled 'How Does Literature Think'. In the end, the analysis fizzles out and ends up restating Susan Sontag's thesis in *Against Interpretation* (1966; here 2001). What do we gain from the notion that anger had been truly and deeply depicted by Homer in the *Iliad*, at a time when psychoanalysis did not exist? We may all readily agree to the idea that the invention of psychology has been parallel to the development of literature, like we will be ready to see in Maupassant and Robert Louis Stevenson convincing predecessors of Freud.

An American take on all this would tend to be more historical and would point, for example, to the links between *Madame Bovary* (1857; here 2002) and the invention of hysteria in French medicine that culminated with Jean-Martin Charcot's discoveries. Bayard notes more importantly that literature became a field of predilection for psychoanalysis at the time that it was being invented, when Freud, Otto Rank, Sándor Ferenczi and others wanted to test its hypotheses by applying them to culture, and thus, synecdochically, to literature. Now that this discourse has been over-systematized, the issue is: how to continue being inventive. I agree with Bayard that there has been an exhaustion of unconscious hermeneutics after Freud (2004: 157). Bayard believes that the solution lies on the side of literature, and that the future task for criticism consists in generating new theoretical forms from purely literary models. All this remains vague and quite programmatic, as Bayard gestures in the direction of new marginal conceptions of subjectivity found in literary texts, which might avoid the closure of dominant models (ibid.: 160). Finally, given its riches, its diversity and its subversive potentialities, literature would signal the disappearance of psychoanalysis as an interpretive paradigm (ibid.: 164). In the end, the only chance of success of 'applied literature' would be both to acknowledge its paranoid tendencies—meaning its wish to postulate a new and grandiose system able to replace all previous ones—and its inability to say 'we' inspite of its conviction that it has to speak only in the first person.

I had used a similar argument when concluding a presentation on Lacan's reading of Joyce with the idea that, if I wanted to answer clearly the question I had posed: '*Qui jouit de la jouissance de Joyce?*' (Who enjoys Joyce's jouissance?), I could not avoid answering in the first person: '*Moi, je jouis de la jouissance de Joyce*' (I enjoy Joyce's jouissance).' However, I could only do this because I was punning on *ego* (I) and *egaux* (the plural of equal): '*Tous ego devant la jouissance*' (All equal/all egos facing jouissance) (Rabaté 2005: 177). Here, my answer anticipates Lacan's reading of Joyce as an Ego-Symptom, to indicate briefly the direction that I want to take. More broadly, I would want to state my disagreement with the drift of Bayard's argument, even if we do agree that, ideally, it is literature that should be applied to psychoanalysis, and not the other way round. Moreover, we are both aware that the task, if not impossible, may at least have to be pushed back to an indefinite future.

The debate about psychoanalysis and literature has not been resolved satisfactorily by Bayard. My dissatisfaction grew when I reached the end of the book, which concludes with an evocation of reading in a Montaigne-inspired solitude:

> It is not true indeed that literature, after it has, once and for all, delivered its knowledge about psychology, would have nothing to teach us. And it is wrong to believe that having learnt from its multiple thoughts, there would remain nothing that could help us read and love. And wrong above all to imagine that my wish to listen to it would be destroyed by my own criticism, even when—for I keep my own reserve nevertheless—I have discovered a way that would allow me to be taught by books, in the tranquility found at last in the absence of dialogue, alone at last (Bayard 2004: 173; my translation).

On the contrary, I would suggest that once we have begun splicing literature and psychoanalysis, we cannot be left alone in peace, we cannot continue pottering round the stacks in the meditative peace of Montaigne's walled-in library. My inclination will thus be to find a different way out, notably via Lacan's use or uses of literature. Now I want to focus on one key issue: why is Lacan relentless in his critique of Freud's strategy of 'verifying' psychoanalysis by 'applying' it to literature? Can Lacan himself avoid applying psychoanalysis to literature? Is he really consistent on this point? This would be the core of Derrida's reproach in his 1975 'Le facteur de la vérité' (here 1987). Very cogently, Derrida accuses Lacan of reducing literary texts to examples that confirm a pre-established truth. Such a tendency would seem, indeed, to have been generalized by the proliferating readings of Slavoj Žižek that multiply examples proving Lacan's mathemes to be true. In the course of my essay, this will imply making another detour via the old debate that opposed Lacan and Derrida in the 1970s.

However, I will suggest that Lacan's later theory of the *sinthome*, even when it flirted with psychobiography, did aim at pushing psychoanalysis away from the danger of exemplarity; that is the reduction of textual singularity to dogmatic schemes. If a symptom is less what a patient wants to be cured of than the condensed statement of his or her individuality, literature, in so far as it leads to the *sinthome*, tends to disclose the most proper element of the human dimension. Joyce's writing practice thus offers Lacan less a field to be ploughed following a predictable and repeatable procedure than a model of linguistic equivocation in which the psychoanalytic cure finds renewed youth.

Lacan argues for the centrality of the letter and literature in psychoanalysis while dismissing anything that looked like applied psychoanalysis, especially when applied to the field of literature. How can we make sense of this seeming contradiction? Several attempts have been made in the last decade to produce Lacanian readings of literary texts with the view of applying Lacanian insights to literature. Apart from a few exceptions, they tend to be disappointing, and I have had the opportunity of pointing out what I see as misguided in Ben Stoltzfus' 1996 *Lacan and Literature: Purloined Pretexts* (see Rabaté 2001: 216). On the whole, I saw in Stoltzfus a case of classical Freudian criticism disguised as Lacanian discourse. Stoltzfus' issues hinge round Oedipal desire and the fear of castration in a hermeneutics founded upon character analysis. Typically, Lacanian concepts are invoked to update an exhausted critical vocabulary.

It does not matter if theoretical asides reveal misreadings of Lacan's concepts like S1 and S2 (presented as a variation on the classical semiotic triangle)—S1 is depicted as a master signifier whose signified is 'the sea' while S2 is equalled to a repressed 'referent', the mother as *la mère* (Stoltzfus 1996: 97–9). For Lacan, there would be only one signifier in this case, something that would sound like *lamer*, and then its sliding along the signifying chain would create a polysemy in which one could then, indeed, distinguish a master signifier or S1 from the S2 of unconscious knowledge. The thesis underlying all of Stoltzfus' readings is that literary texts repeat past traumas by re-enacting primal fantasies, even though, thanks to Freud's insights, these traumas may never have taken place at all (ibid.: 95).

All this is purely Freudian, even if a latent Jungianism is perceptible in remarks about why the dream functions like an 'iconic, masked mirror of the unconscious' which then faces a 'linguistic reflector' provided by fiction (ibid.: 2). This is why it is important to show discrepancies between pre-Freudian or non-Freudian psychoanalytic approaches, Freudian approaches and finally Lacanian strategies facing literature. Lacan often advances his theses by reading Freud closely and then dramatically changing the perspective. One can see this process at work most revealingly when Lacan revisits Freud's central insight that Hamlet is a modern-day version of an older, starker and more uninhibited Oedipus. It took Lacan some close reading of *Hamlet* (here 2003) to hit upon a snag in the usual Freudian reading, namely its dependence upon an unexamined and also questionable psychology, which is why it will never be sufficient to say, like Bayard, that literature's function is to provide a parallel account of human psychology. Lacan throws into light the dependence of Freud's Oedipal model upon a psychological reasoning that can easily be reversed:

> [About *Hamlet*] What does the psychoanalytic tradition tell us? That everything hinges round the desire for the mother, that this desire is repressed and that this is the cause for which the hero could not approach the act that is requested of him, namely, revenge against a man who is the current possessor, now illegitimate because a criminal, of the maternal object. If he cannot strike the person who has been pointed out for his vindication, it is because he himself has already committed the crime to be avenged. Inasmuch as there is, in the background, the memory of an infantile desire for the mother, of the Oedipal desire to murder the father, Hamlet would in a sense become an accomplice of the current owner, *beatus possidens*, in his eyes. He could not attack this owner without attacking himself. Is this what they mean?—or he could not attack this possessor without reawakening in himself the old desire, felt as a guilty one, in a mechanism that makes obviously more sense.

Let us not get fascinated by such a non-dialectical scheme. Could we not say that everything could be reversed? If Hamlet were to jump immediately on his stepfather, could one not say that he finds in this an opportunity to quench his guilt? (Lacan 1982: 19; my translation).

With one deft thrust, Lacan punches a hole in Freud's central contention: Hamlet cannot kill his uncle in revenge for his father's murder because the uncle has accomplished his (Hamlet's) deepest incestuous wishes. This, for Lacan, is a 'non-dialectical' argument, since it rests on an unquestioned psychology of imitation. Freud's psychologization of the main characters' French triangle (as Joyce would say) has been founded on a common-sense view, hence it can be easily turned into the opposite. It is no stretch of imagination to suppose that Hamlet would want to punish a successful rival—the notion was brought home to Lacan in his study of the mirror stage and of the role of aggressivity in psychoanalysis. Lacan's shift from an objective genitive (*'désir de la mère'* means 'desire for the mother') to a subjective genitive (*'désir de la mère'* is read as 'her desire for another man') is a 'dialectical' reversal refuting a psychology of mimetism that assumes that one would not want to punish someone who acts out one's deepest longings. Hamlet's inhibition will thus be seen to stem from his archaic desire for his mother, but more because the paralysis derives from his fixation with the riddle of Gertrude's desire for another man, whether his uncle or father.

In order to avoid relying undialectically on common-sense psychology, Lacan argues, one has to read the text carefully, closely and pay attention to its recurrent signifiers such as 'Ophelia' and 'phallus', 'foils' and 'foil', so as to connect dynamically these linguistic *Knotenpunkte* in a phenomenology of the desiring subject. Hamlet's false start as a desiring subject who questions the very source of desire will have to pass beyond the archaic object, or the mother, to then meet the phallus and death, before reaching an awareness of the place of the Other as determining desire. Such a complex phenomenology of stages will lead finally to an ethics of the desiring subject.

In this context it is worth rehearsing Lacan's critique of applied psychoanalysis—especially to literature. Having understood the need for such dialectic of subjectivity, one can re-contextualize staple psychoanalytical interpretations that take psychobiography as an unavoidable starting point or framework. Marie Bonaparte's monumental psychobiography of Poe published in 1933 was introduced by Freud in glowing terms. His foreword stated:

> In this book my friend and pupil, Marie Bonaparte, has shone the light of psycho-analysis on the life and work of a great writer with pathologic trends.
>
> Thanks to her interpretive effort, we now realize how many of the characteristics of Poe's works were conditioned by his personality, and can see how that personality derived from intense emotional fixations and painful infantile experiences. Investigations such as this do not claim to explain creative genius, but they do reveal the factors which awaken it and the sort of subject matter it is destined to choose. Few tasks are as appealing as enquiry into the laws that govern the psyche of exceptionally endowed individuals (1949: xi).

Clearly, Freud was enthusiastic when he saw the concept of a single author's psychobiography completed. His approach was very close to this, as can be verified from his texts on Leonardo da Vinci, Dostoyevsky and other writers. Biographical readings appear as a condition for the discovery of the deep links between creations and neurotic or pathological features in their creators. In his foreword, Freud's use of the term personality could call up its use in Lacan's doctoral thesis on paranoia and its relation to personality, published in 1932, only one year before Bonaparte's book on Poe.

Breaking with this endorsement of applied psychoanalysis, Lacan repeatedly attacks the very idea of applying psychoanalysis to literature which he thought was misguided at best and at worst a symptomatic failure leading to the 'hogwash' of common psychoanalytic criticism. In a discussion on literature at Yale University, Lacan opposed the 'letter' to 'literature' and added that if Freud needed literature to define the unconscious, the readings that Freud produced were dated or limited in their scope. In the 1956 'Seminar on "The Purloined Letter"' (1957; here 1988), he rails against Marie Bonaparte, who seemed to believe that Poe was simply a precursor of Freud:

Just so does the purloined letter, like an immense female body, stretch out across the Minister's office when Dupin enters. But just so does he already expect to find it, and has only, with his eyes veiled by green lenses, to undress that huge body.

And that is why without needing any more than being able to listen in at the door of Professor Freud, he will go straight to the spot in which lies and lives what that body is designed to hide, in a gorgeous center caught in a glimpse, nay, to the very place seducers name Sant'Angelo's castle in the innocent illusion of controlling the City from within it. Look! Between the cheeks of the fireplace, there's the object already in reach of a hand the ravisher has but to extend [. . .] The question of deciding whether he seizes it above the mantelpiece as Baudelaire translates, or beneath it, as in the original text, may be abandoned without harm to the inferences of those whose profession is grilling (1988: 48).

Lacan appends a note at the end of the last sentence with the even more enigmatic remark: 'And even to the cook herself' (ibid.: 14n).

Marie Bonaparte was here the butt of Lacan's satire, since it was she who had corrected Charles Baudelaire's mistranslation in her French book on Poe. Even if she had Freud's ear, Bonaparte is reduced to an ancillary 'cook' or, even worse, to a torturer who 'grills' suspects until they confess the crimes that they have been framed for. In a sense, this previous reading by Bonaparte had been a blessing for Lacan, who was spared the trouble of 'interpreting' literature because of the negative model set by her all-too-eager quest for unconscious truths and Oedipal resolutions. It is Derrida who later accuses Lacan of repeating and simplifying Bonaparte's argument, thereby missing the richness of psychobiographical criticism—for example, attention to a series of images that migrate from story to story (Derrida 1987: 442–54).

In Lacan's seminar on Poe, a salient feature of the story is its logical structure, its pattern of ironic repetitions. Three scenes are superposed: in the first scene, we have a 'blind' king, who embodies the Law but is unable to understand that anything is happening at all, a 'seeing' queen who suffers but remains impotent while the daring minister profits from the interaction between the first two. He puts his letter on the table, leaves with the coveted prize, knowing that the queen cannot ask for it without awakening suspicions.

The second scene details the futile efforts by the police to retrieve the letter on behalf of the queen. This time, the 'blind' character is the prefect of police and, by extension, his men, who cannot find the letter because they assume that it must be hidden. They are projecting as a reality their notion of what 'hiding' means, never imagining that the letter could be hidden by being left in full view. The 'seeing' character who cannot do much in this case is the minister who basks in the imaginary security afforded by the letter's possession. The active agent is Dupin who identifies creatively with the minister, reconstructs his mental process, sees all, prepares an exact double of the stolen letter and devises the strategy to distract the minister.

The third scene reverses the first theft. The minister has now turned into a 'blind' man unaware of what is happening, while Dupin acts and, moreover, signs his substitution by quoting lines from Prosper Jolyot de Crébillon that will identify him as soon as the minister decides to check the contents of the missive. Caught up in brotherly rivalry, Dupin is animated less by honour or greed than by the wish to settle an old account. He thus exposes himself to the gaze of the author, Poe, and his readers, including Lacan. One will need to reconstitute the tale's logic and follow its psychical economy if one wants to avoid 'stealing' the letter by imposing a meaning or a content on it.

The force of Lacan's structuralist reading is undeniable, although it may lead to its undermining. How can one prevent another 'turn of the screw' and stop the triangular permutations at any point? Such a pattern cannot provide a Hegelian resolution that would bring the dialectic of blindness and vision to a point of absolute knowledge. As Barbara Johnson masterfully demonstrates, when Derrida accuses Lacan of translating the contentless letter into a content, a 'truth' defined by femininity and castration, he himself sees too much, translates too soon, reduces Lacan's stylistic games and thus misreads a seminar that was no less 'literary' than Poe's story (Johnson 1977).

What matters therefore in Lacan's reading is not the series of imaginary projections that each moment or position entails but the careful mapping out of a symbolic structure that determines each subject's position facing the others and the Other. This symbolic structure is described as a chain of effects determined by the revolving displacements of a signifier. In Poe's story, the letter allegorizes the itinerary of a signifier whose signified remains inaccessible. Lacan stresses the issue of intersubjectivity, a term that may sound dated, but is nevertheless indispensable: it is used in the sense of 'intersubjective complex' or 'intersubjective repetition', so as to point out that no single subjective position can be described in isolation. The subjective positions are caught in a repetition automatism ensuring that the letter comes back to the same place at the end. Quite logically, Derrida voices doubts as to the legitimacy of this postulated economy: can we say with Lacan that 'a letter always reaches its destination?' Do not letters get lost, stolen or destroyed?

However, let us note that Derrida always links his critique with a repudiation of anything that resembled applied psychoanalysis, thus repeating Lacan's gesture. Derrida resists the idea that one could use literary texts as mere examples:

> From the outset, we recognize the classical landscape of applied psychoanalysis. Here applied to literature. Poe's text, whose status is never examined—Lacan simply calls it 'fiction'—, finds itself invoked as an 'example.' An 'example' destined to 'illustrate', in a didactic procedure, a law and a truth forming the proper object of a seminar. Literary writing, here, is brought into an illustrative position: 'to illustrate' here meaning to read the general law in the example, to make clear the meaning of a law or of a truth, to bring them to light in striking or exemplary fashion. The text is in the service of the truth, and of a truth that is taught (1987: 425–6).

According to Derrida, psychoanalytic criticism cannot but reduce the form of a text to a teleology. Žižek has answered to these objections very cogently in *Enjoy your Symptom!* (1992), showing that at an imaginary level, a letter always reaches its destination because whoever receives the letter retroactively believes he or she is the addressee, in a movement similar to Althusserian interpellation. On a symbolic level, the circulation of the letter itself assures that it has already reached its destination, the Other or the symbolic order itself. This is enhanced by an important detail that Žižek does not discuss. Even if Minister

D recognizes the handwriting on the address and infers from it the real cause of the queen's embarrassment—he 'fathoms her secret' in one gaze (Poe 1983: 210)—we are never told the identity of the sender. The only thing we know about the identity of the sender is that he is a duke whose name begins with the letter S. We are deprived of any information as to the contents of the letter. We do not know what links the sender has with the queen. Not only is the letter always in circulation as far as the story is concerned, but it seems impossible that the letter be returned to its actual writer. Only a bold scribbler like Alexandre Dumas would dare to disclose to the readers that the sender might be identified as Georges Villiers, the English lover of Queen Ann of Austria, to superimpose here the plot of another novel, a famous novel to be sure, *The Three Musketeers* (here 2008), in which part of the twisted story concerns jewels that would betray the queen. *The Three Musketeers* began being serialized in 1844 which, by an uncanny coincidence, was the year when Poe published for the first time 'The Purloined Letter' in an American magazine.

Since Poe wrote, deliberately or not, the exact inverse of the Romantic historical novel by going directly at the core of the textual logic of exchanges underpinning such easy fantasies, we witness a letter that cannot be sent back to an empirical sender while nevertheless reaching its destination, which is the locus of the Other, the birthplace of all desires and fantasies. The 'agency of the letter' at work in Poe's tale does not entail an ideality of a closed economy, as Derrida contends, but guarantees that the workings of language displaces identities thanks to the constant sliding away of the signifier. For in the end, as Žižek states, the third reading of the 'destination' of the letter can only be death; since this signifier, seemingly immortal, brings mortality to the fore. This is indeed the point where Derrida and Lacan meet—when both emphasize the lethal dimension of the letter's endless self-erasure.

Thus, if the letter always returns to its destination, it is not to its sender (which would effectively close off the circle of an accomplished 'economy' of the gift) but to its addressee, which implies that such a 'destination' is already 'destined'. Both ends of the letter's trajectory are thus open, as we may even wonder whether the prefect will actually hand back the letter to the queen! He might have had personal motivations for enlisting Dupin's help, and we cannot be so sure that the poor queen can be allowed to sleep safely after all is said and done. At least, it has reached one addressee, Lacan, and by implication, all of us. While it is not true, as Derrida asserts, that Lacan fails to address the issue of the narrator of the story, both Derrida and Lacan wish—differently, it is true—to integrate the act of interpretation into the system of the text. The intersubjective triad interpellates Lacan as a reader: the third repetition of the triangular pattern implies that Lacan has perceived that Dupin has shifted to an imaginary position. Contrary to what Derrida states, neither in the second nor in the third triad does the analyst withdraw from the symbolic circuit— the reader as analyst tries to inhabit the blind spot of the text, which allows for the perception of the letter not in so far as its contents matter, but in so far as it moves along the chain to impact the very act of interpretation. When Lacan sees Dupin see himself and thus turn into a good example of the rule that the *non-dupes errent* (those who do not want to be duped are erring or mistaken), since it entails a constant floating away of the *nom du père* (Name-of-the-Father), he effectively takes part in the mechanism of the passage of a symptom. He will be the next one to be implicated in imaginary delusion if he believes that he too possesses a secret knowledge lying too visibly on the surface.

Perhaps because he believes that there is something like the ownership of this secret, perhaps because he is jealous of such a position of analytic mastery, Derrida strives to adopt the position of the analyst, who finds a solution to a subjective problem of interpretation by facilitating a repetition with a crucial difference. However, against his strictures, Lacan's reading of 'The Purloined Letter' never fully abandons the textuality of the text, whether Poe's text or the seminar's. Fundamentally, what he chooses to ignore as the 'scene of writing' implying the narrator derives from a deliberate effort to avoid the pitfalls of Bonaparte's psychobiographical reading. Against Bonaparte, against Derrida, Lacan had to repress the fact that the tale was written by Poe in a given historical period, with clearly identifiable literary clichés, models and genres. These were aspects of textuality and of literariness in which Lacan was not interested, precisely because it was the text's literality that engaged him at the level of a riddle, or as the tip of an allegory's sunken mass.

If there is a site in the unconscious in which Lacan does not situate himself in the seminar on Poe, it is the unconscious of the text, an unconscious that he skirts in favour of the knowledge that he gleans there. Does Derrida escape such a repression? Derrida opposes the undecidability and infinity of literature to any idealization aiming at modelizing it in the name of a pre-established truth that simply confirms its presuppositions. He sees Lacan as his other, a would-be purveyor of truths. But as most commentators have pointed out, one cannot produce a reading of any text without reducing or suppressing certain elements—pure textuality will always have to be streamlined to offer something like a theme, a structure, a plot or a narrative. This is what we have to be ready to account for: a certain loss, without which we would not even be able to talk about texts in general. There is a certain impossibility of remaining at the level of pure textuality, we cannot stay always with the text qua text, and we will inevitably need modelizations, exemplifications—and why not—a few conceptual handles. Which sends us back all the more violently to the question of applying anything to texts—such as psychoanalytical concepts, for example. It might thus be the case that whoever attacks applied psychoanalysis will end up applying it but without knowing it, and more insistently as a symptom.

Jean-Luc Nancy and Philippe Lacoue-Labarthe have suggested, in a similar critical assessment as Derrida's, that it is because Lacan's theories do not form a totalizing system that they avoid reductionism, idealization and psychoanalytic mastery of truth. Lacan's theses do not exploit literary examples to confirm Freud's insights since they present themselves as 'literary' and not as 'scientific' as Freud hoped his theories were, which implies that literature has a more loaded role to play in Lacanian discourse. Literature would inhabit the theory from the beginning so as to make it tremble, hesitate and complicate its own status. Literature ruins the mirage of a pure and clean theory fitting neatly well-chosen 'examples'. In other words, it is important to distinguish an 'application' from a pure 'exemplification'. The application imports some of the dynamism of literary devices into the theory whereas exemplification merely seeks the confirmation of pre-established truths.

Thus Nancy and Lacoue-Labarthe conclude an analysis of Lacan's elaboration on metaphor in these terms:

It is certainly not by chance if, along with the usual meaning of the word 'metaphor', Lacan also incorporates the literary genre where we seem to find it most often—namely poetry, and more precisely poetry circumscribed by two references: Hugo and surrealism. [. . .] That is, the poetry that we are able to designate, in its own terms, as that of the Word—of Divine Speech or of speech—and of the 'power' or 'magic' of words. An entire poetics of this order and an entire poetic practice of this style indeed subtend Lacan's text, here as elsewhere, in its literary references, its peculiar stylistic effects, and finally its theoretical articulations (1992: 74).

True, they point out Lacan's equivocations about the role of Martin Heidegger in his discourse and his invocation of a hidden truth accessible to the psychoanalyst. However, they understand why Lacan is reluctant to found his discourse rigorously except in a practice of reading (of Freud's texts), moving strategically between a pragmatics of therapy and philosophy, of linguistics, rhetoric and anthropology. This forces him in the end to stand out as a 'literary' theoretician, a home-made *bricoleur* of theory, whose conceptual borrowings create a singularly syncretic writing which is less the definitive statement of a 'founder' of discursivity than the textual experiments of a quester often doubled by a jester.

Our current debate should assess the consequence of Lacan's central contention that there is 'no metalanguage': truth can never be uttered fully in a philosophical or scientific discourse buttressed upon axioms, basic definitions and fundamental concepts. Even the 'four fundamental concepts' of Freudian psychoanalysis cannot be unearthed or isolated from the dense tissue of Freudian texts as evinced in *The Seminar of Jacques Lacan. Book XI. The Four Fundamental Concepts of Psychoanalysis, 1961* (1973; here 1981). These concepts describe a movement, which, even if it can be stabilized at various points and in various graphs, will go on. Lacan staunchly refuses to sum up Freud's 'basic terms' in an axiomatic vocabulary as is done too often. In order to avoid reductive views, he shows how to reopen Freud's texts. Reading them as literally as possible often entailed reading them as literarily as possible, at times indeed against the grain of their explicit intentions. Literature is the site in which no intentional fallacy will ever obtain. If Freud's works are indistinguishable from literature, Lacan becomes a literary critic who applies the knowledge gained thereby to one precise situation, that of clinical practice. Such literature is to be grasped fundamentally as made up of letters.

In the context of the discussion regarding Poe, this sends us back to the way in which Lacan's argument implies a conception of the letter as an entity that is truly 'uncuttable'. In a long semantic analysis based on a few French idioms, he shows that one can speak of 'letters' in the plural but one cannot say 'there is letter' (*de la lettre*) or 'there is some letter' in the same fashion as 'there is time' or 'there is butter here.' Like literature, the letter is what in linguistics is called 'uncountable'. Whether singular or plural, it cannot be divided or cut into pieces—even if it was, it would still be a collection of fragments belonging to a letter. This is why the police starts from the wrong assumption that the minister's room can be divided into smaller and smaller units, including all the objects, books, frames, table legs, etc. it contains, so that they may be examined with needles, magnifying glasses and all the technical apparatus of scientific detection.

Similarly, 'letter' either in French or in English entails a homophony that it does not in languages such as German. A 'letter' (*Brief*) can be made up of 'letters' as written signs (*Buchstaben*), but even if it has been destroyed—as Lacan shows when analyzing André Gide's personal letters to his wife in *Écrits* (1966a)—the letters remain present by their absence: they are made 'whole' by the 'hole' that they left in Gide's heart. Hence Lacan refused to distinguish any of the three meanings as he stressed in the seminar on Poe: 'as for the letter—be it taken as typographical character, epistle or what makes a man of letters' (1988: 39). If the 'Seminar on "The Purloined Letter"' sketches a topology of the letter, the review of Gide's biographies circumscribes an ontology of the letter—and both function as the mainstays of the volume of *Écrits*.

This ontology is dominated from the beginning by the key term of jouissance. As Lacan reads it in Gide, the letter circumscribes the edges of a hole left open by jouissance and then closed by the symbolic system. I will briefly traverse Lacan's discussion of Gide, and his focus on the scene of Gide's mourning after his wife had burnt their correspondence. The occasion for this was Lacan's double review of Jean Delay's *La Jeunesse d'André Gide* (1956–57) and of Jean Schlumberger's *Madeleine et André Gide* (1956). Recently, Eric Marty has denigrated the all-too-obvious 'literary' features of this essay (2005: 125–46). I would like to argue that its literalness is, in fact, a structural factor in what I see as the deployment of an ontology with which the later Lacan will renew himself.

The review pays homage to Delay's eminence as a psychiatrist and literary craftsman. Lacan does not share Delay's aim to produce a psychobiography, but recognizes that by exploring in depth a particular subject, Gide, one will get to the core of one person by throwing new light on 'the rapport between man and the letter' (1966a: 739; my translation). Delay's biography devotes 1,300 pages to Gide's life between 1869 and 1895 only, in the attempt to open Gide's secrets. Lacan portrays Jean Delay as a James Boswell for Samuel Johnson or a Johann Peter Eckermann for Goethe and reminds his readers of the fact that Charles Augustin Sainte-Beuve was not dead. Lacan alluded to the nineteenth century scholar who had made biographic criticism his speciality. Sainte-Beuve incurred Proust's rejection in *Against Sainte-Beuve* (1954; here 1988), a collection of essays that contained the seeds of the entire *In Search of Lost Time* (1913–27; here 2003): after all, *contre* means 'against' not only as an opposition but also in the sense of 'leaning against a wall'. It is exactly in that sense that Lacan may be said to be 'against psychobiographical criticism'. Christopher Prendergast has recently analyzed the lasting impact of Sainte-Beuve on French academic circles, connecting it with the invention of modern literary criticism (see Prendergast 2008).

Without frontally attacking such a biographical ambition, Lacan qualifies it. Proust's example tends to prove that one can hardly separate the matter of *In Search of Lost Time* from the author's life, a fact that is also visible in Joyce's quasi-autobiographies. Gide's, Proust's and Joyce's lives have contributed rough material to be treated and transformed by the texts. Thus there is no 'message' to be read in an author's life, except that this life would be subject to further elaboration:

> The only thing that counts is a truth derived from what is condensed by the message in its development. There is so little opposition between this *Dichtung* [fiction] and the *Wahrheit* [truth] in its bareness, that the fact of a poetic operation should rather bring us back to

a feature that is forgotten about every truth, namely that it is produced as truth (*qu'elle s'avère*) in a structure of fiction (Lacan 1966a:
741–2; my translation).

Gide was right to make fun of the de Gouncourt brothers, Edmond and
Jules, whose stupidity was revealed by the fact that they thought that one needs
to give 'proofs' and adduce all the time the factual reality of everything one
writes (ibid.: 742, 1n; my translation).

Lacan focuses on one episode—a textual gap mentioned by Delay, in the
acknowledgements, signalling the absence of any correspondence between
Gide and his wife. Delay's psychological reconstitution is indeed a 'marriage
of psychology and the letter', which finally proves that it is the letter that dom-
inates the author's psychology (ibid.: 747; my translation). In his extensive
biography, Delay, who was not ignorant of psychoanalysis, refused to produce
a work of 'applied psychoanalysis'. Lacan comments:

> He first rejects what this absurd phrase ['applied psychoanalysis'] re-
> veals of the confusion reigning there. Psychoanalysis can be applied
> in a strict sense only as treatment and therefore to a speaking and
> hearing subject. In this case, it can merely be a psychoanalytic
> method, proceeding to the deciphering of signifiers without paying
> any attention to the presupposed existence of the signified (ibid.:
> 747–8; my translation).

Delay's honesty and rigour in his biographical method allows him to expose the very 'structure of the subject' that psychoanalysis has outlined. Gide
himself had been introduced—briefly—to psychoanalysis, and even if he remained ironical or sceptical (he called Freud an 'idiot of genius' and made fun
of a 'wave of oedipedemics'), his works probe the complexities of human sexuality with a rare candour.

Gide's ambivalence facing his wife came to the fore in the text he published
after the death of Madeleine, *Et nunc manet in te* (1947). The riddle that Lacan,
like Delay and Schlumberger, tries to solve is the writer's obstinacy to marry
Madeleine, a slightly older cousin who was like a sister for him. Did Gide want
to protect her from a sexual scandal brought about by the aunt? He stuck to his
decision even after he had been made aware of his homosexual inclinations

and had been initiated in Biskra by Oscar Wilde and Lord Alfred Douglas. How could Gide, whose sensuality had developed early and whose homosexuality was blatant, decide to marry a cousin in an almost incestuous union, knowing full well that her sexuality would always remain unsatisfied? Did he believe in a 'mystical love' based upon sexual renunciation, did he want to reach a higher jouissance with a religious partner? In fact, the unconsummated marriage exacted its toll on Madeleine, who was kept in the dark as to her husband's sexual preference. In *Et nunc manet in te*, Gide admits that his wife soon appeared prematurely aged, saying that they were often taken for mother and son.

Delay's psychobiography examines all the factors that contributed to this fateful union while Lacan focuses on the drama generated by the deception: in 1918, Madeleine burnt all of Gide's letters to her in her rage after he left with Marc Allégret. Gide's reaction took excessive forms: he kept crying for one week, he claimed that it was worse than if he had lost a 'child'—'I am suffering as if she had killed our child' (Gide 1947: 80; my translation). Lacan describes this as 'the wail of a primate's female companion who has been struck in the belly' (1966a: 761; my translation). Madeleine knew that these letters were 'her most precious possession' as Gide had been in the habit of writing long letters daily since they were in their teens. The letters were kept as a shared treasure in a huge chest of drawers. But Madeleine had felt that she had to do something after Gide's betrayal in order not to become mad (Gide 1947: 81; my translation). Gide regained some distance facing his letters, meanwhile asserting proudly that 'Maybe there never was a more beautiful correspondence' (ibid.: 84; my translation).

The cult of the love letters became a 'passion', the alienation of desire by a fetishized object. Indeed, Madeleine noted that passion would suddenly distort the features of her husband, as when during their wedding trip to Algiers, Gide would, once in a while, go to the window in the train and furtively caress the arms and shoulders of seductive Arab boys. 'You looked like a criminal or a madman,' she confided to him (ibid.: 42; my translation). More fundamentally, Gide's perversion did not come from homosexual desire but from a desire to be the little boy that he once was, more precisely, the 'desired child' who had been the object of his aunt's sexual attentions.

André Gide's perversion consists in this that he can only constitute himself [. . .] by submitting himself to this correspondence that is the heart of his work—by being one whose importance increases if he is in his cousin's place, by being the person whose every thought is turned towards her, the one who literally gives her at every moment what he does not have, but nothing more than that—who constitutes himself as a personality only thanks to her. [. . .] This wife whom he does not desire becomes the object of a supreme love, and when this object with which he has filled up the hole of a love without desire comes to disappear, he cries out the miserable shout whose connection I have pointed out with the comical cry par excellence, that of the miser—*My casket! My dear casket!* (Lacan 1998b: 260–1; my translation, italics in the original).

The 'hole of a love without desire' refers to the love letters that were destroyed, and fundamentally shows the crucial place of jouissance in literature. Gide only understood what happened to the strange couple they formed after Madeleine's death. His lost letters replaced vanished desire, and they send us in the direction of jouissance.

This particular structure allows one to become a 'man of letters', whose 'truth' is also valid for the general reader. Lacan quotes *Et nunc manet in te*, and practises an almost deliberate misreading. In 1939, Gide had written in his diary:

Before leaving Paris, I was able to revise the proofs of my *Diary*. Rereading it, it appears to me that the systematic excision (until my mourning at least) of all the passages concerning Madeleine have in a way *blinded* the text. The few allusions to the secret drama of my life thus become incomprehensible because of the absence of what could throw light on them. Incomprehensible or inadmissible, the image of my mutilated self I give there, offering only, in the burning place of the heart, a hole (1947; my translation, italics in the original).

When he saw this passage, Lacan believed that Gide was referring to the burnt correspondence. He later realized his mistake but came to the conclusion that he had been right in his first assumption: Gide's texts also point to the same structural function of the hole. This is the point at which Gide's famous irony, displayed in many different texts, finds a radical limit. 'The letters into which he poured his soul had . . . no double. And when their fetishistic nature appears, this provokes the laughter that always accompanies a subjectivity at a loss. Everything ends in comedy, but what will make laughter end?' (Lacan 1966a: 763; my translation) It would be easy to superimpose this analysis with that of 'The Purloined Letter' and the threefold analysis of 'destination' that we have seen as sketched by Žižek.

The 'hole' left by destroyed letters accounted for Gide's amazing productivity as a writer. Lacan, who notes that Delay announces another book on Friedrich Nietzsche, concludes with a question: 'It will only stop, this movement, at the rendezvous you already know since you are going towards it, to the question concerning the figure offered by words beyond comedy when it turns into farce: how can one know who, among the tumblers, is holding the real Punchinello?' (ibid.: 764; my translation) Once more, death looms as the 'absolute master' of the 'destination' and it will mark Madeleine's place. Death does not preclude parody as witnessed by Nietzsche's cry of 'Ecco, ecco, il vero pulchinello!' (Here, here is the true pulchinello) as he was pointing to a cross. Parody does not spare the letter of desire. Nietzsche implied so much in his last letters, narrating that he would go round in the streets in Turin, tap people on the shoulder and say: 'I am god, and I made this caricature' (1976: 687; translation modified).[2]

This leads us to the re-emergence of the letter in 'Lituraterre', an essay written for a special issue on 'Literature and Psychoanalysis' of a new quarterly, *Littérature*. I will quote a few passages from this difficult text, in which the same old attack on psychobiographical readings can be recognized. 'For psychoanalysis, the fact that it be appended to the Oedipus, does not qualify it in any way to find its bearing in Sophocles' text. The evocation by Freud of a text by Dostoyevsky is not enough to assert that textual criticism, hitherto a private

---

2 Nietzsche's statement was in Italian: '*Siamo contenti? Son dio ho fatto questa caricatura.*' which was translated by Walter Kaufmann in the footnote (1n) as 'Are we content? I am the god who has made this caricature.'

hunting ground reserved to academics, has received any fresh air from psychoanalysis' (Lacan 1971: 3–4; my translation).

Lacan contrasts the 'ironic' title that he had given to *Écrits* with any attempt by literary minded psychoanalysts to engage with literature. He does not prohibit them the interpretation of literary texts, but their judgements should not carry more weight because of their profession. He stresses the lack of content of the 'purloined letter' to distinguish the letter from the signifier it carries:

> My criticism, if it can be called literary, can only bear (I hope) on what makes Poe a writer when he gives us such a message about the letter. Clearly, if he does not tell this as such, this is not a defect but an all-the-more rigorous avowal.
>
> Nevertheless, such an elision could not be elucidated by some feature in his psychobiography: rather, it appears blocked to us. (Thus, the kind of psychoanalysis that has cleaned up all the other texts of Poe declares here that its housecleaning meets a limit.)
>
> No more could my own text be solved by my own psychobiography: as for instance by the wish I reiterate of being at last read correctly. For, in order to think this, one would have to develop what I say that the letter carries so as to *always* reach its destination.
>
> It is sure that, as always, psychoanalysis receives from literature a less psychobiographic conception even when taking repression as its main spring. As for me, if I propose to psychoanalysis the idea of a letter in sufferance, it is because this shows its own failure. And here is where I bring some light: when I invoke the enlightenment, I demonstrate where it makes a *hole*. This is well known in optics, and the recent physics of the photon is underpinned by it.
>
> This is a method by which psychoanalysis might justify its intrusion better: for if literary criticism could indeed renew itself, it would be because of the presence of psychoanalysis forcing texts to measure up to it, the enigma remaining on the side of psychoanalysis (ibid.: 4).

Once more, Lacan's refusal to reduce the meaning of any text to a psychobiographical 'housecleaning' as done by Bonaparte is coupled with a wish to leave literature in the domain of riddles and enigmas.

For Lacan, finally, literature is made up of holes and erasures. He glosses the etymology of 'literature' via the Latin, in which the plural form (*literae*) signifies 'writing, epistle, literature', while literatura in the singular means 'writing, learning, literature'. The noun derives from the verb lino whose meanings call up 'I smear', 'I cover' or 'I erase.' As Freud indicated in his 1910 'The Antithetical Sense of Primal Words', the oldest roots of any language contain 'antithetical meanings'—in German, for example, one finds links between *stimme* (voice) and *stumm* (mute) (see Freud 1958). Literature would belong to this category in so far as its roots leave us with a double image: we see a hand covering a tablet with wax, the same hand will then erase the tablet so that it be free to register other signs. Finally, *literatura* brings us closer to *litus*—as a noun, the act of smearing or covering a surface, as a participle, the same meaning as *lino*, as a noun, *litus*, *litoris*, the 'littoral' or seaside, or the edge of a land. 'Literature' generates a double pun by suggesting both letters and their erasure (a pun that is more obvious in French, since one can always hear *rature*—erasure or crossing out—in the very signifier) and a space with its limit or border, a territory that reaches its limit, be it the sea or an abyss.

Finally, the letter appears as constitutive of the human subject and of sexuality as a whole: Lacan's text concludes with an enigmatic reference to an 'it is written' underpinning sexual relationship or, rather, the lack of it. The same 'it is written' also refers to the transformation of knowledge into jouissance 'through the edge of the hole in knowl-edge' (Lacan 1971: 5; my translation).

Lacan returned to 'Lituraterre' in *The Seminar of Jacques Lacan. Book XX. Seminar on Encore: On Feminine Sexuality, The Limits of Love and Knowledge, 1972–73*, (1975; here 1998a) when he discussed the 'solitude' that any person can experience once in a while:

> That solitude, as a break in knowledge, not only can be written but it is that which is written par excellence, for it is that which leaves a trace of a break in being.
>
> That is what I said in a text, certainly not without its imperfections, that I called '*Lituraterre*.' 'The cloud of language', I expressed myself metaphorically, 'constitutes writing.' Who knows whether the fact that we can read (*lire*) the streams I saw over Siberia as the

metaphorical trace of writing isn't linked (*lié*)—beware, *lier* (to link) and *lire* consist of the same letters—to something that goes beyond the effect of rain, which animals have no chance of reading as such? (1998a: 120).

Lacan stresses again 'the impossibility of inscribing the sexual relationship between two bodies of different sexes' (ibid.: 120). Such a writing takes the form of a simple knot, which 'has all the characteristics of writing—it could be a letter' (ibid.: 122). With Joyce, the letter ends up figuring the trefoil of Trinity. We are already in the realm of the Borromean knot, whose particularly graceful coils can show without words the enigma of the sexual *non*-rapport.

This is the concept of the *sinthome* that Lacan develops at length in *Le Séminaire. Livre XXIII. Le Sinthome, 1975–76* (2005). It was in this very seminar that he scorns 'applied psychoanalysis', even though he remains very close to Joyce's biography. On 13 January 1976, he attacks a Freudian interpretation of Joyce in Mark Shechner's *Joyce in Nighttown: A Psychoanalytic Inquiry* (1974), which was for Lacan an egregious counter-model:

> [Shechner] imagines that he is a psychoanalyst because he has read many psychoanalytic books. This is a rather widespread illusion, especially among analysts. And then he analyzes *Ulysses*. [. . .] This gives you the impression that the imagination of the novelist, I mean the novelist's imagination, the imagination that constructed *Ulysses*, is to be trashed. Which is not my sense at all (2005: 71; my translation).

In the same passage, Lacan does not spare Freud, although he feels that Freud had the merit of 'restraining himself' by never analyzing long novels nor analyzing too systematically (ibid.: 71).

Thus Lacan refrained from reading the 'unconscious' of characters like Stephen or Bloom, and showed the greatest respect for critics like Hugh Kenner, Clive Hart or Robert M. Adams whose books illuminated issues like 'motif', 'structure', 'surface', 'symbol' or 'consistency' (see Adams 1962). I adduce them to show that Lacan was not at all opposed to literary criticism on principle and appreciated it when it threw light on textual processes. Fundamentally, Lacan used literary texts and their commentaries to eschew the danger of a reductive structuralism limited to the 'logics of the signifier'. When he became more interested in confrontations with the real, perversion, the jouis-sance of the Other, the term symptom condensed what he had to say about lit-erature, as is obvious with Joyce. It was as if the 'symptom' had taken the place of the 'letter' in the earlier formulations, or as if it allowed Lacan to bridge the gap between the loop of the letter and the function of psychotic discourse. Joyce was also a good pretext for him to revisit his early essay on psychotic discourse, 'Les Écrits Inspirés' (Inspired Writings, 1931), which already showed how the 'letter' can be inspired by as well as addressed to the Other. I do not want to discuss Joyce at length here, as this would take us too far, and as there is still today a disagreement as to his fundamental role for Lacanian psychoanalysis: was Joyce a psychotic like his daughter who showed Lacan how to deal with psy-chotic discourse (as Jacques-Alain Miller and Colette Soler believe) or is he a writer who was miming psychotic discourse so as to come close to his daughter's disease and reach a 'language of the night' (as Néstor Braunstein and Colin MacCabe think)?[3]

I would like to conclude with the idea that we need to read with Lacanian psychoanalysis and not literally apply it to literature. I have just used the word perversion and to say something about such a concept, a concept which is too rarely mentioned in the context of Lacanian discussions of literature, I will thus return to Nabokov, whose *Lolita* (1955; here 1974), for one, is a novel about which I would be at a loss in my pedagogical practice if I did not have Lacanian discourse at my disposal. One could examine it in the context of Roudinesco's recently published history of perversion. True to the Lacanian motto that perversion is a structure, Roudinesco sketches a chronicle in which literature—Gustave Flaubert's *Madame Bovary*, Honoré de Balzac, Victor Hugo, Emile Zola –figures next to real-life case studies—Gilles de Rais, a Nazi like Rudolf Höss, medieval mystics like Mary Alacoque (see Roudinesco 2007). She does not limit her scope to a history of the conceptions of perversion, of the ideological projections branding the enemy as evil. Indeed, the 'perversion' invoked by the judges who condemned Joan of Arc to the stake has little to do with the 'perversion' that sent Oscar Wilde to jail. However, one cannot

---

3 See Braunstein (1997 and 1998), MacCabe (2003), Miller (1987) and Soler (1993).

understand perversion from a culturalist perspective only. Psychoanalytic discourse, in so far as it respects the model of scientific discourse, cannot lose itself
in baroque catalogues as compiled by Richard von Krafft-Ebing. Perversion appears as a disposition that goes back to the personal evolution of young men
and women and thus is so 'natural' that, for Freud, young children could be
called 'polymorphous perverse'. With Lacan, the stress is laid on an avoidance
of the law. The pervert illustrates creatively or stereotypically the transgressive
nature of the sexual drive. Marquis de Sade provides a logical access to the
structure: in Lacan's 'Kant avec Sade' (1966b), a refused norm is postulated,
necessary even for the construction of the divine Marquis's system. Thus it is
not a coincidence that at the end of *Philosophy in the Bedroom* (1795; here 1994),
Madame de Mistival, the mother of Eugénie, a novice debauchee whom she
vainly attempts to pry from the group of Libertines, is tortured and sent home
infected with smallpox after her sex has been sewn tight by her daughter. Eugénie closes off the passage that gave birth to her, which paradoxically confirms the old maxim: '*Noli tangere matrem*' (it is forbidden to touch the mother).
In the end, the mother remains out of reach, which signals Sade's submission
to the law of prohibition of incest (Lacan 1966b: 790; my translation). A perverse structure confirms the law by deriding it, and Sadian libertines identify
with an evil and cruel God. This sends them on an exhausting quest for a jouissance that always remains inferior to the absolute jouissance that they imagine
in the Other.

This brief synthesis should help contextualize the issue of perversion and
sublimation in *Lolita*. The lasting appeal of the novel can be understood in that
it stages a certain jouissance, a universal jouissance which is connected with an
exploration of the world of nubile femininity. *Lolita* was certainly the result of
Nabokov's love affair with US, even though the idea came to him prior to his
American exile. By forcing us to enter the fantasy world of Humbert Humbert,
a poet doubled by a pervert, and a paedophile indeed, Nabokov at once seduces
us and destroys the seduction. In the story, it is in fact Lolita who appears much
closer to reality—she is the one who technically seduces Humbert, she manip-
ulates him and spends a whole year on the road, being pampered and indulged.
And also, she is the one who quickly finds the true name for their relationship:
'The word is incest' (Nabokov 1974: 111).

As for Humbert, he explains that he was planning to drug Lolita so as to satisfy his lust while she is unconscious, 'a completely anesthetized little nude' (ibid.: 114). He then begins a tirade to explain what he has done:

> The whole point is that the old link between the adult world and the child world has been completely severed nowadays by new customs and new laws. Despite my having dabbled in psychiatry and social work, I really knew very little about children. After all, Lolita was only twelve, and no matter what concession I made to time and place— even bearing in mind the crude behavior of American schoolchild-ren—I still was under the impression that whatever went on among those brash brats, went on at a later age, and in a different environ-ment. Therefore [. . .] the moralist in me by-passed the issue by cling-ing to conventional notions of what twelve-year-old girls should be. The child therapist in me (a fake, as most of them are—but no mat-ter) regurgitated neo-Freudian hash and conjured up a dreaming and exaggerating Dolly in the 'latency' period of girlhood. Finally, the sensualist in me (a great and insane monster) had no objection to some depravity in his prey. But somewhere behind the raging bliss, bewildered shadows conferred—and not to have heeded them, this is what I regret! (ibid.: 114–15).

In conformity to his general rejection of psychoanalysis, Nabokov is fond of punning on 'therapist' and 'the rapist' (ibid.: 105). In this passage, the cate-gory of the monstrous is marked by an invasive 'bliss', a perverse jouissance that momentarily cancels out 'moral' feeling, any empathy with another's pain:

> Reader must understand that in the possession and thralldom of a nymphet the enchanted traveler stands, as it were, *beyond happiness.* For there is no other bliss on earth comparable to that of fondling a nymphet. It is *hors concours*, that bliss, it belongs to another class, an-other plane of sensitivity. Despite our tiffs, despite her nastiness, de-spite all the fuss and faces she made, and the vulgarity, and the danger, and the horrible helplessness of it all, I still dwelled deep in my elected paradise—a paradise whose skies were the color of hell-flames—but still a paradise (ibid.: 152).

In fact, Humbert is much less of a pervert than he thinks—in the novel, the true pervert is Quigley, a devotee of Sade who organizes orgies with children as participants. Humbert's magic is quickly soiled, debased, lost. What he fears most is the perversion of his 'perversion'. For him, perversion has the positive effect of sidetracking normality and its attendant social repression. Art implies a certain proximity with perversion since artists manipulate, lie, distort facts, explore inner erotic longings without timidity. In the end, it is literature that saves Humbert, ideally at least. For Nabokov, if Proust and Joyce are the two main literary models—*Ulysses* (1922) with the unforgettable Gerty on the beach, *In Search of Lost Time* with Albertine, a model for the later Lolita, the masterpieces that stage perversion in a grandiose manner—the other model, the model that he both rejects and loves, is that of Freud. After all, the whole novel is presented as a sick man's confession or a psychoanalytic case study in the grand manner of Freud's major studies.

To condense my main thesis, I will say that what really changes, what will keep on changing in a productive sense is literature. As for theories, they follow fashion, they are discarded after a while and do not need to transform themselves continuously. They are readings, translations that can and will be replaced. Like translations, theories are useful, necessary even, but always to be revamped. Thus Lacan has, in my view, transformed less theory (in the sense of psychoanalytic theory) than literature as such.

This is an idea that Lacan himself entertained. One can observe this in a discussion he had about literature at Yale University, where he opposed the letter to literature, saying that he was not sure what the latter consisted of (he mentioned, as we saw, that Freud needed literature to grasp the unconscious). After a few disparaging remarks on Freud's psychoanalytic reading of Wilhelm Jensen's 1903 novel *Gradiva*[4], Lacan added:

> There is a new inflection of literature. Today, it does not mean what it meant in Jensen's time. Everything is literature. I too, produce literature, since it sells: take my *Écrits*, this is literature to which I have imagined I could give a status which was different from what Freud

---

4 See Freud (1921).

imagined. [. . .] I do not think I am producing science when I produce literature. Nevertheless, this is literature because it has been written and it sells. And this is also literature because it has effects, even effects on literature (1976: 34; my translation).

Lacan was aware of the impact of his theories on contemporary avant-garde writers, especially on the group of writers gathered by *Tel Quel*. This implied that this new literature was not to be 'psychoanalyzed' even if their authors might be—at times by him! Lacan repeated this at the close of *Le Séminaire. Livre XVIII. D'un discours qui ne serait pas du semblant, 1971* (A Discourse that Might not be a Semblance, 2007): if one should never 'analyze' written texts, one should 'criticize' them (Lacan 2007: 161; my translation). Curiously, and most revealingly, at that very moment, Lacan was talking of . . . *Totem and Taboo*!

References

ADAMS, Robert M. 1962. *Surface and Symbol. The Consistency of James Joyce's Ulysses*. New York: Oxford University Press.

BRAUNSTEIN, Néstor. 1997. 'La clinica en el nombre proprio' in *El Laberinto de las structuras* (Heli Morales Ascensio ed.). Mexico: Siglo 21, pp. 70–96.

———. 1998. 'El ego Lacaniano' in *En Las Suplencias del Nombre del Padre* (Heli Morales and Daniel Gerber eds). Mexico: Siglo 21, pp. 53–74.

DERRIDA, Jacques. 1987. 'Le Facteur de la Vérité' (Alan Bass trans.) in *The Postcard: From Socrates to Freud and Beyond*. Chicago: The University of Chicago Press, pp. 411–96.

DUMAS, Alexander. 2008. *The Three Musketeers* (Richard Pevear trans.). London and New York: Penguin Classics.

FLAUBERT, Gustave. 2002. *Madame Bovary* (Geoffrey Wall trans.). Rev. edn, London and New York: Penguin Books.

FREUD, Sigmund. 1921. *Delusion and Dream* (Helen M. Downey trans.). London: George Allen and Unwin.

——. 1926. *Die Frage der Laienanalyse*: *Unterredungen mit einem Unparteiischen*. Vienna: Internationaler Psychoanalytischer Verlag, p. 116.

——. 1949. 'Foreword' to Marie Bonaparte, *The Life and Works of Edgar Allan Poe* (John Rodker trans.). London: Imago, p. xi.

——. 1950. *The Question of Lay Analysis* (Nancy Procter-Gregg trans.). New York and London: W. W. Norton.

——. 1958. 'The Antithetical Sense of Primal Words' (M. N. Searl trans.) in Benjamin Nelson (ed.), *On Creativity and the Unconscious*: *The Psychology of Art, Literature, Love, and Religion*. New York: Harper, pp. 55–62.

JENSEN, Wilhelm. 1918. *Gradiva*: *A Pompeiian Fancy* (Helen M. Downey trans.). New York: Moffat, Yard and Company.

JOHNSON, Barbara. 1977. 'The Frame of Reference: Poe, Lacan, Derrida'. *Yale French Studies* 55/56 (Literature and Psychoanalysis): 457–505.

JOYCE, James. 2000 [1922]. *Ulysses*. London: Penguin Classics.

LACAN, Jacques. 1981. *The Seminar of Jacques Lacan. Book XI. The Four Fundamental Concepts of Psychoanalysis, 1964* (Jacques-Alain Miller ed., Alan Sheridan trans.). New York and London: W. W. Norton.

——. 1988. 'Seminar on "The Purloined Letter"' (Jeffrey Mehlman trans.) in John P. Muller and William J. Richardson (eds), *The Purloined Poe*: *Lacan, Derrida, and Psychoanalytic Reading*. Baltimore, MD: The Johns Hopkins University Press, pp. 28–54.

——. 1998a. *The Seminar of Jacques Lacan. Book XX. Encore*: *On Feminine Sexuality, The Limits of Love and Knowledge* (Jacques-Alain Miller ed., Bruce Fink trans.). New York and London: W. W. Norton.

MACCABE, Colin. 2003. *James Joyce and the Revolution of the Word* (2nd edn). London: Palgrave Macmillan.

NABOKOV, Vladimir. 1974 [1955]. *Lolita*. New York: Crest Books.

NANCY, Jean-Luc and Philippe Lacoue-Labarthe. 1992. *The Title of the Letter*: *A Reading of Lacan* (François Raffoul and David Pettigrew trans). Albany: State University of New York Press.

NIETZSCHE, Friedrich. 1976. 'Letter to Jacob Burckhardt (dated 6 January 1889)' in *The Portable Nietzsche* (Walter Kaufmann ed., and trans.). New York: Penguin Books, p. 687.

POE, Edgar Allan. 1983. 'The Purloined Letter' in *The Complete Tales and Poems of Edgar Allan Poe*. Harmondsworth: Penguin, pp. 208–22.

PRENDERGAST, Christopher. 2008. *The Classic: Sainte-Beuve and the Nineteenth-Century Culture Wars*. New York: Oxford University Press.

PROUST, Marcel. 1988. *Against Saint-Beuve and Other Essays* (John Sturrock trans.). Reprint, London and New York: Penguin.

———. 2003. *In Search of Lost Time* (C. K. Scott Moncrieff, Terence Kilmartin and Andreas Mayor trans). New York: Modern Library Classics.

RABATÉ, Jean-Michel. 2001. *Jacques Lacan: Psychoanalysis and the Subject of Literature*. Hampshire and New York: Palgrave.

SADE, Marquis de. 1994. 'Philosophy in the Bedroom' in *Justine, Philosophy in the Bedroom, and Other Writings* (Richard Seaver and Austryn Wainhouse trans). New York: Grove Press, pp. 177–370.

SHAKESPEARE, William. 2003. Philip Edwards (ed.), *Hamlet: The Prince of Denmark* (2nd edn). Cambridge: Cambridge University Press.

SHECHNER, Mark. 1974. *Joyce in Nighttown: A Psychoanalytic Inquiry*. Berkeley: University of California Press.

SONTAG, Susan. 2001 [1966]. *Against Interpretation: And Other Essays*. New York: Picador.

STOLTZFUS, Ben. 1996. *Lacan and Literature: Purloined Pretexts*. Albany: State University of New York Press.

ŽIŽEK, Slavoj. 1992. *Enjoy your Symptom! Jacques Lacan in Hollywood and Out*. Oxford and New York: Routledge Classics.

FRENCH SOURCES

BAYARD, Pierre. 2004. *Peut-on appliquer la littérature à la psychanalyse?* Paris: Les Éditions de Minuit.

BELLEMIN-NOËL, Jean. 1979. *Vers l'inconscient du texte*. Paris: Presses Universitaires de France.

DELAY, Jean. 1956–57. *La Jeunesse d'André Gide*. 2 vols. Paris: Éditions Gallimard.

GIDE André. 1947. *Et nunc manet in te*. Paris et Neuchatel: Ides et Calendes.

KOFMAN, Sarah. 1985. *L'enfance de l'art: une interprétation de l'esthétique freudienne* (3rd edn). Paris: Éditions Galilée.

LACAN, Jacques. 1931. 'Écrits Inspirés: Schizographie'. *Annales Médico-Psychologiques* 2: 508–22.

———. 1932. *De la psychose paranoïaque dans ses rapports avec la personnalité.* Paris: Le Français.

———. 1957. 'Le séminaire sur "La Lettre Volée"'. *La Psychanalyse* 2: 1–44. Subsequently published in *Écrits* (1966).

———. 1958. 'Jeunesse de Gide ou la lettre et désir'. *Critique* 131: 291–315. Subsequently published in *Écrits* (1966).

———. 1963. 'Kant avec Sade'. *Critique* 191: 291–313. Subsequently published in *Écrits* (1966).

———. 1966a. 'Jeunesse de Gide ou la lettre et le désir' in *Écrits*. Paris: Éditions du Seuil, pp. 739–64.

———. 1966b. 'Kant avec Sade' in *Écrits*. Paris: Éditions du Seuil, pp. 765–90.

———. 1971. 'Lituraterre'. *Littérature* 3(3) (October): 3–10.

———. 1973. *Le Séminaire. Livre XI. Les quatre concepts fondamentaux de la psychanalyse, 1964* (Jacques-Alain Miller ed.). Paris: Éditions du Seuil.

———. 1975. *Le Séminaire. Livre XX. Encore, 1972–73* (Jacques-Alain Miller ed.). Paris: Éditions du Seuil.

———. 1976. 'Conférences et Entretiens dans des universités nord-américaines'. *Scilicet* 6/7: 7–63.

———. 1982. 'Le désir et son interprétation'. *Ornicar? Bulletin périodique du champ freudien* 25: 13–36.

———. 1998b. *Le Séminaire. Livre V. Les formations de l'inconscient, 1957–58* (Jacques-Alain Miller ed.). Paris: Éditions du Seuil.

———. 2005. *Le Séminaire. Livre XXIII. Le Sinthome, 1975–76* (Jacques-Alain Miller ed.). Paris: Éditions du Seuil.

———. 2007. *Le Séminaire. Livre XVIII. D'un discours qui ne serait pas du semblant, 1971* (Jacques-Alain Miller ed.). Paris: Éditions du Seuil.

MARTY, Eric. 2005. 'Lacan et Gide, ou l'autre école' in Eric Marty (ed.), *Lacan et la littérature*. Paris: Le Marteau sans maître, pp. 125–46.

MILLER, Jacques-Alain. 1987. 'Préface' in *Joyce Avec Lacan* (Jacques Aubert ed.). Paris: Navarin, pp. 9–12.

RABATÉ, Jean-Michel. 2005. 'Qui jouit de la jouissance de Joyce?' in Eric Marty (ed.), *Lacan et la littérature*. Paris: Le Marteau sans maître, pp. 157–80.

ROUDINESCO, Élisabeth. 2007. *La Part obscure de nous-mêmes: Une histoire des pervers.* Paris: Éditions Albin Michel.

SCHLUMBERGER, Jean. 1956. *Madeleine et André Gide.* Paris: Éditions Gallimard.

SOLER, Colette. 1993. 'L'expérience énigmatique du psychotique, de Schreber à Joyce'. *La Cause Freudienne* 23: 50–9.

PART 2
From Literature

'To Be, or Not …'
Lacan and the Meaning of Being in Shakespeare's Hamlet
MATTHEW SHARPE

'To be, or not to be, that is the question,' intones William Shakespeare's Hamlet, immortally:

> Whether 'tis nobler in the mind to suffer
> The slings and arrows of outrageous fortune,
> Or to take arms against a sea of troubles,
> And by opposing end them. To die, to sleep—
> No more; and by a sleep to say we end
> The heart-ache and the thousand natural shocks
> That flesh is heir to (Shakespeare 2003: 3.1.56–63).

Arguably the greatest philosopher of the last century, Martin Heidegger, made his name by claiming that we have forgotten the proper, abyssal meaning of 'Being' in the modern age. It is telling that, for all of Heidegger's staggering erudition and his later worship of the poets, to my knowledge, he never refers to Shakespeare, arguably, the poet of poets. Nor does the philosopher refer to Shakespeare's *Hamlet* (1603; here 2003), written at the very inception of the modern age and arguably the bard's greatest creation. For *Hamlet* is a poetic masterpiece in which the *Seinsfrage* (question of the meaning of Being) is explicitly raised by Shakespeare's most famous hero—indeed, it fairly torments the troubled prince of Denmark from the play's first moments. Arguably the greatest psychoanalytic thinker of the last century, Jacques Lacan, was by contrast in little doubt about the importance of *Hamlet* as a poetic masterpiece, or about the centrality of the *Seinsfrage* to its eponymous hero:

> For Hamlet, [what is central] is that he is guilty of being. He cannot tolerate being. Before the drama of *Hamlet* even begins, Hamlet is aware of the crime of existing [. . .] for him the problem of existing [. . .] is posed in terms which are his own: namely the 'to be or not to be' which is something which engages him irredeemably in being as he very clearly articulates it (Lacan 1958–59a: Session 13, p. 212).

Lacan devoted the best parts of eight sessions of 'The Seminar of Jacques Lacan. Book VI. Desire and its Interpretation, 1958–59' (1958–59a) to Shakespeare's masterpiece. Hamlet's eloquent laments on the 'mortal coil' 'are not meant to leave us unmoved', he wryly comments, punctuating the famous soliloquy from the beginning of the third act (ibid.: Session 13, p. 213). Indeed, Lacan notes, there is something singularly striking—'stupefying'—about Shakespeare's most uncanny tragedy: '[I]t is something that knocks you over backwards, makes you bite the carpet and roll on the ground, it is something unimaginable' (ibid.: Session 14, pp. 221–2). It is then fair to say with Jean-Michel Rabaté that when Lacan turns to *Hamlet* in his sixth seminar, it is less to illustrate preformed dogma, than to be *struck* by what it can teach psycho-analysis about human desire. 'I maintain [. . .] and I think I am in accord with [Sigmund] Freud in saying this,' he comments in concluding his first session on the play, 'poetic creations engender rather than reflect psychological creations' (ibid.: Session 13, p. 214).

Lacan's sessions on *Hamlet* from 3 March to 13 May 1959 certainly come at a culminating point in a sequence of four stunning seminars, in which Lacan had established his status as a strikingly independent, if abidingly faithful, reader of Freud. *Le Séminaire. Livre IV. La relation d'objet, 1956–57* (The Object Relations, 1994) and 'The Seminar of Jacques Lacan. Book V. The Formations of the Unconscious, 1957–58' (1957–58) had seen Lacan's systematic refiguring of Freud's fundamental notions of the Oedipus and castration complexes. In the process, as we shall see, Lacan had formulated many of his key distinctions: the imaginary versus real and symbolic fathers; the phallus as the signifier of the desire of the mother; and desire versus demand and need. 'Desire and its Interpretation' also contains some of Lacan's earliest formative thoughts on the role of fantasy anticipating his later, central concept of the *objet petit a*, cause of desire. *Hamlet* confronts Lacan at this decisively important, generative juncture in his development, as 'this kind of network, of birdcatcher's net in which the desire of man is essentially articulated' (1958–59a: Session 14, p. 222).

Lacan's reading of *Hamlet* begins by addressing, with Freud, the problem that everyone faces, and that Hamlet poses to himself, amid fiery self-recriminations, namely, that he is in no doubt that he ought to kill the usurper Claudius and avenge his murdered father. Yet, though heaven itself might enjoin him, not to mention all-too-human motives of rivalry, vengeance and the word of his revered father, Hamlet cannot bring himself to act (ibid.: Session 13, p. 210). He has 'cause, and will, and strength and means to do't', 'yet I live to say this thing's to do' (Shakespeare 2003: 4.4.45–6, 44).

There are libraries of critical essays written on this topic. *Hamlet* is one of the most written-about works of literature in Western history.[1] Lacan's response and his interpretation of the play take bearing, here as elsewhere, from that of Freud. For all the oceans of ink that have been spilt on *Hamlet*, Lacan notes, it is striking that no one before Freud, circa 1897, had remarked the kinship between *Hamlet* and Sophocles' *Oedipus Rex*. Freud wrote of *Hamlet* in three places: in his letters to Wilhelm Fliess (1887–1904; here 1985), in the later paper 'Mourning and Melancholia' (1917; here 1963) and centrally in *The Interpretation of Dreams* (1899; here 1953). Freud's observations were then importantly developed by Ernest Jones' 1910 piece 'The Oedipus-Complex as an Explanation of Hamlet's Mystery'. Let us cite Freud's paradigmatic formulations from

---

1 Nearly every possible motive or angle has been explored, down to Edward P. Vining's bold speculation in *The Mystery of Hamlet* (1881), that the key is that Hamlet was secretly a woman dressed as a man, whose real aim throughout the play was to seduce Horatio! (see Lacan 1958–59a: Session 14, pp. 217–18). Hamlet is the archetypal modern whose crippling self-doubts reflect the fast-emerging doubts of an age that would live without God or religion. Or Hamlet is the man of knowledge, educated at Wittenberg, no less, where [Martin] Luther studied. But he knows too much. He is the one who has peered into the Dionysian abyss at the heart of Being, and so he is paralyzed: 'sicklied o'er with the pale cast of thought' (Shakespeare 2003: 3.1.85). For other critics, the mystery of *Hamlet* is that there is no mystery. However celestial the bard's famed wit, it was not up to giving sufficient reason for the actions and inaction of his listless hero. And there are other readings, or rationalizations, for Hamlet's failure to live up to his name (see Lacan 1958–59a: Session 14, pp. 215–21).

The Interpretation of Dreams at some length, since they will frame all that follows, even as we will see Lacan moving beyond Freud's position:

> Another of the great creations of tragic poetry, [. . .] Shakespeare's *Hamlet*, has its roots in the same soil as *Oedipus Rex* [. . .]. Strangely enough, the overwhelming effect produced by the modern tragedy has turned out to be compatible with the fact that people have remained completely in the dark as to the hero's character. The play is built up on Hamlet's hesitations over fulfilling the task of revenge that is assigned to him; but its text offers no reasons or motives for these hesitations and an immense variety of attempts at interpreting them have failed to produce a result. [. . .] The answer, once again, is that it is the peculiar nature of the task. Hamlet is able to do anything—except to take vengeance upon the man who did away with his father and took the father's place with his mother, the man who shows him the repressed wishes of his own childhood realized. Thus the loathing which should drive him on to revenge is replaced by self-reproaches, by scruples of conscience, which remind him that he himself is literally no better than the sinner whom he is to punish. Here I have translated what was bound to remain unconscious in Hamlet's mind (Freud 1953: 264; quoted in Lacan 1958–59a: Session 13, pp. 204–5).

There is something remarkably 'balanced' about Freud's reflections on *Hamlet* 'in this half-page in which one could say that when all is said and done everything is already there', Lacan contends (ibid.: Session 14, p. 216). Freud's observations neatly put in their place those readings that see Hamlet as incapable of action, and which thereby fail to notice that when it comes to Polonius and Rosencrantz and Guildenstern, he acts as promptly and ruthlessly as any Machiavellian prince. More deeply, Freud's interpretation situates the play at what Lacan proposes is exactly the right level: namely, as what he terms a 'tragedy of desire' (ibid.: Session 17, p. 264; Session 19, p. 295): 'of desire in so far as man is not simply possessed, invested, by it but that he has to situate, has to find this desire' (ibid.: Session 14, p. 223).

Before Freud, Lacan goes so far as to venture that '*Hamlet* remained a complete literary enigma' (ibid.: Session 13, p. 207). What Freud showed us is that—as we might reprise Friedrich Nietzsche and Johann Wolfgang von Goethe—at the very least, if Hamlet is so disoriented for having stared into the abyss of Being, it is also because the abyss stared back at him with an uncannily familiar, if not familial, gaze. If Freud is right, that is, the truth of the play is revealed in the seemingly contingent fact that when Hamlet does come to his appointed hour, it is while acting as the champion, in a duel, of the very man who is his true enemy. It is along the axis of the rivalrous identification of Hamlet with Claudius that we can understand why Hamlet could not raise his hand against the usurper, until he himself had been fatally wounded, in the process littering the stage with corpses. To strike at Claudius would be, for Freud, to have struck a blow at the man who had fulfilled in reality what Hamlet had only dreamt of.

Nevertheless, Lacan's perspective on *Hamlet* typically moves beyond that of his master, Freud's, even as it takes its initial bearings from it. Indeed, the two thinkers' responses to the play could almost provide a 'royal road' into understanding the reorientation of psychoanalysis introduced by Lacan's reframing of the Freudian field. In an addendum to the interpretation of *Hamlet* cited above, Freud suggested that the differences between the Hamlet story and the Oedipus myth—the fact that, in the former, the parricidal-incestuous crime is performed not by the hero, but by an other, and it is known to Hamlet, and before him to this other, from the beginning—reflect the higher levels of repression characterizing modern civilization, and its malaises.[2] Lacan's reading of the play, with qualifications, suggests an almost opposed orientation that, in fact, approaches more closely Freud's passing designation of Hamlet as a melancholic in 'Mourning and Melancholia'. *Hamlet* 'opens up a new dimension on man' in this work, Lacan claims (ibid.: Session 15, p. 237). And this dimension is predicated on a certain failure of the symbolic order in the play's early modern conception and setting, rather than its more thoroughgoing historical instauration. If our modern Oedipus feigns madness, we might say, there is neurosis, if not madness, in his feigning:

---

2 Noting, of course, that Claudius' crime is fratricidal, although Lacan suggests that Hamlet Senior was as a father figure to him, both as older sibling and as king.

What Hamlet finds himself confronted with in this 'to be or not to be' is the encountering of the place taken by what his father has said to him. And what his father has said to him qua ghost, is that he had been surprised by death 'in the blossoms of my sin' [Shakespeare 2003: 1.5.76]. It is a matter of encountering the place taken by the sin of the other, the unpaid sin. The one who knows is on the contrary, the contrary of Oedipus, someone who has not paid for this crime of existing (Lacan 1958–59a: Session 13, p. 213).

Lacan's reading then sets itself, as the red thread into the mystery of the play, a question asked less often in *Hamlet* reception: what are 'the paths by which [Hamlet] can rejoin [the act to which he is called], which will make possible the act which in itself is impossible'? (ibid.) Lacan wants to answer why Hamlet does finally act, as well as why he for so long does not. And it is in this light that his reading, at its heart, pays close attention to a figure and a relationship which is absent from Freud's interpretation: 'namely Hamlet's relations to [. . .] the conscious object of his desire', Ophelia (ibid.: Session 13, p. 211). It is not for nothing that Ophelia's very name evokes *ho phallos* in the Greek, Lacan boldly claims, thereby invoking the very signifier of life or Being at the hidden heart of the ancient mysteries, which he was at this point in his career elevating to the central stake or foil in the Oedipal complex. If Hamlet's 'time is out of joint' (Shakespeare 2003: 1.5.189), Lacan argues, it is above all because this phallus is not in its rightful place for him. And if Being presents itself in such gruesome aspects to him in his strangely methodical madness, it is because this phallus has not been properly mourned or symbolized, so that it can only return in the real as a dangerous Thing—or, as Lacan interprets one of Hamlet's 'schizophrenic' remarks, shortly after he has killed Polonius who was lurking behind the curtains in Gertrude's chamber:

The body is with the King [the phallus],
But the King [the phallus] is not with the body (ibid.: Session 14, p. 230).

In order to begin to fathom Lacan's reading of *Hamlet*, then, and how he conceives the *Seinsfrage* within it, we need to start with the 'piece of bait' called Ophelia whom Hamlet treats so symptomatically.

Regarding Hamlet's relations to his conscious object of desire, Lacan comments, Shakespeare begrudges us little. Ophelia is 'one of the most fascinating creations which have been proposed to human imagination' (ibid.: Session 13, p. 211). Hamlet is clear that he 'did love [her] once' (Shakespeare 2003: 3.1.114). Ophelia's testimony to her brother Laertes and to her absurd father Polonius attests as much, alongside her maidenly affections for the prince. The letter from Hamlet which Ophelia dutifully delivers up to Polonius, and he deceptively to the king, poetically confirms it: 'doubt truth to be a liar,' the prince enjoins his sweetheart, 'but never doubt I love' (ibid.: 1.2.117–18). Finally, in the famous graveyard scene in the last act to whose decisive importance for Lacan we will return in the final section below, Hamlet weighs his devotion for the dead woman 40,000 times greater than Laertes' brotherly affection (ibid.: 5.1.236)—exactly twice the number of Fortinbras' contingent against Poland whose valour rebukes Hamlet's inaction in the central scene of the fourth act (ibid.: 4.4.56–61).

It is what transpires between these two seasons of Hamlet's evanescent affections for Ophelia that concerns Lacan. The precipitating moment is Hamlet's encounter with his father's ghost. When next he comes to his beloved, everything has changed. In Ophelia's affecting words, here is what transpired:

> My Lord, as I was sewing in my closet,
> Lord Hamlet, with his doublet all unbraced,
> No hat upon his head, his stockings fouled,
> Ungartered, and down-gyvèd to his ankle,
> Pale as his shirt, his knees knocking each other,
> And with a look so piteous in purport
> As if he had been loosed out of hell
> To speak of horrors—he comes before me.
>
> (ibid.: 2.1.75–82). [. . .]

> He took me by the wrist, and held me hard;
> Then goes he to the length of all his arm,

And with his other hand thus o'er his brow
He falls to such perusal of my face
As a would draw it. Long stayed he so;
At last, a little shaking of mine arm,
And thrice his head thus waving up and down
He raised a sigh so piteous and profound
As it did seem to shatter all his bulk
And end his being. That done, he lets me go,
And with his head over his shoulder turned
He seemed to find his way without his eyes,
(ibid.: 2.1.85–96).

It is not too much to say that something 'properly pathological' transpires for Hamlet at this instant, Lacan comments (1958–59a: Session 17, p. 277). What follows is a complete transformation in his relations to Ophelia. 'I did love you once,' he tells her when they next meet, and then corrects himself: 'I loved you not' (Shakespeare 2003: 3.1.114, 116). Indeed, everything he has to say to Ophelia or about her from this point onwards until her death is characterized not simply by a 'disgust at sexuality', as Freud put it, but is moved by what Lacan calls more specifically a 'horror of femininity':

Namely, what he uncovers [. . .] before the very eyes of Ophelia as being all the possibilities of degradation, of variation, of corruption, which are linked to the evolution of a woman's very life in so far as she allows herself to be drawn into all the actions which little by little make a mother of her. It is in the name of this that Hamlet rejects Ophelia in the fashion which appears in the play extremely sarcastic and extremely cruel (1958–59a: Session 13, p. 211).

Conception is a blessing, the prince advises Polonius, 'but as your daughter may conceive—Friend, look to't' (Shakespeare 2003: 2.2.183). To Ophelia, in whose madness Hamlet's outrage will indeed find its destination as he desires (ibid.: 3.1.88–9), there is a famous counsel: 'If thou dost marry, I'll give thee this plague for thy dowry: be thou as chaste as ice, as pure as snow, thou shalt not escape calumny. Get thee to a nunnery, go. Farewell' (ibid.: 3.1.131–3):

I have heard of your paintings too, well enough; God hath given you one face, and you make yourselves another. You jig, you amble, and you lisp, you nickname God's creatures, and make your wantonness your ignorance. Go to, I'll no more on't, it hath made me mad. I say we will have no mo marriages. Those that are married already, all but one shall live, the rest shall keep as they are. To a nunnery, go (ibid.: 3.1.137–43).

If *Hamlet* as a whole is the drama of the eponymous hero's failing desire, of there being something wrong with his desire, as Lacan gently puts it (1958–59a: Session 13, pp. 210–11), Lacan's contention is that Ophelia becomes the symptom of this repudiation of desire:

[T]he object in question [Ophelia] is no longer treated as she should be, as a woman. She becomes for him the bearer of children and of every sin, the one who is designated to engender sinners, [. . .] woman conceived here uniquely as the bearer of this vital tumescence which it is a question of cursing and putting an end to. A nunnery could just as well at the time designate a brothel. Semantic usage shows it (ibid.: Session 17, p. 278).

It is in this light that Lacan makes one of his maverick linguistic interpretations. With the help of Boissade's *Dictionaire Étymologique Grec*, he notes that in Homer, we can find the signifier *Ophelio*, which has the sense of 'to make pregnant, to impregnate', and also 'this molting, vital fermentation, which is described more or less as allowing something to change, or to thicken' (ibid.: Session 16, 262). Boissade goes further and ties *Ophelio* to the nominative form *ho phallos*, and thereby to the Thing (*la Chose*) which Lacan had spent much of the previous two years elevating to the heart of the psychoanalytic lexicon: 'it is thus moreover that Hamlet qualifies it, situates it, in order to reject it: you will be the mother of sinners, this image precisely of vital fecundity, this image [. . .] illustrates for us more I think than any other creation the equation [. . .] *Girl=Phallus*' (ibid.: Session 16, p. 262).

In order to understand Lacan's conception of the significance of Ophelia in Hamlet's tragedy, we need to turn for a moment to his burgeoning conception of the phallus, which dates from exactly this period of his teaching. To cite the key passage in 'The Signification of the Phallus' (1966; here 2006b), Lacan's famous contention concerning the phallus in psychoanalysis is:

> In Freudian doctrine, the phallus is not a fantasy, if by that we mean an imaginary effect. Nor is it such an object (part-, internal-, good, bad, etc.) in the sense that this term tends to accentuate the reality pertaining in a relation. It is even less the organ, penis or clitoris, that it symbolizes. [. . .] the phallus is a signifier (2006b: 579).

Yet, Lacan illustrates in several sessions of 'The Formations of the Unconscious', that this revelation is primarily neither his, nor psychoanalysis'. He continues in 'The Signification', written at the same time as 'The Formations of the Unconscious': 'it is not for nothing that Freud used the reference to the simulacrum that it represented for the ancients' (ibid.). The fact that 'our very ancient' cultures, for example, made so much of elevated standing stones shows 'the world of difference there is between this relationship of a certain animal species more or less upright in stature to what is hanging from the bottom of his belly', than that of our Darwinian forbears (Lacan 1957–58: Session 27, p. 447). In pagan cultures, the phallus was the central object in fertility cults from the beginning and thus something highly symbolic: 'In short, what is striking is [sic.] the very special function of this object which, for the ancients, beyond any doubt, played the role in the mysteries, of the object [. . .] [to which] initiation lifted the last veils, namely of an object which for the revelation of meaning, was considered as a final significant character' (ibid.: Session 20, p. 332).[3]

---

3 The murals on the walls of the Villa of Mysteries at Pompeii to which Lacan refers in the session of 23 April 1958 (ibid.: Session 20, p. 333) show the price the initiate paid for the unveiling of the phallus in the mystery fertility cults (ibid.: Session 21, p. 350): 'everything which refers to the phallus is the object of amputations, of marks of castration, or of more and more accentuated prohibitions, [up to] the eunuch character of the priests of the great goddess' (ibid.: Session 20, p. 333). Do these ritual instances not show us, Lacan asks, that from the beginning, the phallus—far from being only the tumescent male organ—'represents [. . .] desire in its most manifest form [. . .] namely that which makes the human being who does not have [it] be considered as castrated, and inversely which for the one who has something which can claim to resemble it, as menaced by castration' (ibid.: Session 20, pp. 332–3)?

But what did this phallus signify for the ancients, according to Lacan, which meant that its approach—except in such stylized simulacra as those worn by the ancient comic actors (ibid.: Session 20, pp. 331–2)—ineluctably provoked the winged demons graphically depicted at Pompeii? Since man is a being caught up in 'this *logos* business', Lacan contends, he unfailingly 'perceives himself as excluded from the totality of desires [. . .] as a link in the chain of life, as only being one of those through whom life passes' (ibid.: Session 26, p. 427). Nevertheless, this same being-in-language means that humans can envisage this chain of life from which we have been constitutively cut as a single vital whole:

[L]ife as such [. . .] not so much a particular species as the essence of what it means to be a species, to be a creature, a natural being—[. . .] Nature incarnate or sublimed [. . .] the natural realm understood as utterly subordinated to, utterly exhausted by, the twinned Darwinian drives to survive and reproduce (Mulhall 2008: 18).

The meaning of Being, we might say in Heidegger's language, is first of all, for Lacan, associated with the primordial plenitude that the subject fantasizes is lost to it, the object of both its most intimate desires and the symbolic prohibitions undergirding primary repression. And it is exactly this primordially lost register of Being or being alive that Lacan designates as the 'signification of the phallus' as a signifier in the article bearing the same name:

The phallus is the privileged signifier of this mark in which the role of the Logos is wedded to the advent of desire. One could say that this signifier is chosen as the most salient of what can be grasped in the sexual intercourse as real as well as the most symbolic [. . .] sense [. . .] since it is the equivalent in intercourse to the (logical) copula. One could also say that by virtue of its turgidity, it is the image of the most vital flow as it is transmitted in generation (2006b: 581).

Lacan's typically maverick wager in this period of his teaching, that is, was to resituate this ancient signification of the phallus in the psychoanalytic orbit, or—beyond Freud and Jones—to see in the Freudian field an experiential ground for what the pagans figured in the mythological other scene. The way he does this involves a wholesale refiguring of what Freud had aimed to describe in the Oedipus complex and its dissolution, where, the little boy finds himself in an ambivalent position of rivalry towards the father, in competition for possession of the mother. This is how Freud asks us to imagine Hamlet and to see the reason for his inability to strike down Claudius, his rival/alter ego. The stake or pivot that will allow the boy out of this complex is his ownership of what Little Hans eloquently dubbed a 'widdler'. When he sees that mother, or perhaps a sister or little girlfriend, lacks this privileged endowment, he comes in fear and trembling to conceive that he might lose it too.

So we note two things. First, the mother figures in the Freudian understanding of the Oedipus complex principally as the object of the child's and the father's, competing desires. Freud is also almost silent on what we might call the 'father-mother axis' of the Oedipal triangle. The father claims her as his. And, aided by the child's castration fears, that ought to be enough to impress upon the child the prohibition against incest that will from here on form the nucleus of the boy's superego. Second, Freud's emphasis on the penis leads him into notorious difficulties when it comes to accounting for the sexual development of little girls: 'what women want'.

The Oedipus complex plays itself out differently for Lacan. The founding reason is that desire, for him, is always the desire of the Other. From the mirror stage onwards, he claims, the child shapes its sense of identity round the images of its significant others. In this imaginary register, desire is always tinged with aggression and identification, with deep ambivalence: as Freud had grasped in his formulation of the oral, anal-sadistic and Oedipal-phallic stages. The reason is that the child necessarily comes to desire what others desire, since its observations of what they want configure its wishes in the first place. This affects Lacan's re-conception of the Oedipus complex in two ways, which correspond to the two points noted above about Freud's understanding. First, the pivotal stake in the child's desire is not simply possession of the mother qua object. The child desires above all the mother's desire as a subject, wants to be desired by her and ultimately, to be 'everything' for her—the phallic Thing which might fully satisfy her. With all these anthropological resonances in mind, Lacan proposes that the 'phallus' is the signifier of this desire of the mother. As such, this is what both the boy and the girl child most ardently desire to be in the phallic or Oedipal stage: 'In the first moment and at the first stage [of the Oedipus complex], this is what happens: it is in a way in a mirror that the subject identifies himself with what is the object of desire of the mother' (Lacan 1957–58: Session 10, p. 169).

So, for Lacan, as the phallus replaces the penis as the key stake in the Oedipal drama, castration fear becomes primarily the fear of losing the mother's desire, rather than any biological endowment. His emphasis on the intersubjective constitution of desire has, however, a second consequence for the Oedipus complex. Since it is the mother's desire, rather than her being, that is 'the Thing', correlatively a weight falls on the father-mother axis of the Oedipal triangle that is absent in Freud. Castration will primarily involve an intervention of the father in what Lacan calls the discourse of the mother. Simply put, how the mother responds to the father, particularly to his words, becomes the decisive given for Lacan in the resolution of the Oedipus complex. For example, when Little Hans' father talks to his mother, Lacan notes, he may as well be whistling—and this is central to why Hans developed his phobia. If the child is to assume an identification which will, given time, allow it to peaceably negotiate sexual difference, Lacan claims that the father needs to intervene—not as the more potent rival—in the symbolic register in the name of a Law which will mediate and limit the desire of the mother, as it is perceived by the child. He must present himself to the child as someone who, as the bearer of the Law against incest, *has* the phallus—and for that reason— *is not* the phallus. In what Lacan calls the paternal metaphor, this Law must take the place of the signification of the phallus—as we have said above, the primordial meaning of Being for the subject, which the symbolic order primordially debars.

The differing direction that Lacan's reading takes from Freud's—to which Hamlet's relations to Ophelia indeed provide the outer key—can now be approached more directly. The emphasis in *Hamlet*, for Lacan, falls primarily on the Hamlet-Gertrude axis of the Oedipal triangle, rather than on what directly concerns Hamlet's relations to Claudius. More specifically, it is only in so far as Hamlet cannot see *what Claudius might be for his mother* that he fails to stand up to this incestuous imposter, instead inflicting his rage on everything and everyone else, including his most vicious treatment of Ophelia. It is to the question of Gertrude's desire and what it signifies for Hamlet, that we turn now.

GERTRUDE'S DESIRE, OR THE MEANING OF BEING (S[Ø])

So, as Lacan puts it paradigmatically, if he is right: '[U]ndoubtedly the least that can be said to count for [Hamlet] is that he is fixed on his mother—it is the most certain and obvious thing in Hamlet's role' (1958–59a: Session 15, p. 241); '[W]hat Hamlet is grappling with, is a desire which should be regarded, considered where it is in the play, namely [. . .] very far from his own, that it is not the desire for the mother, but the desire of the mother' (ibid.: Session 15, p. 243). That this is a step beyond Freud is not something Lacan advertises, as Rabaté comments. Nevertheless, in the same seminar, Lacan makes it very clear, even gently disputing Freud's reading of the play *en passant*: 'I mean one might just as well say, that if Hamlet immediately hurled himself on his stepfather, that he would find here after all the opportunity [to salve] his own guilt by finding outside of himself the really guilty party' (ibid.: Session 15, p. 241).

It seems astonishing that no one before Lacan had stressed the importance of this desire of the mother, Gertrude, in putting Hamlet's time and desire out of joint. From the very beginning, before he has heard anything of his father's ghost, Hamlet speaks very frankly concerning the matter. If the whole business of life appears 'sterile, stale, flat and unprofitable' to him, he is not silent as to why it strikes him thus:

> That it should come to this!
> But two months dead—nay not so much, not two—
> So excellent a king, that was to this
> Hyperion to a satyr, so loving to my mother
> That he might not beteem the winds of heaven
> Visit her face too roughly—heaven and earth,
> Must I remember? [. . .] and yet within a month—
> Let me not think on't; frailty, thy name is woman—
> A little month, or ere those shoes were old
> With which she followed my poor father's body,

Like Niobe, all tears, why she, even she—

O God, a beast that wants discourse of reason

Would have mourned longer—married with my uncle,

My father's brother, but no more like my father

Than I to Hercules—within a month,

Ere yet the salt of most unrighteous tears

Had left the flushing in her gallèd eyes,

She married. Oh most wicked speed, to post

With such dexterity to incestuous sheets.

It is not, nor it cannot come to good.

But break, my heart, for I must hold my tongue

(Shakespeare 2003: 1.2.137–43, 145–59).

Shortly afterwards, when his father's ghost appears to Hamlet it is not simply to fire his anger against Claudius. Hamlet is also charged, in very direct terms, by his father's perturbed spirit to end Gertrude's 'luxury' with Claudius, who is designated here as 'that incestuous, that adulterate beast' (ibid.: 1.5.41 and 81–91). Although Lacan does not remark on it, it is remarkable that Hamlet's harsh repudiation of Ophelia decisively situates her not simply qua mother —already a surely deeply telling fact in the maiden who had previously attracted his amorous desire. Ophelia is calumnied by him as in effect nothing short of the very representative of maternity per se, that she might give birth to such sinners as he: 'Get thee to a nunnery—why wouldst thou be a breeder of sinners? I am myself indifferent honest, but yet I could accuse me of such things, that it were better my mother had not borne me. [. . .] What should such fellows as I do crawling between earth and heaven?' (ibid.: 3.1.119–25). We see here the positioning of Ophelia as mother, if not as Gertrude herself, in order then to deride her as proxy for the sins of the other.

At the heart of Lacan's interpretation, however, lies his reading of the astonishing, infamous exchange between Hamlet and Gertrude in the central scene of the third act, wherein Hamlet comes to his mother's chambers, after the conceit of the *Schauerspiel* or play within the play. Lacan notes that having abjured her, again in the most explicit term, to desist from sleeping with his uncle, Hamlet hesitates or, at the very least, waxes ambivalent. 'What shall I do?', Gertrude asks Hamlet, her heart 'cleft in twain' (ibid.: 3.4.182; 157). Lacan replies by observing that, at this decisive moment when Hamlet directly confronts the question of his mother's desire, he can only fail:

> [H]aving got to this summit that is in question, there is in Hamlet a sudden collapse which makes him say: and then after all, now that I have told all that to you, do whatever you want, and go and tell all this to Uncle Claudius. Namely you are going to let him give you a little kiss on the cheek, tickle your neck a little, scratch your tummy a little, and the pair of you are going to end up in bed as usual [. . .] we see here [. . .] the disappearance, the dying away of his appeal, into something which is a consenting to the desire of his mother, laying down his arms before something which seems ineluctable to him: namely that the mother's desire here takes on again the value of something which in no case, and by no method, can be raised up (1958–59a: Session 15, p. 244).

The different elements of the Lacanian reading of *Hamlet* as then turning on Hamlet's inability to symbolize Gertrude's desire unfold themselves with astonishing explanatory power. After Hamlet's passion towards Gertrude has provoked her to ask him 'What wilt thou do? thou wilt not murder me?' (Shakespeare 2003: 3.4.21), Lacan notes that Hamlet's father's ghost asks him to mediate, or render straight again, the errant desire of his widow. In Shakespeare's verse, the ghost asks Hamlet to use all his considerable wit to 'step between her and her fighting soul. Conceit in weakest bodies strongest works' (ibid.: 112–13). Again, when Ophelia compliments the acuity of Hamlet's interpretation of the 'mousetrap' play he stages to catch the king's conscience, Lacan notes that his response almost literally anticipates his father's demand to rectify Gertrude's desire, and ruefully reflects his inability to do it. 'I could interpret between you and your love,' Hamlet says to the shunned Ophelia, 'if I could see the puppets dallying' (ibid.: 3.2. 255).

Yet, this is the problem and source of the great mystery of Hamlet's inability to act as he ought, Lacan contends. He cannot step between his mother's desire and her fighting soul, since he cannot see the puppets of her desire dallying. Nor can he comprehend what might be pulling the strings of this libidinous woman who could fail to mourn a husband and to take his brother and rival so soon to bed. In Lacan's defense, a great deal of what Hamlet says—together with his scurrilous persecution of Ophelia as proxy for the sins of his mother—makes the importance of this troubling enigma of Gertrude's desire clear. The central exchange with Gertrude, already raised, highlights his disbelieving bewilderment at his mother's ability to love Claudius. The mirror that he holds up to her fighting soul juxtaposes the counterfeit images of the queen's two lovers. Claudius for Hamlet is less than a shadow of his father, scarcely 'a King of shreds and patches' (ibid.: 3.4.102), and he cannot pour enough derision upon his head. So what can Gertrude possibly *see* in him?

Look you now what follows.

Here is your husband, like a mildewed ear

Blasting his wholesome brother. Have you eyes?

Could you on this fair mountain leave to feed,

And batten on this moor? Ha! have you eyes?

(ibid.: 3.4.63–7)

The very 'value of *Hamlet*', Lacan ventures on 8 April 1959, is that it allows us to gain access to the meaning of the S(Ø)in the graph of desire—which he had been developing in the previous two seminars. This S(Ø), Lacan explains, stands as the signifier of the final inconsistency of the Other. It marks the absence of some final guarantor or 'Other of the Other' that could answer the *che vuoi*? [what do you want?] question that every child addresses to the Other. To evoke what Nietzsche says about the play, we could say that this S(Ø) is Lacan's more analytic figuring of the abyss into which Hamlet is alleged to have stared, at the heart of the enigma of Being:

The meaning of what Hamlet learns from his father is [. . .] the irredeemable, absolute, unplumbable betrayal of love. Of the purest love, the love of this king who perhaps of course, like any man, may have been a great rogue but who with this being who was his wife would go so far as to keep the wind away from her face. At least according to what Hamlet tells us (Lacan 1958–59a: Session 16, p. 256).

It is Hamlet's inability to fathom this S(Ø) that sees him as 'fixed' in the tendrils of his mother's desire. Since he cannot move this mountain, he remains 'nothing but the reverse side of a message which is not his own' (ibid.: Session 17, p. 265). *Hamlet*, Lacan argues, is a play that comes from the underworld, in the precise sense of the Acheron that Freud tells us he would move, in the epigraph to *The Interpretation of Dreams*, since it was not given to him to be able to move heaven. In terms of Lacan's development of Freudian theory, this play is about what persists when the symbolic order fails and what ensues when there is something rotten at the heart of this order.[4]

When Hamlet's father's ghost appears, his appearance itself attests, in the terms that Lacan develops, that there is an unpaid symbolic debt of the exact type that psychoanalysis confronts in neuroses. The ghost cannot find peace until this debt has been paid, his story has been told, and his memory has been mourned as it ought to be:

> What Hamlet finds himself confronted with in this 'to be or not to be' is the encountering of the place taken by what his father has said to him. And what his father has said to him qua ghost, is that he had been surprised by death 'in the blossoms of my sin' [Shakespeare 2003: 1.5.76]. It is a matter of encountering the place taken by the sin of the other, the unpaid sin. The one who knows is on the contrary, contrary to Oedipus, someone who has not paid for this crime of existing (Lacan 1958–59a: Session 13, p. 213).

---

4 From its very first lines, Lacan notes, there are extraordinary indicators of this failing of the symbolic in Hamlet's Denmark (ibid.: Session 14, p. 223). In a choice instance of the transitivity that characterizes the imaginary, it is the visitor Bernardo at the play's opening who, approaching the guard, asks: 'who's there?', necessitating a correction by Francisco, the rightful protector of the realm: 'Nay, answer me, stand, and unfold yourself' (Shakespeare 2003: 1.1.1–2). And what, after all, are all those oppressions that speak to Hamlet about the desirability of suicide, if not an inventory of abuses against the order of the symbolic Law:

> Th'oppressor's wrong, the proud man's contumely,
> The pangs of disprized love, the law's delay,
> The insolence of office, and the spurns
> That patient merit of th'unworthy takes (ibid.:3.1.71–4).

Unlike the father of Freud's dream who did not know he was dead, the uncanny thing about the ghost is that he has seen exactly how he met his mortal end. More than this, Hamlet's father is all-too-awake to what Lacanians describe as the real of jouissance ('father, can't you see I'm burning' [Freud 1953: 509]), to which the father in the Freudian dream remains in the dark. The text intimates that Hamlet senior is, indeed, suffering things well beyond the order of the pleasure principle, or mortal imagination:

I am thy father's spirit,

Doomed for a certain term to walk the night,

And for the day confined to fast in fires,

Till the foul crimes done in my days of nature

Are burnt and purged away. But that I am forbid

To tell the secrets of my prison house,

I could a tale unfold whose lightest word

Would harrow up thy soul, freeze thy young blood,

Make thy two eyes like stars start from their spheres,

Thy knotted and combined locks to part

And each particular hair to stand an end,

Like quills upon the fretful porpentine.

But this eternal blazon must not be

To ears of flesh and blood

(Shakespeare 2003: 1.5.9–22).

For Hamlet, Lacan hence notes, this question, 'to be or not to be', is not as simple or as general and abstract a matter as a philosopher might take it to be. He is no atheist, whatever they taught him at Wittenberg. At the very least, Hamlet illustrates the popular (mis)reading of Lacan's dictum that the true formula of atheism is 'God is unconscious' (1998a: 59). The agnosticism Hamlet professes about what lies beyond the grave in the 'to be or not to be' soliloquy gives way only too readily when the opportunity of killing Claudius arises as he sits praying, after the *Schauerspiel*. In Lacan's words, Hamlet is very worried about 'the eternal "to be" of Claudius' (1958–59a: Session 14, p. 228).

And this is what stays his hand, nothing like the supposed doubts of a would-be atheist or fledgling modern man unable to act absent theological orientation.

On one level, in layman's terms, we can rightly say that Hamlet wants Claudius to go to hell, which his father's ghost has attested very clearly as a prospect. What interests us, from the Lacanian perspective, is what is at stake in this undying 'to be'—and so what of Claudius might be involved in that other scene, beyond the mortal coil, where he might go to heaven or to hell. For this undying 'to be', Lacan contends, lies exactly in the register of what in the first part of this essay we saw as the signification of the phallus, veiled in the ancient mysteries and primordially repressed with the instauration of the symbolic order in the life of each subject. This uncanny 'to be' is what lies beyond or beneath the symbolic order: in the real of unmediated desire wherein Hamlet's father suffers without cease for unspeakable sins, and wherein a woman, the mother, can unspeakably pass over a noble husband's memory for a usurper's bed. For Hamlet, it fairly obtrudes in the unmediated desire his mother bears for Claudius, who he is thus systematically unable to act against.

Lacan's unifying claim is that, above all, *Hamlet* ought to be considered, if not exactly a *Trauerspiel* (tragedy), a play about the failure to mourn. 'From the beginning of *Hamlet*,' he comments at the beginning of his last session on the play, 'there is nothing but talk of mourning' (ibid.: Session 19, p. 295). In the first instance, it is Gertrude's failure to mourn her first husband that shapes what follows: 'the funereal baked meats did coldly furnish forth the marriage tables' (Shakespeare 2003: 1.2.180–1). As Lacan puts it:

> [W]ith respect to the dead person, the one who has just died, something has not been performed which are called rites: rites assigned, when all is said and done, for what? What are funeral rites? The rites through which we satisfy . . . the memory of the dead person. What are they if not the total, massive intervention from earth to heaven of the symbolic operation (1958–59a: Session 18, pp. 292–3).

Later, he points out that Hamlet will to try to *scream* out this failure to mourn his father by preventing Polonius' slain body from being properly buried. Instead, he drags it round by the feet, hides it absurdly and then taunts those who would find him: 'hide fox, and all after' (Shakespeare 2003: 4.2. 27). This is in effect how Gertrude's failure to mourn Hamlet Senior has demeaned his memory, as if he were little better than a hunted animal: such surely is the message Hamlet's acting out tries to convey to the Other.

Through unfolding the neurotic consequences for Hamlet of this failure to properly mourn his father, though, Shakespeare's tragedy for Lacan stages what ensues whenever any subject has failed to symbolize the loss of our most intimate wishes, this being the universal stake of acceding to the symbolic order. However regal Hamlet idealizes his father to be, it is Gertrude's 'o'er-hasty marriage' that has unhinged the young prince, so that 'the fact is that the phallus is completely outside its usual position compared to our analysis of the Oedipal position' (Lacan 1958–59a: Session 19, p. 308). The phallus is with the new king, Claudius, indeed. But the phallus at stake is not the signifier of the symbolic Law, whose installation would keep jouissance at bay. Claudius is instead the rival who enjoys the desire of the mother, as Freud recognized. He is the one who from Hamlet's perspective has achieved in reality what Hamlet has only fantasized about: the *pere jouisseur*, rather than a bearer of symbolic authority; the man who is or would be the phallus as Thing, rather than its representative qua signifier of the symbolic order and the order of Law.

So this is why Hamlet will not strike Claudius when he can, as the latter sits at prayer. For he wants to strike at that which he symptomatically derides in Ophelia, under the repulsive aspect of everything that is nauseating in life itself: what we might term King Claudius' second phallic body, the body invested in him by Gertrude's unregulated passion. 'The phallus, well and truly real here, must be attacked as such. He always stops' (ibid.). Moreover, as Lacan echoes Polonius, there is method in Hamlet's madness. For the phallus, 'even when it is here well and truly real, is a shade', something which 'always slips through your fingers', or in Hamlet's telling quip is a 'Thing of Nothing'.

> We are not so much dreaming with [Hamlet] of what happens on the other side, but simply saying this, that to put in the final full stop in something does not prevent the being remaining identical to everything that he has articulated by the discourse of his life, and that here there is no 'to be or not to be': that the 'to be', whatever it is, remains eternal (ibid.: Session 14, p. 228).

'NOT TO BE': THE PRICE OF HAMLET'S DESIRE

Towards the end of the session of 18 June 1958, discussing obsessional neurosis, Lacan comments that what is basically at stake is an inability to fully engage in the symbolic order except 'by this sort of repetition which a humorist portrayed in the famous "to be or not", and the chap scratches his head in order to be able to continue: "to be or not . . .", "to be or not . . ." And it is in repeating that he is able to find the end of the sentence' (1957–58: Session 26, p. 435). There are multiple Lacanian resonances at play in this telling instance of wit. He himself associates this inability to end the sentence—at least at one remove—with Daniel Paul Schreber's chattering birds, whose miraculous sentences would often not achieve a closure: 'lacking now is [. . .]' More broadly, the *vel* (either-or) Hamlet confronts between being and non-being speaks to the dilemma Lacanian psychoanalysis tells us we all face, as beings born into the discourse of the Other. Either we in effect choose being, with the refusal of the symbolic. Or we opt for an acceptance of the non-being of subjectivity through symbolic castration that will give us access to whatever civilization and discontents we can find in the order of Law and the signifier. The obsessional, Lacan tells us, opts for the order of the signifier. But his best intentions are troubled by what Freud identified as a preponderance of aggressivity in the construction of his desire. We think of the hypothetical violence ('what if you were to take the razor and cut yourself') that visited themselves upon the Rat Man (see Freud 1955: 151–318), which meant that he was forced finally to abbreviate his prayers so that they could be repeated so quickly that no doubt about his pious intentions had time to intervene: 'to be or not . . .', 'to be or not . . .', 'to be or not . . .'.[5]

Lacan is hesitant about 'diagnosing' Hamlet as a literary character. Indeed, the session in 'Desire and its Interpretation' of 18 March 1959 contains some of Lacan's most extended comments on his approach to literature and his rejection of the paradigm of 'psychobiography' which, for example, Ella Sharpe brought to her reading of Shakespeare (Lacan 1958–59a: Session 15, pp. 387–94). We can surmise, Lacan speculates, that some event or other must

---

5 See Lacan (1957–58: Session 22–7) for extended passages on the obsessional.

have impressed itself upon Shakespeare around 1603, which led to the unflattering presentation of so many of his heroines from after *Hamlet*, and the extraordinary shaping of this play. *Hamlet* is known to have been written soon after the death of his son Hamnet, a deep trauma for any man. But what is decisive, for Lacan, are the texts that Shakespeare has bequeathed to us. These have compelling logics that, we have seen, are amply sufficient to detain our psychoanalytic attention.

All this said, Lacan notes that there is more than something of the obsessional about Hamlet's inaction, as the bard presents it to us. The obsessional, according to Lacan's reformulation of Freud in the previous year's seminar, is someone who has from the beginning encountered the desire of the Other in the register of threatening rivalry. His manifold defences—rituals, reaction formations, the cancellation and isolation of aggressive thoughts—embody a demand for the death of the Other as this threatening, desiring being. His signature doubts and oscillations arise from the fact that like the hysteric, his flagging desire nevertheless depends on the Other's desire. The compromise formations of his neurosis all serve to delay the hour of confronting this desire, and all that it provokes within him. In the meanwhile, he sets himself to the laborious task of presenting up to the Other as so many gifts, the spectacles of his multiple feats and achievements.

Similarly, everything Hamlet does or does not do, Lacan comments, takes place in the time of the Other:

> It is in his parents' good time that he remains [in Denmark rather than leaving for Wittenberg]. It is on the time of other people that he suspends his crime: it is in his stepfather's time that he embarks for England; it is in Rosencrantz and Guildernstern's time that he is led, evidently with an ease which astonished Freud, to send them to their death thanks to a piece of trickery which is carried out very cleverly (ibid.: Session 17, p. 274).

Even when he does enter into the final confrontation whose multiple twists will lead him to his act, it is at the beck and call of Claudius: 'Sir, I will walk here in the hall. If it please his majesty, it is the breathing time of day with me. Let the foils be brought, the gentlemen willing; and the King hold his purpose,

I will win for him, and I can' (Shakespeare 2003: 5.2.153–6). In the meanwhile, throughout the majority of the play, there is Hamlet's veritable wall of discourse whose manic qualities Lacan remarks, and which effortlessly accommodates all the nuances of language to denounce and confound all who encounter him (1958–59a: Session 18, pp. 288–9).

What is it then that projects Hamlet, albeit in the apparently most unlikely way, towards his act? We noted above that Lacan's posing of this question represents one of the unique features of his reading of the play. Here again, the acuity of Lacan's analytic framework is amply attested. The desire of the obsessional, Lacan summarizes, 'is characterised by the function of an impossible desire' (ibid.: Session 17, p. 272): it can only be safely maintained if the object is off limits or 'dead' to him. And just so, his evanescent desire for Ophelia returns, as if by chance, when, returning from his incomplete sojourn in England, Hamlet comes across the funeral procession for Ophelia, who has been driven to probable suicide by his derision and Polonius' murder. Laertes has leapt into the grave and, clutching her corpse, is making great protestations of brotherly love. At precisely this moment, something gives in Hamlet. He leaps into the grave and fires off an inventory of proofs of his love for the dead girl he has so recently demeaned, in which Lacan invites us to see attestations of the imaginary identification with Laertes which will play itself out in the final encounter:

> 'Swounds, show me what thou't do
> Woo't weep? woo't fight? woo't fast, woo't tear thyself?
> Woo't drink up eisel, eat a crocodile?
> I'll do't. Dost thou come here to whine,
> To outface me by leaping in her grave?
> Be buried quick with her, and so will I
> (Shakespeare 2003: 5.1.241–6).

Yet, more finally important, for Lacan, is how Hamlet, as it were, quilts this remarkable series of challenges or boasts:

> He concludes by saying: who is giving these cries of despair in connection with the death of this young girl. And he says: the one who is crying 'is I, Hamlet the Dane' [Shakespeare 2003.: 5.1.224]. We have

never heard him saying that he is a Dane; he hates the Danes. All of a sudden we see him absolutely converted [. . .]. It is in the measure that something S [of the signifier] is here in a certain relationship with o [the little o of the other] that all of a sudden he makes this identification which makes him discover for the first time his desire in his totality (1958–59a: Session 14, p. 231).

In short, in this encounter with Laertes which explicitly anticipates the elaborate challenge in the final scene, Hamlet, for the first time, accedes to something like a symbolic identification. In mourning Ophelia, or through seeing Laertes truly mourn, Hamlet is finally able to accede to the 'not to be' of a symbolic identity. There is something in this 'Hamlet the Dane', as we might say, which trumps all of his imaginary loves and hates, and finally puts at a proper distance the cloying desire of the mother that has clung to him ever since she too hastily spurned his father's name. Instead, this paradigmatic symbolic attestation situates Hamlet in the dimension of a cause and ideal, that of being a Dane, a political subject. It is an identification in which there is something ineluctably transpersonal and normative, and which points towards a mandate for which one might give up his life and his private conceits. Hamlet, Lacan comments, at this moment precisely can '[take] the bit between his teeth' and become a man (ibid.: Session 15, p. 247).

It is this symbolic register, too, that veritably frames the action of the final scene. The stakes Claudius and Laertes pit on the latter's duel with Hamlet, Lacan notes—the Barbary horses, the ornate French rapiers complete with ornamental carriages (ibid.: Session 18, pp. 284–5)—are all of the order of beautiful and useless things which Marcel Mauss showed were the privileged objects in the highly symbolic systems of gift exchange in early societies: 'vases made to remain empty, shields too heavy to be carried, sheaves that will dry out, lances that are thrust into the ground—[. . .] all destined to be useless, if not superfluous by their very abundance' (Lacan 2006a: 225). And what occurs in the final exchange, so that Hamlet finally, too late, becomes as good as his father's name? Beyond all the symbolic tokens that mark off the duel between Laertes and Hamlet as what Georg Wilhelm Hegel called a struggle for pure prestige: 'beyond this, there is played out the drama of the accomplishment of Hamlet's desire, beyond this there is the phallus' (Lacan 1958–59a: Session 18, p. 287).

'I'll be your foil, Laertes,' says Hamlet, punning on three senses of the word: the swords the two will wield; how Hamlet will, like a jewel case, set off his rival's brilliance; but also, thirdly, how he will be Laertes' nemesis in the duel (ibid.: Session 18, pp. 287–8). He does not know that the tip of Laertes' sword or foil has been laced with poison, and that he will shortly indeed wield it fatally against both Laertes and the king, having been poisoned himself. The price, then, of his assumption of the capacity to act is that he is mortally wounded by this death-dealing phallus and knows himself to be dying. Hamlet's accession to his symbolic mandate remains an accession which is too late, and the final belated, successful act remains 'a botched piece of work' (ibid.: Session 13, p. 214). Or, in the language of Lacan's thinking, the 'not to be', that we can say should have been stabilized in the symbolic order by the rightful, timely mourning of the Name-of-the-Father, has to return in the real before Hamlet can fully accede to the rightful action. This is the key to the story Hamlet delegates to Horatio to tell, certainly as it is retold by Jacques Lacan.

References

ENGLISH SOURCES

FREUD, Sigmund. 1953. *The Interpretation of Dreams* in *The Standard Edition of the Complete Psychological Works of Sigmund Freud*, VOLS 4 and 5 (James Strachey ed., and trans.). London: Hogarth Press and the Institute of Psycho-Analysis, pp. ix–630.

———. 1955. 'Notes upon a Case of Obsessional Neurosis' in *The Standard Edition of the Complete Psychological Works of Sigmund Freud*, VOL. 10 (James Strachey ed., and trans.). London: Hogarth Press and the Institute of Psycho-Analysis, pp. 151–318.

———. 1963. 'Mourning and Melancholia' in *The Standard Edition of the Complete Psychological Works of Sigmund Freud*, VOL. 14 (James Strachey ed., and trans.). London: Hogarth Press and the Institute of Psycho-Analysis, pp. 237–60.

————. 1985. *The complete letters of Sigmund Freud to Wilhelm Fliess, 1887–1904* (J. M. Masson ed., and trans.). Cambridge, MA: Harvard University Press.

JONES, Ernest. 1910. 'The Oedipus-Complex as An Explanation of Hamlet's Mystery: A Study in Motive.' *The American Journal of Psychology* 21(1) (January): 72–113.

LACAN, Jacques. 1957–58. The Seminar of Jacques Lacan. Book V. The Formations of the Unconscious, 1957–58. Unofficially translated by Cormac Gallagher from the unedited French typescripts of the seminar that was published in 1998. Available at http://www.valas.fr/IMG/pdf/THE-SEMINAR-OF-JACQUES-LACAN-V_formations_de_l_-in.pdf (Last accessed on 22 August 2012.)

————. 1958–59a. The Seminar of Jacques Lacan. Book VI. Desire and its Interpretation, 1958–59. Unofficially translated by Cormac Gallagher from the unedited and unpublished French typescripts of Le Séminaire. Livre VI. Le désir et son interprétation, 1958–59. Available at http://www.lacaninireland.com/web/wp-content/uploads/2010/06/-THE-SEMINAR-OF-JACQUES-LACAN-VI.pdf (Last accessed on 22 August 2012.)

————. 1998a. *The Seminar of Jacques Lacan. Book XI. The Four Fundamental Concepts of Psychoanalysis, 1964* (Jacques-Alain Miller ed., Alan Sheridan trans.). Reprint, New York and London: W. W. Norton.

————. 2006a. 'The Function and Field of Speech and Language in Psychoanalysis' in *Écrits: The First Complete Edition in English* (Bruce Fink trans.). New York and London: W. W. Norton, pp. 197–268.

————. 2006b. 'The Signification of the Phallus' in *Écrits: The First Complete Edition in English* (Bruce Fink trans.). New York and London: W. W. Norton, pp. 575–84.

MULHALL, Stephen. 2008. *On Film* (2nd edn). New York: Routledge.

SHAKESPEARE, William. 2003. Philip Edwards (ed.), *Hamlet: The Prince of Denmark* (2nd edn). Cambridge: Cambridge University Press.

VINING, Edward P. 1881. *The Mystery of Hamlet*. Philadelphia: J. P. Lippincott and Co.

ŽIŽEK, Slaovj. 2006. *How to Read Lacan*. London: Granta Books.

FRENCH SOURCES

LACAN, Jacques. 1956. 'Fonction et champ de la parole et du langage en psychanalyse'. *La Psychanalyse* 1: 81–166. It was subsequently published in *Écrits*
(1966).

———. 1958–59b. Le Séminaire. Livre VI. Le désir et son interprétation,
1958–59. Some sessions published in 1982.

———. 1966. 'La Signification du Phallus' in *Écrits*. Paris: Éditions du Seuil,
pp. 685–96.

———. 1973. *Le Séminaire. Livre XI. Les quatre concepts fondamentaux de la psychanalyse, 1964* (Jacques-Alain Miller ed.). Paris: Éditions du Seuil.

———. 1982. 'Le désir et son interprétation'. *Ornicar? Bulletin périodique du
champ freudien* 25: 13–36.

———. 1994. *Le Séminaire. Livre IV. La relation d'objet, 1956–57* (Jacques-Alain
Miller ed.). Paris: Éditions du Seuil.

———. 1998b. *Le Séminaire. Livre V. Les formations de l'inconscient, 1957–58*
(Jacques-Alain Miller ed.). Paris: Éditions du Seuil.

Lewis Carroll and Psychoanalytic Criticism: Why Nothing Adds Up in Wonderland

CHRISTOPHER LANE

In 1966, in a short radio tribute to Lewis Carroll conveying why the surrealists had championed the quirky Victorian, Jacques Lacan explained that their admiration sprang from Carroll's interest in 'all kinds of truths—ones that are certain even if not self-evident' (2002a: 9, translation modified).[1] The truth snared in his fiction is that our culture adopts rules that can seem ridiculous from too close. Moreover, while a lot of fiction strives to imitate those rules, Carroll upended them to cast a wry light on their sometimes-ludicrous foundations. Much of Lacan's tribute amplifies the ensuing paradox to assess what counterintuitive insight it gave the young Alice as she and her writer meditated on Wonderland.

This essay adopts a similar course, asking what Carroll's nonsense is about and wherein lies its overall effect. What does it tell us about the social world in which he lived and the divergent, often-surreal realm of fantasy that he delighted in depicting and overturning? In asking these questions I hope to show that, several decades before Sigmund Freud, Carroll found a profoundly counterintuitive and psychoanalytic way of thinking about fantasy and symbols: he put fantasy at odds with law and pushed meaning to the limits of sense, to the point where it unravels to reveal the fantasies and signs that help make it operate.

---

1 Lacan first presented this homage on 31 December 1966 on France Culture (French radio), under the title 'A Psychoanalyst Comments'. The text entitled 'Hommage rendu à Lewis Carroll' published in *Ornicar? Revue du champ freudien* in 2002 is based on Marlène Belilos's transcription of the talk from a tape recording of it, edited by Jacques-Alain Miller. The page numbers in my essay correspond to the French text.

The effect of Carroll's doing so is of lasting importance for psychoanalysis, this essay argues, because he found a way to relay through fiction the price and difficulty of adaptation. His works let us imagine a different outcome, where rules and precepts are briefly suspended so that the ones we are used to seem strange, even foreign and unnatural.

All this attention to the most 'surreal' aspects of our culture led Lacan to return to André Breton's argument: that Carroll's use of nonsense was like a 'vital solution to the deep contradiction between an acceptance of madness and the exercise of reason' (quoted in Marret-Maleval 2002: 342; my translation). To Breton, Carroll was in fact the surrealists' first 'master in the school of truancy', because he juxtaposed the 'poetic order' against the madness— even supposed tyranny—of rationalism. But rather than simply repeat that line, which downplays much of the profundity of Carroll's philosophy, Lacan's tribute to him aimed at something more: he wanted to rescue Carroll's insight into the way human beings are compelled to adapt to broader cultural demands. As Lacan put it, almost pitting his reading against generations of devoted readers who have derived only innocent pleasure from the Alice stories, Wonderland generates 'unease', even a kind of 'malaise', by revealing the ordeal of such a process (Lacan 2002a: 9).

The idea that Wonderland is a platform for anxiety and malaise complicates Breton's more free-and-easy celebration of Carrollian nonsense, hinting at an underside to the latter that generates suffering as well as bliss (see Fig.1). Yet this double-edged assessment is central to how Lacan saw the paradoxical insights that certain fictions generate, including those by Edgar Allan Poe, Carroll, James Joyce, Jean Genet and Marguerite Duras. As he put it in 'Homage', the doors on which the fictive pushes often reveal 'discordances of personality'. What matters in the *Alice* stories is that the text prepare Alice Liddell—and the reader—for the powerful, counterintuitive insight, 'One only ever passes through a door one's own size' (ibid.: 11, translation modified; see Fig. 2).

Could the same be said about the way we approach Carroll's fiction and life? Perhaps more than most writers, Carroll invites such questions, not merely because of his affection for Alice Liddell but also because he tried to draw a sharp line between his pseudonym and his identity as Charles Lutwidge

FIGURE 1 (*left*): From *Through the Looking-Glass* (1872). FIGURE 2 (*right*): From *Alice in Wonderland* (1865). Illustrations by Sir John Tenniel.

Dodgson, Oxford don, Anglican clergyman and eccentric logician. That line has only increased speculation on what, exactly, Dodgson was so intent on separating off and assigning to his other, pseudonymic identity.

Lacan frustrated that line of enquiry, displacing the question of psychobiography altogether. His homage was given entirely to Carroll, the invented name, without even mentioning his namesake, Charles Dodgson. Yet the *Alice* stories confound that move, forcing the author back into view, because Carroll/Dodgson wrote himself obliquely into *Through the Looking-Glass and What Alice Found There* (1872; here 1998b) as the bumbling, doting White Knight (see Fig. 3). No analysis of the *Alice* stories, therefore, can proceed without at least noting the space, even gulf, that Dodgson tried to create between his names and their respective identities.

At least initially, psychobiography bears quite heavily on our approach. We cannot ignore that Dodgson's talent for nonsense and philosophical games is nearly as famous as his passion for the seven-year-old Alice Liddell, on whom his protagonist was carefully modelled (see Fig. 4). The passion was so ardent that Liddell's concerned parents finally prevented the 30-year-old from seeing

119

FIGURE 3 (*left*): The White Knight from *Through the Looking-Glass*. Illustration by Sir John Tenniel. FIGURE 4 (*right*): Alice Liddel (1852–1934), dressed as a beggar maid. Photograph by Charles Lutwidge Dodgson.

her. Published after this ban, Dodgon's text seems to be partly an attempt at overstepping it, in reminiscence, to record the happiness it effectively disabled. As Carroll/Dodgson writes at the beginning of *Looking-Glass*, representing his and the girl's age differences, her maturation and the parental ban as a type of fatality: 'I and thou / Are half a life asunder . . . No thought of me shall find a place / In thy young life's hereafter' (1998b: 117). The Victorians were more accepting of the reality of child brides than we are today, but that Liddell's parents drew a line indicates that even by Victorian standards Dodgson had overstepped it.

With Carroll, by contrast, the praise we bestow on his fiction seems commensurate with its keen artistry, philosophical adventurousness and semantic genius. It is to Carroll that we attribute such outsized flights of fancy as a mad tea party peopled by raucous, acrimonious creatures—almost a mini society in dissensus. He also gives us philosophically minded insects imitating classical Athens, babies that turn into pigs, the grin of a cat projected across the sky and the queen of a chess game who is transfigured miraculously into a sheep dressed as a grandmother, before she morphs into a kitten whom Alice asks, in turn, whether it dreamed the whole crazy adventure (see Figs 5 and 6).

'Which dreamed it?' is indeed the fascinating ontological question that concludes *Looking-Glass*, with implications for our wondering whether Dodgson or Carroll should—even can—claim authorship of the whole madcap fantasy (ibid.: 238). Such issues are vital to determining who or what is responsible for such vertiginous fantasies and, thus, whether they belong to a besotted Oxford don, manifest themselves from the mind—and unconscious—of a remarkably original thinker, circulate in the brain of a cat or arise, as if unbidden, from the imagination of an inquisitive yet precociously self-assertive girl (see Fig. 7).

Many of the antics that Carroll relays in Wonderland pointedly flatter Alice into believing that she sees through the many escapades, to what is beyond them—as if she were partly outside the worlds of each novella and thus able to gauge them from a position of relative mastery. Yet, we soon learn, the comparison that Carroll sets up between Wonderland and the Victorians' symbolic order does not render the latter less nonsensical. The comparison—and associated philosophy—is extended still further in *Sylvie and Bruno* (1889; here 1991), Carroll's proto-Joycean novel, which styles Fairyland and Outerland as largely interchangeable. As Carroll declares in the novel's appendix,

FIGURE 5 (*left*): The Cheshire-Cat from *Alice in Wonderland*. FIGURE 6 (*right*): The sheep in *Through the Looking-Glass*. Illustrations by Sir John Tenniel.

FIGURE 7: Alice, from *Alice in Wonderland*.
Illustration by Sir John Tenniel.

I have supposed a Human being to be capable of various psychical states, with varying degrees of consciousness, as follows:—

—the 'eerie' state, in which, while conscious of actual surroundings, he is *also* conscious of the presence of Fairies;

—a form of trance, in which, while *un*conscious of actual surroundings, and apparently asleep, he (i.e., his immaterial essence) migrates to other scenes, in the actual world, or in Fairyland, and is conscious of the presence of Fairies (1991: 389).

Three additional criteria convey the novel's imagined states of being, implying that Carroll was clearly serious about their ontological distinctions.

Meanwhile, Dodgson was busy advocating mathematics as a palliative for 'mental trouble'. In later years, after a life of conventional—even fervent— piety, including his decision in 1861 to be ordained, he struggled intensely with religious doubt. He also made an odd habit of returning mail addressed to Lewis Carroll, saying the figure was to him 'unknown'. We might reckon this last move a strategy for coping with unwanted notoriety, a sign of anguish over an increasingly buried chapter of his life or even, plausibly, a form of dissociation whereby two identities (Carroll and Dodgson) could flourish only because Dodgson held them so rigidly apart.

Art and biography seem to part company over these interpretive dilemmas. For *how* we interpret the enigmas attached to both registers is, the *Alice* stories show, central to determining what questions she and, later, the reader can ask about them. As Lacan put it in the passage cited earlier, Carroll seems to want to 'prepare' her for the lesson that 'one only ever passes through a door one's own size' (*on ne franchit jamais qu'une porte à sa taille*) (Lacan 2002a: 11)—a statement hinting that an answer can emerge only after one has discovered how to ask the question attached to it. Approach such a portal from the wrong direction, with the wrong premise or at the wrong time, Carroll implies, and passage through it is unlikely. The idea is almost like that of Wonderland itself, in which much happens the wrong way round, playing havoc with cause and effect, inference and interpretation. Alice has to shrink or expand to enter a different ontological realm. She has to adapt to circumstances and indeed, sometimes does so with relative ease, but not always.

One of the questions that Carroll implicitly poses at such moments, bearing heavily on psychoanalysis, is whether interpretation can unlock and resolve such conundrums. In Wonderland, as in Outerland, these conundrums persist not only because both realms are thoroughly imbued with nonsense, but also because investigation into both novellas chases but finally cannot limit interpretation. Additionally, Carroll leaves undecided whether interpretation is a key that unlocks secrets, or whether secrets are enigmatic signifiers that taunt and seduce us into a world of symbols which, as readers and children, we are not fully equipped to understand.[2] In *Looking-Glass*, for example, in a significant metatextual moment, Humpty Dumpty adopts a hermeneutic code that is comically incapable of addressing what other characters say and mean. As Carroll's overeager interpreter declares, 'When *I* use a word, it means just what I choose it to mean—neither more nor less [. . .]. The question is [. . .] which is to be master—that's all' (Carroll 1998b: 186).

---

2 See Laplanche (1999) and Ricoeur (1970: 20–36).

A successful outcome to such voluntarism and mastery is of course as elusive to Humpty Dumpty as it is to other figures in Wonderland. Oblivious, however, he veers down another idiosyncratic track: how words assume—then almost literally contain—a life of their own. Carroll himself dubs some of them portmanteau words, capturing the idea that meaning is encased in them and Freud took such terminology as his preferred figure for the dream. But Humpty Dumpty's observations are much more prosaic: 'They've a temper, some of them,' he asserts, 'particularly verbs [. . .]—however, *I* can manage the whole lot of them! Impenetrability! That's what *I* say!' (ibid.).

Impenetrability would mean different things a generation later, when Carroll was finishing *Sylvie and Bruno* and writers such as Henry James, George Meredith and Joseph Conrad were cultivating a style of difficulty intent on signalling what, in life and relationships, is most opaque and resistant to meaning. Yet in the end, as all these writers demonstrated in their fiction, opacity is not a mask to screen intention. As Freud understood (and described in his important 1899 essay 'Screen Memories'; here 1962), the screen ends up representing a wish that the ego can struggle assiduously to hide. When, for example, the Red King blurts out that he is engaging in a kind of automatic writing—his pen recording 'all manner of things that [he does not] intend—' (Carroll 1998b: 131), Carroll displaces the ego and indicates that it is through language that the unconscious speaks, revealing truths that we conventionally veil, including—a final tease—that there often *is not* that much to hide.

This too represents Lacan's interest in Carroll: a fascination with surfaces as well as hidden depths and an agility with thought that is finally more adventurous than even Carroll's almost literal transfiguration of the mirror-stage, in *Looking-Glass* (see Figs 8 and 9). So, despite the apparent distance between Carroll and Dodgson regarding the *Alice* stories, the 'malaise' that Lacan identified in both works of fiction highlights a remarkable set of strategies to describe and mask loss. The *Alice* stories are, we might say, both a brilliant solution to the pain Dodgson experienced over Alice Liddell and an intense meditation on the broader consequences of that loss when we adapt to a social order whose laws and customs teeter between meaning and nonsense.

Comedy was not the only genre in which Dodgson voiced doubts about the price of adaptation. He wrote plaintively in the preface to his late, strikingly

FIGURE 8 (*left*) and 9 (*right*): Alice, from *Through the Looking-Glass*. Illustrations by Sir John Tenniel.

named *Pillow Problems Thought Out During Sleepless Nights* (1893), 'There are sceptical thoughts, which seem for the moment to uproot the firmest faith; there are blasphemous thoughts, which dart unbidden into the most reverent souls; there are unholy thoughts, which torture with their hateful presence, the fancy that would fain be pure. Against all these some real mental work is a most helpful ally' (quoted in Lennon 1972: 108–9).

In this form of uncertainty, nonsense—like mathematics—becomes a compensatory anchor. As Hugh Haughton put it perceptively in his introduction to the stories, 'Nonsense can convert the disorderly world of unbalanced feeling into externalized absurdity' (1998: xxiii). By Dodgson's reckoning, mathematics brings to a halt his zany fantasies, because it wards off the 'unholy', the 'sceptical', the 'blasphemous'—and surely also the erotic. In distinguishing then between real and ersatz 'mental work', Dodgson seemed to want to eliminate *internal* challenges to his faith and duty. Yet those challenges persist—even thrive—in his fiction, which carefully elaborates fantasies completely at odds with the model of professional stability he tried to present to the world.

That discrepancy is startling and a challenge to his readers. From at least one perspective, Dodgson's struggle—and the model of repression to which it

125

gave rise—sounds classically Victorian. It implies that he represented desire as an irrational temptation that undermined his tenuous stability as an Oxford don. Certainly, as we'll see, this belief guided several early Freudian readings of the stories by William Empson, Phyllis Greenacre and Paul Schilder, each of whom saw Alice as a stand-in for an Oedipal drama that Dodgson acted out unconsciously in his fiction.

Yet, this critical model is itself the cause of some misunderstanding about that fiction. To begin with, it downplays the philosophical complexity of the writing, which thematizes quite brilliantly how little control and understanding authors have over their creations, and why adaptation may not be such a good or desirable outcome after all. When Lacan focused on Carroll's proto-surrealism, he captured the work's philosophy, even as he left key psychobiographical questions hanging, because unasked.

Fascinated by the gap between these approaches, including what they presume and permit in literary and psychological analysis, I hope to establish something of a middle way between them. Especially in the case of Carroll/ Dodgson, one cannot rule out psychobiography, not least because the author flirts with a version of it that tests its veracity. Still, some forms of psychobiography, including analysis of details and events in Dodgson's life, cannot account for all of the effects in Carroll's astonishing fiction. In the *Alice* stories and *Sylvie and Bruno*, for example, the model of ontology that Carroll adopts represents the unconscious as external and disembodied, as Lacan would later argue, and the symbolic order as brittle, precarious and often painfully arbitrary. The idea that the work correlates simply with its author's unconscious desires misses Carroll's larger point about how fantasies help define us and why blind spots in our thinking manifest themselves in the culture at large.

Largely overturning the depth model of subjectivity, Carroll's fiction most often focuses on the play and limits of meaning across numerous semantic and ontological registers. As the narrator observes in *Sylvie and Bruno*, almost doffing his hat at the myriad philosophical and metafictional questions that ensue: '"Either I've been dreaming about Sylvie," I said to myself, "and this is the reality. Or else I've really been with Sylvie, and this is a dream! Is Life itself a dream, I wonder?"' (Carroll 1991: 10).

Like Carroll, Poe and several others, Lacan also presented life as a kind of dream, with the unconscious structured as its language and the symbolic order as imbued with myths, fantasies and beliefs that are almost oneiric in quality. Additionally, Carroll's philosophy, a full century before Lacan engaged with it, renders that language by such idiosyncratic signifiers as 'Boojum', 'Snark' and 'slithy toves'. Not all such neologisms are nonsensical in his case. 'Chortled' has since entered our language as a delightful verb. But the vertigo created by this second Carrollian model does much besides, including to dramatize a difficulty for Alice—and us—in adapting to the world of language and symbols. That is because the rules and rituals governing everything seem both whimsical and arbitrarily enforced. They serve as a check on contingency and freedom in Wonderland, while casting the adult world as undesirable, authoritarian and almost willfully perverse. Consider the angry Queen of Hearts, whose face explodes with rage the moment others question whether her capricious, unjust orders are reasonable (see Fig. 10).

In *Looking-Glass*, the problems stemming from such arbitrary authority and meaning greatly intensify. The novella is structured like a game of chess, with Alice qua pawn dreaming of becoming queen as she tries, like a child, to

FIGURE 10 (*left*): Alice and Queen of Hearts from *Alice in Wonderland*. FIGURE 11 (*right*): Alice's fellow passengers in the train, from *Through the Looking-Glass*. Illustrations by Sir John Tenniel.

negotiate the moves and aims of other pieces (or characters). But in the coun-terintuitive *Looking-Glass* world, nothing is quite as it appears and any sugges-tion that it follows the logic and order of chess proves deceptive. As Alice tries progressing from the third to fourth squares on the chessboard, for example, little that she's told adds up to a coherent proposition or truth.

She tries to complete this part of the journey by train, a surreal idea in it-self, but when the train guard 'angrily' demands to see her ticket, she is scolded for replying quite reasonably, 'There wasn't room for one where [I] came from. The land there is worth a thousand pounds an inch'. Instead of heeding her, the ticket inspector morphs disturbingly into an inner chorus, with 'a great many voices [saying] all together [. . .], "Don't keep him waiting, child. Why, his time is worth a thousand pounds a minute"' (Carroll 1998b: 146).

The incident represents a troubling, almost threatening, intrusion by the adult world into an ostensibly child-like narrative. Indeed, immediately after the guard berates Alice, a gentleman strongly resembling Benjamin Disraeli (whose first term as prime minister shortly preceded the novella's publication) begins gratuitously to hector her. He is dressed from head-to-toe in white paper, almost anticipating the 'papier-mâché Mephistopheles' of Conrad's Kurtz. And unusually, in Tenniel's illustration of the scene, Alice looks chas-tened and bashful, drawn to scale diminutively against the overbearing adults (see Fig. 11). Next to the papered Disraeli is a goat who pipes up that Alice may not know her alphabet, but she ought to know her way to the ticket office (again, overlooking that there was not one). And next to the goat is a beetle—too small to be featured in the sketch—who seems compelled to ratchet up the criticism by adding, comically, 'She'll have to go back from here as luggage!' (ibid.: 147).

Using all available Victorian optics to gauge and fathom her, the guard peers at her 'first through a telescope, then through a microscope, and then through an opera glass'. At last he says, 'You're travelling the wrong way,' shuts the window, and goes away. But by this point, Alice thinks to herself, 'There's no use in speaking' for most of her attempts at communication bring neither understanding nor accountability. The 'voices didn't join in, *this* time, as she hadn't spoken, but, to her great surprise, they all *thought* in chorus [. . .]. "Better say nothing at all. Language is worth a thousand pounds a word!"' (ibid.: 146).

The demand that Alice hears, even though nothing is said at this point, is also for a response in the adult world that does not make much sense; she cannot reasonably comply with it (she cannot create a ticket office where none exists). Yet, since the demand intensifies, the choric relentlessness takes on the attributes of an irrationally judgmental supplement to an irrationally chaotic Wonderland. The two arguably go hand-in-glove in Carroll's world, underscoring demands that Alice cannot fulfil, much less resolve.

Since these issues surpass biographical details, engaging the many intellectual and philosophical currents that swirl round them, Carroll's interest in the asymmetry between Wonderland and the adult world seems to teach Alice that the symbolic order does not—indeed, cannot—add up.[3] Documented especially by the train guard, the gnat, the carpenter and a bewildered White Knight, the ensuing disjuncture in the novella drives Carroll's already counterintuitive perspective, making an already off-kilter world seem ruled by a truly senseless rationale.

In his tribute to Carroll, Lacan claimed that psychoanalysis alone grasps the strangeness and paradoxical quality of such fiction. Early Freudians thought so too—albeit with a different sense of the reason for and effect of that strangeness. So much so, in fact, that Paul Schilder came close to denouncing Carroll's text for the very emphasis that Lacan later saw as grounds for praise: its willingness to suspend disbelief so radically that it amounts almost to a 'refusal of reality' (Lacan 2002a: 10).

Writing in the years immediately before Freud's death, when ego psychologists began modifying his theory of the unconscious into an adaptive programme for the ego, Schilder largely pathologized Carroll for the dearth of consolation his fiction offers children, asking:

> How did Carroll come to this queer world? It is a world without real love. The queens and kings are either absurd or cruel or both. We would suspect that Carroll never got the full love of his parents [. . .]. Are some of the animals also representatives of the parents? [. . .] Do

---

3 For three quite different perspectives on this, see Holquist (1969), Lecercle (1994) and Holbrook (2001).

the insects represent the many brothers and sisters who must have provoked jealousy in Carroll [. . .]?

Then Schilder's analysis truly goes off the rails:

What was his relation to his sex organ anyhow? [. . .] There may have been in Carroll the wish for feminine passivity and a protest against it [. . .]. As in all forms of primitive sexuality, the promiscuity in Carroll's relation to children is interesting (1938: 165, 166).

After lamenting Dodgson's fairly 'immature' understanding of family dynamics, Schilder delivers a similar verdict on his fiction, which would equally apply to any literary work that is broadly surreal, uncanny or simply fantastical: 'I suspect that nonsense literature will originate whenever there are incomplete object relations and a regression to deep layers involving the relation of space and time on the basis of primitive aggressiveness' (ibid.: 167). Somewhat ridiculously, Schilder deems even vaguely experimental fiction morbidly pathological; only classic realism holds sway in his mind for its apparent commitment to psychical maturity.

But while psychoanalytic literary criticism in the 1930s tended to seek the answers to literary enigmas in the psyches of the relevant author, it wasn't monolithic in its reasons for doing so. In 1935, William Empson conceded—without dismissing—the strangeness of Carroll's fiction. But since the latter still troubled him he invoked psychoanalysis in hopes of demystifying it. For Empson, Carroll gives us 'the child as swain' who passes through a bewildering landscape peopled by fantastic creatures, in order to arrive wiser and more mature at the other end (Empson 1950). Accordingly, Alice should be relieved that the quixotic fantasies of execution that Queen of Hearts has remain oneiric; she awakens to a world that is apparently more rational and coherent.

But Empson's stress on the symbolic logic of the world misses part of what makes Carroll so uncanny as a writer and thinker: the nightmarish quality of the *Alice* stories whose almost Kafkaesque undertones hint that such irrational aggression will not end, but will continue to haunt Alice through waking life. Donald Rackin famously described Alice as 'the reader's surrogate on a frightful journey into meaningless night', where 'practically all pattern, save the consistency of chaos, is annihilated,' leaving the works to affirm only 'the sane madness of ordinary existence' (1966: 314, 313 and 325). Empson's apparently Freudian hermeneutics also end up alarmingly close to the model that Carroll parodies through Humpty Dumpty. Alice is, he claims, 'a father in getting down the hole, a foetus at the bottom, and can only be born by becoming a mother and producing her own amniotic fluid' (1950: 272–3). Moreover, 'The famous cat is a very direct symbol of this ideal of intellectual detachment; [. . .] it appears only as a head because it is a disembodied intelligence, and only as a grin because it can impose an atmosphere without being present,' and so on (ibid.: 273).

Although Empson's and his deductions are in different ways off-the-mark, Schilder does usefully mention, in an implicit rebuttal to Empson's psychoanalytic pastoral: 'One is astonished to find in [Carroll's] pleasant fairy stories the expression of enormous anxiety.' Alice, he comments, is frequently depicted as 'standing bewildered', 'She does not know what to do,' 'She does not even know her name,' 'She cannot find the word "tree".' When she wants to repeat a poem, 'another poem comes out, to her distress'. 'She moves and comes back to the same place' (1938: 161). Schilder was surely correct, moreover, in noting that 'most of her anxieties are connected with a change of her body'—its size, appetites and the threats it receives from relentless, unreasoning adults. The anxiety here would seem to be largely about Alice's ability to adapt to a world to which she feels peculiarly ill suited. Wonderland, in a comic rendition of the aggression circulating in the Victorian world beyond, does not exactly go out of its way to make room for her. (Nor, perhaps, should it.) The interest is in the friction, conflict and anxiety that ensue.

Phyllis Greenacre was astute in describing the cruelty and violence of Wonderland, yet finally as limited as Schilder in her attempts at interpreting it. She declared:

> The great charm of the tale lies in the panorama of grotesque caricature expressed in the general mixture and fusion of identities of the animals, insects and strange human beings whom Alice meets. Through all this is a cacophony of cruelty so extreme as to be ridiculous: animals eat each other up, a baby turns into a pig and is abandoned to wander away into the forest, decapitation is a general threat,

and a Cheshire Cat does appear smiling though separated from its own body (1955: 182).

But she reduced the intelligence of Carroll's parody to an unresolved Oedipal drama, which manifests itself not as anxiety, adaptive distress or voyeuristic pleasure, but rather as superegoic guilt and self-recrimination:

> The controlling and encasing functions of his superego were paramount and in themselves unbelievably aggressive—toward him. They seem to have been derived from the extreme intensity of his pregenital aggressions; from the way in which these engulfed and carried with them the normal phallic urges; and from the enforced precocity of the conscience development which prohibited so widely and so devastatingly. His nonsense, detached and meaningless as it consciously appeared to him and as he intended it to be for others, nonetheless contained his innermost secrets, the primal-scene excitations, the oral-anal-phallic urges bringing their complementary fear of punishing destruction (ibid.: 275).

One reason these quasi-Freudian typologies do not correspond to the fiction itself, Lacan later made clear, is that Carroll's novellas complicate, even to the point of conceptual collapse, the notion of a lucid, unidirectional ontogenesis. What is truly psychoanalytic—even Lacanian—about them is that the young girl's bizarre, unpredictable experiences work themselves out without tragedy, teleology or recourse to a preordained fate. Chance and necessity are thus interesting variables in the fiction, sometimes colliding with moments of extraordinary, capricious cruelty—'Off with their heads' being also the most memorable (Carroll 1998a: 72). At other times, Alice tries to fathom whether the symbolic order is hiding an enigma or, indeed, hiding that it doesn't have one. In this respect, the drama over adaptation is not worked out in advance; it is staged throughout as a problem that Alice and the reader cannot easily overcome. Individual pathology is thus, to a degree, beside the point. The issue is more a structural problem about the limits of sense and reason in a world that often abides by neither.

For this reason, the relationship between malaise and joy in Carroll's fiction reveals far more than surreal, sometimes-absurd ontological dilemmas (though those still abound, often hilariously). In using literature to pinpoint what is most paradoxical about the symbolic order—that it arises out of and then comes to rely upon nothingness—Lacan helps us see the hermeneutic and ethical stakes of psychoanalytic literary criticism in focusing on a writer drawn to representing what is most senseless, contentless and finally insoluble about that nothingness.

'It isn't trifling,' Lacan observes, 'that Alice appeared at the same time as [Charles Darwin's] *The Origin of Species* [1859], to which she is, one could say, the opposition' (2002a: 12, my translation). Six years in fact fell between their publication, though the idea for Alice came to Carroll three years after Darwin's treatise caused a minor earthquake in Victorian thought and culture. But Lacan's overall point holds: while Darwin expounds on lineage and genealogy to address the evolution and atavism of species, Carroll pushed the analogy in the opposite direction, inverting endings and beginnings to readjust psychic time, while coming close to unravelling the sequences by which we try to fathom ontogenesis belatedly, after the fact. As one unnamed lady 'exclaims enthusiastically' in *Sylvie and Bruno*, 'A development worthy of Darwin! [. . .] Only you reverse his theory. Instead of developing a mouse into an elephant, you would develop an elephant into a mouse!' (Carroll 1991: 31).

Tenniel's illustrations nicely capture this ontological density and elasticity, emphasizing not only the *difficulty* but also the *price* of Alice's attempt to conform and adapt to circumstances. She is first too small, then too big for the world she wants to inhabit (see Figs 12 and 13). She is unprepared for it, yet joins it long after it has established rules and laws with which she struggles to comply.

What Carroll anticipates so deftly here is a radical idea that Freud would later popularize: we miss the 'right moment' of biology, given our capacity for reflection and consciousness. We arrive *too soon* into a symbolic order that we piece together and understand, if at all, only quizzically and belatedly. Carroll also doubtless plays a Darwinian joke in having the then-extinct Dodo not only vibrantly alive in Wonderland, but also likened, with amusing ludicrousness, to William Shakespeare.

In these ways, Carroll's non-Darwinian ontology makes unexpected patterns of meaning and resemblance collide in Wonderland. Its many creatures

FIGURE 12: Alice, from *Alice in Wonderland*.
Illustration by Sir John Tenniel.

miraculously share the same language yet rarely communicate straightforwardly. As Alice remarks about the 'Jabberwocky' (not the monster, but the
famous parody of Tennysonian sentimentalism that comically misrepresents
it), 'It seems very pretty [. . .] but it's rather hard to understand!' 'Somehow it
fills my head with ideas,' she adds, 'only I don't exactly know what they are!'
(Carroll 1998b: 134).

The provocation of enigmatic signifiers and the task of deciphering them
extend to Wonderland's legal apparatus, moreover, with its presumption of
guilt long preceding any state of innocence. The inversion of guilt and innocence thereby acquires a strong psychical inflection, with accusations of wrongdoing predating even the *fantasy* to act. 'Sentence first—verdict afterwards'
—shouts Queen of Hearts, demanding punishment whether or not a 'crime'
even of mild impropriety has occurred (Carroll 1998a: 107).

In all senses, then, nothing quite adds up in Wonderland. None of
the creatures in Wonderland easily coexists—they are all fractious, peevish,

irrepressible, but for the most part insistently singular. At the same time, nothingness amounts to an ontological dimension that Carroll and Lacan ultimately take very seriously. The hilarity and tragedy of life is held, they show, pincers-like by the real. To confront the limits of the latter—as Alice does repeatedly, with her pointed questions, quirky imagination, preternatural respect for rules and, sometimes, whimsical joy in breaking them—is to expose, in the nineteenth century no less, an extremely rickety structure held together by desire, illusion and force, a volatile brew at the best of times.

One reason for Lacan's admiration for Carroll's fiction is that the novelist tended to celebrate in children an unwillingness, even stubborn refusal, to adapt to the world (a feature that is especially notable in a writer who was, in most respects, a logician and stickler for rules). Similar pockets of refusal pepper Victorian fiction, of course, from the mavericks traversing so many Charles Dickens novels to startling disjunctures in Rudyard Kipling's profoundly complex 1901 novel *Kim*. Yet Carroll's brilliance in making that refusal almost ethical is truly idiosyncratic, and doubtless gave rise to the *joie singulière* [singular joy]—even *jouis-sens*—that Lacan later felt compelled to revisit.

FIGURE 13: Alice, from *Alice in Wonderland*.
Illustration by Sir John Tenniel.

Examples of this type of glee recur throughout the *Alice* stories, from the Gryphon urging everyone to break into song, to the Mock Turtle and Lobster Quadrille who caper about with unselfconscious pleasure. But when the games fall away in Carroll's fiction, as they do on several striking occasions, a brooding melancholy replaces them, creating a jarring effect. Without the crazy banter, Alice (as Paul Schilder recognized) is also left at the mercy of inexplicable forces. One then sees a greater rationale for the melancholia, for the fiction tends to lament the consequence of that adaptation, even to the point of asking whether such a heavy sacrifice ultimately is worth it.

Perhaps the clearest source of bewildered sadness in *Looking-Glass* is the hapless, semi-ridiculous White Knight, a fictional counterpart of Carroll himself. He arrives in a bid to 'rescue' Alice from a competing Red Knight, then falls off his horse so many times that she ends up rescuing *him*. White Knight is plodding, kind and something of a philosopher. 'What does it matter where my body happens to be?' he ponders (Carroll 1998b: 213). 'My mind goes on working all the same. In fact, the more head-downwards I am, the more I keep inventing new things' (ibid.). He sings to Alice a song alternately called 'The Aged Aged Man' and 'Ways and Means' and she, the narrator insists, rather emphatically, is so moved that she takes in '[the scene] like a picture' and sits 'listening, in a half-dream, to the melancholy music of the song' (ibid.: 214).

The interlude with White Knight comes just before Alice crowns herself queen, as he himself notes forlornly, and his song is full of questions and injunctions such as 'How is it you live?' and 'Come, tell me how you live!'—lines said to be 'cried' several times (ibid.: 215, 216). The knight and new queen part shortly thereafter. Yet in his bumbling courtly love and earnest solicitude, the knight tries to warn her about something he cannot openly say, which he sings instead: 'I'll tell thee everything I can: / There's little to relate' (ibid.: 214). This, he seems to be underscoring, teasingly, is all that he can relay as content. But the meaning of his caution is more structural than substantive. In seeking to depersonalize the information, Carroll gives it greater ontological cogency.

A similar idea runs through the surreal, quasi-cannibalism of 'The Walrus and the Carpenter' interlude, whose explicit warning to children appears to be 'Avoid talking to strangers,' but whose broader meaning extends all the way to religious discipleship. The little oysters—their 'coats [. . .] brushed, their faces washed, / Their shoes [. . .] clean and neat'—eagerly follow the walrus and the carpenter, eventually waiting in a row for further instructions from them, as if they were lined up in a church pew (ibid.: 160, 161). It is then that the adult figures 'feed' on the youngsters, gorging on them so relentlessly that they eat every one (see Fig. 14). Coming from an Anglican clergyman, the image is jarring in a poem otherwise focused on children's necessarily meek submission to orders.

Any relation between White Knight's warning and the allegory of the walrus and the carpenter is of course conjectural. But their shared thread arguably is that adaptation to the world of adults is risky and not without cost. As Lacan would put it, one receives some meaning for the 'being' one is forced to give up, but it is not a fair exchange and much is lost in translation. Those witnessing the loss cannot symbolize it completely, because recognition of what is gone comes too late. As Carroll decried, 'Even *men* very often fail to "desire" what is, after all, the best thing for them to *have*' (quoted in Gattégno 1976: 169). The qualifier 'even *men*' makes this already profound aphorism striking, implying that men are not exceptional in this respect; the disjuncture they experience is instead exemplary of humanity at large.

FIGURE 14: The walrus, the carpenter and the oysters, from *Through the Looking-Glass*. Illustration by Sir John Tenniel.

Masked as an allegory about children and being 'wrong' for the world, the *Alice* stories subtly reveal the deceits and falsehoods of the symbolic order. In refusing to imitate the comic pretensions of a system bound by the contingency of signifiers, Carroll gives us that world aslant and askew. His oblique perspective underscores the drives and psychical effects that exceed symbolization—drives that in his fiction come to assume an ardent, impossible meaning.

References

ENGLISH SOURCES

CARROLL, Lewis. 1991. *The Complete Sylvie and Bruno* (Thomas Christensen ed.). San Francisco: Mercury House.

————. 1998a. *Alice's Adventures in Wonderland* in Hugh Haughton (ed.), *Alice's Adventures in Wonderland and Through the Looking-Glass and What Alice Found There* (The Centenary Edition). London: Penguin Classics, pp. 9–110.

————. 1998b. *Through the Looking-Glass and What Alice Found There* in Hugh Haughton (ed.), *Alice's Adventures in Wonderland and Through the Looking-Glass and What Alice Found There* (The Centenary Edition). London: Penguin Classics, pp. 111–241.

EMPSON, William. 1950. 'Alice in Wonderland: The Child as Swain' in William Empson, *Some Versions of Pastoral: A Study of the Pastoral Form in Literature*. Reprint, London: Chatto and Windus, pp. 253–94.

FREUD, Sigmund. 1962. 'Screen Memories' in *The Standard Edition of the Complete Psychological Works of Sigmund Freud*, VOL. 3 (James Strachey ed., and trans.). London: Hogarth Press and the Institute of Psycho-analysis, pp. 301–22.

GATTÉGNO, Jean. 1976. *Lewis Carroll: Fragments of a Looking-Glass from Aristotle to Zeno* (Rosemary Sheed trans.). New York: Crowell.

GREENACRE, Phyllis. 1955. *Swift and Carroll: A Psychoanalytic Study of Two Lives*. New York: International Universities Press.

HAUGHTON, Hugh. 1998. 'Introduction' in Hugh Haughton (ed.), *Alice's Adventures in Wonderland and Through the Looking-Glass and What Alice Found There* (The Centenary Edition). London: Penguin Classics, pp. ix–lxv.

HOLBROOK, David. 2001. *Nonsense against Sorrow: A Phenomenological Study of Lewis Carroll's 'Alice' Books*. London: Open Gate Press.

HOLQUIST, Michael. 1969. 'What Is a Boojum? Modernism and Nonsense'. *Yale French Studies* 43 (The Child's Part): 145–64.

LACAN, Jacques. 2002a. Homage to Lewis Carroll. Unpublished translation by Russell Grigg of 'Hommage rendu à Lewis Carroll'.

LAPLANCHE, Jean. 1999. 'Interpretation between Determinism and Hermeneutics: A Restatement of the Problem' in John Fletcher (ed.), *Essays on Otherness*. New York and London: Routledge, pp. 138–65.

LECERCLE, Jean-Jacques. 1994. *Philosophy of Nonsense: The Intuitions of Victorian Nonsense Literature*. New York and London: Routledge.

LENNON, Florence Becker. 1972. *The Life of Lewis Carroll: Victoria Through the Looking Glass* (3rd edn). New York: Collier Books.

RACKIN, Donald. 1966. 'Alice's Journey to the End of Night'. *PMLA* 81(5) (October): 313–26.

RICOEUR, Paul. 1970. *Freud and Philosophy: An Essay on Interpretation* (Denis Savage trans.). New Haven, CT: Yale University Press.

SCHILDER, Paul. 1938. 'Psychoanalytic Remarks on Alice in Wonderland and Lewis Carroll'. *Journal of Mental and Nervous Disease* 87(2) (February): 159–68.

FRENCH SOURCES

LACAN, Jacques. 2002b. 'Hommage rendu à Lewis Carroll'. *Ornicar? Revue du champ freudien* 50: 9–12.

MARRET-MALEVAL, Sophie. 2002. 'Lacan sur Lewis Carroll, ou "Tandis qu'il lourmait de suffèches pensées"'. *Ornicar? Revue du champ freudien* 50: 335–59.

Joyce: Lacan's Sphinx[1]

GEOFF BOUCHER

What is important to me is not to pastiche *Finnegans Wake*—one will always be inferior to the task—but to say how I give to Joyce, in formulating this title, *Joyce-the-Symptom*, nothing less than his proper name, a name in which, I believe, he would have recognized himself in the dimension of nomination (Lacan 1987a: 22, my translation).

'We have learned to see Joyce as Lacan's own symptom,' writes Jean-Michel Rabaté, 'and as the Sinthome par excellence' (2006: 26). This duality of Joyce as an unreadable text permeated with enjoyment and, at the same time, as an enigma that Lacan wants to decipher supplies the key to an understanding of *Le Séminaire. Livre XXIII. Le Sinthome, 1975–76* (2005). Lacan's addition of a fourth term, the *sinthome* (Σ), to the triad of the real, the symbolic and the imaginary strengthens his late shift from the 'speakingbeing' (*parlettre*, a Lacanian neologism that indicates the insertion of the human being into the signifying chain) to MAN (*LOM*, a Lacanian play on *l'homme*). Instead of the human being as *inserted* into the symbolic order, this seminar presents Joyce as *inserting* himself into language, tying the signifier to the body in a special, unique way. For Lacan, the *sinthome* is eccentric to the registers of the real, symbolic and imaginary, yet, paradoxically, it links them when the Name-of-the-Father fails. The implication is carried in the concept of nomination, which means the construction of a replacement for the paternal function, that the Name-of-the-Father (or its structural equivalents, such as Woman, God, and Joyce) makes language possible for the individual.

---

1 A version of this essay has appeared in 2011 as '"The Compositor of the Farce of Dustiny": Lacan Reading, and Being Read By, Joyce'. *Analysis* 16 (October): 99–118.—Ed.

Lacan's final complete seminar on Joyce represents a last, convulsive revision of the entire corpus of Lacanian psychoanalysis. Prompted by an invitation to speak at an international Joyce conference by leading French Joyce scholar, Jacques Aubert, Lacan turned the seminar of 1975–76 into an exploration of the questions raised by the paper delivered the previous year. Rabaté's comment sums up the findings of a torrent of recent scholarship on what is perhaps Lacan's most perplexing seminar.[2] Thanks to this material, we can now draw some conclusions about the status and implications of Joyce-the-Symptom, both regarding psychoanalytic theory and his reading of Joyce. But there are two main unresolved problems in the current debate on this seminar—whether Lacan regarded Joyce as a psychotic (stabilized or otherwise)[3] and the degree to which Lacan's final seminar represents a belated *rapprochement* (reconciliation) with Jacques Derrida on the question of 'generalized writing'.[4] This essay provides a brief overview of the major discussions of Lacan's intervention and then probes some of the findings, especially regarding the Joycean text.

I will position Lacan's enquiry in the context of his research into the unconscious, centred on the *objet petit a* as the epistemological object of psychoanalysis and then bring out the opposed character of the psychoanalytic and deconstructive readings of Joyce. While highlighting the insights that Lacan's reading of Joyce enables, I will question Lacan's basic strategy, namely, to interpret not the unconscious in the text but the activity of writing as a symptom. This commits Lacan to a biographical approach about which he is sceptical elsewhere, with the consequence that he is forced to regard the Joycean text itself as situated in the dimension of unreadability.[5] A perhaps overlooked

---

2 See Rabaté (2001: 154–82), Harari (2002), Thurston (2002), Dravers (2005), Ronen (2005), Miller (1987) and Ragland-Sullivan (1990).

3 This problem is an explicit tension in Harari's otherwise excellent introduction to Lacan's 'The Sinthome' (Harari 2002). It is equivocally treated by Luke Thurston's (2004) brilliant expositions of both Lacan and Joyce.

4 This position is best stated in Rabaté 2001: 154–82.

5 See Lacan (1987b: 31–6). Lacan speaks of Joyce's *Scribbledehobble* in terms of 'inconceivably private jokes' (1976–77a: Session 5, p. 35) that he elsewhere describes as located in the real which 'forecloses meaning' (ibid.: Session 8, p. 46).

result of this is that not only does Joyce become Lacan's symptom, but also that the Lacanian seminar becomes dominated by a literary trope—that of inversion and reversal in the mirror of the doppelgänger. Lacan locates Joyce as both a saint of letters and a literary Sphinx, declaring him unanalyzable on the basis that he enjoys without suffering, because Joyce believes in his Thing, the *sinthome* of his work. Lacan thinks that the Joycean riddle can be solved with a fourth loop in the notorious Borromean knot. But, of course, with truly Sophoclean irony, it is Lacan who is the riddle. As Lacan's theoretical prose becomes increasingly Joycean, the Joycean relation to the literary father is transposed onto Lacan's relation to Freudian psychoanalysis.

THE JOYCEAN *SINTHOME*

Certainly, the seminar on Joyce is remarkable for its intellectual energy. Although the seminar is interrupted by Lacan's trip to America, it is clear that he reread the central works by Joyce during the year—*A Portrait of the Artist as a Young Man* (1916), *Ulysses* (1922) and *Finnegans Wake* (1939)—in their entirety. Lacan had also clearly read *Exiles* (1918), *Dubliners* (1914) and *Stephen Hero* (1944). He also made his way through the scholarly volumes populating Aubert's extensive library, where caches of books were delivered weekly. He made regular midnight visits to Aubert to question him on recondite points of Joyce interpretation. At one point, Lacan declares to his audience: '[Y]ou must be thinking that when it comes to Joyce, I'm a fish out of water.' And he explains: '[H]e writes with such peculiar subtlety in English that he disarticulates it' (1976–77a: Session 5, p. 23). That Lacan was defeated by Joyce's language seems unlikely—this is the same Lacan who, a few weeks before this mock admission, declares to his American audience that he has been practising his English by reading Joyce in the original (see Rabaté 2000). Lacan dives into the wonderland of Joyce's works, principally concerned with its implications for psychoanalytic research and clinical practice. If he is finally defeated by what we might call Joycean *lalangue*, it is not a consequence of English but of the peculiar structure of these riddling texts.

In the process, Lacan produces an enigmatic series of new concepts within a completely fresh 'turn' in his thinking. If Lacan's trajectory is characterized by the progression through the imaginary (from 'The Discourse of Rome'[6] to

The Seminar of Jacques Lacan. Book II. The Ego in Freud's Theory and in the Technique of Psychoanalysis, 1954–55 [1978; here 1988], the symbolic (the 'structuralist' Lacan of *The Seminar of Jacques Lacan. Book III. The Psychoses, 1955–56* [1981; here 1993] to *The Seminar of Jacques Lacan. Book XI. The Four Fundamental Concepts of Psychoanalysis, 1964* [1973; here 1998a]) and the real (the 'post-structuralist' Lacan of 'Le Séminaire. Livre XII. Problèmes cruciaux pour la psychanalyse, 1964–65' [Critical issues for Psychoanalysis; unpublished], to *The Seminar of Jacques Lacan. Book XX. Encore: On Feminine Sexuality, The Limits of Love and Knowledge, 1972–73* [1975; here 1998b]), then *Le Sinthome* cements a fourth and final Lacan—the Lacan of 'nomination' and the *sinthome*, the fourth loop in the Borromean knot; of the *sinthome* and *MAN* (Žižek 1989: 132–3); of the Joycean ego as alternative to psychosis; and, of the radically individual character of the unconscious and the replacement of Lacanian *linguistrickery* by a new *faunetics*. Now, the loops of the real, symbolic and imaginary cannot be knotted together without the intervention of the *sinthome*, which, more than simply an archaic spelling of symptom, is the centre of gravity of the human being, the kernel of enjoyment sustaining the individual.[7] For Lacan, the *sinthome* is 'the most proper element of the human dimension' (Rabaté 2001: 165) and the referent or result of nomination. The *sinthome* connects the real, symbolic and imaginary through the nomination (in the sense of election) of a functional equivalent for the Name-of-the-Father. Nomination involves both the election by the human being of their singular insertion into language and the process whereby the subject 'makes a name for himself', up to and including Joyce's evasion of psychosis, despite the absence of the paternal function, through his nomination of his own ego as the functional equivalent of the Name-of-the-Father. Joyce-the-Symptom in the first place signifies that the

---

6 It is the popular name for the essay 'The Function and Field of Speech and Language in Psychoanalysis' (1956). See Lacan (2006). See also Lacan 2001a.—Ed.

7 Already in 'Le Séminaire. Livre XXI. Les non-dupes errent /Les noms-du-pére, 1973–74' (The Non-dupes Err/ The Names-of-the-Father; unpublished), Lacan had proposed that the Name-of-the-Father was the fourth loop in the knot. *Le Sinthome* complements this conjecture and fleshes it out as a theoretical innovation.

proper name nominated by James and made through the literary works of Joyce is coextensive with the *sinthome* of a radically private use of language: Joyce (the literary name) *is* the symptom of Joyce (the man); the works of Joyce are the replacement for a radically deficient paternal signifier that keeps Joyce the man sane. Who can doubt Lacan's intellectual courage? Can there be any real uncertainty about this being a fundamental revision of the conceptual armature of the previous decade? Surely, this is a last, catastrophic rupture with everything that had been established in so-called 'Lacanianism'—almost, one might say, a handful of suggestive brushstrokes on a fresh canvas.

Along the way there are also the opaque topological ruminations, Duchampian wordplays and intellectual meanderings that characterize the final period. Lacan regrets that he has nothing to say and wonders whether Joyce was mad. He wonders with strategic naivety why Joyce bothered to publish *Scribbledehobble* (1961). Gone are the dazzling insights into the texts of William Shakespeare and Paul Claudel, Sophocles and André Gide. Instead of textual commentary that suddenly blazes into the heart of a new understanding of the literary work, we have pages and pages of multicoloured diagrams, word salads, neo-Dadaesque provocations to the audience, numerological speculations and diagrammatic conjectures. It is not simply that Lacan cannot absorb the entire library of Joyce scholarship in a hectic year of teaching. In place of a new reading, the biographical interpretation of the Joycean work becomes more insistent as Lacan's perplexity at the texts increases. At the same time, Lacan's own text becomes ever more openly Joycean: acrostic rather than aphoristic, inscrutable rather than enigmatic, hermetic rather than hermeneutic. Joyce-the-Symptom—whose symptom is this Joyce that seems forced on Lacan? If Lacan baptizes Joyce with his proper name—as he claims to do— then who prepares the way for whom? Joyce might indeed have had, as Lacan suspects, a redeemer delusion. But the redeemer's mission is primed by comparatives—'one will always be inferior to the task'—if not superlatives. This is Lacan's position of enunciation throughout the seminar: 'I have need to be baptized of thee, and comest thou to me?' (Matthew 3:14).

It is not that Lacan lacked intellectual power in his final seminar, but that his theoretical position lacked penetration—at least, into Joyce's texts. I do not accept the condescending theory of the advancing senility of the final years

(Roudinesco 1997). The reduction of language to its letters, the condensation of complex discursive motifs into a series of deceptively simple sigla—these I would describe as perfectly Joycean, rather than intellectually enfeebled.[8] I completely discount the theories of 'Lacanian delusion' and the master's sterility returning with a vengeance at the end of his life, offered to account for the cryptic nature of 'Joyce-the-Symptom'. These notions of a deficiency in Lacan's intellectual energies are contradicted by the text of the seminar at every point. Rabaté's reading of Joyce as Lacan's symptom has immense potential. It highlights the relative difference in their respective powers of insight—where Lacan's interpretation of Joyce remains within the ambit of biographical criticism and traditional scholarship, the encounter with Joyce provokes one last cataclysmic revision of Lacanian psychoanalysis.

As Rabaté observes, throughout the seminar, Lacan's concern is not to position Joyce's work within the discourse of the university, as the object of a scholarly knowledge that barely conceals its will to mastery even as it puts the intimidated clerks to work (2001: 160).[9] Instead, Lacan operates within analytical discourse, where the analyst positions himself or herself as the 'trash' (the *trashitas* rather than the pious *caritas*), the remainder of enjoyment left over from the signifying operations of the subject.[10] Lacan identifies the *objet petit a*, the *sinthome*, with the saintly man (*saint-homme*) who has renounced mastery, and then with St Thomas Aquinas (*sinthomaquinas*) who is just as crazy as Joyce—and Lacan ('Joyce displaces the *saint homme* from my *madaquinisme*').[11] Employing only such mythical knowledge, the analyst, as the agent within an

---

8 For a fascinating introduction to these in Joyce, see McHugh (1976).

9 See Jacques Derrida's introduction to the Joyce symposium for an example of how an admission of intimidation and incompetence, that is, of the impotence of the clerical as a declaration of membership within the university discourse, functions as a password (1988: 42).

10 The *caritas/trashitas* opposition is elaborated in Lacan (1990). For a full exposition of Lacan's discourse theory, see Lacan (2007). For valuable explanatory essays, see Clemens and Grigg (2006).

11 Lacan (erroneously) claims that by substituting the 'splendour of Being', which Lacan does 'not find very striking', Joyce removes the *sinthome* from the Thomist doctrine of *claritas* (a doctrine of the radiance of the aesthetic object):

analytical discourse, is positioned in dialogue with the divided subject of the unconscious, and by insisting on the place of the symptom—the *objet petit a*— the analyst allows the subject to produce those master signifiers that are, rather than its symptom, the course of its suffering. Yet, the twist is that in *Le Sinthome*, it is Joyce who occupies the place of the *sinthomaquinas*, whose language is the *madaquinisme* of acrostic re-combinations, trans-linguistic homophonies and untranslatable puns.[12] Joyce is Lacan's literary saint, whose letters reduce the English language to litter even as they generate a 'Joyce' who is entirely distributed across the ruins of the signifier. In the *faunetics* of Lacan's version of *Finnegans Wake*, the text is traversed by a major movement whose *tropology* is highly literary: ironic reversal and the chiasmatic exchange of properties.[13] As Lacan becomes ever more Joycean—moving, indeed, towards what some have called a post-Joycean conception of the end of analysis (Harari 2002: 359)— Joyce increasingly occupies the position of Lacan's divine *trashitas*.

A focus on language and the operations of literary irony in the seminar implies acceptance of the position of, for instance, Philippe Julien, that the Borromean knots are a distraction, a lure for the desire to directly comprehend the transmitted message in the form of a spatialized schema. Indeed, I consider the entire departure into the Borromean topology—Lacan admits to being 'the prey of the knot'—to exhibit an imaginary captivation. Along these lines, Julien proposes that these diagrams, initially introduced as mnemonic devices to support a uniform pedagogy, usurp their cognitively subordinate status and posture as non-symbolizable mathematical objects (see Julien 1994). Yet, they are used by Lacan everywhere as visual representations for linguistically conveyed concepts. Accordingly, their topological value is nil, because they

---

One should state things clearly: as far as philosophy goes, it has never been bettered. That is not even the whole truth [. . .]. In *sinthomadaquin* there is something termed *claritas*, for which Joyce substitutes something like the splendour of Being—this is the weak point in issue. Is this a personal weakness? I do not find the splendour of Being very striking (Lacan 1976–77a: Session 1, p. 3).

12 For a study on Joyce and Aquinas see Noon (1957).

13 And should we also mention, as a literary trope in the seminar, the gigantic *vanitas* grinning out of the hole in *LOM*, Lacan's final play on *l'homme* (*MAN*)?

are not generated by formal mathematical reasoning but through the symbolic postulation of analogies, although as images of theoretical positions their utility is unquestionable. Lacan's fundamental insight is that the unconscious is structured like a language, not like a mathematical surface. That Lacan decided to express this deep theoretical insight through quasi-mathematical diagrams is potentially unfortunate. Instead of his mathematical reflections, we can interpret the ruination of the signifier and the endlessly suggestive enjoymeant of the recombination of letters into portmanteau words and polyvocal, multilingual jokes, that characterize *Finnegans Wake* as a final model for the operations of the unconscious.

LACAN'S ENCOUNTER WITH JOYCE

In his lecture to Aubert's symposium, Lacan stresses that the encounter between him and Joyce happened in reality—in 1921, they met in a Paris bookstore—as well as in a certain relation to language, one that ruptures the everyday pragmatics of what Lacan calls the chatterbox, and which instead facilitates the emergence of equivocation and polyvocality. We can specify that this encounter with Joyce involves both subjective identification and theoretical revision.

In *Le Sinthome*—although not for the first time—Lacan stages a profound identification with Joyce. According to Néstor Braunstein, Joyce is Lacan's literary alter ego.[14] Yet, perhaps, this formulation is not quite accurate. Lacan maintains that Joyce is indifferent to his reception yet highly narcissistic. Despite his lack of human sympathy for Joyce, in the Joyce seminar, Lacan highlights a cluster of shared symbolic traits—their rejection of Catholicism, their style in language, their reduction of labyrinthine signifying complexity to a series of elementary diagrams. In other words, Joyce functions here for Lacan not as the imaginary other but as the bearer of a symbolic identification. Joyce, Lacan declares, 'is like me: a heretic' (1976–77a: Session 1, p. 3). But the Lacanian heresy (*heresie*—Lacan's pun on R. S. I., the real, symbolic and imaginary) is to be supplemented by the Joycean apostasy.

---

14 See Rabaté (2001: 174) and Braunstein (2003: 102–15).

Lacan's identification with Joyce determines the transposition of this relation into the text, with frequent elision of the distinction between Joyce and
his characters. 'Stephen,' Lacan announces, 'is in other words, Joyce as he
imagines himself'; and again: 'Stephen is Joyce as he solves his own riddle'
through the search for an absent/lacking father in the progress of *Ulysses*. '*Ulysses*
bears witness to the way in which Joyce remains rooted in his father, even as he
denies him—and this is exactly his symptom' (ibid.: Session 4, pp. 20–1). Yet,
strangely, at the same time, Lacan announces his intention to interpret the
symptom of the work rather than the unconscious within the text. His question
is not about the meaning of these texts but the function of his art for Joyce. If
the fertility of a Lacanian approach has been abundantly demonstrated by Rabaté, Lacan's own strategy is based on a frankly biographical approach.[15]

Guided by an attentive reading of Richard Ellmann (1983) and Aubert's
patient scholarship and close analysis of Joyce's letters, Lacan's thesis, based
on the crucial datum of failure of the paternal function on the part of John
Joyce, is that Joyce's writing supplements the deficient Name-of-the-Father.
Lacan appears to have interpreted both *Portrait* and *Ulysses* as autobiographical. Joyce, as the thesis goes, 'makes a [N]ame (of the Father) for himself'
through his endless writing, thus fathering himself. The Lacanian discourse
on Joycean 'original sin' interprets this motif in terms of the failure of the R.
S. I. to knot together round the Name-of-the-Father, so that writing acts as a
prosthetic paternity, a rejoining of the sundered links. Joyce's literary career
is interpreted externally as the symptom of a compensation for the paternal
deficiency, based in a wish for a real father.

In the field of Joyce studies, at least, Lacan's theoretical compass is determined by his respect for traditional literary scholarship, especially that of
Robert M. Adams and Clive Hart. Lacan also makes use of Aubert's edition of
Ulysses. Adams proposes in *Surface and Symbol* (1962) that most of the texture
that provides narrative verisimilitude in the novel is superficial detail (some
of it factually wrong) rather than 'luminous symbol' (1962: xvii). Accordingly,

---

15 See Rabaté (1991a and 1991b), and aside from the already mentioned work by Luke
Thurston, Leonard (1993).

the 'meaningless is deeply interwoven with the meaningful' (ibid.: 245) and the novel 'does not make a neat allegorical pattern' (ibid.: 256). Lacan's interpretation of this is that Adams has identified the distinction between the imaginary consistency of the diegetic world formulated in the symbolic medium of the narration, and the Joycean epiphanies that appear at right angles to the symbolic texture as interruptions where meaning and meaninglessness interpenetrate. But like Adams, Lacan does not fully take up the implications of Stephen's (highly Lacanian) equation of William Shakespeare with the ghost in *Hamlet*. One result is that the Oedipal dynamics of the struggle over literary progenitors for Joyce (the name, not the man) are missed by Lacan and consequently, *Ulysses* begins to seem like a text transitional towards psychosis. Hart uses the motif of the crossed circle in *Structure and Motif in Finnegans Wake* (1962) to describe the cosmological structure of *Finnegans Wake*. The quartered circle symbolizes the Viconian division of history into four ages (including the *ricorso* as an age as Joyce does), while the cyclical structure adumbrates the narrative circle of *Finnegans Wake* itself. All of this thematizes the circularity of a text that returns on itself in the first and last lines, yet constantly generates new interpretations with every traversal of the textual surface. Finally, the motif of the crossed circle indicates the problem of squaring the circle, that is, a mathematical problem involving infinite recursion, which adequately summarizes the generative matrix of this most important Joycean work. But for Lacan, the elaborate manipulation of rings of string and quasi-geometrical figures is not intended to summon up the 'bad infinity' of deconstructive dissemination. Instead, the act of abstraction from the textual surface to its generative problematic discloses the mechanism by which the whole work forms a 'consistency without unity'—that is, a style of the subject.

Lacan is wary of what we might call 'psychoanalysis and other ruses'—depth hermeneutics, father–son patterns and the collective unconscious. He excoriates Mark Shechner's *Joyce in Nighttown* (1974), on the basis that it trivializes the actual text, reducing it to a schema external to the significations of the nighttown sequence. Shechner is taken as illustrative of 'applied psychoanalysis' which involves not an encounter with the text with the potential to transform theory, but the application of an interpretive grid to the text so as to validate a hermeneutic result determined outside the work itself. Lacan is also highly suspicious of the psychoanalytic motifs nested within the text. He rejects the conception of Bloom as father to Stephen and dismisses Joyce's dalliance with occultism and obscurantism (Blavatsky). His comment on the relation between *Finnegans Wake* and the collective unconscious is profound and damning: the idiosyncrasy of the text is a precise refutation of the speculations of Jungian psychoanalysis, which itself stands unveiled as a symptomatic defense against the unconscious. Finally, and perhaps too definitively, Lacan rejects the mythological structuration of *Ulysses* and *Finnegans Wake* (Homer and Vico).

Lacan's intuition is that Joyce is a literary saint—on the one hand, meaningless trash, an objectival remainder of the signification process; on the other hand, a figure who 'is' only as text, that is, who dissolves into the Joycean writing. According to Lacan, 'in his art, Joyce, in a privileged manner, aimed at the fourth term of the knot' (1976–77a: Session 2, p. 10). At one level, what this means is fairly clear: 'Joyce compensated for the lacking father.' Lacan writes: 'what I proposed very gently last time was that Joyce has a symptom whose origin is this: that his father was lacking, radically lacking—he speaks of nothing but this' (ibid.: Session 7, p. 42); and again: 'it turns out in *Ulysses* that Joyce has to support the father's subsistence' (ibid.: Session 1, p. 6).

Yet, before we conclude with Catherine Millot that the opposition between analysts and critics entails a division in the reception of Joyce between the meaninglessness and the meaningfulness of the texts, we need to consider Lacan's interpretation of the enigma of Joyce's work (Millot 1988: 207–9). Again, Lacan does not fully observe his own stricture regarding the distinction between an external approach (the enigma of Joyce's work; art as symptom) and an internal hermeneutic (the enigmas in Joyce's work; the textual unconscious). The acrostics of the Joycean text fascinate Lacan as a new riddle of the Sphinx—that is, Joyce is an anti-Oedipus for Lacanian psychoanalysis. Aubert's reading of the Stephen–Bloom relation as a puzzle whose solution is 'the Name-of-the-Father' is indicative of the fascination, as is Lacan's own interpretation of the moment in *Portrait* where Stephen is beaten by his friends in terms of the bodily ego as a detachable envelope.

Lacan is interested, for instance, in the riddle that Stephen tells his class (Lacan 1976–77a: Session 4, p. 22):

The cock crew
The sky was blue:
The bells in heaven
Were striking eleven.
Tis time for this poor soul
To go to heaven (Joyce 2000: 32; italics in the original).

The 'solution' to the riddle is 'the fox burying his grandmother under a hollybush'. But as Roberto Harari notes, this riddle is preceded by another that has a clearer bearing on psychoanalysis (2002: 134–6):

Riddle me, riddle me, randy row.
My father gave me seeds to sow (Joyce 2000: 31; italics in the original).

The rest of the riddle (not supplied) is: 'the seed was black and the ground was white/ Riddle me that and I'll give you a pipe.' The solution to this riddle is 'writing a letter'. The paternal seed only germinates in the form of letters. According to Lacan, the distinction between Joyce and Oedipus is that because Joyce believes in his *sinthome*, he does not desire to solve the riddle of himself (see Harari 2002: 135). But it is not clear that Lacan can entirely resist the temptation.

Lacan's Confrontation with Deconstruction

Perhaps for this reason, at the moment of the turn in avant-garde theory, during the mid-1970s, to textual formalism and 'revolutions of the word', Lacan is not interested in the liberation of the signifier. Unimpressed by the ruptures with the dominant ideology said to spring from the dissolution of the subject into the textual network, Lacan's objective is exactly the opposite of the literary experimentalism of Philippe Sollers and the critical vanguardism of Roland Barthes.[16] Lacan's question is: *given* the generation of the identity of the speaking subject in the anonymity of the signifying chain, through a contingent series of identifications, *how* can we account for the evident style of

---

16 In English, this tendency is adequately represented in MacCabe (2003).

the subject, its idiosyncratic adoption of language, expressive of a unique subjectivity? Such a question means that Lacan is ineluctably involved in a theoretical confrontation with Derrida. Indeed, the various 'revolutions of the word' supposedly heralded by the Joycean text, although often enlisting Lacan as a theoretical authority, in actuality employ deconstructive rather than psychoanalytic insights.

One dimension of this confrontation dates from *Encore* and the reading of Lacan by deconstructionists Philippe Lacoue-Labarthe and Jean-Luc Nancy (1992). The basic accusation made in that text is that Lacan reinstates the unitary subject of the Cartesian *cogito* by means of the ruse of placing it 'under the bar' of signification, that is, in the unconscious. The elementary Lacanian rejoinder to this frank misreading is that the subject of the unconscious is excentric to itself—its substance is external to its existence as a product of the chain of signification, lying as it does in the *objet petit a*. Hence the Lacanian subject cannot be conceptualized as a Cartesian unity of thinking and being—however disguised, buried or repressed—because it is by definition divided between these alternatives. This is the entire meaning of Lacan's tortuous excursions into the topic of the forced choice and his restatement of the Cartesian *cogito* as a disjunctive syllogism, from *The Four Fundamental Concepts of Psychoanalysis* onwards. According to Lacan, the *cogito* does not run: I am thinking, therefore I am; but—where I am thinking, there I am not, and where I am, there I am not thinking (1998a: 224–5). This rejoinder is not explicitly provided in *Encore*— Lacan has other things on his mind and only says that although Lacoue-Labarthe and Nancy read 'with the worst of intentions', they are effectively addressing a love letter to him by assuming that he has full knowledge of the unconscious (1998b: 65). Yet, it is easy to see how *Le Sinthome* completes a Lacanian rejoinder: Joyce, the subject, as Joyce-the-Symptom, has all of his being, his substance, outside him, in the *sinthome* of the Joycean work.

The apparent *rapprochement* with Derrida in *Le Sinthome*—Lacan declares that some of their insights are in accord, on the basis of Lacan's prior demonstration of the existence of the bar of signification—therefore conceals a deep underlying difference. Derrida reads Joyce as an instance of the dissemination generated by the 'infrastructures', deep textual quasi-structures supporting and subverting the signifier with their limitless and anarchic play

(1988: 27–75).[17] Accordingly, Derrida positions Joyce in the lineage of textual experimentation running through Antonin Artaud, Stéphane Mallarmé and Paul Celan. Indeed, from his opening work on Edmund Husserl onwards, Derrida steadfastly maintains that Joyce's project was the opposite of the Husserlian reduction of multiplicity to univocal self-presence—the Joycean work is taken to represent a dispersion of the self-present intentionality of the ego into the textual network that supports and subverts consciousness (1978: 102). In grouping Derrida's interpretive strategy with his own insights, Lacan is probably rather generous—just as he had previously recommended to his audience that they all read Lacoue-Labarthe and Nancy, despite the hostility of these authors. For in actuality, Lacan is highly sceptical of the deconstructive effort to demonstrate that the dissemination of the textual infrastructures explains the Joycean text, that is, to claim Joyce as the broadcast mechanism for a grammatological demonstration. While the Derridean record tends to grind out the same threnody irrespective of the literary author in question, it is manifestly evident that Joyce is exactly the opposite of what he should be for deconstruction—a signature.[18]

That the Joycean liberation of the signifier brings the unconscious into play is not for a moment questioned by Lacan but his interest lies in the proper name of the author, that is, in the emergence of a distinctive style of the subject *despite* the 'subversion of the subject in the dialectic of desire'. The limitations of the deconstructive position, by contrast with Lacanian psychoanalysis, have been explored in detail by Peter Dews in *Logics of Disintegration* (1987). According to Dews, the problem faced by Derrida is that the endless dissemination of the textual infrastructures prevents the emergence of meaning and therefore blocks the identity of the subject. By contrast, Lacan can explain the emergence of meaning without reverting to the fiction of the self-present intentionality of the speaking subject, because Lacan proposes that the *objet*

---

17 For an exposition of the relation between the deconstruction of signifying binaries and the dissemination of the infrastructures, see Gasché (1986).

18 See for example the eerie resemblance that emerges between Mallarmé and Artaud in Derrida's treatment of them (Derrida 1978).

petit a is a non-specular double for the subject. In the 'lost' object, the divided subject can unconsciously recognize themselves without involving a transparent, Cartesian ego.

Lacan's theorization of the *objet petit a* happens in relation to the concepts of alienation and separation. Conceptually, the entry of the 'speakingbeing' into language requires the transformation of the linearity of instincts into the circularity of the drives, through the cutting out of any determined object of the instincts and its replacement by a signifier that acts as the ideational representative of the drives. But this logically requires two steps (although simultaneous): the creation of a 'hole in the real' and the emplacement of a signifier in that hole. We can relate these two steps to alienation and separation, as well as to Lacan's earlier schema of the metaphor of the Name-of-the-Father, developed in 1959 in 'On a Question Preliminary to any Possible Treatment of Psychosis' (here 2001b), where Lacan proposed that 'the metaphor of the Name-of-the-Father [. . .] is the metaphor that substitutes this Name in the place first symbolised by the operation of the absence of the mother' (2001b: 152). This process can be schematized as follows:

$$\frac{\text{Name-of-the-Father}}{\text{Desire of the Mother}} \cdot \frac{\text{Desire of the Mother}}{\text{Signified to the Subject}} \longrightarrow \frac{\text{Name-of-the-Father}}{} \cdot \frac{\text{O}}{\text{Phallus}}$$

But Lacan continues:

> Let us now try to conceive of a circumstance of the subjective position in which, to the appeal of the Name-of-the-Father responds, not the absence of the real father [. . .] but the inadequacy of the signifier itself. [. . .] The presence of the signifier in the Other is, in effect, a presence usually closed to the subject, because it usually persists in a state of repression [. . .]. [But, for the psychotic,] [t]o the point at

which the Name-of-the-Father is called [. . .] may correspond in the Other, then, a mere hole, which, by the inadequacy of the metaphoric effect, will provoke a corresponding hole at the place of phallic signification (ibid.: 153).

The paternal 'No!' has not repressed the mother as enjoyment, and so the Name-of-the-Father cannot operate as a phallic signification. Instead, it is foreclosed. The consequences of this are familiar to us from *The Psychoses*: the imaginary status of the phallic signifier, the degeneration of language into reified objects and sentence fragments of a *Grundsprache* ('basic language' or 'mother tongue') profoundly permeated with enjoyment, the invasion of the real in the form of hallucinations and a paranoiac relation to the Other.

But in his subsequent considerations of the dialectic of desire, in 'Le Séminaire. Livre VI. Le désir et son interprétation, 1958–59' (Desire and its Interpretation), Lacan appears to develop this notion of a paternal 'No!' in the form of the unary trait, the mark of lack in the Other, symbolized as $S(\emptyset)$. The initial mark that occupies the place of the hole in the real created by the absence of the mother as enjoyment cannot be a signifier, because it is itself the *condition* for entry into language. This implies that the $S(\emptyset)$ is neither articulable nor differential: it is non-fungible and silent, yet it marks the place of the infant's entry into language. We can conjecture that the *objet petit a*, the object of the drive and also the object of desire, is the phantasmatic 'referent' of this impossible, primordial 'ur-signifier', $S(\emptyset)$. Like $S(\emptyset)$, the *objet petit a* is non-symbolizable, yet always returns to the same place and, unlike it, the *objet petit a* has an imaginary component, appearing as it does foremost in the other.

The non-fungible mark that creates a hole in the real and makes it possible for the infant to enter the symbolic order occupies the position of the *objet petit a*—the ideational representative of the drives—only to be displaced by the object signified by the paternal signifier, is also not a part of the real (it makes a hole in the real). Nor is it a part of the imaginary order, although it has an imaginary aspect in so far as it appears through the other. Otherwise expressed, the unique entry point of the human being into the field of the signifier happens—right from the beginning of Lacan's thinking—through the intervention of something that is not imaginary, symbolic or real.

In other words, alongside the cataclysmic revision of Lacanian psycho-analysis, there is a return to the concepts elaborated in *The Psychoses*. Here, Lacan sees Joyce as a proof *a contrario* of the hypothesis that the Name-of-the-Father is the key to the entry into the symbolic order.

LACAN'S INSIGHTS INTO THE JOYCEAN TEXT

For Lacan, the foreclosure of the Name-of-the-Father is the basic key to the Joycean text—with the difference, compared to the figure of Daniel Paul Schreber investigated in *The Psychoses*, that Joyce engages in nomination. The liberation of the signifier in Joyce's work is accomplished through an aberrant relation to the paternal function, so that art is the process by which Joyce 'makes his name'. The 'original sin' in Joyce is therefore interpreted as a sign of paternal failure and, in particular, paternal perversion, which describes the father-son relation in terms of a turn to the father, as a defense against the mother that generates filial masochism. In particular, the deficiency of the real father leads James Joyce to seek replacement paternal figures with sufficient gravity to supplement the lack in the Name-of-the-Father.[19] This leads Lacan to interpret Bloom and Stephen as sons rather than as father–son figures, with the consequence that the literary fathers (Homer, Dante and especially Shake-speare) are the problem posed by the Joycean text.

Yet, paradoxically, Lacan does not fully follow up this insight into *Portrait*, *Ulysses* and *Finnegans Wake*, perhaps because of his determination to interpret art as symptom rather than the unconscious in art. Instead, the accent in his reading falls on the fabrication of a paternal signifier through the artifice of 'making a name'.

Lacan's reading of the transition from *Portrait* to *Ulysses* demonstrates that the Name-of-the-Father and the lack of a sexual relation are correlates, just as the lack of the Name-of-the-Father can be correlated with the existence of a sex-ual relation. Joyce *forges* a Name-of-the-Father for himself and consequently, there *is* a sexual relation between James Joyce and Nora Joyce (née Barnacle).

---

19 The key index of this is HCE's sexual misdemeanour in Phoenix Park (Joyce 1964: 008.08–010.23).

Roberto Harari summarizes this economically in the chapter 'Eve in the Labyrinth of Daedalus' in his *How James Joyce Made His Name* (2002: 37–70), which sets itself the task of interpreting the 'beginnings of Joyce's literary project' in *Stephen Hero* and *Portrait*. In *Portrait*, the accent falls on the 'artificer' whose artisanal production is aestheticized through Joyce's 'Thomist' aesthetics. Stephen Dedalus is linked through naming to artifice in a lineage that connects him to Daedalus (an inventor) and then Hephaestus (*the* artificer). These inventive artificers fatally father their own sons as extensions of their creativity, just as, Stephen Dedalus argues in *Ulysses*, Shakespeare fathered himself to protect himself from his own cuckolding at the hands of his wife. The father is the fiction of the son. The idea that paternity is artificial, together with the possibility that the son might therefore father himself, is prolonged into *Ulysses* as the notion that 'fatherhood [. . .] is unknown to man. It is a mystic state [. . .] founded [. . .] upon the void' (Joyce 2000: 266). Dedalus concludes that '*Amor matris*: subjective and objective genitive, may be the only true thing in life' (ibid.). The notion that the love of the mother enjoys the ambivalence of the genitive (love of and love for) is reminiscent of the desire of the Other, as is Joyce's conclusion that '[p]aternity may be a legal fiction' (ibid.). But in the section on Shakespeare, Stephen elaborates that Shakespeare, in writing the character Hamlet, 'was not the father of his own son merely but, being no more a son, he was and felt himself the father of all his race, the father of his own grandfather, the father of his unborn grandson [. . .]' (ibid.: 267). What is at stake here is the fabrication of an Other of the Other, expressed in terms of a fantasy of auto-genesis. The father begins when and where the son ends. Correlatively, to become a father the son must destroy his own father, and father himself, as the only possible way to be son and father at once.

For Lacan, the Name-of-the-Father is located in the place of lack. But Joyce does not really lack. Evidence for this comes from his relationship to Nora with whom *there exists a sexual relationship*. For Joyce, Lacan stresses, Nora is the Woman: she 'fitted' him like a glove—that is, there is nothing contingent about their encounter (1976–77a: Session 6, p. 38).[20] In the letters pointed to by Harari

---

20 Harari notes that the probable source for this observation is the letter in Joyce (1975: 176 [1 November 1909]).

we find some bizarre sexual practices that highlight this fitting—Joyce wants to savour 'every secret and shameful part of [Nora's body], every odour and act of it' (Joyce 1975: 181)—and when children intrude into the relationship, there is trouble, because there is no space in the glove for three (Harari 2002: 167–9).

So, the existence of a sexual relation means that there is a necessary rather than contingent connection between real and symbolic, drive and desire.[21] Lacan diagnoses the existence of a sexual relation in Nora/Molly and uses this as the key to understanding Joyce's women, including Eve/Issy. The presence of a sexual relation in the absence of a paternal function means that a scission opens between Joycean enjoyment and the enjoyment of Woman.

JOYCE'S CHALLENGE TO LACAN

The problem for the Lacanian reading of *Portrait*, *Ulysses* and *Finnegans Wake* is that according to the considerations outlined so far, Joyce should be psychotic. Yet, as Rabaté stresses, Joyce scholars are reluctant to consider these works as productions of a psychosis (2006: 26–42). Indeed, Lacan himself has serious reservations as to whether the texts are authentic productions of a psychotic state—he considers most of it to engage in a sort of mimicry of schizophrenic discourse.

Before examining the implications of this, I want to simply gather the evidence that this is indeed, and despite strong reservations, the overall direction of Lacan's thinking. Lacan regards Joyce as the author of a progression of documents—*Stephen Hero*, *Portrait*, *Ulysses*, *Finnegans Wake*—that testify to a struggle against psychosis. 'In fact,' Lacan maintains:

[I]n the continuing progress of his art—namely that speech (*parole*) which comes to be written, to be broken, to be dislocated, so that in the end to read him seems an encounter with a continuing progress, from his first efforts in the critical essays, then in *Portrait of the Artist* and again in *Ulysses*, concluding with *Finnegans Wake*—it is hard not

---

21 For instance, Bloomsday, the day of *Ulysses*, that is, the temporal space of a universal and necessary moment, is the day of Joyce and Nora's first sexual union (16 June 1904).

to see that a certain relation to language is increasingly imposed on him, to the point where he ends up breaking or dissolving language itself, by decomposing it, going beyond phonetic identity (1976–77a: Session 7, p. 43).

I have already mentioned the deficiency of the paternal name and the existence of a sexual relation. Lacan also mentions three other decisive symptoms of psychotic process in Joyce: hallucinations (imposed voices and a redeemer delusion), the disintegration of language into letters and the irruption of the real in the form of epiphanies. Finally, implied in Lacan's discourse and supported by Joyce's biography, there are strong aetiological indications of a schizophrenic situation in the family background, which, taken together with Lucia's schizophrenic break, appear to ground Lacan's position in a clinically solid diagnostic supposition.

Hallucinations: Lacan seems convinced that Joyce suffered from a redeemer delusion—not to redeem God, but to redeem the father at God's behest. Indeed, the 'barmy idea' of redemption happens in so far as 'there is a relation of the son to the father' (ibid.: Session 6, p. 39). Lacan proposes that this results in Joyce's language (or *lalangue*, pre-symbolic babble) that he calls *jouis-sens* (enjoy-meant) and links this to 'imposed speech'—the voice of 'Them' in paranoid hallucination as well as the inspired wordplays of Joycean artifice. The real—the register of the Thing (*la Chose*)—is *ab-sens* (absent meaning), present in Joycean *lalangue*. According to Lacan, Joyce accepted the 'calling' (by God) to break up the English language and eliminate mindless routinization from it.

Lacan also considers that Joyce transposed his own symptom of imposed voices onto Lucia when he maintained that she was capable of marvellous forms of communication. Lacan interprets this as a claim about telepathy and understands that Joyce thereby implicates himself in his daughter's symptom. For Lacan, Lucia is an extension of Joyce's symptom/*sinthome*. Joyce believed in Lucia as in his writing: for him, she was more intelligent than others, capable of miraculously informing him about others' fate; she is merely eccentric, she does not hear voices but is capable of telepathy (ibid.: Session 7, p. 42).

Language: According to Lacan, Joyce allows himself to be 'invaded by the phonemic qualities, by the polyphony of language (*la parole*)' (ibid.: Session 7,

p. 43). The implication is that in Joycean portmanteau words and linguistic puns, we are dealing not with metaphors but with moments where the 'knot' of the *sinthome* momentarily fails. The implication is that in the place of metaphor, Joyce maintains endless chains of metonymic equivocation which are punctuated, not by metaphors, but by moments where the meaningless real discloses itself. Accordingly, his text is an archipelago of epiphanies in a sea of metonymy, which Lacan understands to consist of moments of the 'splendour of Being' or irruption of the real, into the banality of corrupted speech or everyday experience. In this sense, the Joycean practice of annihilating English with a fundamentally Other language that would make way for these isolated moments of radiance is not unlike Schreber's *Grundsprache* in *The Psychoses*.

Epiphanies: Indeed, the epiphanies are interrupted moments of speech reminiscent of the fragmented discourse of Schreber's rays. Epiphany must be rigorously opposed to equivocation, where (especially in punning) the meaning emerges only with a saturation of context; in epiphanies, the radiance emerges as a rupture with a context defined in advance as meaningless (banal). As Harari observes:

> The extasis that comes over being at the moment of the epiphany does not generate meaning. This would also imply—as we have observed in Joyce's work—a failure of metaphorical production. [. . .] The evacuation of phallic signification from what surges up in the epiphany, touching on mysticism and devoid of all meaning, means that it can be categorised [. . .] as being in contact with the Thing (2002: 73 and 77).

Aetiology: In aetiological terms, there is plenty of evidence to support Lacan's contention of Joyce's lifelong struggle against psychosis. There appears to be a crisis between *Portrait* and *Ulysses* in so far as Joyce's conviction that 'one great part of every human existence is passed in a state which cannot be rendered sensible by the use of wideawake language, cutanddry grammar and goahead plot' represents a radical departure from the aesthetics of *Portrait* (1975: 318). Between *Ulysses* and *Finnegans Wake* a fresh crisis intervenes: the death of Joyce's father and Lucia's collapse into schizophrenia. It is reasonable to suppose that the radical derangement of the signifier into constituent letters in *Finnegans Wake* bears some relation to these events.

If *Ulysses* stages an abortive return to the father, then *Finnegans Wake* is an exploration of the 'original sin' of his lack. The riddle Joyce poses throughout is that of writing a letter (as a result of a mandate from his father). In psychotic style, this writing a letter becomes a writing of letters, (de-)composed of letters and decomposed into letters. Hence the portmanteau words, the bilingual puns, the acrostic character of the Joycean text. Joycean ambition—summarized as the creation of the uncreated conscience of his race (genealogical not ethnic)—is immortality, the destiny of a unique writing, which Lacan finally identifies with the role of the Joycean ego in tying together the real, the symbolic and the imaginary. To summarize: the Joycean *sinthome* is his own ego, considered in its almost megalomaniacal character as the bearer of a special destiny.

Now we come, though, to the crucial interpretive decision. A basic question facing anyone confronting *Le Sinthome* is whether the *sinthome* appears when the standard Name-of-the-Father is lacking (that is, when an individual might otherwise slide into psychosis), or whether every person has a *sinthome*. We can say that Lacan prefers the second option—he talks of the *sinthome* as the elementary human dimension and the psychotic kernel of every individual—and that the commentators have followed Lacan in this. From this perspective, Lacan performs on his own work the same conceptual operation of abstraction and generalization that he had previously performed on the Freudian father in the Oedipus complex. Lacan, from at least *The Psychoses* onwards, maintains that it is not the empirical father who is decisive, but the signifier representing the paternal function. This means that the Oedipus complex, with its requirement of identification with the imago of a specific individual, is a myth, a specious generalization of a particular instance, but one that nonetheless accurately reflects something important about the underlying universal process.

The fourth knot is originally the Name-of-the-Father (but no longer considered as an element of the symbolic order. See Lacan 1973–74). Reconceptualizing it outside the symbolic order as the *sinthome*, the fourth loop of the quadruple Borromean knot, implies a new generalization, of which the

Name-of-the-Father is but one specification (others include Woman, God and Joyce). Hence, Lacan asks: '[w]as it not in compensation for this paternal abdication, this *Verwerfung* [foreclosure] in fact, that Joyce felt himself imperiously called—this is the very word, resulting from a mass of things in his text—to valorise his proper name at the father's expense?' (1976–77a: Session 6, pp. 40–1). Joyce writes to compensate for the lacking Name-of-the-Father, to make himself a proper name as well as to make a name for himself; and, 'Joyce's art is so particular that the term *sinthome* is very fitting for it' (ibid.: Session 7, p. 42). *Sinthome*, the concept, is a high-level generalization, a functional element that knots together the real, the symbolic and the imaginary. *Sinthome*, the particular thing that every individual clings to, is something absolutely singular, that functions as or in the place of the Name-of-the-Father. Does not nomination (of a *sinthome*) perform the same operation of abstraction and generalization on the paternal function?

Elegant as this might seem, we should sound a note of caution. Lacan says explicitly that the *sinthome* in Joyce emerges through nomination, a peculiar operation that happens because of the failure of the Name-of-the-Father. Lacan is then consistent when he characterizes Joyce's condition as a de facto foreclosure—that is, not *de jure*, according to the Law. Joyce mimics the Law in his practice of nomination, thus operating so deep within the standard coordinates of the Oedipus complex that it is quite possible to read *Finnegans Wake* in terms of an Oedipal address to the father and as an Oedipal staging in relation to the literary father, Shakespeare (see Cheng 1984). At the same time, Joyce is 'disinvested from the unconscious', according to Lacan. He is not, in other words, a divided subject. For Lacan, because Joyce believed in his *sinthome*, he is not analyzable—he does not suffer from his symptom, rather, it cures him (or keeps him sane).

All of this suggests that rather than looking for a fourth and final Lacan, we should warily regard Joyce as a proof *a contrario* of Lacan's earlier theses on psychosis and the phallus.

One reason for this interpretive strategy is supplied by efforts to do otherwise. In so far as commentators such as Harari accept the notion of a fourth register as something that applies to every individual, they begin to adopt anti-Freudian positions. Harari notes that:

The splendour of the *Wake* has to do, not with metaphor, but with *jouissance*. This is the fundamental point about Joyce: he managed to work on his own *jouissance*, all the while convinced that what he was producing was something exceptional and deserving of being recognised by the whole world. This amounts to a complete reversal of the Freudian view of art (2002: 82).

But other, larger reversals loom into view with this. The unconscious becomes radically individual, rather than formed in the intersubjective space of the discourse of the Other. The faunetics of language implies mimicry, rather than entry into a web of differential relations. Individuals with a complementary *sinthome* can enjoy a sexual relationship. *MAN* does not lack. These entirely reasonable propositions when applied to the individual Joyce, become rather suspect (at a minimum, they are radically under-motivated by the clinical data) when applied to everyone. Along this radical path, finally, the global effectiveness of psychoanalysis is questioned, and with the real, according to Harari, 'Lacan sought to distance himself from what Freud dreamt up' (ibid.: 295).

In so far as such a catastrophic position is motivated by Lacan's own remarks—and I have said that they are hedged with qualifications and conjectures, representing a work in progress rather than a 'final state'—I want to draw attention to how this is in actuality a Joycean anti-psychoanalysis. For these positions—suspicion towards both Carl Jung and Freud, rejection of the unconscious as operating at any level other than the collective/mythical, the radical individual ability to transcend linguistic determinations, insistence on the possibility of a harmonious sexual relation, the belief that it is possible after all to fabricate a paternal signifier and thereby choose one's own destiny—are Joyce's positions first and foremost.

I suggest that this ironic reversal, where Joyce acts as a literary Sphinx that Lacan believes he solves, only to end up as the riddle himself, is generated by means of his own strategy. Adopting a biographical approach, Lacan trembles on the threshold of declaring the Joycean text psychotic. He runs from this oracular determination, determined to find the text unreadable rather than to declare the author insane. Then he hesitates, not only because he is impressed by Joyce, but also because he is unsure how authentic this text actually is in terms of its testamentary value. But this is of course to state both the dilemma and its solution at the same time, for literary texts are not literal, no matter how much they might approach the status of letters. There is no contradiction between Joyce's lifelong struggle against psychosis and literary genius, not just because there is no a priori opposition between these terms, but also for the more straightforward reason that a literary work is not entirely the product of authorial intentions. The entire dimension of mythological structuration and references to literary father figures—Homer, Dante and Shakespeare foremost—is overlooked by Lacan, who then ends up with something perilously close to a Joycean reading of Joyce, rather than a Lacanian interpretation of *Ulysses* and *Finnegans Wake*. We should be careful, I think, before we ascribe to this interplay of misreadings and reversals the status of a wholly new psychoanalytic theory.

References

ENGLISH SOURCES

ADAMS, Robert M. 1962. *Surface and Symbol: The Consistency of James Joyce's Ulysses*. New York: Oxford University Press.

BOUCHER, Geoff. 2011. '"The Compositor of the Farce of Dustiny": Lacan Reading, and Being Read By, Joyce'. *Analysis* 16 (October): 99–118.

BRAUNSTEIN, Néstor. 2003. 'Desire and jouissance in the teachings of Lacan' in Jean-Michel Rabaté (ed.), *The Cambridge Companion to Lacan*. Cambridge: Cambridge University Press, pp. 102–15.

CHENG, Vincent. 1984. *Shakespeare and Joyce: A Study of Finnegans Wake*. University Park: Pennsylvania State University Press.

CLEMENS, Justin and Russell Grigg (eds). 2006. *The Other Side of Psychoanalysis: Reflections on Seminar XVII*. Durham, NC: Duke University Press.

DERRIDA, Jacques. 1978. *Edmund Husserl's Origin of Geometry: An Introduction* (John P. Leavey, Jr trans.). Stony Brook and New York: N. Hays.

————. 1988. 'Ulysses Gramophone: Hear Say Yes in Joyce' (Shari Benstock trans.) in Bernard Benstock (ed.), *James Joyce: The Augmented Ninth*. Syracuse, NY: Syracuse University Press, pp. 27–75.

DEWS, Peter. 1987. *Logics of Disintegration: Poststructuralist Thought and the Claims of Critical Theory*. London and New York: Verso.

DRAVERS, Philip. 2005. 'Joyce and the *Sinthome*: Aiming at the Fourth Term of the Knot'. *Psychoanalytical Notebooks: A Review of the London Society of the New Lacanian School* 13 (May): 93–116.

ECO, Umberto. 1989. *The Middle Ages of James Joyce: The Aesthetics of Chaosmos* (Ellen Esrock trans.). London: Hutchinson.

ELLMANN, Richard. 1983. *James Joyce* (2nd revised edn). Oxford: Oxford University Press.

GASCHÉ, Rodolphe. 1986. *The Tain of the Mirror: Derrida and the Philosophy of Reflection* (5th edn). Cambridge and London: Harvard University Press.

HARARI, Roberto. 2002. *How James Joyce Made His Name: A Reading of the Final lacan* (Luke Thurston trans.). New York: Other Press.

HART, Clive. 1962. *Structure and Motif in Finnegans Wake*. London: Faber and Faber.

JOYCE, James. 1914. *Dubliners*. London: Grant Richards Ltd.

————. 1918. *Exiles: A Play*. New York: B. W. Huebsch.

————. 1960 [1916]. *A Portrait of the Artist as a Young Man*. Harmondsworth: Penguin.

————. 1961. *Scribbledehobble: The Ur-Workbook for Finnegans Wake* (Thomas E. Connelly ed.). Evanston, Ill: Northwestern University Press.

————. 1964 [1939]. *Finnegans Wake* (3rd edn). London: Faber and Faber.

————. 1969 [1944]. *Stephen Hero*. Rev. edn, London: Jonathan Cape.

————. 1975. *Selected Letters of James Joyce* (Richard Ellmann ed.). New York: Viking.

————. 2000 [1922]. *Ulysses*. London: Penguin Classics.

JULIEN, Philippe. 1994. *Jacques Lacan's Return to Freud: The Real, the Symbolic and the Imaginary* (Devra Beck Simiu trans.). New York: New York University Press.

KENNER, Hugh. 1980. *Ulysses*. London and Boston: Allen and Unwin.

LACAN, Jacques. 1976–77a. Le Sinthome. Unpublished translation by Luke Thurston of the sessions of 'Le Séminaire. Book XXIII. Le Sinthome, 1975–76' published in *Ornicar? Bulletin périodique du champ freudien* 6–11. Available at http://www.mediafire.com/?wmymynnzty5 (Last accessed on 22 August 2012.)

————. 1988. *The Seminar of Jacques Lacan. Book II. The Ego in Freud's Theory and in the Technique of Psychoanalysis, 1954–55* (Jacques-Alain Miller ed., Sylvana Tomaselli trans.). Cambridge: Cambridge University Press.

————. 1990. *Television: A Challenge to the Psychoanalytic Establishment* (Joan Copjec ed., Denis Hollier, Rosalind Krauss and Annette Michelson trans). New York and London: W. W. Norton.

————. 1993. *The Seminar of Jacques Lacan. Book III. The Psychoses, 1955–56* (Jacques-Alain Miller ed., Russel Grigg trans.). New York: W. W. Norton; London: Routledge.

————. 1998a. *The Seminar of Jacques Lacan. Book XI. The Four Fundamental Concepts of Psychoanalysis, 1964* (Jacques-Alain Miller ed., Alan Sheridan trans.). Reprint, New York and London: W. W. Norton.

————. 1998b. *The Seminar of Jacques Lacan. Book XX. Encore: On Feminine Sexuality, The Limits of Love and Knowledge, 1972–73* (Jacques-Alain Miller ed., Bruce Fink trans.). New York and London: W. W. Norton.

————. 2001b. 'On a Question Preliminary to any Possible Treatment of Psychosis' in *Écrits: A Selection* (Alan Sheridan trans.). New York and London: Routledge Classics, pp. 137–72.

————. 2006. 'The Function and Field of Speech and Language in Psychoanalysis' in *Écrits: The First Complete Edition in English* (Bruce Fink trans.). New York and London: W. W. Norton, pp. 197–268.

————. 2007. *The Seminar of Jacques Lacan. Book XVII. The Other Side of Psychoanalysis, 1969–70* (Jacques-Alain Miller ed., Russell Grigg trans.). New York and London: W. W. Norton.

LACOUE-LABARTHE, Philippe and Jean-Luc Nancy. 1992. *The Title of the Letter: A Reading of Lacan* (François Raffoul and David Pettigrew trans). Albany: State University of New York Press.

LEONARD Garry. 1993. *Reading Dubliners Again: A Lacanian Perspective*. Syracuse, NY: Syracuse University Press.

MACCABE, Colin. 2003. *James Joyce and the Revolution of the Word* (2nd edn). London: Palgrave Macmillan.

MARINI, Marcel. 1992. *Jacques Lacan: The French Context* (Anne Tomiche trans.). Brunswick, Maine: Rutgers University Press.

MCHUGH, Roland. 1976. *The Sigla of Finnegans Wake*. Austin: University of Texas Press.

MILLER, Jacques-Alain. 1987. 'Préface' in Jacques Aubert (ed.), *Joyce avec Lacan*. Paris: Navarin, pp. 9–12.

MILLOT, Catherine. 1988. 'On Epiphanies' in Bernard Benstock (ed.), *James Joyce: The Augmented Ninth*. Syracuse, NY: Syracuse University Press, pp. 207–09.

NOON, William T. 1957. *Joyce and Aquinas*. New Haven, CT: Yale University Press.

RABATÉ, Jean-Michel. 1991a. *James Joyce, Authorized Reader*. Baltimore, MD: The Johns Hopkins University Press.

————. 1991b. *Joyce Upon the Void: The Genesis of Doubt*. London: Macmillan.

————. 2000. *Lacan in America*. New York: Other Press.

————. 2001. *Jacques Lacan: Psychoanalysis and the Subject of Literature*. Hampshire and New York: Palgrave.

————. 2006. 'Aspace of Dumbillsilly: When Joyce Translates Lacan'. *Critical Quarterly* 48(1) (Spring): 26–42.

RAGLAND-SULLIVAN, Ellie. 1990. 'Lacan's Writings on James Joyce: Writing as Symptom and Singular Solution' in Richard Feldstein and Henry Sussman (eds), *Psychoanalysis and . . .*. New York and London: Routledge, pp. 76–86.

RONEN, Ruth. 2005. 'Art and Anxiety, or: Lacan with Joyce'. *(Re)-turn: A Journal of Lacanian Studies* 2 (Spring): 143–56.

ROUDINESCO, Élisabeth. 1997. *Jacques Lacan* (Barbara Bray trans.). New York: Columbia University Press.

SHECHNER, Mark. 1974. *Joyce in Nighttown: A Psychoanalytic Inquiry into Ulysses*. Berkeley: University of California Press.

THURSTON, Luke. 2002. *Re-Inventing the Symptom: Essays on the Final Lacan*. New York: Other Press.

———. 2004. *James Joyce and the Problem of Psychoanalysis*. Cambridge: Cambridge University Press.

ŽIŽEK, Slavoj. 1989. *The Sublime Object of Ideology*. London and New York: Verso.

FRENCH SOURCES

LACAN, Jacques. 1956. 'Fonction et champ de la parole et du langage en psychanalyse'. *La Psychanalyse* 1: 81–166. Subsequently published in *Écrits* (1966).

———. 1958–59. Le Séminaire. Livre VI. Le désir et son interprétation, 1958–59. Some sessions published in 1982.

———. 1959. 'D'une question préliminaire à tout traitement possible de la psychose'. *La Psychanalyse* 4: 1–50. Subsequently published in *Écrits* (1966).

———. 1964–65. Le Séminaire. Livre XII. Problèmes cruciaux pour la psychanalyse, 1964–65. Unpublished seminar.

———. 1966. *Écrits*. Paris: Éditions du Seuil.

———. 1973–74. Le Séminaire. Livre XXI. Les non-dupes errent/ Les noms-du-pére, 1973–74. Unpublished seminar.

———. 1973 as *Le Séminaire. Livre XI. Les quatre concepts fondamentaux de la psychanalyse, 1964* (Jacques-Alain Miller ed.). Paris: Éditions du Seuil.

———. 1974. *Télévision*. Paris: Éditions du Seuil.

———. 1975. *Le Séminaire. Livre XX. Encore, 1972–73* (Jacques-Alain Miller ed.). Paris: Éditions du Seuil.

———. 1976–77b. 'Le Séminaire. Book XXIII. Le Sinthome, 1975–76' published in *Ornicar? Bulletin périodique du champ freudien* 6–11.

———. 1978. *Le Séminaire. Livre II. Le moi dans la théorie de Freud et dans la technique de la psychanalyse, 1954–55* (Jacques-Alain Miller ed.). Paris: Éditions du Seuil.

———. 1981. *Le Séminaire. Livre III. Les Psychoses, 1955–56* (Jacques-Alain Miller ed.). Paris: Éditions du Seuil.

———. 1982. 'Le désir et son interprétation'. *Ornicar? Bulletin périodique du champ freudien* 25: 13–36.

———. 1987a. 'Joyce le Symptôme I' in Jacques Aubert (ed.), *Joyce Avec Lacan*. Paris: Navarin, pp. 21–9.

———. 1987b. 'Joyce le Symptôme II' in Jacques Aubert (ed.), *Joyce Avec Lacan*. Paris: Navarin, pp. 31–6.

———. 1991. *Le Séminaire. Livre XVII. L'envers de la psychanalyse, 1969–70* (Jacques-Alain Miller ed.). Paris: Éditions du Seuil.

———. 2001a. 'Discours de Rome' in Jacques-Alain Miller (ed.), *Autres écrits*. Paris: Éditions du Seuil, pp. 133–64.

———. 2005. *Le Séminaire. Livre XXIII. Le Sinthome, 1975–76* (Jacques-Alain Miller ed.). Paris: Éditions du Seuil.

PART 3

To Lituraterre

A Literary Introduction to 'Lituraterre'

SANTANU BISWAS

'Lituraterre' arguably constitutes the most significant turning point in the fairly long interface between psychoanalysis and literature. It is both the title of an essay written by Jacques Lacan, possibly in early May 1971, and the seventh session (held on 12 May 1971) of his then-ongoing seminar which was published in 2007 as *Le Séminaire. Livre XVIII. D'un discours qui ne serait pas du semblant, 1971* (On a Discourse that Might not be a Semblance).[1] In course of developing on certain crucial aspects of his later teachings on psychoanalysis, such as, separation and the littoral condition of the letter, a discourse that might not be a semblance, the impossible-to-write sexual relationship, etc., Lacan explores in the essay four questions that are of great significance in the fields of literary studies and psychoanalysis alike, which are:

1   How might literature turn towards *lituraterre* in search of a discourse that might not be a semblance?

2   What should be the concern of psychoanalytic literary criticism that is not a university discourse?

3   Is the literature of the littoral a discourse that is not a semblance?

4   How might writers try to instal the sexual relationship?

---

1 The essay was published about five months later as the introductory chapter of the third issue—devoted to the theme of literature and psychoanalysis—of a literary quarterly, *Littérature*. It was reprinted in 1987 in *Ornicar? Revue du champ freudien* 41, before being given its proper place at the beginning of the posthumously published second volume of Lacan's writings, *Autres écrits* (2001), by its editor Jacques-Alain Miller, following Lacan's lead in the *Écrits* (1966). I have used Jack W. Stone's translation of the essay from *Autres écrits*.

I shall try to comprehend Lacan's answers to these questions with the help of 'On a Discourse that Might not be a Semblance' in general and the essay 'Lituraterre' in particular.

Lacan's neologism *lituraterre* might appear to be the combination of the Latin words *litura* (deletion or erasure) and *terre* (earth, soil or ground) but is actually the result of a spoonerismic rendition of *littérature* (literature).[2] Owing to this and other associations with literature, *lituraterre* stands for: [writing] deletion [on the] ground, or [writing] erasure [on] earth. At the broadest level, 'Lituraterre' deals with writing erasure on earth and with the littoral condition of the letter that writes it. Of the two conditions of the letter mentioned by him in this essay—the literal, or the letter as erasure; and the littoral, or the edge of the letter as erasure—the letter is literal, Lacan specifies, 'because it is founded on the littoral' (1971: Session 7, p. 136).

'Lituraterre' begins with the clarification that, although *lituraterre* has been legitimized in Ernout and Meillet's French etymological dictionary of Latin—Lacan referred to its 1959 edition and mentions it for the second time in his seminar, after 'The Seminar of Jacques Lacan. Book IX. Identification, 1961–62' (1961–62)—it came to him by way of a spoonerism (Lacan 2001a: 1). In this dictionary, the entry on *littera*, which variously means letter of the alphabet, writing character, literature, culture, etc., begins by stating that 'the spelling [. . .] *litera* is due to a false comparison with *lino, litum* [. . .]' (Ernout and Meillet 2001: 363; my translation). They had thus mentioned the erro-neous spelling and acknowledged the false association forged thereby between the letter or literature and coating, deletion or erasure. But, as mentioned earlier, *lituraterre* is the spoonerismic inversion of *littérature*.

Apart from *lino* and *litura*, the third word that Lacan asks his readers to look up in Ernout and Meillet is *liturarius*, which, as Dany Nobus explained, means 'that which shows deletions' and is 'homophonic with *litorarius* (from *litus* and *litoris*), which means shore, coast, littoral' (Nobus 2002: 27). In these

---

2 Named after the Reverend William Archibald Spooner (1844–1930), Warden of New College, Oxford, who was notoriously prone to this tendency, 'spoonerism' is a play on words in which the corresponding consonants, vowels or morphemes are transposed—for example, 'it is *kiss*tomary to *cuss* the bride.'

three senses therefore—the transformation of *littérature* into *lituraterre*; the erroneous conjunction of literature and erasure; and the erasure of the letter bringing about its littoral condition—the very title of Lacan's essay is the first indicator of how 'literature may be in the process of turning towards *lituraterre*' (Lacan 1971: Session 7, p. 138).[3]

Lacan then relates the misspelling of *littera* as *litera* to the 'equivoque' by which '[James] Joyce slips from a letter to a litter' (2001a: 1), which is similar to a point he had made in passing in the *Écrits*: '"A letter, a litter": in Joyce's circle, they played on the homophony of the two words in English' (2006a: 25). While the whole of *Finnegans Wake* (1939; here 1975) is as much 'A comedy of letters!' (Joyce 1975: 425) as it is a comedy of litter, the word litter itself, as well as several Joycean derivatives of it, figures throughout the novel, often in connection with writing, literacy, literature or storytelling: 'illitterettes' (ibid.: 284), 'laying out his litterery bed' (ibid.: 122), 'concoct an equo-angular trillitter' (ibid.: 286), 'the twattering of bards in the twitterlitter' (ibid.: 37), 'countlessness of livestories have netherfallen by this plage, flick as flowflakes, litters from aloft . . .' (ibid.: 17), 'what a jetsam litterage of convolvuli of times lost or strayed' (ibid.: 292), 'a litteringture of kidlings' (ibid.: 570), 'artis litterarumque patrona' (ibid.: 495) and so on. But, perhaps, Joyce best ratified his slippage from a letter to a litter in the following three excerpts: 'writing and with

---

3 Jean-Michel Rabaté explained how the Latin word *literatura* denotes writing, erasure and a shore, which indicates how literature appears to tend towards *lituraterre* in another sense:

> In Latin the plural *literae* signifies writing, epistle, literature, while *literatura* in the singular means writing, grammar, learning or literature. However the latter noun comes from the verb *lino*, whose meaning is contradictory since it calls up 'I smear', 'I cover' or 'I erase' [. . .]. As Lacan pursues the image, *literatura* as a signifier leads us closer to the Latin word *litus*—a word that has different meanings: as a noun, the act of smearing or covering a surface; as a participle, the same meaning as *lino*; as another noun, (*litus*, *litoris*), the 'littoral', a shore or coastline. 'Literature', then, generates a double pun: it suggests both letters and their erasure (a pun that is more obvious in French since one can always hear *rature*—erasure or crossing out—in the very signifier) and the limit or border of a territory, be it the sea, a hole or even another territory (2001: 33–4).

lines of litters slittering up and louds of latters slettering down' (ibid.: 114), 'the heroticisms, catastrophes and eccentricities transmitted by the ancient legacy of the past; type by tope, letter from litter, word at ward, with sendence of sundance' (ibid.: 614–15) and 'And so it all ended. Artha kama dharma moksa. Ask Kavya for the kay. And so everybody heard their plaint and all listened to their plause. The letter! The litter! And the soother the bitther!' (ibid.: 93)

In the 1975 'Joyce the Symptom I' (here 1987a), Lacan attributed Joyce's equivocation in *Finnegans Wake* to the peculiarity of English spelling: 'And if there weren't this kind of spelling, so peculiar to the English language, three quarters of the effects of *The Wake* would be lost' (1987a: 6). 'The letter! The litter!' then represent the two forms of the letter: as semblance and as refuse or trash. The latter is explained by Jean-Louis Gault as Joyce's 'relation to the elementary phenomenon of *lalangue* prior to any subjective implication' (Gault 2007: 76).

There exists another piece of equivoque that Lacan must have been aware of—the book in which it figures is cited by him in *Écrits* (see Lacan 2006a: 47, 11n)—in the form of the letter written on 9 February 1929 to Joyce in response to the published fragments of his *Work in Progress* (1928–37) by an America-based Russian reader, Vladimir Dixon. Dixon described his letter as 'a litter' and referred to James Joyce as 'Mister Germ's Choice' and 'mysterre Shame's Voice' in it, which illustrates Joyce's fall from the letter to the litter in yet another form (Beckett et al. 1929: 193–4).

From the name of Joyce in conjunction with litter as trash or excreta, Lacan 'recalls' Joyce's temporary patroness at Zurich, Edith Rockefeller Mc-Cormick, and the 'shower' she had offered him in September 1919 in the form of a psychoanalysis with Carl Jung (Lacan 2001a: 1), possibly upon the latter's request. Joyce, going by his report to his friend Claud Sykes, found this 'unthinkable' and refused straightaway (Thurston 2004: 130), for which his stipend was promptly terminated by her, possibly following Jung's advice.[4]

---

4 Edith Rockefeller McCormick (1872–1932) was the fourth daughter of John D. Rockefeller and an analytic psychologist analyzed by Jung at Zurich from 1913 to 1921. See also Cambray and Carter (1977: 240), Thurston (2004: 104–48) and McLynn (1996: 324).

Lacan thinks that Joyce would have gained nothing from a psychoanalysis, for he had already managed to achieve the best one could expect at the end of it by having arrived there all by himself! (see Lacan 2001a: 1). Here, the end of analysis is related to the subject's construction of his *sinthome* and identification with it as the supplementary fourth ring that holds together the R. S. I. as a three-ring Borromean knot and thus prevents its disintegration. Lacan states in *Le Séminaire. Livre XXIII. Le Sinthome, 1975–76* (2005b) that Joyce had constructed an unanalyzable *sinthome* for himself through his act of writing, especially that of *Finnegans Wake* (1976–77a: Session 8, p. 48). Thus, the composition and, more importantly to Lacan, the publication of *Finnegans Wake* is responsible for the simultaneous destruction of English language and literature, a sin that made Joyce a *sin(t)-homme*, and the construction of his *sinthome*, a synthetic creation that made Joyce a *synth-homme*, that enabled him to make a name for himself. Lacan wonders whether it was Saint Thomas Aquinas returning to Joyce yet again in terms of the expression *sicut palea* (chaff) with which Aquinas had explained why he had stopped writing the *Summa Theologica* (1265–73) (Lacan 2001a: 1).[5] In the final analysis, however, chaff and litter are not identical, nor is Aquinas' declaration on *Summa Theologica* identical to Joyce's writing of *Finnegans Wake*. There is room for doubt as to whether Aquinas, otherwise a major component of Joyce's *sinthome*— Joyce's *SaintThom*(as)—was indeed revisiting him on this particular matter as well. This justifies the interrogative mode of Lacan's sentence and the logical necessity of the next one in which he 'attests' that Joyce's work both inaugurated the space of the literary wastebasket so as to contain polluted literature—which made him Saint Joyce, Joyce the *saint-homme*, for Lacan who, unlike Aquinas, considered the saint's business to be *trashitas* and not *caritas*— and facilitated a spillover of the contents of the wastebasket so as to overtly

---

5 'In December 1273, Aquinas had a mystical experience that prompted him to cancel all his work on the third part of the *Summa Theologica*. [He stopped at question 90, on penance]. Aquinas explained the decision to his secretary [or, confessor] with the famous words: "All the things I have written are like chaff (*sicut palea*) to me, compared with what I have seen and what has been revealed to me." After this event, Aquinas did not put a single word on paper anymore and he died three months later' (Nobus 2002: 39, 31n).

reintroduce into circulation what had been separated by the work of the ancient tie (ibid.).[6]

Lacan had spoken on the sewerage with great emphasis both before and since. In this essay itself, he alludes to his lecture entitled 'Mon enseignement, sa nature et ses fins' (My Teaching, its Nature and its Ends), addressed to interns in psychiatry at Bordeaux's Hôpital Psychiatrique Charles-Perrens on 20 April 1967, where he had enthusiastically spoken on 'the prodigious analogy that exists between sewage and culture':

> Unlike what happens at every level of the animal kingdom [. . .] man is naturally characterized by the extraordinary embarrassment he feels about [. . .] the evacuation of shit. [. . .] A great civilization is first and foremost a civilization that has a waste-disposal system. So long as we do not take that as our starting point, we will not be able to say anything serious. [. . .] when it comes to the equation *great civilization = pipes and sewers*, there are no exceptions. There were sewers in Babylon, and Rome was all sewers. That's how the City began, with *Cloaca maxima* (2008: 64–6).

He returns to this theme in reply to Willard von Orman Quine's question following his lecture at the Massachusetts Institute of Technology in December 1975: 'Refuse (*les déchets*) perhaps comes from the interior, but the characteristic of man is that he doesn't know what to do with his refuse. Civilization is refuse (*déchet*), *Cloaca maxima*. Refuse is the only thing that testifies to our having an interior' (1976a: 7; translation modified). In 'Lituraterre', Lacan 'avows' that his fate as a psychoanalyst is riveted to the 'wastebasket' (*poubelle*)—not only in the sense of the place where analysands dump their trash but also in

---

6 'A saint's business, to put it clearly, is not *caritas*. Rather, he acts as trash (*déchet*); his business being *trashitas* (*il décharite*)' (Lacan 1990: 15). Lacan also pointed to Joyce's reference to the lavatory thus: 'There's something here that Joyce, who is on the list of my current preoccupations, symbolises with the English word *suck*—it is the noise that the lavatory makes when you pull the chain, when it sinks down the hole' (1989: 8). Joyce himself had briefly depicted an indirect connection between litter and the lavatory thus: 'Was it him that suborned that surdumutual son of his, a litterydistributer in Saint Patrick's Lavatory [. . .]?' (1975: 530).

the sense of the analyst's being the waste product at the end of every analy-sis—and playing on the word 'avowal' he arrives at Samuel Beckett (Lacan 2001a: 1). He had referred to *Waiting for Godot* (1952; here 2003d) in passing at least twice before, but he described Beckett explicitly in relation to 'dustbins' in a remark made in his seminar of 1968–69.[7]

Then, going a step further, he writes of 'the avowal (*l'avouer*) or, as pro-nounced of old, the having (*l'avoir*), by which Beckett balances the debt (*doit*) which makes refuse of our being' (2001a: 1, translation modified). Lacan's wordplay in French with *avouer* and *avoir*, beyond the obvious phonetic simi-larity, suggests a relation between the two words that is similar to the one be-tween 'owning up' and 'owning' in English. Beckett owned up to what he owned in order to settle the debt that reduces our being to trash. Lacan's allusion to accountancy in terms of 'balance' is the reason that *doit*, which is closer to 'debit', is translated as 'debt'. But *doit* also means 'must', owing to which the remark can also be translated as follows: 'The avowal or, as pronounced of old, the having, by which Beckett must (*doit*) balance what makes waste of our being'. In this ren-dition too, the relation between *avouer* and *avoir* is not merely phonetic, for the former underlies the latter in so far as we can only avow what we have, which necessarily includes the waste. We cannot exclude it when we 'must' avow all that we have. In both these later texts, Lacan was most probably alluding to Beckett's play *Endgame* (1958; here 2003b), whose title bore a fortuitous resonance of the

---

7 Lacan made a passing remark on *Waiting for Godot* in the context of his discussion on the number two being odd—'the two numbers that have no equal are waiting for Godot' (2006b: 395)—after Beckett had come into prominence following the staging of this play in Paris in 1953. He made another passing remark later in the context of his discussion on God: 'echoing Beckett who one day called him Godot' (1961–62: Session 24, p. 324). But, importantly, in the opening session of 'The Seminar of Jacques Lacan. Book XVI. From an Other to the other, 1968–69' (1968–69), Lacan stated:

> [A] certain number of us [those who are 'labelled' 'structuralist' by 'the publi-cist'], thanks to the labour of this agency ['the publicist'], find ourselves to-gether in the same dustbin (*poubelle*) [. . .]. I could not in any case find myself uncomfortable in it, especially since we know a little bit about what is involved in dustbins in this period dominated by the genius of Samuel Beckett (1968–69: Session 1, p. 1).

'end' (of analysis)—as does *(Fin)negans Wake* in another sense—and throughout which the protagonist Hamm kept his parents, Nagg and Nell, 'bottled' in two dustbins (Beckett 2003b: 103). The end of analysis here concerns the subject having a glimpse of the real of his being as waste, as Beckett may have had with or without the assistance of his analysis with Wilfred Bion round the beginning of his literary career.[8] Whether or not Lacan was aware of it while writing the essay, it is noteworthy that Beckett's 35-second play on 'littered [. . .] rubbish', *Breath* (1969; here 2003a), was written and staged in Paris only two years before 'Lituraterre' was written (Beckett 2003a: 371). More importantly, Lacan thinks that Beckett's act of balancing the debt through his 'avowal', or 'having', saved the 'honour of literature' (2001a: 1). This is to be understood in the light of Lacan's own definition of 'literature' that in so far as it is 'a matter of collecting in a writing, what was first of all, primitively, song, spoken myth, dramatic procession', it is 'only a way of accommodating oneself to leftovers *(restes)*' (1971: Session 7, p. 132)—due to its passage from the spoken to the written, from totality to fragments and from the numerous to the surviving few; that is, from the letter to the litter, or better still, from literature to 'litteringture'. This would explain why in 'Joyce the Symptom I', Lacan does not look beyond Joyce's equivocation on letter and litter to emphasize the weight of the word literature itself: 'And to emphasize the weight of this word *literature*, I'll invoke the equivocation that Joyce often played upon—*letter, litter*. The letter is refuse' (1987a: 6). Lacan thinks Beckett's avowal, or having, also relieved him of the need to believe that the psychoanalyst alone was privileged to know a little bit about the dustbin (2001a: 1). The instances of Joyce and Beckett that are suggestive of two forms of affinity between the letter and the litter in two types of ends of analysis once again indicate how literature appeared to tend towards *lituraterre*.

---

8 'For two years, during 1934–5 Samuel Beckett (or Sam to those who knew him well), aged 28 to 29, underwent a course of psychoanalysis with Bion at the Tavistock Clinic in London, meeting perhaps four times a week' (Anzieu 1989: 163). As if to indicate a relation of contiguity between excreta and trash as the two forms of human refuse, the play which premiered as a curtain raiser to *Endgame* at London's Royal Court Theatre in 1958 was *Krapp's Last Tape*, the protagonist of which, whose name contains a pun on 'crap', suffered from a 'bowel condition' in the form of an 'Unattainable laxation' (Beckett 2003c: 217–18).

On the question of what the primary concern of psychoanalytic literary criticism should be, Lacan classifies it in its existing form as a 'university discourse', and suggests that it should concern itself with the unreadable and the impossible in literary and psychoanalytic works in order to come closer to the psychoanalyst's discourse (ibid.: 1–2). He assesses Freud's works on literature and Marie Bonaparte's work on Poe as inadequate and misdirected respectively, and suggests that his own writing on Poe—the 1956 'Seminar on "The Purloined Letter"' (1957; here 2006a)—could serve as a better example of literary criticism. He thinks this could be best understood in terms of what his critique of Poe bears on: 'what Poe makes of being a writer in forming such a message on the letter' (ibid.: 2). What does Poe make of being a writer—a letter-user—as the writer of this story on the letter? Citing Poe, Lacan claims that a 'writer' is one who avows it all the more rigorously by not saying it as such (1971: Session 7, p. 133). 'What is essential' in his story 'is that one will never know what is in it [the letter]' and yet be able to follow its trajectory in its entirety (ibid.: Session 5, p. 110). In so far as Poe's story is about how a letter belonging to the queen underwent two detours before finally, possibly, returning to her, it shows us how a story can depict the complete trajectory of a letter, including a detour within a detour, 'without having any recourse to the contents of the letter' (ibid.: Session 7, p. 133). Lacan specifies here that the elision of the message cannot be explained with the help of Poe's psychobiography. Appropriately enough, Poe's psychobiographical critic 'Marie [Bonaparte] does not even touch it!' (ibid.: Session 7, p. 134). Similarly, readers of Lacan's writing on Poe will not find any mention of the term phallus in it—'what is not said' there is 'the phallus' (ibid.: Session 6, p. 114)—and yet, they will be able to view the 'effect of feminization' as the consequence of holding the letter or the phallus demonstrated rigorously (ibid.: Session 7, 133; Session 6, pp. 120–1). As a letter in sufferance, as a letter doubly detoured, the purloined letter moreover brings out the 'failure' of the letter in that state—in terms of its non-usability, its effeminizing effect on the holder, the castrating import of its loss and, above all, the delay in its arrival at its destination. Psychoanalytic literary criticism ought, therefore, to learn from the way in which Poe and Lacan shed light on the letter and the phallus respectively—dealing with their failures at their limits—by not bringing them out of their hiding. For the reason that both Poe and Lacan function as 'writers' in this special sense of writing on it with greater rigour by not writing it, Lacan states: 'Poe [. . .] had been guided in his fiction by the same aim (*dessein*) as mine' (2006a: 46). He further states that, following the instance of the letter in Poe that 'takes on its importance from the fact that it is unreadable' (1971: Session 6, p. 123)—where the unreadable content of the letter constitutes an unbridgeable gap in the narrative—one should read the structure of Freud's as well as his own teachings in their 'impossibilities' (ibid.: Session 6, p. 114). He explains that Poe gave Dupin the role of throwing dust into our eyes to make us believe that the 'cutest of the cute exists,' who knows and understands everything, for whom nothing is unreadable, which is untrue (ibid.: Session 6, p. 121). Rather, the important point here is that Poe was able to demonstrate the effects of the letter at its limit so thoroughly because he had effaced its content and thus converted it and the narrative on it into the edges of an unreadable hole, which brings out the letter's littoral condition in the story.

Lacan suggests that psychoanalytic literary criticism ought to compare the impossible and the un-readable in literary and psychoanalytic works with an aim to enable the former to shed light on the edge of knowledge. He thought, partly following Freud, that psychoanalysis had a great deal to receive from literature, especially on the question of the letter. He thought that Poe's depiction of the letter in sufferance from where it showed its failure, and Joyce's depiction of the letter tending towards the littoral by way of litter, could assist in illuminating the letter at its limit for psychoanalysis. He also thought that psychoanalysis has existed since Freud so that literary works could measure themselves against it, with the enigma belonging to the side of psychoanalysis and the source of illumination belonging to the side of literature (see Lacan 2001a: 3). With the help of these remarks and his critique of Poe, Lacan at once indicates how literature appeared to tend towards *lituraterre* where it showed the letter making holes in writing, urged literary criticism in general to shed light on this aspect of literature and advised psychoanalytic literary criticism in particular to compare the holes made by the letter in literary and psychoanalytic writings respectively.[9]

---

9 Lacan points to topology for another instance of how writing made holes in the written: 'There is no topology without writing [. . .]. [T]opology [. . .] consists precisely in making holes in what is written' (1971: Session 5, p. 97).

Lacan then offers a 'literary demonstration' of the idea that 'literature may be in the process of turning towards *lituraterre*' (1971: Session 7, p. 138; translation modified), in terms of a bit-by-bit construction of the apologue that constitutes the most perfect illustration of *lituraterre* in Lacan: while flying back to Europe from Tokyo, at the end of his second visit to Japan shortly before writing the essay, over the otherwise barren Siberian Plain, the only thing that he could see through the window of the aircraft—and from between the clouds—was rivers. He calls these solitary traces in view 'streaming' (*ruissellement*) and writes: 'The streaming is the bouquet of a first stroke (*trait*) and of what effaces it. I have said it: it is from their conjunction that the subject is made, but in that two times are marked there. It is necessary then that the erasure be distinguished there' (2001a: 5).[10] Later, when the aeroplane swerved to sustain itself in isobars, Lacan saw traces of an embankment (ibid.: 6). That is where the literary demonstration ends, with Lacan's emphasis clearly placed on the first stroke and its effacement, and the embankment or the edge of the shore designating the effacement, as a form of *lituraterre*.

How should we read the expression 'a first stroke and of what effaces it', given that the first stroke or the unary trait or the letter in 'Lituraterre' is already an erasure? If the first stroke is a furrow on the ground, an empty river-bed, an erasure written on earth, then the streaming effaces it partially by filling it up with water, which however, does not efface the edges of the erasure. Rather, the water establishes the edges as the two banks of the river which continue to distinguish the erasure. I think, however, that the relation of the letter to its erasure in this passage should be read in the light of an *après-coup* (retroaction), in terms of which the letter is retroactively posited from an erasure. That the subject is made from this conjunction of an erasure-as-letter and a retroactive construction of an erased letter is a radically new way of considering him in so far as he is described not in terms of his representation

---

10 Lacan ratified in *The Seminar of Jacques Lacan. Book XX. Encore: On Feminine Sexuality, The Limits of Love and Knowledge, 1972–73* (1975b; here 1998) that the clouds and the rivers/streams in 'Lituraterre' metaphorically denoted writing: '"The cloud of language," I expressed myself metaphorically, "constitutes writing." [. . .] [and] that we can read (*lire*) the streams I saw over Siberia as the metaphorical trace of writing' (1998: 120).

by the signifier S1 for the signifier S2, as Lacan had done throughout *Écrits* and in all his early works, but in terms of his relation to the real order by way of his separation or extraction from it. This description of the subject as one who procures oneself from the real order constitutes a precise definition of Lacan's subject of separation. Lacan further clarifies that the only decisive thing that he saw in the Siberian Plain was the littoral condition that he was able to perceive so strongly owing to the excess created by Japanese writing, and then contends: 'between knowledge (*savoir*) and jouissance, there is a littoral which only turns to the literal in so far as this turn, we might take it the same at any instant' (ibid.: 5–6). In this wordplay in French and English, with 'littoral' meaning the edge and *littéral* meaning literal or something pertaining to the letter, the littoral is the edge or the bank of a river where the water touches its limit. It is not a border because it does not separate two domains, it is not a letter artificially inscribed by the speaking being between two territories and it is not a third element. Rather, the littoral is the edge that writes the streaming or the river as the letter. In the same way, 'between' does not denote a border nor is it a third element that separates the first and second elements, which are knowledge and jouissance, or water and earth. Rather, it denotes a limit that is indicative of a beyond the limit, in terms of which the jouissance, as something situated beyond the limit of knowledge, refers to itself through the littoral. Finally, when the littoral is viewed literally, it remains unchanged at any instant, for, as a letter, it may be read in the same way every time.

Lacan asks if a discourse can be constituted from the littoral that would not be a discourse emitted from a semblance? But first, to explain what a semblance means in Lacan, Russell Grigg's well-stated answer to this question may be summarized as follows: the English word semblance or semblant means being like, resembling, make believe, seeming and appearance, while the corresponding French word *semblant* has the additional connotations of outer appearance, pretence and imitation, often non-deceptive and useful. In his early teachings, where Lacan described the *objet petit a* as a semblance of the primordial lost object, for example, a semblance is a resemblance that is deceptive because it is not the real thing, and yet non-deceptive because the subject knows that it is a substitute rather than the real thing. Despite these two factors, it provides satisfaction to the subject, which explains its seductive quality and utility. Miller captured these connotations succinctly by stating that the function of a semblance is to 'veil nothing', and to posit something in the place of nothing by *veiling* nothing. Lacan had used the term semblance in 1957 and 1964 but it became an important concept in the 1970s when he used it in the broader sense of a substitute for something, and more importantly, extended its use to radically redefine as semblances some of his important concepts originally not defined as semblances, such as, the Other, the Name-of-the-Father, language and the phallus in the main (Grigg 2007: 131–8). Lacan also pointed to the relations of *objet petit a*, love and jouissance to semblance in *Encore*.

In reply to the above question, Lacan states that avant-garde literature is 'made of the littoral', for it sustains itself by the hole and 'not [. . .] by the semblance' (2001a: 7). Although the Joyce-inspired French avant-garde literature alluded to by Lacan largely rejected traditional notions of character, plot, psychology and narrative style, it was not completely unanchored or unstructured. Much of it was concerned, in different ways, with philosophy, the meaning of language, the need to severely criticize the time and expose the systems of control, the urge to inscribe what was as it was, as announced by the title of the journal *Tel Quel*, and with the reinterpretation of the role of politics, religion, art, literature, sex and the media. However, in terms of its radical departure from traditional forms of narration—by way of unconventional narrative styles, wordplay, condensation, neologism, displacement, pun, riddle, allusion, ideogram, misspelling, combination of incongruous words and phrases, use of words from different languages, absence of punctuation, stress on the sounds of words, the fading self, etc.—avant-garde literature comprised texts that were hallucinatory, chaotic and situated at the edge of meaning. By creating holes in meaning and thus eluding sense, it directed the attention of the readers to the very materiality of the letters and their sounds on the one hand, and to the limit of meaning and the impossible void beyond it as the site of jouissance, on the other. Thus, avant-garde literature comes closest to a form of a discourse that might not be a semblance because, being made of the littoral instead of the literal, it is sustained by the holes in the semblance. However, there is no discourse that is not a semblance, for the organizing point of every discourse begins with a semblance without which it is impossible to qualify what is involved in a discourse. Avant-garde literature is no exception, for, in the final analysis, though it is a discourse of the littoral, it is not a discourse that is not a semblance. It 'proves nothing but the breakage, which only a discourse can produce, with an effect of production' (ibid.).

Of the two levels at which Lacan describes writing in 'Lituraterre'—'Writing, the letter, is in the real, and the signifier, in the symbolic' (1971: Session 7, p. 143)—writing the letter in the real, or writing as 'the furrowing of the signified in the real' (ibid.: Session 7, p. 142) was of greater importance to him at this stage, especially because he was looking for a discourse that might not be a semblance. This is the reason that he states that, whereas literature aspires to turn to *lituraterre* by ordering itself from a scientific movement, where writing 'has made a marvel', he *lituraterres* himself by making us remark that 'writing is this furrowing (*ravinement*) itself' (2001a: 7). He then turns to the 'writing-effect' in the Japanese tongue, more elaborately in 'On a Discourse that Might not be a Semblance' than in 'Lituraterre', for the 'resources' for an 'example' of *lituraterre* (1971: Session 7, pp. 145–9).[11] In the fifth session of this seminar, Lacan singled out the Japanese language for revealing the extraordinary degree 'to which a writing can work upon a tongue' (ibid.: Session 5, p. 108) and explained its speciality:

> What is called the moneme, here, in the middle, is something you
> can change. You give it a Chinese pronunciation, quite different to a

---

11 In order to minimize misunderstanding, Lacan clarified fairly early in 'Lituraterre' that although his 'teaching [. . .] is posted as a slogan for the promotion of the written', what 'agrees with [him] better' is the 'displacement of interest' suggested by the fact that 'it is beginning in our day that finally Rabelais is read [. . .]' (Lacan 2001a: 2). As Éric Laurent explains, Lacan wished to promote not the written but reading, which he did in this case by hailing the interest in reading Rabelais in this epoch. Laurent clarifies that although Rabelais was already a major figure who had moreover been made into 'the great man of the Renaissance' by Jules Michelet, it is the work of Mikhail Bakhtin, who depicted the 'laughter of the people of the Renaissance' in Rabelais on the one hand, and that of Michael Screech who showed that it was rather 'the laughter of the humanists and that Rabelais's most smutty jokes are derived in general [. . .] from a piece of writing by Erasmus' on the other, that has drawn the attention of readers and critics from all over Europe to Rabelais's laughter in this epoch (Laurent 2007: 29).

Japanese pronunciation, so that, when you are in the presence of a Chinese character, you have [to know], if you are initiated, but naturally only the naturals know it, when you pronounce it *on-yomi* or *kun-yomi* depending on the case, which are always very precise [. . .]. That teaches you a lot about the fact that the Japanese tongue is nourished by its writing (ibid.: Session 5, pp. 108–9).

In the session on *lituraterre* that followed, as well as in the essay cited here, Lacan further explains:

If there be included in the Japanese language an effect of writing, the important thing is that this effect remains attached to writing and that [. . .] the carrier of the effect of writing is there a specialized writing in that in Japanese it can be given two different pronunciations: in *on-yomi* its pronunciation as character, the character is pronounced as such distinctly, in *kun-yomi* the fashion in which is said in Japanese what the character means (2001a: 7).

The kanji consists of Chinese characters that can be pronounced in two different ways: the *on-yomi*, or the 'on' reading, and the *kun-yomi*, or the 'kun' reading. *On-yomi* concerns the Chinese pronunciation of the Chinese character, while *kun-yomi* concerns the Japanese pronunciation of what it means in Japanese. The writing-effect in Japanese language remains attached to writing because it is borne by this duplicity in pronunciation. It also divides the Japanese subject in a way whereby one of his registers is satisfied with writing and the other with speech (ibid.: 8). In so far as the Japanese tongue sustains itself as the edge of the erasure of Chinese characters, it is an instance of *lituraterre* in language.[12] Going a step further in 'The Seminar of Jacques Lacan. Book XXI. R. S. I., 1974–75' (1975a), Lacan states with due reference to 'Lituraterre': 'On returning from a trip to Japan, I believed myself to see a certain duplicity in pronunciation, doubled by the duplicity of the system of writing, a special difficulty of the

---

12 Rabaté explained that contrary to Roland Barthes's depiction of Japanese calligraphy in the *Empire of Signs* (1970; here 1983) as a pure void, Lacan thought that 'letters do not point to a pure void of signification but produce a "hole" in which enjoyment [jouissance] of the most excessive type can lurk' (Rabaté 2001: 34).

language to operate at the level of the unconscious, and precisely in what would appear to make it easier' (1975a: Session 6, p. 31; translation modified). The duplicity in pronunciation compounded by the duplicity in writing concerning *hiragana* and *katakana* as its two syllabaries made the Japanese language resist— rather than making it conducive to—the unconscious. He had already clarified in his 1972 'Preface to the Japanese Edition of the *Écrits*' (here 2001b) that, the gap between the unconscious and speech, which is not open in any of the languages pertinent for psychoanalysis, is rendered open and 'tangible at every instant' in Japanese due to its dependence on Chinese writing (2001b: 2). In other words, although this gap posited by the double duplicity characterizing the language should have made it easier for the Japanese language to operate at the level of the unconscious, the perpetually open nature of this gap makes such an action difficult. Pointing to its most pertinent consequence for psychoanalysis, Lacan had remarked that 'no one who inhabits this language has any need to be psychoanalyzed' (ibid.: 2).[13]

Lacan also states for the first time in 'On a Discourse that Might not be a Semblance' what would become one of his most significant later teachings, namely, that the sexual relationship between man and woman cannot be written. He stresses on this impossibility throughout the seminar, especially in the sessions following the one on *lituraterre*, by variously stating that, the sexual relationship cannot be written in the function $F(x)$ when the function itself is not to be written (1971: Session 6, pp. 128–30); that writing is related to foreclusive negation and discordant negation (ibid.: Session 8, p. 164); that there is no sexual relationship in the speaking being since all relationships subsist from the written (ibid.: Session 4, pp. 83–4); that the sexual relationship fails because it cannot be inscribed in language (ibid.: Session 8, pp. 152–3); that the sexual relationship cannot be written because The woman, in so far as she is the signifier

---

13 Lacan claimed at different moments in his later teachings that Joyce, and presumably others like him, speakers of Japanese and practicing Catholics did not need a psychoanalysis (1976–77a: Session 8, p. 48). Shin'ya Ogasawara argues with the support of two clinical examples that, Lacan's assessment of the analyzability of the Japanese subject should be read theoretically, as a 'limit-case of "psychoanalysability"', not literally, for, 'in the Japanese unconscious the instance of the letter is made in hiragana' (1999a: 2–3).

that there is no Other, does not exist (ibid.: Session 6, p. 127); that 'every man' exists only as a signifier, while The woman cannot be inscribed (ibid.: Session 8, p. 165); that language does not take into account the sexual relationship because 'inscription' consists in not being able to comment on the sexual relationship of man and woman as speaking beings who dwell in language and draw from it the usage of the word (ibid.: Session 8, p. 153); that the sexual relationship cannot be written because there is a disjunction between man and woman, or nature and 'it is written' as the written decree of the heavens (ibid.: Session 3, p. 69; Session 4, p. 92); that the sexual relationship is not inscribable, cannot be grounded as a rapport, due to the indetermination caused by its not being measurable (ibid.: Session 8, pp. 150–2); because the phallus as the third term in the relation makes it untenable (ibid.: Session 8, pp. 164–5); that in Freud's writing, the sexual relationship is deficient, or sustained by the composition of jouissance and castration, where castration is the unreadability of the letter (ibid.: Session 10, pp. 5–7); that there is no sexual relationship in 'The Purloined Letter' because the king is imbecile, the minister perfectly realizes his castration and the queen as the owner of the letter does not exist qua the law;[14] that the fictive promotion of the sexual relationship in Poe's story indicates the letter's relationship

14 The king as the destination of the letter is 'the Subject' who is 'distinguished by its very special imbecility'. He 'manifests this function of Subject' and knows nothing. If he got his hands on the letter, however, the one thing he would understand despite knowing nothing is that the contents have a sense, which explains why the letter arrives at its destination because of the message it carries (Lacan 1971: Session 6, p. 120). The minister would 'perfectly realize' his castration by the queen if he opened the facsimile letter, which would be 'the most perfect castration that is demonstrated' (ibid.: Session 6, p. 122) by Poe due to the words from Prosper Jolyot de Crébillon's play inscribed in it by Dupin that would make 'castration [. . .] [end] up with producing a *being-there* [or] *Dasein*' for the minister (ibid.: Session 5, p. 93). And, the queen and her letter did not exist qua the law in two overlapping senses:

a) That the *lettre*—a feminine noun in French—which belonged to the queen and effeminized each of its holders, did not officially exist with respect to the law of the king and the law of the land and

b) Somewhat like the Lévi-Straussian notion of the woman who circulates as a signifier outside patriarchy so as to sustain it, the letter is transmitted outside the field of the law of language that rendered it unreadable.

with a deficiency from which it gets its value (ibid.: Session 8, pp. 153–4); that the sexual relationship is missing in the field of truth (ibid.: Session 10, p. 6); and that logic, a form of writing, carries the same mark of the sexual impasse as does the analytic discourse (ibid.: Session 8, pp. 165–6).[15] In this context, Lacan stated in an earlier session of 'On a Discourse that Might not be a Semblance': 'The fact that there is no sexual relationship, I already fixed under this form that there is not for the rapport any way at present of writing it. Who knows, there are people who dream that one day this will be written; why not?' (ibid.: Session 5, p. 99; translation modified).[16] Following from this remark, Lacan concluded 'Lituraterre' by stating that the only solution for writers who dream of installing the sexual relationship one day might well be 'an asceticism of writing [. . .] rejoining an [impossible] "it is written."' (2001a: 9).

---

15 However, Lacan will go on to say: 'What is Joyce's relation to Nora? Oddly enough, I'd say it is a sexual relationship, even though I say there's no such thing. But it's a funny kind of sexual relationship [. . .]' (1976–77a: Session 5, p. 38). It is a funny kind because:

a) Joyce used the very lack of sexual relationship, which he called 'exiles', in order to remain bound to Nora (ibid.: Session 4, p. 21).

b) In *Exiles* (1918; here 1962), Richard introduced 'jealousy' and 'doubt' in the mediatory place of the third so as to found his sexual relationship with Bertha round it.

c) Joyce imagined the character of 'some other man' and opened for him the choice of 'a woman' with Nora (ibid.: Session 4, p. 21).

d) It is a rapport only from Joyce's side, as Nora is entirely reduced to a tightly fitting inverted glove of his (ibid.: Session 5, pp. 38–9).

16 The reasoning behind Lacan's proposition that it might one day be possible to write the sexual relationship may be understood in terms of the following remark he made on the real order a few years later:

But, after all, why not also think that one day we will be able to know a little bit more about the real?—again owing to calculations. Auguste Comte used to say that we would never know anything about the chemistry of the stars, and lo and behold, along comes a thing called the spectroscope, which lets us know very precise things about the chemical composition of stars. So, we need to be cautious, along come things, absolutely phenomenal points of passage, that one could surely not have imagined or in any way foreseen (2005a: 98; page number correspond to the French essay).

References

ENGLISH SOURCES

ANZIEU, Didier. 1989. 'Beckett and Bion'. *International Review of Psycho-Analysis* 16: 163–9.

BARTHES, Roland. 1983. *Empire of Signs* (Richard Howard trans.). New York: Hill and Wang.

BECKETT, Samuel. 2003a. *Breath* in *The Complete Dramatic Works*. London: Faber and Faber, pp. 369–72.

————. 2003b. *Endgame* in *The Complete Dramatic Works*. London: Faber and Faber, pp. 89–134.

————. 2003c. *Krapp's Last Tape* in *The Complete Dramatic Works*. London: Faber and Faber, pp. 213–23.

————. 2003d. *Waiting for Godot* in *The Complete Dramatic Works*. London: Faber and Faber, pp. 7–88.

————, Marcel Brion, Frank Budgen et al. 1929. *Our Exagmination Round His Factification for Incamination of Work in Progress*. Paris: Shakespeare & Company.

CAMBRAY, Joseph and Linda Carter. 1977. *C. G. Jung Speaking: Interviews and Encounters*. New Jersey: Princeton University Press.

GAULT, Jean-Louis. 2007. 'Two Statuses of the Symptom: Let us Turn to Finn Again' (Heather Menzies trans.) in Véronique Voruz and Bogdan Wolf (eds), *The Later Lacan: An Introduction*. Albany: State University of New York Press, pp. 73–82.

GRIGG, Russell. 2007. 'Semblant, Phallus, and Object in Lacan's Teaching'. *Umbr(a): A Journal of the Unconscious* 1: 131–8.

JOYCE, James. 1962 [1918]. *Exiles*, including Joyce's 'Notes' on the play. London: New English Library.

————. 1975 [1939]. *Finnegans Wake*. London: Faber and Faber.

LACAN, Jacques. 1961–62. The Seminar of Jacques Lacan. Book IX. Identification, 1961–62. Unofficially translated by Cormac Gallagher from the unedited French typescripts of the unpublished seminar Le Séminaire. Livre IX. L'Identification, 1961–62. Available at http://www.valas.fr/IMG/pdf/THE-SEMINAR-OF-JACQ-UES-LACAN-IX_identification.pdf (Last accessed on 22 August 2012.)

———. 1968–69. The Seminar of Jacques Lacan. Book XVI. From an Other to the other, 1968–69. Unofficially translated by Cormac Gallagher from the unedited French typescripts of the seminar which was officially published in 2006. Available at http://www.lacaninireland.com/web/wp-content/uploads/2010/06/Book-16-from-an-Other-to-the-other.pdf (Last accessed on 22 August 2012.)

———. 1971. The Seminar of Jacques Lacan. Book XVIII. On a Discourse that Might not be a Semblance, 1971. Unofficially translated by Cormac Gallagher from the unedited French typescripts of the seminar which was officially published in 2007. Available at http://www.valas.fr/ IMG/pdf/THE-SEMINAR-OF-JACQUES-LACAN-XVIII_d_un_discours.pdf (Last accessed on 22 August 2012.)

———. 1975a. The Seminar of Jacques Lacan. Book XXII. R. S. I., 1974–75. Unpublished translation by Jack W. Stone of 'Le Séminaire. Livre XXII. R. S. I., 1974–75'. Ornicar? Bulletin périodique du champ freudien 2: 87–105; 3: 96–110; 4: 92–106; 5: 17–66). Available at http://www.scribd.com/doc/3312400 1/10 724-The-Seminar-of-Jacques (Last accessed on 22 August 2012.)

———. 1976a. 'Massachusetts Institute of Technology. December 2, 1975' (Jack W. Stone trans.). Columbia, MO: University of Missouri. Available at http://web.missouri.edu/~stonej/-M.I.T.pdf (Last accessed on 22 August 2012.). Available as part of 'Conferences in North American Universities'. Scilicet 6/7: 7–63.

———. 1976–77a. Le Sinthome. Unpublished translation by Luke Thurston of the sessions of 'Le Séminaire. Book XXIII. Le Sinthome, 1975–76' published in Ornicar? Bulletin périodique du champ freudien 6–11. Available at http://www.mediafire.com /?wmymyn-nzty5 (Last accessed on 22 August 2012.)

———. 1987a. Joyce the Symptom I. Unpublished translation by Daniel Collins of 'Joyce le Symptôme I'. Available at http://traceofink. files.wordpress.com/2010/08/joycethesymptom.pdf (Last accessed on 22 August 2012.)

———. 1989. 'Geneva Lecture on the Symptom' (Russell Grigg trans.). Analysis 1 (Australia): 7–26.

———. 1990. Television: A Challenge to the Psychoanalytic Establishment (Joan Copjec ed., Denis Hollier, Rosalind Krauss and Annette Michelson trans). New York and London: W. W. Norton.

————. 1998. *The Seminar of Jacques Lacan. Book XX. Encore: On Feminine Sexuality, The Limits of Love and Knowledge, 1972–73* (Jacques-Alain Miller ed., Bruce Fink trans.). New York and London: W. W. Norton.

————. 2001a. 'Lituraterre' (Jack W. Stone trans.). Columbia, MO: University of Missouri. Available at http://web.missouri.edu/~stonej/Lituraterre.pdf (Last accessed on 22 August 2012.)

————. 2001b. 'Preface to the Japanese Edition of the *Écrits*' (Jack W. Stone trans.). Columbia, MO: University of Missouri. Available at http://web.missouri.edu/~stonej/preface_japanese.pdf (Last accessed on 22 August 2012.)

————. 2005a. The Triumph of Religion. Unpublished translation by Adrian Price of 'Le Triomphe de la Religion'.

————. 2006a. 'Seminar on "The Purloined Letter"' in *Écrits: The First Complete Edition in English* (Bruce Fink trans.). New York and London: W. W. Norton, pp. 6–18.

————. 2006b. 'The Situation of Psychoanalysis and the Training of Psychoanalysts in 1956' in *Écrits: The First Complete Edition in English* (Bruce Fink trans.). New York and London: W. W. Norton, pp. 384–411.

————. 2008. *My Teaching* (David Macey trans.). London: Verso.

LAURENT, Éric. 2007. 'The Purloined Letter and the Tao of the Psychoanalyst' (Marc Thomas and Victoria Woollard trans) in Véronique Voruz and Bogdan Wolf (eds), *The Later Lacan: An Introduction*. Albany: State University of New York Press, pp. 25–52.

McLYNN, Frank. 1996. *Carl Gustav Jung*. New York: St Martin's Press.

NOBUS, Dany. 2002. 'Illiterature' in Luke Thurston (ed.), *Reinventing the Symptom: Essays on the Final Lacan*. New York: Other Press, pp. 19–43.

OGASAWARA, Shin'ya. 1999a. The Instance of the Letter in the Japanese Unconscious (Jack W. Stone trans.). Columbia, MO: The University of Missouri. Available at http://web.missouri.edu/~stonej/Japan-Unc.pdf (Last accessed on 22 August 2012.)

RABATÉ, Jean-Michel. 2001. *Jacques Lacan: Psychoanalysis and the Subject of Literature*. Hampshire and New York: Palgrave.

THURSTON, Luke. 2004. *James Joyce and the Problem of Psychoanalysis*. Cambridge: Cambridge University Press.

FRENCH SOURCES

ERNOUT, Alfred and Alfred Meillet. 2001. *Dictionnaire Étymologique de La Langue Latine: Histoire des Mots*. Paris: Klincksieck.

LACAN, Jacques. 1956. 'Situation de la psychanalyse et formation du psychanalyste en 1956' in a special issue of *Les Études Philosophiques*. Subsequently published in *Écrits* (1966).

―――. 1957. 'Le séminaire sur "La Lettre Volée"'. *La Psychanalyse* 2: 1–44. Subsequently published in *Écrits* (1966).

―――. 1966. *Écrits*. Paris: Éditions du Seuil.

―――. 1974. *Télévision*. Paris: Éditions du Seuil.

―――. 1975b. *Le Séminaire. Livre XX. Encore, 1972–73* (Jacques-Alain Miller ed.). Paris: Éditions du Seuil.

―――. 1976b. '1975-12-02. Massachusetts Institute of Technology'. *Scilicet* 6/7: 53–63. Available as part of 'Conférences et Entretiens dans des universités nord-américaines'. *Scilicet* 6/7: 7–63.

―――. 1976–77b. 'Le Séminaire. Book XXIII. Le Sinthome, 1975–76'. *Ornicar? Bulletin périodique du champ freudien* 6–11.

―――. 1985. 'Conférence à Genéve sur le symptôme'. *Le bloc-notes de la psychanalyse* 5: 5–23.

―――. 1987b. 'Joyce le Symptôme I' in Jacques Aubert (ed.), *Joyce Avec Lacan*. Paris: Navarin, pp. 21–9.

―――. 2001c. 'Lituraterre' in Jacques-Alain Miller (ed.), *Autres écrits*. Paris: Éditions du Seuil, pp. 11–22.

―――. 2001d. 'Préface a l'edition Japonaise des *Écrits*' in Jacques-Alain Miller (ed.), *Autres écrits*. Paris: Éditions du Seuil, pp. 497–9.

―――. 2005b. *Le Séminaire. Livre XXIII. Le Sinthome, 1975–76* (Jacques-Alain Miller ed.). Paris: Éditions du Seuil.

―――. 2005c. 'Le Triomphe de la Religion' in *Le Triomphe de la Religion précédé de Discours aux Catholiques* (Jacques-Alain Miller ed.). Paris: Éditions du Seuil, pp. 69–102.

―――. 2005d. *Mon Enseignement*. Paris: Éditions du Seuil.

―――. 2006. *Le Séminaire. Livre XVI. D'un Autre à l'autre, 1968–69* (Jacques-Alain Miller ed.). Paris: Éditions du Seuil.

————. 2007. *Le Séminaire. Livre XVIII. D'un discours qui ne serait pas du semblant, 1971* (Jacques-Alain Miller ed.). Paris: Éditions du Seuil.

OGASAWARA, Shin'ya. 1999b. 'L'instance de la lettre dans l'inconscient japonais'. *Ornicar? Digital* 67 (19 January): 1–4.

The Littoral Condition of the Letter[1]

JEAN-PIERRE KLOTZ

It cannot be other than interesting to speak of Jacques Lacan in Calcutta, which is such a new place, but also a very ancient one. India is an ancient country becoming a new one. It has had a type of division that could be relevant to our references in this conference and to the references of psychoanalysis as that which looks both for ancient ways—it was established by Sigmund Freud concerning an ancient point—and for new ones; and to try and find old references in the new and untrodden ways, with there existing, always, a gap between the new and the old. The gap between the new and the old or between the immediate and the historical began that way and continues to exist. At the centre of the analytical experience also is something at the level of a gap that has to be permanently surrounded, to be approached, but which remains until the end of analysis (and it is the end to establish it) impossible to name as such. This central hole or gap is absolutely fundamental.

This is a conference on literature, which is not my speciality, for as a clinician, I read only because I like literature and hence, I am not very learned on philosophical culture or the arts. However, I understand certain aspects of culture since psychoanalysis with Lacan obliges me to not only travel all over the world, but also to undertake many journeys in culture, in knowledge and round knowledge to always find and grasp the limits of what we try to enter into. Since our enterprises are interesting but limited, we try to find the limit and to see how, in their plurality, the limits are arranged one with the other. That is significant at the level of culture—that is, at the level of literature—

---

1 I have transcribed the essay from a video recording of the lecture with the assistance of Sukhaloka Mukerjee and edited the transcription—Ed.

for psychoanalysis. And the title of this conference—'From Literature to Litu-raterre' is based on that point.

'Lituraterre' (written in 1971; here 2001b), written for a literary journal, is a rather difficult text. Lacan, though interested in literature, was rather cautious about not *illustrating* psychoanalysis with literature. He stated at the beginning of 'Lituraterre' that psychoanalysis has nothing to say about literature and can in no way improve literary criticism. Psychoanalysis has in common with literature, as well as with other disciplines and other domains of culture, only what is at its limit. Beyond its limit is something impossible to say (as I have said often), as the state of psychoanalysis too indicates (see Lacan 2001b: 11–12). Perhaps not known to everyone, nor understood, is that the aim of psychoanalysis is not to provide any ultimate, marvellous, perfect speech. It is not at the level of something that can be said but of the impossible to say. We speak regularly in an analysis for years together, during the sessions, during years on papers, on conferences, on courses, seminars, etc. But we speak also, always, to encounter an 'impossible to say', to surround it, to approach it and to try to demonstrate as well as possible, this dimension of the impossible. That is the reason Lacan begins with an address to literature in 'Lituraterre', saying that he has to learn from literature; and that he hopes writers and people who deal with literature would interest themselves in psychoanalysis because literature has in common with it this something which is impossible to say (ibid.). I will summarize or interpret what was being said at that moment about the special state of psychoanalysis.

What is interesting at that level and in what is surrounded or approached by the text is precisely the problem of the letter. Usually in literature, the criticisms or the [theoretical] approaches are attempts to find meaning in general. And the approach to the exploration of the dimension of meaning—even if it goes on to the beyond of the meaning—can be through the limits of the meaning. Lacan makes an allusion in the essay to avant-garde literature. Avant-garde literature, especially in France, developed from the tradition largely inaugurated by James Joyce, who had lived for quite a lot of time in France, and had written much while there. Joyce became an important reference of Lacan afterwards, beginning at the moment of 'Lituraterre'. In avant-garde literature, the dimension of meaning is pushed to its limit and beyond, to put a new accent on what usually produces meaning. With Joyce and with avant-garde literature, a point is reached where meaning does not function any more. We read the text but do not understand it and we are also obliged to look at the text itself—its functions, translatability, etc. It became increasingly difficult, nearly impossible, to translate Joyce's works, *Finnegans Wake* (1939) becoming the summit of intranslatability. The translation became a new text—a mixture of several languages as a sort of a permanent witticism, a permanent play on words and a mixing of words culminating in the production of an unreadable text.

From this tradition, avant-garde literature became, increasingly, a literature of non-meaning in which accent was put on the letter; that is, on the writing as material. It was also the big book of materialism and focusing on the letter as *material* can interest psychoanalysis or, rather, it can make writers of avant-garde literature interested in psychoanalysis. Because in psychoanalysis, and especially in it, as Lacan reiterated Freud at the beginning of his teaching, the accent was first on the language, on the unconscious as structured by the signifier, by the signifying chain; and for the first 10 years of his teachings, the problem of writing, of the letter, of what is written, of what is said was not so different. Even some well-known psychoanalysts—pupils of Lacan—as Serge Leclaire, for example, said in the 1950s, 'Where Lacan speaks of the signifier, I speak of the letter. For me it is the same.' He did not repeat it afterwards, but at the moment when Lacan moved in his teaching—in the 1970s and the 1980s, that is to say the moment until his death and the dissolution of the École Freudienne de Paris—many of the pupils and analysands of Serge Leclaire followed a way different from the Lacanian way towards the real, towards the impossible to say. Lack of distinction between the letter and the signifier can produce confusion after a time, which prevents us from grasping something of the specificity of the real, which became, increasingly, Lacan's aim approximately after *The Seminar of Jacques Lacan. Book XI. The Four Fundamental Concepts of Psychoanalysis, 1964* (1973; here 1981) after the excommunication, when the *objet petit a* emigrated in *Le Séminaire. Livre X. L'angoisse, 1962–63* (Anxiety; 2004) from the imaginary to the real in the analytical experience.

It was precisely in *L'angoisse* and *The Four Fundamental Concepts of Psychoanalysis* that Lacan restated the set of his teaching through what he called the four fundamental concepts: the unconscious, repetition, transference and the drive, and to stress that transference and repetition are not the same—as it is classically the case in Freud—because of the difference between what is said and a precise account of how it is said, to explain it simplistically. The difference between transference and repetition is also a movement that induces a specificity of the real state of the experience which would be developed by Lacan until the end of his teaching. It is possible to say that in Lacan's teaching the first 10 years comprise the return to Freud and the second part, following *The Four Fundamental Concepts of Psychoanalysis*, comprises the return to himself; that is, a return to what he had said before. He deconstructs what he had built before, to sum it up quickly so as to fix the period. It is very important to read Lacan periodically. Jacques-Alain Miller has taught us to read Lacan against Lacan, to point out that Lacan first said something and then said something completely to the contrary 10 years later, of course in a different context. We can demonstrate with the texts of Lacan how he contradicted later what he had demonstrated at the beginning, which can be difficult at times to sustain, although interesting. But why? Because it is *with* contradiction, *with* something that cannot be unified together that one can surround and approach what Lacan called the real as an impossible to say. A hole is introduced between the two signifiers of the elementary couple of signifiers, S1 and S2, and this hole is the only unary place, which is symbolized by the unary trait—however, that does not make the unary trait a real as such. There is a shifting aside, which is written by the bar, but it is not the same. The only thing that can be the same in the analytic experience is the real, which, when called, named or situated, is always in terms of the lie—that is the reason we say that it is only possible to lie about the real. And what we have to look for is less the dimension of truth and more of the real as approached as a lie, knowing the dimension of the lie with which one is speaking of it. We can try to write it in scientific ways—the relationship between psychoanalysis and science is a very old and important question.

Lacan always maintained that psychoanalysis is *not* a science. It is not, nor can it be, scientific. This is established on the grounds that it would not exist without science. The ambition of Freud was, of course, to make it a science; its ethics are not completely different from that of science, *but* psychoanalysis takes an account of what science leaves aside—to summarize it, the subjective dimension. The subject is what has to be foreclosed, ejected, rejected to establish science, because the results of science have to be established universally, for everyone—they must be valid for every case. If they are scientific they are universal, whereas subjectivity, with its singularity, is a protestation of an individual against universality. And to take an account of the subject of the unconscious at the beginning—the subject which is the stake of psychoanalysis—one has to take an account of the singular, not only of the universal. There is no universal truth of the subject. There is only, for every subject, the possibility of separating the singular and the universal, and of working with one's singularity as discovered by oneself through the analytical experience. That is the main reason it is necessary to do an analysis to become a psychoanalyst—to elect, to choose the singularity in one's subjectivity. It is not a criticism of science, nor does it put aside or go against science, but is *alongside* science. It is *with* science and has a link—what I call a link of separation—with it.

And the problem of the link of separation—the paradox of a link which is a separation and not a unification—is present in the famous formula 'There is no sexual relationship' as the paradigm of the real in Lacan. It is also present elsewhere in Lacan, especially at the level of what we have to consider a letter, and what Lacan tries to depict through the apologue of Siberia, the streaming of water in the Siberian rivers and the shore that he saw from the plane, the littoral. And the littoral is precisely something that is at the level of a link, of separation and in the way of an apologue. The paradox of the letter, defined that way, is that the letter is what Lacan called *le ravinement*—the furrowing of the signified—but what is important here is not to believe that the letter is primary. It is, rather, an *effect* of the language even if *as* a letter it does not belong to that language. It is something that is separated from what belongs to the signifying battery, from the dimension of language. The letter can be read, but what is read is never the whole letter. This is what allows several readings of the letter, because no reading is ever equivalent to the letter as such. And the letter is the effect, or in terms of the discourse of Lacan, it is produced by the signifier and the language as something that is outside but not without.

Lacan calls the littoral condition the shore, which is, in the apologue, the shore of the rivers in the emptiness of the Siberian plain, where there is no litter, because it is completely without any asperity, without anything. Only rivers can be seen there, and what one sees of the rivers are the shores. And this shore (because if the river has no shore it is not a river, it is an ocean, and an ocean is as empty as the Siberian plain—it is necessary therefore to see a shore) is a litter! The shore, as such, is a littoral. But what is interesting is that 'littoral' is close to 'literal'—that is, to letter, litter and so on—and that it is a litter, something that is cutting. The apologue insists on the clouds and the plain between the clouds that he could see from the flight. It is owing to the shore, the edge, that one sees, from an aeroplane, that there is a river—the streaming, *ruissellement*—a river on the plain. And what *is* the letter there as such? It is not the water of the river that demonstrates it, but the two shores without the water. The letter as such, as a real, is what is hollowed by the water. This hollow is the interesting point: the materiality, the real of the letter is a gap, it is a hollow which can be filled by meaning, signifiers, language and all the phenomena of language. But what remains when one takes away the water is the hollowed letter. The hollow is an aspect of the littoral—when there is a littoral there is always something that is hollowed.

Lacan's definition of the *objet petit a* as real—from the lost object of Freud—sees it as the lost *objet petit a* as present here and now. It is not a natural object. It is produced by the fact of the speaking being. Nevertheless, it is an object which he sometimes tried to locate as hollowed. Although the *objet petit a* has no middle and form, is infinite and both nothing and more than everything, it always presents itself as an object with a gap or hollow in the middle, which allows us to say that it can be the frame—the only positive frame of the experience but also of the identity for any speaking being, every identity being different from the name given to the man who speaks of it.

This littoral condition is encrypted in the text of 'Lituraterre'—even if it is present as an apologue with many literary effects and written in a way that is very difficult to follow or to translate well. But 'Lituraterre' is also the beginning of Lacan's later teachings, which is one of the reasons Jacques-Alain Miller had put this text at the head of *Autres écrits* (2001a), like the 1956 'Seminar on "The Purloined Letter"' (1957; here 2006) had been placed at the beginning of *Écrits* (1966), non-chronologically, although the other texts in *Écrits*, barring another, were arranged in chronological order. The texts comprising *Autres écrits* are all treated in the same way except 'Lituraterre', which has the same status of a sort of apologue, like the 'Seminar on "The Purloined Letter"', for the later Lacan, who is no more the Lacan of the signifier but of the *objet petit a*. And the Lacan of the *objet petit a* becomes more and more prominent after 'Lituraterre', developing on the Borromean knot in *Le Séminaire. Livre XXIII. Le Sinthome, 1975–76* (2005) and in all the seminars following it—which Jacques-Alain Miller called the very last of Lacan's teachings.

What is important in this is the symptomatization of the experience, or of analysis. To be in a relation with the real, even if it is a relation of separation with the *objet petit a*, every subject has a tool: his or her subjectivity, which is the symptom. The main discovery of psychoanalysis is the way to transform the symptom that is dysfunctioning—the symptom one is suffering from or that is being used in a wrong way for enjoyment, *jouir* (which is the occasion of the demand for or beginning of psychoanalysis)—to the symptom as functioning.

I once wrote about the therapy of the symptom and the therapy through the symptom. The only therapeutic thing in psychoanalysis is the symptom; and in analysis, the symptom one is suffering from can be transformed into a symptom one is no longer suffering from. Suffering does not characterize the symptom, which is not a trouble one has to eradicate. This knowledge is very important in the present moment when we are required to struggle—and our ambition is worldwide—against the eradication of the symptom, against people who want only the universal goodness. The only possibility to support the goodness, to deal with the goodness or the badness, is the symptom; that is to say the singular way one can take with one's partner, with others, with the world and especially with oneself, firstly with oneself, as a symptom. The symptom links a subject with a dimension of the real—it was inaugurated by Lacan with the definition of the *objet petit a* through the letter and it became increasingly functional—which he called the *sinthome*, the real part of the symptom that cannot be interpreted and is situated at the main point of one's intimacy as well as outside. Lacan tried to define with the term *extimacy* (*extimité*)—it indicates that which is both inside the being and, in an imaginary way, is without any limit with what is most outside—that there is no limit at the level of the innermost and the most external; that it is a separation which is present inside as well as outside, between an individual, what he or she imaginarizes as himself or herself, and the outside. That characterizes the real for Lacan, as well as this littoral condition defined for the letter in the real outside but not without the structure—the language structure, the unconscious, the subject—without which there is no subject. Without jouissance, without the body, without all that is imaginarized everywhere, the subject remains a pure abstraction.

That it is not a border or a frontier characterizes the littoral condition—or it is a border that is *inside*—because a border or a frontier is indicated by an Other, by a way of discourse. It is a symbolic trait. A true border separates two equivalent domains, for example, a border between two countries. A littoral is different. No one has traced on a map the limit of the shore of the river. There are two shores but only one limit, which is the letter as a hollow, as I have explained about the river. But the littoral, the shore, separates the earth or ground from the water and it can move according to the season. It is not a line that is written, if it is possible to put it like that, rather, it is a letter that is written; that is, it is on the limit of what is written. Lacan taught many important things using it, such as, how he was impressed by his trip to Japan at that moment, the calligraphy, how he was also impressed by his discussions with François Cheng—the Cheng references were very important to Lacan but not discussed seriously that often. An English translation of the article by Éric Laurent on the Tao of psychoanalysts has been included in *The Later Lacan* (2007), where Laurent insists on them—one does not usually speak or think about the Japanese and the Chinese references—and compares the Hindu emptiness with the Chinese emptiness. He finds in the former something that still belongs to the occidental way, which puts on stage the 'being', which is not the case in the Tao of the Chinese. And we are on the shore, on the littoral of that here! We are not so far from China.

References

ENGLISH SOURCES

JOYCE, James. 1964 [1939]. *Finnegans Wake* (3rd edn). London: Faber and Faber.

LACAN, Jacques. 1981. *The Seminar of Jacques Lacan. Book XI. The Four Fundamental Concepts of Psychoanalysis, 1964* (Jacques-Alain Miller ed., Alan Sheridan trans.) New York and London: W. W. Norton.

———. 2006. 'Seminar on "The Purloined Letter"' in *Écrits: The First Complete Edition in English* (Bruce Fink trans.). New York and London: W. W. Norton, pp. 6–48.

LAURENT, Éric. 2007. 'The Purloined Letter and the Tao of the Psychoanalyst' (Marc Thomas and Victoria Woollard trans) in Véronique Voruz and Bogdan Wolf (eds), *The Later Lacan: An Introduction*. Albany: State University of New York Press, pp. 25–52.

FRENCH SOURCES

LACAN, Jacques. 1957. 'Le séminaire sur "La Lettre Volée"'. *La Psychanalyse* 2: 1–44. Subsequently published in *Écrits* (1966).

———. 1966. *Écrits*. Paris: Éditions du Seuil.

———. 1973. *Le Séminaire. Livre XI. Les quatre concepts fondamentaeux de la psychanalyse, 1964*. Paris: Éditions du Seuil.

———. 2001a. Jacques-Alain Miller (ed.), *Autres écrits*. Paris: Éditions du Seuil.

———. 2001b. 'Lituraterre' in Jacques-Alain Miller (ed.), *Autres écrits*. Paris: Éditions du Seuil, pp. 11–22.

———. 2004. *Le Séminaire. Livre X. L'angoisse, 1962–63* (Jacques-Alain Miller ed.). Paris: Éditions du Seuil.

———. 2005. *Le Séminaire. Livre XXIII. Le Sinthome, 1975–76* (Jacques-Alain Miller ed.). Paris: Éditions du Seuil.

PART 4

And Beyond

Cogito *in Literature: Descartes with Beckett*

SLAVOJ ŽIŽEK

One can understand James Joyce, with all the obscenities that permeate his writings, as the ultimate Catholic author, 'the greatest visionary of the dark underground of Catholicism, an underground embodying a pure transgression, but one which is nevertheless a profoundly Catholic transgression' (Altizer 1997: 101). Catholicism is legalistic and, as Paul knew it so well, the Law generates its own transgression. Consequently, the staging of the obscene underground of the Law, the travesty of the Black Mass—or, in Joyce's case, the elevation of Here Comes Everybody into Christ who has to die in order to be reborn as the eternal Life-Goddess from Molly Bloom to Anna Livia Plurabelle—is the supreme Catholic act.

This achievement of Joyce simultaneously signals his limit, the limit that pushed Samuel Beckett to break with him. If there ever was a kenotic writer, the writer of the utter self-emptying of subjectivity, of its reduction to a minimal difference, it is Beckett. We touch the Lacanian real when we subtract from a symbolic field all the wealth of its differences, reducing it to a minimum of antagonism. Jacques Lacan sometimes gets seduced by the rhizomatic wealth of language beyond—or, rather, beneath—the formal structure that sustains it. It is in this sense that, in the last decade of his teaching, he deployed the notion of *lalangue* which stands for language as the space of illicit pleasures that defy normativity, of the chaotic multitude of homonymies, wordplays, 'irregular' metaphoric links and resonances. Productive as this notion is, one should be aware of its limitations. Many commentators have noted that Lacan's last great literary reading, that of Joyce to whom his late seminar, *Le Séminaire. Livre XXIII. Le Sinthome, 1975–76* (2005) is dedicated, is not at the level of his previous great readings, such as of *Hamlet, Antigone* or the Coufontaine trilogy. There is effectively something fake in Lacan's fascination with late Joyce, with *Finnegans Wake* (1939; here 1964) as the latest version of the literary *Gesamtkunstwerk* with its endless wealth of *lalangue* in which not only the gap between singular languages but the very gap between linguistic meaning and jouissance seems overcome and the rhizome-like *jouis-sens* (enjoyment-in-meaning: enjoy-meant) proliferates in all directions. The true counterpart to Joyce is, of course, Beckett. After his early period, in which he, more or less, wrote some variations on Joyce, the 'true' Beckett constituted himself through a true ethical act, a cut, a rejection of the Joycean wealth of enjoy-meant, and the ascetic turn towards a minimal difference, towards a minimalization, subtraction, of the narrative content and of language itself—this line is most clearly discernible in his masterpiece, the trilogy *Molloy* (1951; here 2009b), *Malone Dies* (1951; here 2009a), *The Unnamable* (1953; here 2006a). Beckett is effectively the literary counterpart of Anton Webern: both are authors of extreme modernist minimalism, who extract a minimal difference from a wealth of material. Beckett's *Texts for Nothing* (1955; here 2006b) is the fourth term that supplements this trilogy. Beckett himself referred to *Texts* as 'the grisly afterbirth of *L'innomable* [*The Unnamable*]', the 'attempt to get out of the attitude of disintegration [of the trilogy] but it failed' (quoted in Boulter 2004: 333). The obvious link is that the first line of the first text—'Suddenly, no, at last, long last, I couldn't any more' (Beckett 2006b: 295)—echoes the famous last line of *The Unnamable*—'you must go on, I can't go on, I'll go on' (Beckett 2006a: 407)—which is a true Kantian imperative, a paraphrase of Kant's '*Du kannst, denn du sollst*' ('You can, because you must'). The voice of conscience tells me: 'You must go on.' I reply, referring to my weakness: 'I can't go on.' But as a Kantian, I know that this excuse does not count, so I nonetheless decide that 'I'll go on,' doing the impossible. Is then *The Unnamable* by Beckett not to be opposed to Alain Badiou's version of it? In Beckett, *l'innomable* is not the excessive multitude that cannot be forced thoroughly, but the ethical fidelity itself, its persistence embodied in the 'undead' partial object. Since, for Beckett, what 'must go on' is ultimately writing itself, the Lacanian version of the last line of *The Unnamable* is something that *ne cesse pas a s'ecrire* (doesn't cease writing itself)—a necessity, the first term in the logical square which also comprises impossibility (that which *ne cesse pas a ne pas s'ecrire*, does not cease not writing itself), possibility (that which *cesse a s'ecrire*, ceases to write itself) and contingency (that which *cesse a ne pas s'ecrire*, ceases not writing itself) (see Lacan 1998: p. 94, pp. 144–5). It is crucial to note here the clear distinction between possibility and contingency: while possibility is the opposite of necessity, contingency is the opposite of impossibility. In Badiou's terms of the attitudes towards a Truth-Event, necessity stands for the fidelity to truth, impossibility for a situation with no truth, possibility for the possibility of a truth-procedure to exhaust its potentials and to stop, and contingency for the beginning of a new truth-procedure.

So what does *Texts* register, a possibility or a contingency? A possibility, definitely—a possibility to 'cease writing', to betray fidelity, to cease going on. The failure of *Texts* is thus good news: the texts in it are failed betrayals, failed attempts to get rid of the ethical injunction. They are a comical supplement to the great triad—an opportunist's attempt to squeeze out of the call of duty, somewhat like Søren Kierkegaard's 'sickness unto death', where a mortal human being attempts to escape immortality, its unbearable ethical burden or injunction. In this sense, they are an optimistic work—their message is that one cannot but 'go on' as an immortal bodiless drive, as a subject without subjectivity: 'No, no souls, or bodies, or birth, or life, or death, you've got to go on without any of that junk' (Beckett 2006b: 329).

Jonathan Boulter thus got it right—on condition that we strictly distinguish between subject and subjectivity. The whole of the trilogy can be read as a gradual getting rid of subjectivity, a gradual reduction of subjectivity to the minimum of a subject without subjectivity—a subject which is no longer a person, whose objective correlative is no longer a body (organism) but only a partial object (organ), a subject of 'drive' which is Sigmund Freud's name for immortal persistence, 'going on'. Such a subject is a living dead—still alive, going on, persisting, but dead or deprived of body—undead. *Texts* is a comical attempt to re-subjectivize this subject—among other things, to provide him with a body, to travel back the road from Cheshire-Cat's smile to its full body. Boulter is right to correct Alfred Álvarez who claimed that *Texts* is written in the same 'breathless, bodiless style' as *The Unnamable*:[1]

---

1 See Álvarez (1973).

One of the things the reader notices about *Texts* from its outset is that the body (of the narrator/narrated) has made an uncanny return from its near obliteration in *The Unnamable*: the narrator of *The Unnamable* is disembodied (it may be that 'he' is merely a brain in an urn). At the very least, the issue of subjectivity is a complex one in the trilogy because the relation between voice (of narrator) and body (of narrator) is continually called into question. We may in fact argue that the trilogy in toto is about the dismantling of the physical body: in *Molloy*, the body is ambulatory but weakening; in *Malone Dies* the body is on its last legs, immobile and dying; in *The Unnamable* the physical body may in fact have ceased to be an issue as the narrator floats between personalities and subject positions. All of which is to indicate that in *Texts*, the body has made [. . .] an unexpected comeback (Boulter 2004: 333–4).

The subject without subjectivity, this 'living dead', is also timeless when we reach this point: 'time has turned into space and there will be no more time till I get out of here' (Beckett 2006b: 320)—note how Beckett repeats here Richard Wagner's precise formula of the sacred space of the Grail's castle from *Parsifal*: 'Here time becomes space', which Claude Lévi-Strauss quotes as the most succinct definition of myth. The subject we thus reach, a subject without subjectivity,

cannot maintain with any certainty that the experiences he describes are in fact his own; we have a narrating subject who cannot discern if his voice is his own; we have a subject who cannot tell if he has a body; and most crucially, we have a subject who has no sense of personal history, no memory. We have, in short, a subject whose ontology denies the viability of mourning and trauma, yet who seems to display the viability of mourning and trauma (Boulter 2004: 337).

Is this subject, deprived of all substantial content, not the subject—in the exact sense of the word and at its most radical—of the Cartesian *cogito*? Boulter's idea is that, for Freud, trauma presupposes a subject to whom it happens and who then tries to narrativize it, to come to terms with it, in the process of mourning. In the case of the Beckettian narrator, on the contrary,

there is no hope of establishing a link between his own present condition and the trauma that is its precondition. Instead of having a
story seemingly given to him unawares—as in the case of the victim
of trauma who cannot recognize his past as his own—the Beckettian
narrator can only hope (without hope [. . .]) for a story that will re-
connect his present atemporal [. . .] condition to his past (ibid.: 341).

This is the division of the subject at its most radical: the subject is reduced
to $ (the barred subject), even its innermost self-experience is taken away from
it. This is how one should understand Lacan's claim that the subject is always
'decentred'—his point is not that my subjective experience is regulated by objective unconscious mechanisms that are decentred with regard to my self-
experience and, as such, beyond my control (a point asserted by every materi-
alist), but, rather, something much more unsettling: I am deprived of even my
most intimate subjective experience, the way things 'really seem to me', that
of the fundamental fantasy that constitutes and guarantees the core of my
being, since I can never consciously experience it and assume it. One should
counter Boulter's question, 'To what extent do trauma and mourning require
a subject?' (ibid.: 337), with a more radical one: to what extent does (the very
emergence of) a subject require trauma and mourning?[2] The primordial
trauma, the trauma constitutive of the subject, is the very gap that bars the
subject from *its own* 'inner life'.

This inner and constitutive link between trauma and subject is the topic
of Beckett's late masterpiece *Not I*, a twenty-minute dramatic monologue written in 1972 (here 2003a), an exercise in theatric minimalism. There are no
'persons' here, intersubjectivity is reduced to its most elementary skeleton, that
of the speaker —who is not a person, but a partial object, a faceless Mouth
speaking—and Auditor, a witness of the monologue who says nothing throughout the play. All that Auditor does is repeat four times, in 'a gesture of helpless
compassion', the simple gesture of sideways raising of arms from sides and
their falling back (Beckett 2003a: 375). (Asked if Auditor is Death or a guardian
angel, Beckett had shrugged his shoulders, lifted his arms and let them fall to

---

2 See Butler (1997).

his sides, leaving the ambiguity intact—repeating the very gesture of Auditor).
Beckett himself pointed to the similarities between *Not I* and *The Unnamable*
with its clamouring voice longing for silence, circular narrative and concern
about avoiding the first person pronoun: 'I shall not say I again, ever again'
(Beckett 2006a: 348). Along these lines, one could agree with Vivian Mercier's
suggestion that, gender aside, *Not I* is a kind of dramatization of *The Unnamable*—one should only add that, in the former, we get the talking partial coupled or supplemented with a minimal figure of the big Other.[3]

Beckettology, of course, did its job in discovering the empirical sources
of the play's imagery. Beckett himself provided the clue for the 'old hag', but
also emphasized the ultimate irrelevance of this reference: 'I knew that woman
in Ireland. I knew who she was—not "she" specifically, one single woman, but
there were so many of those old crones, stumbling down the lanes, in the
ditches, besides the hedgerows' (quoted in Bair 1978: 622). But, replying to the
queries, Beckett said: 'I no more know where she is or why thus than she does.
All I know is in the text. "She" is purely a stage entity, part of a stage image
and purveyor of a stage text. The rest is [Henrik] Ibsen' (Ackerley and Gontarski
2006: 411). As to the reduction of the body of the speaker to a partial organ
(mouth), in a letter from 30 April 1974, Beckett gave a hint that the visual image
of this mouth was 'suggested by [Michelangelo] Caravaggio's "Decollation of St
John in Valetta Cathedral"' (Brater 1975: 50). As for the figure of Auditor, it
was inspired by the image of a djellaba-clad 'intense listener' seen from a cafe
in Tunis (see Knowlson 1996: 589)—Beckett was in North Africa from February
to March 1972. James Knowlson conjectured that this 'figure coalesced with
[Beckett's] sharp memories of the Caravaggio painting' which shows 'an old
woman standing to Salome's left. She observes the decapitation with horror,
covering her ears rather than her eyes'—a gesture that Beckett added in the
1978 Paris production (see Knowlson and Pilling 1979: 195).

Much more interesting are Beckett's uncertainties and oscillation with regard to Auditor, who is generally played by a male, although the sex is not
specified in the text: when Beckett came to be involved in staging the play, he

---

3 See Mercier (1977).

found that he was unable to place Auditor in a stage position that pleased him and, consequently, allowed the character to be omitted from those productions. However, he chose not to cut the character from the published script and left the decision whether or not to use the character in a production to the discretion of individual producers. He wrote to two American directors in 1986: 'He is very difficult to stage (light–position) and may well be of more harm than good. For me the play needs him but I can do without him. I have never seen him function effectively' (Beckett 1999: xxiv). In the 1978 Paris production, he did reinstate the character but from then on abandoned the image, concluding that it was perhaps 'an error of the creative imagination' (quoted in Knowlson 1996: 617). From the Lacanian perspective, it is easy to locate the source of this trouble: Auditor gives body to the big Other, the Third, the ideal addressee-witness, the place of truth which receives and thereby authenticates the speaker's message. The problem is how to visualize or materialize this structural place as a figure on the imaginary of the stage: while every play—or even speech—needs it, every concrete figuration of it is, by definition, inadequate; that is, it cannot ever 'function effectively' on stage.

The basic constellation of the play is thus the dialogue between the subject and the big Other, where the couple is reduced to its barest minimum: the Other is a silent, impotent witness which fails in its effort to serve as the medium of the truth of what is said, and the speaking subject itself is deprived of its dignified status of 'person' and reduced to a partial object. And, consequently, since meaning is generated only by means of the detour of the speaker's word through a consistent big Other, the speech itself ultimately functions at a pre-semantic level, as a series of explosions of libidinal intensities. At the premiere in Lincoln Centre in 1972, Mouth was played by Jessica Tandy, who had played the mother in Alfred Hitchcock's *Birds* (1963). Debating the piece with her, Beckett demanded that it should 'work on the nerves of the audience, not its intellect' (quoted in Brater 1974: 200), and advised Tandy to consider the mouth 'an organ of emission, without intellect' (quoted in Bair 1978: 625).[4]

---

4 In the 2000 filmed production, directed by Neil Jordan, we see Julianne Moore come into view, sit down and then the light hit her mouth—this makes us aware that a young woman as opposed to an 'old hag' is portraying the protagonist.

Where does this bring us with regard to the standard postmodern critique of dialogue, which emphasizes its origin in Plato, where there is always the one who knows—even if only that he knows nothing—questioning the other—who pretends to know—to admit he knows nothing. There is, thus, always a basic asymmetry in a dialogue—and does this asymmetry not break out openly in Plato's later dialogues, where we are no longer dealing with Socratic irony, but with one person talking all the time, with his partner merely interrupting him from time to time with 'So it is, by Zeus!', 'How cannot it be so?', etc. It is easy for a postmodern deconstructionist to show the violent streak even in Jürgen Habermas' theory of communicative action which stresses the symmetry of the partners in a dialogue: this symmetry is grounded in the respect of all parts for the rules of rational argumentation but are these rules really as neutral as they claim to be? Once we accept this and bring it to its radical conclusion— the rejection of the very notion of objective truth as oppressive, as an instrument of domination—the postmodern path to what Jean-François Lyotard called *le différend* is open: in an authentic dialogue, there is no pressure to reach a final reconciliation or accord, but merely to reconcile ourselves with the irreducible difference of perspectives which cannot be subordinated to any encompassing universality. Or as Richard Rorty put it: the fundamental right of each of us is the right to tell his/her story of life-experience, especially of pain, humiliation and suffering. But, again, it is clear that people not only speak from different perspectives, but that these differences are grounded in different positions of power and domination—what does the right to free dialogue mean when, if one approaches certain topics, one risks everything, even his/her life; or, worse, when one's complaints are not even rejected but dismissed with a cynical smile? The left-liberal position here is that one should especially emphasize the voices that are usually not heard, are ignored, oppressed or even prohibited within the predominant field—sexual and religious minorities, etc. But is this not all too abstract-formal? The true problem is: how are we to create conditions for a truly egalitarian dialogue? Is this really possible to do in a 'dialogic'/respectful way, or is some kind of counter-violence needed? Furthermore, is the notion of (not naively 'objective', but) universal truth, really, by definition a tool of oppression and domination? Say, in the Germany of 1940, the Jewish story of suffering was not simply an oppressed minority's view to be heard, but a complaint whose truth was in a way universal; that is, which rendered visible what was wrong in the entire social situation.

Is there a way out of this conundrum? What about the dialogic scene of the psychoanalytic session, which weirdly inverts the coordinates of the late-Platonic dialogue? As in the latter case, here also one—the patient—talks almost all the time, while the other only occasionally interrupts him with an intervention which is more of a diacritical order, asserting the proper scansion of what was told. And, as we know from Freud's theory, here, the analyst is not the one who already knows the truth and only wisely leads the patient to discover it himself/herself: the analyst precisely does not know it, his knowledge is the illusion of transference which had to fall at the end of the treatment.

And with regard to this dynamic of the psychoanalytic process cannot Beckett's play be said to begin where the analytic process ends? The big Other is no longer 'supposed to know' anything, there is no transference and, consequently, 'subjective destitution' has already taken place. But does this mean that, since we are already at the end, there is no inner dynamic, no radical shift possible anymore—which would nicely account for the appearance of the circular movement in this play (and others) by Beckett? A closer look at the content of the play's narrative in this 20-minute-long monologue, seems to confirm this diagnostic: Mouth utters at a ferocious pace a logorrhoea of fragmented, jumbled sentences which obliquely tells the story of a woman of about 70 who, having been abandoned by her parents after a premature birth, has lived a loveless, mechanical existence and who appears to have suffered an unspecified traumatic experience. The woman has been virtually mute since childhood apart from occasional winter outbursts part of one of which comprises the text we hear. She relates four incidents from her life: lying face down in the grass on a field in April; standing in a supermarket; sitting on a 'mound in Croker's Acre' (a real place in Ireland near Leopardstown racecourse) and 'that time at court'. Each of the last three incidents somehow relates to the repressed first 'scene' which has been likened to an epiphany—whatever happened to her in that field in April was the trigger for her to begin talking. Her initial reaction to this paralyzing event is to assume that she is being punished by God. Strangely, however, this punishment involves no suffering—she feels no pain, as in life she felt no pleasure. She cannot think why she might be punished but accepts that God does not need a 'particular reason' for what He does. She thinks she has something to tell though she does not know what but believes that if she goes over the events of her life for long enough she will stumble upon that thing for which she needs to seek forgiveness. However, a kind of abstract, non-linguistic and continuous buzzing in her skull always intervenes whenever she gets too close to the core of her traumatic experience.

The first axiom of interpreting this piece is not to reduce it to its superficial cyclical nature—endless repetitions and variations of the same fragments, unable to focus on the heart of the matter—imitating the confused mumbling of the 'old hag' who is too senile to get to the point: a close reading makes it clear that, just before the play's end, there is a crucial break, a decision, a shift in the mode of subjectivity. This shift is signalled by a crucial detail: in the last (fifth) moment of pause, Auditor does not intervene with his mute gesture—his 'helpless compassion' has lost its ground. Here are all five moments of pause:

1 'all that early April morning light . . . and she found herself in the— . . . what? . . . who? . . . no! . . . she! . . . [*Pause and movement 1*.]' (Beckett 2003a: 376–7)

2 'the buzzing? . . . yes . . . all dead still but for the buzzing . . . when suddenly she realized . . . words were— . . . what? . . . who? . . . no! . . . she! . . . [*Pause and movement 2*.]' (ibid.: 378–9)

3 'something she— . . . something she had to— . . . what? . . . who? . . . no! . . . she! . . . [*Pause and movement 3*.]' (ibid.: 381)

4 'all right . . . nothing she could tell . . . nothing she could think . . . nothing she— . . . what? . . . who? . . . no! . . . she! . . . [*Pause and movement 4*.]' (ibid.: 382)

5 'keep on . . . not knowing what . . . what she was— . . . what? . . . who? . . . no! . . . she! . . . SHE! . . . [*Pause.*] . . . what she was trying . . . what to try . . . no matter . . . keep on . . . [*Curtain starts down*.]' (ibid.: 383)

Note the three crucial changes here:

1 The standard, always identical series of words which precedes the pause with Auditor's movement of helpless compassion (' . . . what?

. . . who? . . . no! . . . she! . . .') is here supplemented by a repeated capitalized 'SHE'.

2   The pause is without Auditor's movement.

3   It is not followed by the same kind of confused rambling as in the previous four cases, but by the variation of the paradigmatic Beckettian ethical motto of perseverance ('no matter . . . keep on').

Consequently, the key to the entire piece is provided by the way we read this shift: does it signal a simple—or not-so-simple—gesture by means of which the speaker (Mouth) finally fully assumes her subjectivity, asserts herself as 'SHE'—or, rather, as I—overcoming the blockage indicated by the buzzing in her head? In other words, in so far as the play's title comes from Mouth's repeated insistence that the events she describes or alludes to did not happen to her and that therefore, she cannot assume them in first person singular, does the fifth pause indicate the negation of the play's title, the transformation of 'not I' into 'I'? Or is there a convincing alternative to this traditional-humanist reading which so obviously runs counter to the entire spirit of Beckett's universe? Yes, on condition that we also radically abandon the predominant cliché about Beckett as the author of the 'theatre of the absurd', preaching the abandonment of every metaphysical sense (Godot will never arrive), and the resignation to the endless circular self-reproduction of meaningless rituals (the nonsense rhymes in *Waiting for Godot*, 1952; here 2003b).

This, of course, in no way implies that we should counter the 'theatre of the absurd' reading of Beckett with its no-less-simplified, upbeat mirror-image; perhaps, a parallel with 'Der Laienmann', the song that concludes Schubert's *Winterreise* (1828), may be of some help here. 'Der Laienmann' displays a tension between form and message. Its message appears to be utter despair of the abandoned lover who has finally lost all hope, even the very ability to mourn and despair, and identifies with the man on the street automatically playing his music machine. However, as many perspicuous commentators have noticed, this last song can also be read as the sign of forthcoming redemption: while all other songs present the hero's inward brooding, here, for the first time, the hero turns outwards and establishes a minimal contact, an emphatic identification, with another human being, although this identification is with another desperate loser who has even lost his ability to mourn and is reduced to performing blind mechanic gestures. Does something similar not take place with the final shift of *Not I*? At the level of content, this shift can be read as the ultimate failure both of the speaker (Mouth) and the big Other (Auditor): when Mouth loses even the minimal thread of the content and is reduced to the min-imalist injunction that the meaningless babble must go on ('keep on . . . not knowing what'), Auditor despairs and renounces even the empty gesture of helpless compassion. There is, however, the opposite reading that imposes itself at the level of *form*: Mouth emerges as a pure (form of) subject, deprived of all substantial content (depth of 'personality'), and, pending on this reduction, the Other is also de-psychologized, reduced to an empty receiver, deprived of all affective content ('compassion', etc.). To play with Kazimir Malevich's terms, we reach the zero level of communication—the subtitle of the play's finale could have been 'white noise on the black background of immobile silence'.

In what, then, does this shift consist? We should approach it via its coun-terpart, the traumatic 'x' round which Mouth's logorrhea circulates. So what happened to 'her' on the field in April? Was the traumatic experience that she underwent there a brutal rape? Asked about it, Beckett unambiguously rejected such a reading: 'How could you think of such a thing! No, no, not at all—it wasn't that at all' (quoted in Bair 1978: 624). We should not take this statement as a tongue-in-cheek admission, but literally—that fateful April, while 'wander-ing in a field . . . looking aimlessly for cowslips', the woman suffered some kind of collapse, possibly even her death—definitely not a real-life event, but an un-bearably intense 'inner experience' close to what C. S. Lewis described in his *Surprised by Joy* (1955; here 1977) as the moment of his religious choice. What makes this description so irresistibly delicious is the author's matter-of-fact 'English' sceptical style, far from usual pathetic narratives of mystical rapture: Lewis refers to the experience as the 'odd thing'; he mentions its common lo-cation—'I was going up Headington Hill on the top of a bus'—the qualifications like 'in a sense', 'what now appears', 'or, if you like', 'you could argue that [. . .] but I am more inclined to think [. . .]', 'perhaps', 'I rather disliked the feeling':

> The odd thing was that before God closed in on me, I was in fact of-
> fered what now appears a moment of wholly free choice. In a sense.

I was going up Headington Hill on the top of a bus. Without words and (I think) almost without images, a fact about myself was somehow presented to me. I became aware that I was holding something at bay, or shutting something out. Or, if you like, that I was wearing some stiff clothing, like corsets, or even a suit of armor, as if I were a lobster. I felt myself being, there and then, given a free choice. I could open the door or keep it shut; I could unbuckle the armor or keep it on. Neither choice was presented as a duty; no threat or promise was attached to either, though I knew that to open the door or to take off the corset meant the incalculable. The choice appeared to be momentous but it was also strangely unemotional. I was moved by no desires or fears. In a sense I was not moved by anything. I chose to open, to unbuckle, to loosen the rein. I say, 'I chose,' yet it did not really seem possible to do the opposite. On the other hand, I was aware of no motives. You could argue that I was not a free agent, but I am more inclined to think this came nearer to being a perfectly free act than most that I have ever done. Necessity may not be the opposite of freedom, and perhaps a man is most free when, instead of producing motives, he could only say, 'I am what I do.' Then came the repercussion on the imaginative level. I felt as if I were a man of snow at long last beginning to melt. The melting was starting in my back— drip-drip and presently trickle-trickle. I rather disliked the feeling (1977: 174–5).

In a way, everything is here: the decision is purely formal, ultimately a decision to decide, without a clear awareness of *what* the subject decides about; it is a non-psychological act, unemotional, with no motives, desires or fears; it is incalculable, not the outcome of strategic argumentation; it is a totally free act, although one could not do it otherwise. It is only *afterwards* that this pure act is 'subjectivized', translated into a (rather unpleasant) psychological experience. From the Lacanian standpoint, there is only one aspect which is potentially problematic in Lewis' formulation: the traumatic event (encounter of the real, exposure to the 'minimal difference') has nothing to do with the mystical suspension of ties that bind us to ordinary reality, with attaining the bliss of radical indifference in which life or death and other worldly distinctions no longer matter, in which subject and object, thought and act, fully coincide. To put it in mystical terms, the Lacanian act is, rather, the exact opposite of this 'return to innocence': the original sin itself, the abyssal *disturbance* of the primaeval peace, the primordial 'pathological' choice of the unconditional attachment to some singular object (like falling in love with a singular person which, thereafter, matters to us more than everything else). And does something like *this* not take place on the grass in *Not I*? The *sinful* character of the trauma is indicated by the fact that the speaker feels punished by God. What then happens in the final shift of the play is that the speaker *accepts* the trauma in its meaninglessness, ceases to search for its meaning, restores its extra-symbolic dignity, as it were, thereby getting rid of the entire topic of sin and punishment. This is why Auditor no longer reacts with the gesture of impotent compassion: there is no longer despair in Mouth's voice, the standard Beckettian formula of the drive's persistence is asserted ('no matter . . . keep on'), God is only now truly love, not the loved or loving one, but Love itself, that which makes things going. Even after all content is lost, at this point of absolute reduction, the Galilean conclusion imposes itself: *eppur si muove* (and yet it moves).

This, however, in no way means that the trauma is finally subjectivized, that the speaker is now no longer 'not I' but 'SHE', a full subject finally able to assume her Word. Something much more uncanny happens here: Mouth is only now fully destituted as subject—at the moment of the fifth pause, the subject who speaks fully assumes its identity with Mouth as a partial object. What happens here is structurally similar to one of the most disturbing TV episodes of *Alfred Hitchcock Presents*, 'The Glass Eye' (the opening episode of the third year). Jessica Tandy (again, the actress who was the original Mouth!) plays here a lone woman who falls for a handsome ventriloquist, Max Collodi (a reference to the author of *The Adventures of Pinocchio*, 1883). Having gathered courage to approach him alone in his quarters, she declares her love for him and steps forward to embrace him, only to find that she is holding in her hands a wooden dummy's head. After she withdraws in horror, the 'dummy' stands up and pulls off its mask and we see the face of a sad older dwarf who begins to jump desperately on the table, asking the woman to go away—the ventriloquist is in fact the dummy, while the hideous dummy is the actual ventriloquist. Is this not the perfect rendering of 'organ without bodies'? It is the detachable 'dead' organ, the partial object, which is effectively alive, and whose dead puppet the 'real' person is: the 'real' person is merely alive, a survival machine, a 'human animal', while the apparently 'dead' supplement is the focus of excessive Life.

References

ENGLISH SOURCES

ACKERLEY, Chris J. and Stanley E. Gontarski (eds). 2006. *The Faber Companion to Samuel Beckett*. London: Faber and Faber.

ALTIZER, Thomas Jonathan Jackson. 1997. *The Contemporary Jesus*. London: State University of New York Press.

ÁLVAREZ, Alfred. 1973. *Samuel Beckett*. New York: Viking.

BAIR, Deirdre. 1978. *Samuel Beckett: A Biography*. San Diego, CA: Harcourt Brace Jovanovich.

BECKETT, Samuel. 1999. *The Theatrical Notebooks of Samuel Beckett: The Shorter Plays*, VOL. 4 (Stanley E. Gontarski ed.). London: Faber and Faber; New York: Grove Press.

——2003a. *Not I* in *The Complete Dramatic Works*. London: Faber and Faber, pp. 373–83.

——. 2003b. *Waiting for Godot* in *The Complete Dramatic Works*. Reprint, London: Faber and Faber, pp. 7–88.

——. 2006a. *The Unnamable* in *The Grove Centenary Editions of the Complete Works of Samuel Beckett*, VOL. 2 (Paul Auster ed.). New York: Grove Press, pp. 283–407.

——. 2006b. *Texts for Nothing* in *The Grove Centenary Editions of the Complete Works of Samuel Beckett*, VOL. 4 (Paul Auster ed.). New York: Grove, pp. 295–339.

————. 2009a. *Malone Dies* in *Three Novels: Molloy, Malone Dies, The Unnamable*. New York: Grove Press, pp. 171–282.

————. 2009b. *Molloy* in *Three Novels: Molloy, Malone Dies, The Unnamable*. New York: Grove Press, pp. 3–170.

BOULTER, Jonathan. 2004. 'Does Mourning Require a Subject? Samuel Beckett's *Texts for Nothing*' *Modern Fiction Studies* 50(2) (Summer): 332–50.

BRATER, Enoch. 1974. 'The *I* in Beckett's *Not I*'. *Twentieth Century Literature* 20(3) (July): 189–200.

————. 1975. 'Dada, Surrealism and the Genesis of *Not I*'. *Modern Drama* 18(1): 49–59.

BUTLER, Judith. 1997. *The Psychic Life of Power: Theories in Subjection*. Stanford and CA: Stanford University Press.

JOYCE, James. 1964 [1939]. *Finnegans Wake* (3rd edn). London: Faber and Faber.

KNOWLSON, James. 1996. *Damned to Fame: The Life of Samuel Beckett*. London: Bloomsbury.

KNOWLSON, James and John Pilling. 1979. *Frescoes of the Skull*. London: John Calder.

LACAN, Jacques. 1998. *The Seminar of Jacques Lacan. Book XX. Encore: On Feminine Sexuality, The Limits of Love and Knowledge, 1972–73* (Jacques-Alain Miller ed., Bruce Fink trans.). New York and London: W. W. Norton.

LEWIS, C. S. 1977 [1955]. *Surprised by Joy: The Shape of my Early Life*. London: Fontana Books.

MERCIER, Vivian. 1977. *Beckett/Beckett*. New York: Oxford University Press.

FRENCH SOURCES

LACAN, Jacques. 1975. *Le Séminaire. Livre XX. Encore, 1972–73* (Jacques-Alain Miller ed.). Paris: Éditions du Seuil.

————. 2005. *Le Séminaire. Livre XXIII. Le Sinthome, 1975–76* (Jacques-Alain Miller ed.). Paris: Éditions du Seuil.

The Practice of the Letter and Topological Structure

ELLIE RAGLAND

'[E]very truth has the *structure* of fiction,' Jacques Lacan argued in *The Seminar of Jacques Lacan. Book VII. The Ethics of Psychoanalysis, 1959–60* (1986; here 1992: 12; my emphasis). The name he gave to that which joins the structure of truth—that is the real—to fiction is *lettre*, playing on the link in French between *l'être* (being) and *lettre* (letter). By examining what Lacan meant by the word structure in this axiom, we can arrive at a clearer understanding of what he meant by the *lettre*. My larger goal in this essay is to make sense of the Lacanian idea that the topological function of the letter is characteristic of literary language. In Marguerite Duras's fiction, *Moderato Cantabile* (1958; here 1965), one sees at work Lacan's theory that being is connected to language in a point of overlap between the real and a void that dwells *in* language itself.

In '*Mathemes*: Topology in the Teaching of Lacan'[1] (1986; here 2004), Jacques-Alain Miller points out that the concept of topological 'structure' was present in Lacan's writings as early as 1953, in 'The Discourse of Rome',[2] although this concept did not take on its fuller topological sense until *The Seminar of Jacques Lacan. Book XX. Encore: On Feminine Sexuality, The Limits of Love and Knowledge, 1972–73* (1975b; here 1998) (Miller 2004: 30). In 'The Discourse of Rome', Lacan was concerned with the mortal sense of being which shows the presence of death in the subject of the symbolic. He said that such a presence occupies a central place in speech, thereby marking the underlying structure

---

1 It has been translated into English by Mahlon Stoutz from the Spanish version of the essay which was published as 'La Topología en la Enseñanza de Lacan' in Jacques-Alain Miller (ed.), *Matemas*. VOL. 1 (Buenos Aires: Manantial, 1986), pp. 79–104.

2 It is the popular name for the essay 'The Function and Field of Speech and Language in Psychoanalysis' (1956; here 2006a). See Lacan (2006a).—Ed.

of the absence (*ab-sens*) that sustains it. And, Lacan argued, this mortal sense is both central to the exercise of speech and external to language, reminding us that in 1953, he was seeking to distinguish 'speech' (*la parole* of *le langage*) from the system of rules and conventions of grammar that Ferdinand de Saussure had called *la langue* (see Ragland-Sullivan 1986: 209).

Although Lacan used topology to formalize and explicate psychoanalysis in the third period of his teaching from approximately 1974 to 1981, he never developed his early reference to a peripheral and central exteriority represented by the three-dimensional form of a torus. Miller takes the challenge up, after Lacan's death, in his course 'Extimité' (1985–86). In 'Topology in the Teaching of Lacan', Miller points out the following paradox in Lacan's idea advanced in 1953: An empty centre with a conduit to speech has come into play. And this empty centre is neither myth nor metaphor. Indeed, in this concept, the subject lies *beyond* metaphor, in a point that is both central to language and external to it: *extimate*. And Lacan's concern was to find the structure that this spatial disposition implies (see Miller 2004: 32).

I shall advance this hypothesis: that which is central to spoken (or written) language and at the same time external to it, even *organizatory* of it, is the partial drives—the oral, the anal, the scopic, the invocatory—that Lacan first denoted in his formula for drive: ($\$<>D$). Miller points out in 'Extimité' that the drives bring a piece of the real into play, a *Stück* (piece) left over from early experience of the loss of objects that first *cause* desire (see Miller 1985–86). In other words, language cannot entirely cover remnants of the real that first place discontinuity or disturbance in language, indeed, as the cause round which it is organized. In this context, the Lacanian real is not that of his first period of teaching, that which was full and impossible to symbolize. It is, rather, the *re*-pressed part of jouissance that returns as the real to disrupt the would-be consistencies that language expresses.[3] And the real returns most particularly round the objects-*cause*-of-desire and the partial drives to which they give rise.

---

3 For an in-depth discussion of the many meanings of jouissance in Lacan's teaching, see my introduction entitled 'Traduttore emendatore: The Role of Translation and Interpretation in Exegetical Renewal' in Ragland (1995: 1–15).

No fiction writer does a better job than Duras of unveiling the fact that language is organized round the (partial) object, be it the gaze, the voice or the *rien* (nothing). In order to understand the organizing role of the voice in *Moderato Cantabile* which exemplifies the idea that the *objet petit a* denotes a piece of the real in the symbolic, indeed, serves as the signifier of the hole in the Other (Ø) (see Miller 1985–86), it will help to consider the logic behind Lacan's idea that the *objet petit a* refers to an empty place in words and images. The void at the heart of language makes the *a* oscillate in a temporal jouissance movement of anticipation and retroaction from which the affective lines of space devolve as lines on whose fictional bed language lies. Literary fiction might even be described as the particular use of language that aims for an un-mediated relation to the lure object that one hopes will fill the lack signified by desire, once and for all.

I would suggest that Duras exposes to oneself the gap in the heart of the fiction of one's identity. Her characters use a minimalist language to hollow out a meaning of the object(s) that they desire, be it the vacuum *in* love glimpsed behind Maria's drinking manzanillas in Duras's 1960 novel *10:30 on a Summer Night* or the desperate hope for a new love and a new life that subtends the conversations between Chauvin and Anne in *Moderato Cantabile*. Such minimalist language brings the partial objects-*cause*-of-desire into stark focus.

Miller locates the function of language that tries to penetrate to the inner meaning of an object on the slope of the quest for love where seeking a repetition of a lost sense of 'Oneness' is locatable within the sphere of the *extimate* object. Lacan described it in *The Ethics of Psychoanalysis* as that which is closest to you, the most interior, while at the same time being exterior.

Showing how mathematical topology functions to make a logical set or ensemble of Lacanian concepts of the knot, metaphor, structure and the real, Miller writes that with the addition of 'the Thing' (*la Chose*), Lacan brought the three-dimensionality of space into play within language (Miller 2004: 28–48). In the third period of his teaching, Lacan used the Borromean unit to depict the ordering of the real of the drives, the symbolic field of language and the imaginary sphere of images and identifications, showing the three-dimensionality of the interlinkings of mind and body at play in words. *Passage* from one order to another marks the associative meanings of memory, then, as words (the symbolic) seek to represent the real of the body (the imaginary) at a distance from the *objet petit a* whose primary referent is *la chose primordiale* (the primordial thing) of the real.

In a typical *knotting* together of these orders, a subject's thought and memory are constituted as the signifying chain(s) of a Borromean necklace. Words and images function to fill a central gap in the heart of the illusion one has of *being* a whole identity (see Miller 1985–86: 25). Rather, the first signifier on which human beings depend in relation to others is the 'call' made to the other. And the drives, always partial, circle round this structure, born of the illusion that there is a plenitude to be found at the site of an imaginary object. And, language, fictional or not, is structurally materialized for difference in terms of distance from 'the Thing'—the sexual thing, the jouissance thing— which always harkens back to primordial memories surrounding the inexistence of an essential feminine being. The mother, then, is at the centre of the real precisely because the objects that represent her metonymically are lost again and again in primary experiences of the drive.

In this context, literary fiction is most at home on the slope of metonymy referring to the libido that language paradoxically cancels out and it, in turn, seeks to compensate with all the devices we call creative. In his 1965 'Hommage fait à Marguerite Duras, du ravissement de Lol V. Stein' (Homage to Marguerite Duras on the Ravishing of Lol V. Stein; here 1985), Lacan writes for the first time that the unconscious touches on the practice of the letter (1985: 9).

Although Lacan only ever used literature as an instrument to clarify the phenomena of analytic experience, Miller claims in his course, 'Les réponses du réel' (The Responses of Real, 1983–84), that he understands why literary discourses have taken up Lacan, whereas scientific ones have not (1983–84: Session dated 21 March 1984). Not only does literature concern written language and interpretation, it bears more importantly on the *cause* of psychoanalysis which might be described as the desire to end suffering by re-finding a (supposedly) lost object. And the medium of such an endeavour is the *lettre*. And, the voice implies a feminine—harkening back to the primordial mother—a 'beyond' in the language of the symbolic—a 'beyond' the 'law' of the group.

Literary critics have always intuited that literary language contains a 'sense' outside itself, a *sens jouis*. In 1974, Lacan added the category of *jouis-sens* to his two other jouissances, calling it the *jouis-sens* of unconscious meaning produced in the overlap between the symbolic and imaginary orders at the point where a word or an image fails to function as a limit to anxiety. In such encounters, an impasse that presentifies the real appears as a 'sense' outside meaning, a *j'ouis sens* (Lacan 1975a). Such moments, moreover, bring the temporal sense of lack into language, demonstrating that the real has remained unsymbolized precisely because it contains traumatic knowledge. However, in Lacanian thought, traumatic knowledge is not some mysterious primitive scene but an interior knowledge that breaks up the imaginary consistencies to which a given subject clings in a willed *méconnaissance* (misrecognition). This notion of the real as retrievable in bits and pieces is characteristic of Lacan's third period of teaching.

But even in the 1950s, Lacan had already stressed the *creative* function of the 'word' over the phenomenological concern with being. Lacan argued that language digs out hollows within itself and thus allows its own prior effects to return transformed by metaphor and metonymy, and as a function of anticipation and retroaction, rather than as a Derridean overlapping interplay between sound and meaning. The *lettre* reveals that we do not 'have' being, not even as some kind of 'becoming' in the Heideggerean sense of a fluid process of accumulated narcissism or *Dasein* (being-there). In this period, when Lacan used Martin Heidegger's concepts of *logos* and *aletheia* and spoke of his intellectual debt to Heidegger as a work of 'didactical borrowing', he, nonetheless, situated his *hontology*—that is, we are creatures of shame, not of essential being—in a conjuncture between language and its 'function and field'.

Thus, in the 1950s, Lacan had already begun to leave Heidegger behind. Rather, the Lacanian letter attaches the body to language via desire and the objects it motivates one to seek. But more is implied in this idea than simply the function of lack. Because the subject itself is a function of lack ($) — that is, unconscious knowledge is lacking to conscious thought—subjectivity is structured in a ceaseless movement of fantasy, conscious and unconscious, whose goal is to attain some imaginary *objet petit a*.

The paradox Lacanian analysis uncovers—a paradox long familiar to authors—is that individuals seek objects that do not wish their good. Or, if they seek objects meant to rescue them from their own sometimes-desperate life scenarios, the final hurdle to such change yields but one more set of barriers. In Duras's *Moderato Cantabile*, the words that pass between Anne Desbaresdes and Chauvin seek to construct a love castle via the invocatory drive. The voice in its unique proximity to nostalgia, unveils a link to jouissance that owes little to the sounds of words uttered. Through the hollows that Anne and Chauvin's voices dig out in language, one can 'hear' a love castle built by idealizing imaginary traits. But it can only ever be made of sand. And such dark literary realism says far more about how life actually functions—given Lacan's equation of the repetitions beyond the pleasure principle with the negative jouissance of the death drive—than do all the would-be happy-endings dreamt up by the Grimm brothers.

For the Ur-objects that *cause* desire can never correspond to the imaginary objects of fantasy ($\$<>a$) sought at the level of lure object. In so far as the ideal ego first constitutes itself round these primary objects, it is a symbolic order constellation, not an imaginary one. Thus 'happy endings' lie within the sphere of some felicitous combination of symbolic-order traits with the real, not within Anne and Chauvin's imaginary 'Let's pretend.' Yet, subjects respond to the imaginary as if some prefabricated paradigmatic Good could respond to the concrete particularities out of which each unconscious is made. Text by text, literature celebrates the impasses in the imaginary, the failures arising out of it. One might describe literary language as that which best represents a 'beyond' in the imaginary that covers the 'grimace of the real' as it enters the symbolic.

In 'Hommage', Lacan opened the door to a new theory of the relation between art and the artist as well as text and reader, by stating that the unconscious is not entirely repressed or hidden, but operates and *functions* in the text: 'That the practice of the letter converges with the usage of the unconscious is the only thing to which I will attest in rendering homage to her' (1985: 9; my translation). In the first period of his teaching in 'The Instance of the Letter in the Unconscious or Reason since Freud' (1957; here 2006b), Lacan described the *lettre* as a *place* where being resides between the unconscious and language, calling the *lettre* a localized signifier that one can recognize as language converging with the unconscious. He said that it is to be inserted somewhere between the written and speech—'It will be half-way between the two' (2006b: 412).

By the time he rendered his homage to Duras, 'the practice of the letter' had converged with the unconscious. That is, Lacan implies here that the un-symbolized real finds a *place* within language. The unconscious is no longer free-floating or unborn, as Lacan depicted it in *The Seminar of Jacques Lacan. Book XI. Four Fundamental Concepts of Psychoanalysis, 1964* (1973; here 1981) but has concrete *ex-sistence*. Although Lacan's first theory of the letter in 'The In-stance of the Letter' is the one adapted by post-structuralists, his second theory, enunciated in praise of Duras, is commensurate with the final phase of his teaching which valorizes his efforts over decades to tie the real to language in a truth-functional way.

In this same period, Lacan argued in *The Ethics of Psychoanalysis* that the truth of the 'creative function of the word' lies in its trying to unveil the thing that both causes and paradoxically traumatizes desire (1992: 119–20). Heideg-ger took 'the Thing', which adds the dimension of space to the knot, metaphor, structure and the real, to be the void of nothingness encircled by the clay of the Heideggerean vase. Using this metaphor, Heidegger based his concept of reality on a positive material or 'fact'.

Lacan went in the opposite direction from Heidegger, to the point of link-ing the void created by the loss of things to the 'practice of the letter'. This void is not nothingness, however, but inscribes itself as the *jouis-sens* of a unary (identificatory) trait derived from the earliest experiences of object loss which return as the *a*-ffects of nostalgia, mourning, anxiety and so on. Language tries to re-present these identificatory traits that come from each of the three orders. The hole in the symbolic creates a point of conjuncture between the word or image and the real that gives us a strange paradox. The word exists qua word precisely because there is no vase of being encircling or framing a void. There is, rather, a concrete place of inner emptiness that continually seeks to be filled.

In *The Ethics of Psychoanalysis*, Lacan suggested that fiction *resides* in the curve of the real, in the *place* of the void. The drives circle round the void, at the edges of the cut that first constituted the void as a positivity, while language seeks to represent this *savoir* (knowledge) that Lacan called a *connaissance* (imaginary knowledge) (1992: 12). To better understand how the real belongs most particularly to the realm of literary language, one might contrast Lacan's view of the function of language to Heidegger's non-dialectisizable 'x' which is supported by nothing except another process. Lacan's remoulding of the concept of the process by which one knows uncovers *fantasy* as the subjective knowledge that gives objective consistency to the knowledge we call reality.

In 'De la nature des semblants' (The Nature of the Semblance)—his course of 1991–92—Miller rereads Lacan's writing in 1957 to explain what Lacan had not formulated then: that language also introduces the real in the form of sexuality (Miller 1991–92: Session dated 25 May 1992). In 1957, Lacan was concerned with *structure*—the unconscious has the structure of language and the 'letter' includes the two slopes of the signifier required to make meaning dialectical; that is, metaphor and metonymy—not with the content of the unconscious. One could say, Miller continues, that Lacan placed the real outside at that date, even to the point of foreclosing it to the benefit of the symbolic. Yet, the real returns anyway at the point where the symbolic fails—as both fiction and life reveal.

In *Moderato Cantabile*, the love affair built up between Anne and Chauvin reveals the yearning for what lies beyond the prison walls of each one's symbolic. But the 'grimace of the real' in this piece of fiction does not lie so much in the stories told. They are commonplace. She is wealthy and lonely and desperate. He is a worker who aspires to a more glamorous life, a more glamorous love. Duras's genius lies in capturing in a minimalist fashion, the sorrow of yearning expressed in the invocatory drive. In so far as this Lacanian drive is absolute, non-dialectical, she shows the point at which the *jouis-sens* of meaning is a ciphering of the unconscious that seeks to ascertain what death weight the voice carries of the real (see Ragland 1995: 190). And although the real denotes a foreclosure of a certain dimension of the reality of unconscious truth, this dimension emerges anyway as the effect Lacan called the 'practice of the letter'.

When the unconscious speaks at the juncture where jouissance bends itself to the signifier, we might refer to that as the practice of the 'letter' in literary art. In 1992, Jacques-Alain Miller referred to the cause he had named in 1987 that gives rise to the moments of joining between jouissance and the signifier that Lacan called the 'letter': 'Sexuality speaks and jouissance bends itself to the signifier and . . . it is articulated' (quoted in John Miller 1987: 41). Miller's formulation allows us to put forth a new axiom for literary studies, one that views sexuality in the broader contours that subsume language; that is, as organized by the oral, anal, scopic and invocatory partial drives.

Miller's thesis supports Lacan's reconceptualization of sublimation away from the Freudian conflation of sublimation with repression. Miller said in New York City in 1987 that artists and writers try to make the *objet petit a* appear. They try to pierce appearance to the 'essence', in the medieval realist sense, of objects and language. Or, in Lacanian terms, they seek to embrace the cause of jouissance itself, but come up against the paradox that jouissance cannot speak itself. Meanwhile, the truth of the real speaks loudly behind the images and words it shadows.

But how does one grasp the logic of such a statement? In the session on 'Les noms-du-père et le semblant' (The Names-of-the-Father and the Semblance), dated 25 May 1992, as part of his course 'De la nature des semblants', Miller maintains that Lacan first explained the real in trying to conceptualize truth. While the early Lacan taught that the real cannot be heeded except in a point of fiction, this point of *fixion* is precisely what the later Lacan called a *semblant* which can never be destroyed. This indestructible truth—the *objet petit a* as a piece of condensed jouissance, an irreducible kernel of *non sens* meaning (meaning that is seemingly outside sense)—marks the consistency of the truth of the neurotic. That is, neurotics do not lie as well as their less-suffering fellow-creatures who live comfortably enough in the social masquerade that covers the non-rapport of the sexual difference. While I would not argue, by extending this proposition, that literary artists are perforce neurotic, psychotic or perverse, I would suggest that those more normatively adapted to the social masquerade are entertained by art, rather than being producers of art themselves.

But how does one ascertain unconscious truth in a literary text? If fiction resides in the curve of the real, it is the logic of the *objet petit a* that would offer an answer to what Lacan's axiom means. And even though the trajectory between the drive for satisfaction and the object-*cause*-of-desire can be far apart, the characteristic of the *objet petit a* is to always be there, veiled, hidden, wearing different linguistic guises. Lacanian psychoanalyst Anny Cordié writes that this object lies behind Sigmund Freud's contention that the unconscious does not know contradiction. As the inverse of language, the *objet petit a* escapes the principle of contradiction, for it cannot be negativized (Cordié 1993: 205). That is, the jouissance which circles round the *objet petit a* resides between the lines of a fictional weave. This idea gives us the possibility of an entirely new perspective on the power of metonymy within language. It is generally said that metaphor holds sway over metonymy, jouissance (or libido) serving only as a limit or a hint or *soupçon* (suspicion) of something real beyond language. But Miller points to this: the something outside is, nonetheless, *inside* language. Put another way, metaphor can only work by substitution because it is supported by a metonymic corporal real that hooks language indissolubly to the body and the drives, a corporal real that sexualizes language round the oral, anal, scopic and invocatory drives.

'It is not to his consciousness that the subject is condemned,' Lacan writes in *Le Séminaire. Livre X. L'angoisse, 1962–63* (Anxiety; 2004), 'but to his body, which in many ways resists actualizing the division of the subject' (2004: 53; my translation). So ordinary language steps carefully lest it stir up the jouissance of sexuality, death or anxiety. We find most radically, he argues, that there is no metalanguage, only concrete language trying to negotiate desire and avoid the traumata constituted in the wake of the sexual divide.

In 'Hommage', Lacan affirms, as did Freud before him, that the artist has always preceded other thinkers in ascertaining how the human is constituted. Duras does not depend on the force of an argument, the pathos of a story, the beauty of imagery or the skill of a rhetorical device to advance her narrative, but shapes words carefully, sparingly, round the force of one (partial) drive. Duras's *Whole Days in the Trees* (1954; here 1984) is organized round the Lacanian *rien* (nothing), one of the Ur-objects-*cause*-of-desire he named in 'The Subversion of the Subject and the Dialectic of Desire in the Freudian Unconscious' (speech delivered in 1960 and first published in 1966; here 2006c), as the breast, the faeces, the voice, the gaze, the (imaginary) phallus, the phoneme, the urinary flow and the nothing (2006c: 692–3).

Having suggested earlier that *Moderato Cantabile* is organized round the voice, the invocatory drive, round the 'call' made to the other which Lacan considers the first signifier—the infant's call made to the Other—I would add that even the title, which means 'moderately singing', implies the voice, rather than the piano lesson at issue. Against the meaningless, colourless backdrop of an anonymous cafe, Anne and Chauvin's desolate voices take on a vacuous sonority whose impact is metonymic, on the slope of the sense of language that transcends its more obvious significations.

In *L'angoisse*, Lacan described the voice as a sonority coming from elsewhere, as something not commensurable with language: 'A voice does not assimilate itself, but *incorporates* itself' (2004: 320; my translation). Linking the drives to the signifier, incorporation will always include a piece of the real, a truth concerning a fragment of jouissance knowledge that has not been symbolized by language. And 'that gives the voice a function that models our own emptiness,' Lacan writes (ibid.: 318; my translation). In other words, the voice is connected to the hole at the centre of knowledge in a way that the other drives are not. Not the least of the functions of the voice is to calm anxiety, and, indeed, the way in which one is spoken to or spoken of can confer momentary joy or devastation, unwittingly revealing that 'being' is a complex illusion, not an essence or an innate system.

At the level of the narrative line of *Moderato Cantabile*, upper-class Anne Desbaresdes, married for 10 years to the director of Import Export and Seaboard Iron Founderies, meets by accident a labourer named Chauvin. Their first meeting, at the scene of a crime of passion, sets the stage for their involvement. Retiring to a nearby cafe, they ponder the question of how a person could kill someone they love. Soon they meet every week when Anne brings her son to a piano lesson. As they speak haltingly of love, we can hear jouissance between the lines, at the point where the two disembodied voices seek to create a new life out of their dead desires.

We learn that Anne has no voice in her private world of wealth and social glamour. She is the hostess who drinks too much. Chauvin is a poor worker with aspirations of being elevated by a beautiful, wealthy woman such as Anne. One hears a hollowness within their words made of hope coupled with disappointment, resonating with the pain of being. As they invent a space of love beyond isolation, hope grows. But the novel ends with the impossibility of their escaping their old lives. He wants from her what she wants to shed.

At the level where the voice represents Anne and Chauvin as objects of jouissance, rather than as subjects with stories to tell, speech takes on the *extimate* function of being both external and internal, of unveiling an outside on the inside of language and an inside piercing a hole into the surface outside. Miller calls this the point of *extimacy* of this Other of jouissance in relation to which the Other is Other. Put another way, after Lacan dropped the idea of the Name-of-the-Father as being Other, stressing instead on the fictional function of the father, he never succeeded in explaining why there is no Other of the Other, no metalanguage. Miller argues that Lacan could not explain the alterity within the Other because he never understood that it is the repetition of a primary jouissance that individuals seek in the Other (1994–95).

The empty inner space that each character's voice evokes in *Moderato Cantabile* bears on 'the Thing' each one seeks in the other, the sexual attraction serving as the cover over a love quest.

But Anne's questions to Chauvin play on a different register than his to her. She is trying to understand how love between a man and woman dies. The lovers in the first scene, the crime of passion, serve as the basis on which Anne and Chauvin will talk about love right up to the crescendo of his description of how a man quits loving a woman. ' "I'd like you to tell me now how they came not to speak to each other any more", she says. Chauvin knows this waltz by heart, answering: "I don't know. Perhaps through the long silences that grew up between them at night, then at other times, silences they found more and more difficult to overcome." ' (Duras 1965: 86). Anne's response is telling. She hunches her shoulders dejectedly, knowing, probably unconsciously, that if he knows this, she would go through it again with him.

> 'One night they pace back and forth in their rooms, like caged animals, not knowing what's happening to them. They begin to suspect what it is, and are afraid,' she says. 'Nothing can satisfy them any longer.' He says, 'They're overwhelmed by what is happening, they can't talk about it yet. Perhaps it will take months. Months for them to know' (ibid.: 86).

Tired of describing how love dies, Chauvin's interest immediately turns to the interior of Anne's house. What is it like? Whose room lies behind the window on the first floor? A little later, when they meet again, Anne begs Chauvin to tell her if the woman had not wanted her lover to kill her.

> Chauvin went on, in a flat, expressionless voice that she had not heard from him before. 'They lived in an isolated house,' he says, 'I think it was by the sea. It was hot. Before they went there they didn't realize how quickly things would evolve, that after a few days he would keep having to throw her out. It wasn't long before he was forced to drive her away, away from him, from the house. Over and over again.' Anne Desbaresdes stared at that unknown man without recognizing him, like a trapped animal (ibid.: 103).

If literary art can be illuminated by the Lacanian idea that jouissance materializes language, no writer has done more to depict such a functioning of the practice of the letter than Marguerite Duras. And if, as I have already proposed, the particular poignancy of her art comes from her telling stories round the principal objects that cause desire, the ones Lacan called a real Ur-lining of the subject, she gives literary meaning to Lacan's statement in *Encore* that speaking is always a jouissance and that thought is jouissance (Lacan 1998: 70).

Duras's novel might be said to demonstrate Lacan's axiom: 'There is no rapport of sexual Oneness' (ibid.: 50). Between each person and his or her partner lies the absent Other that Lacan calls the *place* of the unconscious. That Anne wants ideal love from Chauvin and that he wants social prestige from her is only one more formula for the myriad versions of the sexual non-rapport. The exquisite conversation between them resonates with the truth of the non-rapport. Intimacy kills the romance in love because each wants something different than what his or her partner wants. One seeks the *extimate* object—the 'more' in her than her—in the partner, hoping to fulfil one's deepest loneliness via another. Yet, the object of fulfilment is not to be had in a relationship, for it is, and has been, since infancy, radically lost. And all the accommodations couples make to this truth cannot completely veil the real of it.

If we think of literary art as a material product, it is not because the practice of the letter links the body to language via phonemes but because jouissance coalesces round the *objet petit a* in language. Any literary text is always on the side of the question, with its unanswered *raison d'être* constituting the field of the literary as itself an enigma. Duras ends her story on a note of despair, at the point where language cannot symbolize or say the beyond in itself. Anne tells Chauvin that she cannot run away with him. ' "I'm frightened," she says. "It is impossible." "I wish you were dead," he replies. "I am," she says' (Duras 1965: 118). The story begins with the actual murder of two lovers and ends with a 'psychic' murder of a love. The cafe owner turns the radio up, too loud for people to overhear their talk. The hope of a new love dies.

The voice actually *falls* out of language in this story. A piece of the real is dropped. Lacan taught that when the *objet petit a* falls out of language, it marks some jouissance effect. But, the fall of an object, in Lacan's teaching, is not on the same level as the flat surface of textual narrative. In 'Hommage', he writes: '[the fact] that the center is not alike on all surfaces, teaches that vision divides itself between the image and the gaze, that the first model of the gaze is the spot from which one derives the radar that offers the cut or cup of the eye to the horizon' (1985: 10; my translation). In other words, vision is divided between the imaginary image and the real of the gaze, which lies outside the imaginary field of vision. The gaze looks at you, Lacan writes, as a *function* of judgment or idealization. And the voice speaks to you from some point beyond its manifest words, decentering you from the apparent stability of being attached to the ground by words.

In April of 1987, Jacques-Alain Miller laid the groundwork for a new orientation in theories of the aesthetic:

> Art does not provide pleasure, but rather jouissance, a satisfaction of unconscious drives. Art is not a product of the unconscious (*pace* Surrealism), but rather that of the most civilizing urge—sublimation— which is popularly confused with repression. For this reason, art can be said to 'respond' to the unconscious. The given art object, which can be equated to the *objet petit a*, lies outside the signifying chain. The precise distinction between art and literature is that literature consists of the effects of such signification while the material specificity of the art object resists these effects (quoted in John Miller 1987: 41).

In life, the subject is framed by a frame that he or she cannot see or hear because denial, repression and semblance cover castration, loss and symbolic holes. Art, on the other hand, takes risks with language that daily conversation cannot. In the sublimation of art, the impossible of impasses peeks through language, straining words and images at threadbare seams. And in its capacity to elicit affective response from others, art, be it visual or literary, attests to the existence of the real in a work. The real can also be found in the respondents to art at the level where it 'ex-sists' as a writing on and of the body. The jouissance effects of the real cluster round the partial drives whose cause is desire.

References

DURAS, Marguerite. 1965. *Moderato Cantabile* in *Four Novels: The Square; Moderato Cantabile; 10:30 on a Summer Night; The Afternoon of Mr. Andesmas* (Richard Seaver trans.). New York: Grove Press, pp. 61–118.

———. 1984. *Whole Days in the Trees* (A. Barrows trans.). London: John Calder.

LACAN, Jacques. 1981. *The Seminar of Jacques Lacan. Book XI. The Four Fundamental Concepts of Psychoanalysis, 1964* (Jacques-Alain Miller ed., Alan Sheridan trans.). New York and London: W. W. Norton.

———. 1992. *The Seminar of Jacques Lacan. Book VII. The Ethics of Psychoanalysis, 1959–60* (Jacques-Alain Miller ed., Dennis Porter trans.). New York and London: W. W. Norton.

———. 1998. *The Seminar of Jacques Lacan. Book XX. Encore: On Feminine Sexuality, The Limits of Love and Knowledge, 1972–73* (Jacques-Alain Miller ed., Bruce Fink trans.). New York and London: W. W. Norton.

———. 2006a. 'The Function and Field of Speech and Language in Psychoanalysis' in *Écrits: The First Complete Edition in English* (Bruce Fink trans.). New York and London: W. W. Norton, pp. 197–268.

———. 2006b. 'The Instance of the Letter in the Unconscious, or Reason since Freud' in *Écrits: The First Complete Edition in English* (Bruce Fink trans.). New York and London: W. W. Norton, pp. 412–41.

————. 2006c. 'The Subversion of the Subject and the Dialectic of Desire in the Freudian Unconscious' in *Écrits: The First Complete Edition in English* (Bruce Fink trans.). New York and London: W. W. Norton, pp. 671–702.

MILLER, Jacques-Alain. 1986. 'La Topología en la Enseñanza de Lacan' in Jacques-Alain Miller (ed.), *Matemas*, VOL. 1. Buenos Aires: Manantial, pp. 79–104.

————. 2004. '*Mathemes*: Topology in the Teaching of Lacan' (Mahlon Stoutz trans.) in Ellie Ragland and Dragan Milovanovic (eds), *Lacan: Topologically Speaking*. New York: Other Press, pp. 28–48.

MILLER, John. 1987. 'Jacques Lacan's Télévision'. *Artscribe International* 66 (November–December): 40–1.

RAGLAND-SULLIVAN, Ellie. 1986. *Jacques Lacan and the Philosophy of Psychoanalysis*. Urbana and Chicago: The University of Illinois Press.

RAGLAND, Ellie. 1995. *Essays on the Pleasures of Death*. New York and London: Routledge.

FRENCH SOURCES

CORDIÉ, Anny. 1993. *Les cancres n'existent pas*. Paris: Éditions du Seuil.

LACAN, Jacques. 1956. 'Fonction et champ de la parole et du langage en psychanalyse'. *La Psychanalyse* 1: 81–166. Subsequently published in *Écrits* (1966).

————. 1957. 'L'Instance de la lettre dans l'inconscient ou la raison depuis Freud'. *La Psychanalyse* 3 (Psychoanalysis and the Sciences of Man): 47–81. Subsequently published in *Écrits* (1966).

————. 1966. 'Subversion du sujet et dialectique du désir l'inconscient Freudienne' in *Écrits*. Paris: Éditions du Seuil.

————. 1973. *Le Séminaire. Livre XI. Les quatre concepts fondamentaux de la psychanalyse, 1964* (Jacques-Alain Miller ed.). Paris: Éditions du Seuil.

————. 1975a. 'La troisième'. *Lettres de l'École freudienne de Paris* 16: 177–203.

————. 1975b. *Le Séminaire. Livre XX. Encore, 1972–73* (Jacques-Alain Miller ed.). Paris: Éditions du Seuil.

————. 1985. 'Hommage fait à Marguerite Duras, du ravissement de Lol V. Stein'. *Ornicar? Bulletin périodique du champ freudien* 34: 7–13.

————. 1986. *Le Séminaire. Livre VII. L'éthique de la psychanalyse* (Jacques-Alain Miller ed.). Paris: Éditions du Seuil.

————. 2004. *Le Séminaire. Livre X. L'angoisse, 1962–63* (Jacques-Alain Miller ed.). Paris: Éditions du Seuil.

MILLER, Jacques-Alain. 1983–84. 'Les réponses du reel'. Unedited course, at the Département de Psychanalyse, Université de Paris VIII, Saint-Denis.

————. 1985–86. 'Extimité'. Unedited course, at the Département de Psychanalyse, Université de Paris VIII, Saint-Denis.

————. 1991–92. 'De la nature des semblants'. Unedited course, at the Département de Psychanalyse, Université de Paris VIII, Saint-Denis.

————. 1994–95. 'Silet'. Unedited course, at the Département de Psychanalyse, Université de Paris VIII, Saint-Denis.

Reading Bhabha, Reading Lacan:
Preliminary Notes on Colonial Anxiety

GAUTAM BASU THAKUR

[T]he moment of political panic, as it is turned into historical narrative, is a movement that breaks down the stereonomy of inside/outside. In doing so it reveals the contingent process of the inside turning into the outside and producing another hybrid site or sign. Lacan calls this kind of inside/out/outside/in space a moment of extimité: a traumatic moment of the 'not there' [. . .] or the indeterminate or the unknowable [. . .] around which symbolic discourse of human history comes to be constituted (Bhabha 1994b: 296).

[T]he first thing to be advanced concerning the structure of anxiety, is something that you always forget in the observations where it reveals itself: fascinated by the content of the mirror, you forget its limits and the fact that anxiety is framed. [. . .] that the horrible, the suspicious, the uncanny [. . .] presents itself through skylights, that it is as framed that there is situated for us the field of anxiety (Lacan 1962–63: Session 6, pp. 65–6).

The first passage typifies the tendentious arguments characterizing much of Homi Bhabha's work on colonialism, especially his essays in *The Location of Culture* (1994). In particular, the passage illustrates what Bart Moore-Gilbert attributes to all of Bhabha's early writings, namely a departure from Edward Said's reading of colonial discourse and colonizer–colonized relationships in *Orientalism* as 'consistent, confident and monologic', and a rearrangement of the colony as a site 'riven by contradictions and anxieties' (Moore-Gilbert 1997:

118). This essay is concerned with the latter; that is, with Bhabha's readings of colonial relationships and imperial discourse as fraught with a constant sense of dislocation and anxiety. Though much has been written on Bhabha's abstruse language and his ideas about ambivalence, stereotype and hybridity, there is hardly any discussion about the important part that the concept of anxiety plays in Bhabha's thinking about colonialism.

Why is it necessary to deliberate the issue of colonial anxiety through Bhabha? The role of anxiety in structuring the colonizer–colonized relationship and in producing psychopathic conditions amongst both have been noted by many, including Frantz Fanon, Alain Grosrichard, Octave Mannoni and, more recently, Henry Kripps and Christopher Lane. Fanon, for example, in *The Wretched of the Earth* (1961; here 2004) remarks how the harsh realities of colonial rule, the indiscriminate torture and execution of natives psychologically affected both the colonizer and the colonized. Similarly, Mannoni has argued that concerns about the native's desire for European women and racial identity haunted the colonizer (1990). Current writings, as Garth L. Green's observations attest, most commonly present colonial anxiety as 'the seemingly constant fear and concern of colonizers with the threat of violence on the part of the colonized' (2002: 813). But Bhabha's perspective is different. He notes in the passage quoted above, and more broadly in his essay 'By Bread Alone' (1994b), that moments of anxiety ('political panic') expose the fragility of the self–Other, inside–outside discourses as binding. He does not say that anxiety surfaces in the experience of the moment itself but, rather, through the act of representation—'the moment [. . .] turned into historical narrative' (1994b: 296). In other words, anxiety is not situated outside the frame of discourse. It emerges paradoxically at the very interstices of imperial *écriture* aimed at designing the catastrophic moment into a discourse of mastery. Therefore, unlike Fanon and Mannoni who situate anxiety in experiences of the other, Bhabha identifies its origin in discourse and in the production of discourse.

By reading Bhabha in cross-reference to Jacques Lacan, I will argue that colonial anxiety is an epiphenomenon of colonial discourse. Anxieties about the colonized are inextricably bound to the very discourses that aim to construct a singular imaginary of the Other abstracted from the plural reality of the other's space and culture. My reading of anxiety vis-à-vis colonial discourse

241

will accentuate how anxiety inhabits the colonial experiential space as a *fundamental signature* affectively reordering colonial relations, practices, imperial representations and ideologies, and the imaginary of the Other. Anxiety, I will note, originates with the founding gesture of colonialism—the lexicalization of the colonized as an Other and the reproduction of the colonizer as a self that is inverse to that Other—the signification of (the colonized as) difference.

This essay is not a critical exposition of either Bhabha or Lacan, and should be read as an exercise in reading, rereading, and/or even misreading both to make some preliminary observations on colonial anxiety. My point of departure is indeed Bhabha, especially the essays 'The Other Question' (1994c) and 'Articulating the Archaic' (1994a), but my reading of Bhabha and Lacan will be selective. In terms of reading Bhabha with Lacan, I will try to accentuate what I consider the key *strophes* in their works in order to arrive at a hypothetical understanding of colonial anxiety.

ANXIETY IN 'THE OTHER QUESTION'

In 'The Other Question' and 'Articulating the Archaic', Bhabha speaks of anxiety from two apparently distinct theoretical perspectives. In the first essay, anxiety is presented as resulting from the disruption of the constitutive metaphors of colonial discourse, most importantly signifiers of difference; whereas in the second, anxiety is shown as surfacing from the limits of discourse, that is, where discourse fails to adequately explain experiences in the colony. The latter, Bhabha writes, is a product of the colonizer's encounter with 'colonial nonsense' (1994a: 177).

How and why are these two types different? 'The Other Question' focuses on two issues: first, the construction of 'fixities' by colonial discourse to consolidate signs of otherness so as to differentiate the self from the Other; and second, the paradoxical nature of the Other thus constructed, since the Other as stereotype escapes the very fixity it propounds, thereby leading to anxious repetitions of Other-ness in discourse (Bhabha 1994c: 94–5). In context of the slippage noted by Bhabha, one can situate anxiety in the fissure arising between discourse as authority and discourse as failing to authorize the Other as authentic. That is to say, anxieties in imperial discourses are bound to the (unsuccessful) epistemic assembling of an Other from the heterogeneous plurality of the colonized masses. The problem lies in univocally describing the variable and heterogeneous cultures, habits and idiosyncrasies of the colonized as singular. The Other as a type, therefore, always remains partially outside the binary logic of colonial discourse.

The best way to support this theoretical extrapolation is to look closely at Bhabha's discussion of the stereotype in the essay. The stereotype as a sign of otherness is fraught with ambivalence that challenges the very ideological premise on which the stereotype is constructed, that is, fixity as the 'sign of cultural/historical/racial difference' (ibid.: 94). As Bhabha explains, the stereotype is 'a form of knowledge and identification that vacillates between what is always "in place", already known, and [yet] something that must be anxiously repeated' (ibid.: 94–5). It is critical to recognize here that the conundrum of colonial discourse—'the essential duplicity of the Asiatic or the bestial sexual license of the African that needs no proof, can never really, in discourse, be proved' (ibid.: 95)—is predicated upon the existence of a gap between representational reality and the reality of the other. Ambivalence, therefore, as 'central to the stereotype' is a product of a representational reality that ignores, denies, represses and/or forecloses the polyphonic reality of the Other by forcing the other into discourse as a stereotype. We can compare this argument with Said's claim that the Orient is 'not simply [an] empirical reality' which can be shaped, exploited and controlled, but a space that must be continually arranged, governed and articulated through a 'battery of desires, repressions, investments, and projections' (Said 1979: 8). But unlike Said who identifies in exercises of Orientalist imagination a conscious effort to maintain the 'regular constellation of ideas' about the Orient against the 'mere [heterogeneous] being' of the Other, Bhabha reads such exercises as symptoms of the impossibility to construct the Orient/Other as monolithic (ibid.: 5). At this point, a detour into Lacan to consider some observations made by him about identity and anxiety in the essay, 'The Mirror Stage as Formative of the *I* Function as Revealed in Psychoanalytic Experience' (1949; here 2006) and, later, in 'The Seminar of Jacques Lacan. Book X. Anxiety, 1962–63' (1962–63), will better explicate the argument made by Bhabha. Lacan writes in the essay:

For the total form of his body [which is the specular image of the infant in the mirror], by which the subject anticipates the maturation
of his power in a mirage, is given to him only as a gestalt. That is, in
an exteriority [by which is united] the I with the statue onto which
man projects himself, the phantoms that dominate him, and the au-
tomaton with which the world of his own making tends to achieve
fruition in an ambiguous relation (2006: 76–7).

There are three critical ideas here: first, the specular image in the mirror
forms the ego or 'I'; second, this process of identification alienates the self qua
its inverse specular image as belonging to the locus of the Other (to be variously understood as not possible without the intervention of the (m)Other's
support, the agency of the *trotte-bébé* etc.) and third, following from the first
two, the division of the child into an ego and a subject. Identity thus formed is
ex-centric and dependent on misrecognition of the small other as the big
Other. 'After the mirror stage,' as Ellie Ragland-Sullivan observes, 'sights,
sounds, words, dicta, and familial and cultural myths add up to the narcissistic
[moi] fixations that sustain the sense of having an identity during adulthood,
even though they were put in place in childhood' (1986: 21).

In 'Anxiety', Lacan returns to the mirror stage argument while detailing
the relation between the subject and *objet petit a* in anxiety.[1] Identifying the *objet
petit a* as defining the radical otherness of the Other, he notes that it allows the
subject to identify the other as Other, the primary care-giver as the (m)Other
and then 'grasp' through the specular form of its own (mis)recognized image
in the 'mirror' the identity of the self as different from the Other. This interior-
ization of what is outside in the Other constitutes the subject as irrevocably
split—the ego or 'I' and the subject of the unconscious that desires that thing
(*objet petit a*) in the Other (Lacan 1962–63: Session 8, p. 90). This process of
identity formation is further elaborated in *The Seminar of Jacques Lacan. Book XI.
The Four Fundamental Concepts of Psychoanalysis, 1964* (1973; here 1981) where
Lacan introduces two critical concepts, namely, alienation and separation, as

1 The concept of *objet petit a* in Lacan evolved in the course of his career. For a discussion on some these developments see Fink (1996; especially chapter 7: 83–97).

central to the formation of the subject. He explains the first in terms of the alienation of the infant from an imaginary relationship with the mother. This is achieved through an identification of the otherness of the (m)Other. Whereas, separation involves the complete severance of the infant from the (m)Other. The *objet petit a* in context of these stages passes from being the signifier of the other's Otherness (that which the (m)Other has and the subject is prohibited from having) to being the fantastic object of the subject's (unconscious) desire.

How does this theoretical map help us in making sense of colonial discourse and the formation of the native as the Other? And, more importantly, how can we make sense of Bhabha's claim about the anxiety provoking instability of the Other-as-stereotype? One way is to read colonial discourse as a symbolic space and differential identities constructed within that symbolic space as imaginary positions. If we agree that colonialism demands a separation between the colonizer and the native, and that it is advocated in discourse by attributing to the native an essential otherness in context of which the self as 'not same' can be defined, then, this metaphorization of the other as Other, or the condensation of the plural colonized culture into a single identifiable component of difference, enacts a forced separation between the colonizer and the colonized that is prone to implosion by virtue of the fact that these imaginative discourses are challenged in the course of the daily interactions between the colonizer and the native. Colonial anxiety, then, is produced at the instance of the forced metaphorization of the colonial space and exists as a nascent fault threatening the collapse of imperial identity. And every time the colonized announces its desire or breaks out of its objectified positions (that is, whenever it *speaks!*), such as in the times of armed anti-colonial resistance, the colonial imaginary breaks round this fault. To repeat a point made earlier: anxieties about the Other, therefore, do not surface from its phenomenological reality, but from the threat posed by a *return* of the reality *repressed* by the discourse that constructs an expunged image of the Other.

Psychoanalytically speaking, anxiety here is over the intrusion of the real into the symbolic order of the subject. It breaks down the subject's phantasmatic relationship with the Other qua the *objet petit a* as the object of desire—which is characterized by Lacan as $(\$<>a)$—and involves a sudden transformation of this imaginary object of fantasy to an object revealing the real to the subject. This argument is in line with Sigmund Freud's thesis on signal or neurotic anxiety in 'Inhibitions, Symptoms, and Anxiety' (1926; here 1959), where he changed the earlier view about anxiety as caused by accumulated libido to claim that anxiety surfaces when a threat of dissolution is felt by the ego. Signal or neurotic anxiety, by definition, sends out signals of danger threatening the ego's imaginary sense of security and oneness or unity. Importantly though, the actual object or objects posing the threat, unlike in realistic anxiety, is or are absent or lacking (ibid.: 165). This theory of anxiety has found commonplace acceptance in academic and philosophical discussion—anxiety is caused by the realization of a lack, both at the phenomenological level and at the level of the ego. However, as Richard Boothby observes, in spite of sincere attempts at defining the particular nature of the threat, Freud never succeeded in offering an acceptable answer to the question: *what* precisely constitutes the threat? (cited in Shepherdson 2001: xxv). Therefore, with Freud, we cannot go any further than stating that colonial anxiety is a threat felt by the colonizer's ego in terms of the systems of knowledge and power on which this ego is built. But what is the object-cause of this threat? In 'Anxiety', Lacan addresses this problem left unanswered by Freud when he focuses on the alteration of the *objet petit a* from imaginary to the real in anxiety. For Lacan, 'anxiety is not without an object' (1962–63: Session 10, p. 117). *Pas sans* or 'not without' does not imply that the object is absent; rather, it qualifies the object's alteration from imaginary to the real as a 'conditional liaison' linking being to having (ibid.: Session 7, p. 78). Anxiety, he writes, is 'the striking manifestation' of this change and a 'signal of the intervention' of the real object in place of the fantastic object (ibid.: Session 7, p. 75). In other words, Lacan postulates anxiety as resulting from a 'moment of moulting', that is, the moment when the imaginary 'situatable', 'locatable' and 'exchangeable' object, and the 'private, incommunicable and [. . .] dominant [or real] object' appear interchangeable (ibid.: Session 7, p. 77; see also pp. 79–80). This interchangeability of the object, a scenario central to horror films, leads to the 'dawning of a feeling of strangeness which opens the door to anxiety' (ibid.: Session 7, p. 77).

This shift also carries another serious concern for the subject enveloped in his secure shell of the ego. Lacan mentions that anxiety is the object's 'only subjective expression' (ibid.: Session 8, p. 88). The object speaks in anxiety! (Again, an all-too-familiar situation found in horror stories.) Psychoanalytically speaking, objects articulate the lack in the Other. The subject who comes into being by phantasmatically situating the Other as complete, definitive and without any lack shirks at horror in face of this articulation. When Freud says in 'Analysis Terminable and Interminable' (1937; here 1964) that anxiety is caused by a traumatic situation (say, objects speaking!) that poses a threat to the ego, it is again the unanticipated intrusion of the real that is the subject of his comment (1964: 209–53). It is an intrusion for which the subject is not prepared, a sudden infringement that deconstructs the imaginary order of the ego to reveal the subject as bereft of will, power, authority and volition.

The history of European colonialism offers the most illustrative examples of this. John William Kaye (1814–76), the imperial historian who wrote the voluminous history of the Indian Mutiny, *A History of the Sepoy War in India, 1857–1858*, (1864–76, here 1865) speaks about the panic caused by the *lotah*—a metal vessel used by certain classes of Indians in the nineteenth century for storing and drinking water out of. However, in colonial discourse, it was not a simple article of daily use, but, rather, a signifier representing the schismatic, regressive social politics of the colonized Other—people from each of the four castes carried and zealously guarded their own *lotah* so as not to be polluted by sharing, touching or using one carried by a member of another caste.[2] The *lotah*, as represented in colonial discourse, was one more signifier to understand the social and caste prejudices of the Other, and to pin down the Other in a knowledge necessary to adapt colonial rule to the specific demands of the colonized's culture.[3]

---

2 It must be mentioned, of course, that the notion of a rigid fourfold caste hierarchy, as Partha Chatterjee has noted, represented a skewed vision of the colonial space and indigenous culture. Imperial knowledge was thus from the very beginning false knowledge, founded on misrecognition, misreading and deliberate mistranslation of the indigenous culture (Chatterjee 1989).

3 For references to the *lotah* in ethnographic studies on Indian culture, see Shore (1837: 477); Gait (1902); Whitworth (1885: 182); and Yule et al. (1903: 522). Interestingly, there is no separate entry on the *lotah* in William Crooke's 1906 book, *Things Indian*, but the preface explains the regular reference to the object in other works (Crooke 1906: v).

Kaye mentions the lotah while writing about the signs of native discontent that were already present before the outbreak of the 1857 uprising. He writes:

A Hindoo, or a Hindooised Mahomedan, is *nothing without* his Lotah. A Lotah is a metal drinking-vessel, which he religiously guards against defilement, and which he holds as a cherished possession when he has nothing else belonging to him in the world. But a brass vessel may be put to other uses than that of holding water. It may brain a magistrate, or flatten the face of a gaoler, and truly it was a formidable weapon in the hands of a desperate man (1865: 198–9; my emphasis).

The anxiety in this passage over the transformation of the *lotah* and the failure of the administration to prevent that change is important for our purposes here. The dramatic transformation of known objects—objects that had been variously researched, classified, known and represented through the study of the Other's culture and character—into dangerous things via undocumented and unanticipated use metaphorically represents an anxiety over the failure to know and control the indigenous space. The anxiety about the use of the *lotah* as a weapon is tied to an anxiety over inhabiting a shifting symbolic order where signifiers are characteristically unstable and knowledge, impossible to uphold. Moreover, the *lotah* as a signifier for defining the Other becomes problematic since it insists a third category into existence—the Hinduized Muslim. This category designates the Other space and its history as impossible to divide in terms of religion and culture, but as open to co-option and syncretism, thereby posing a serious challenge to the British practice of 'divide and rule.' The conjunction 'but' in the text functions to represent the moment when imperial sovereignty is threatened by the surfacing of a supernumerary detail. In this example, it is not the object per se that is unstable but the object and universe of the colonized as constructed in a discourse. The real of the Other *speaks* through the object!

But what does the Other speak of? It is not dissent, for dissent can be accommodated within the logic of the signifier. The Other speaks of barred jouissance. Jouissance of the Other expresses itself through the articulation of the Other's mysterious, radical otherness that is beyond the straitjacket of the subject's discourse, and reappears as 'an obstacle to the dialectic and logic of the signifier' (Miller 2005: 22). Anxiety is the signal of this sudden appearance of the Other's jouissance as an 'insoluble' remainder in discourse. It signals the 'constriction of the gap between desire and *jouissance*' (Harari 2001: 258), or the symbolic and the real. And as Jacques-Alain Miller reminds us, in 'Anxiety', Lacan's formulation 'anxiety is the signal of the real' pivots on a second formulation: namely, anxiety is the 'sign of the desire of the Other' (Miller 2006: 22).

To clarify this I would turn to Mahasweta Devi's 1987 short story 'Strange Children' (here 1990) which revolves round the experiences of a central-government relief officer sent to distribute supplies in a drought-stricken tribal area adjoining the districts of Ranchi, Palamau and Sarguja in Chhattisgarh. In the course of his work, the officer witnesses the impoverished existence of the indigenous population. The sights and sounds of their plaintive songs and the 'naked, emaciated' bodies with 'bellies swollen with worms and thick spleen' conflict with the officer's preconceived romantic 'images of tribal life' that had been 'drawn from the movies' (1990: 230). He learns about local myths and legends, about the confrontation between the government and tribals over land acquisition, the subsequent massacre of government officials at Kuva by some disgruntled tribals, police reprisals and the sudden disappearance of an entire village population accused for the slaughter at Kuva. Similarly, he learns about a horrifying rumour: 'strange-looking small children' visit the camp at the dead of the night to steal the supplies. These children, he is told, are 'not like human children' (ibid.: 233). Though dismissive of this story at first, one night he confronts these rumoured apparitions escaping with stolen supplies. But as he approaches them, he realizes to his bewilderment that they are not children but the full-grown adults who had carried out the massacre at Kuva and sought refuge in the impenetrable jungles to escape the authorities, and whose bodies have shrunk from years of survival on a frugal diet of leaves and roots. Encircling the officer they recount their tale, all the while rubbing their 'dry and repulsive' genitals deliberately against his body—'We're down to just these fourteen. Our bodies have shrunk. The men can't do anything with it except piss. The women can't get pregnant. That's why we steal food. We must eat to grow bigger again [. . .] We're like this because of the massacre of Kuva' (ibid.: 240). At one level, the speech of the Other articulates discontent against the elitist state official ('We must eat to grow bigger again'), but at another it is an articulation of the lack in the Other. The gesture of rubbing their genitals against the body of the relief officer/State is an expression of the absence of (phallic) jouissance in the lives of the indigene. Confronted with the 'unbearable rubbing' of the Other, the officer is left questioning the reality of the 'Copernican system, science, the twentieth century, the Independence of India, the five-year plans, all that he had known to be true' (ibid.: 240). Unable to negotiate, he decides to let out a scream. Yet, he cannot 'make his voice scream'—his speech dries up in face of the real (ibid.: 241).

Meaning and identity in colonial discourse is extended in two different directions: the signifier and jouissance, that is, towards a symbolic sign of the Other and the sign as the signature of the real. The bar separating the two is critical for sequestering meaning, signification and identity, and keeping anxiety over the dissolution of these at bay.[4] Schematically put, anxiety represents the anguish of encountering what is buried or repressed by the bar, namely, the real. When the bar disappears to reveal the real, as it did in the case of the relief officer, anxieties surface.

The stereotype as a 'complex, ambivalent, mode of representation, as anxious as it is assertive' illustrates this tenuous condition (Bhabha 1994c: 100). While the notion of the stereotyped Other goes some way in satisfying the colonial desire to know the inscrutable natives in their peculiar or different specificity, it also always resists such facile conjugations prompting endless monitoring of the cosmetic margins of the colonial world by the colonizer. Bhabha explains repetition as directly related to the objectification/stereotyping through a process of 'binding' which constructs 'the discursive and political practices of racial and cultural hierarchization' within colonial discourse (ibid.: 96). Repetition enters the colonial experiential space at the same time as discourse captures an alien culture as fixed. Anxiety, consequently, is about the Other as 'an impossible object [. . .] at once a substitution and a shadow' (ibid.: 116–17).

---

4 As Freud shows, meaning of a word is never finite, for it is subjected to co-option by other nonsensical words and this creates bridges between the symbolic certainty and the real's nonsensical uncertainty. See the 'Rat-Man' case in Freud (1955).

INTERLUDE: HISTORICIZING COLONIAL ANXIETY

Given that postcolonial theorists like Said and Bhabha have often been charged with ignoring history, we can read the hypothetical propositions made above with an eye on history. Historically, we can read anxious repetitions in colonial discourse in relation to the ideological shift that attends European territorial aspirations beginning in the eighteenth century—the moment when ethics of territorial occupation collided with the new-found morals of Enlightenment modernity. I characterize this moment as illustrating a turn in colonial discourse—a movement that is best explained as the desire to rationally explain colonialism by veiling the greed for territorial expansion. The emphasis on production of knowledge distinguishes 'modern' or European colonialism from earlier forms of invasive 'no quarter given to the natives' colonization of other lands. However, the weakness for justifying territorial approximation through rational knowledge earmarks modern-day colonialism as a highly neurotic experience fraught with anxiety and driven by compulsive reconstructions of imaginary origins of power, race, gender and modernity. Following Ania Loomba, one can posit the difference between old and modern colonialisms in terms of the restructuring of culture, politics and economy of the colonized by the colonizer, which involves 'drawing [the colonized] into a complex relationship with [the colonizer's]' supposedly superior socio-politico-ideological cultures (Loomba 2005: 9). It is the Manichean character of colonialism—the impossibility of negotiating ground realities of colonialism and violent exploitation of the Other with the help of discourses sanitizing such acts in terms of scientific reason or divine design—which makes colonial discourse analogous to the neurotic's discourse.

It is possible to fine-tune this argument through a discussion of Lacan's seminar on the 'four discourses' (see Lacan 2007). What Lacan terms the Master's discourse, that is, discourse as it served the rule of supreme kings, can be read as the discourse of old colonialism. By contrast, the subsequent form of discourse, university discourse, characterizes the shift in European history and realpolitik towards science, reason and democracy. It is a movement from the tyranny of absolutist regimes to that of science and knowledge, and is indicative of the shift in political economy from feudalism to capitalism. In the 'regime'

251

of this discourse, the position of the supreme authority is occupied by knowledge as a neutral force and as founded on rational, objective authority, which, in turn, defines it both historically as well as conceptually. And it is from this position of objective knowledge that the university discourse addresses the indigenous other. The similarity between Lacan's university discourse and Said's arguments on the strategic use of knowledge as power in *Orientalism* hardly needs to be stressed here. The complicity between Western Enlightenment knowledge and colonial discourses is an established fact in the annals of postcolonial studies. Knowledge posing as scientific and neutral, and devised independently or from within the parameters of Universities and other such institutions, constructed the Orient and the oriental as the Other. In their so-called scientific and rational pursuits, Europe produced knowledge of the Other as different through detailed examinations of 'otherness'. Knowledge thus produced not only served science, but also worked to consolidate the imaginary discourses of colonialism so as to claim the superiority of the West over the colonized. The act of othering as fiction remains hidden in the university discourse. As colonial discourse seeks to establish an acceptable (rational) social link between the forceful act of colonization and the ideals of European liberal modernity, it gives birth to a tension by way of the question: how to veil brute articulations of power with a self-righteous posture?

ANXIETY AND THE ARCHAIC

In 'Articulating the Archaic', anxiety is associated with the *unrepresentable* in the locus of the Other. If the stereotype provokes anxiety by challenging discourse, it also drives incessantly towards re-construction. (Kaye, for example, situates the incident of the *lotah* within the linear grand narrative of the Indian Mutiny. The relief officer in Devi's story vents himself through weeping.) By contrast, the nonsensical ambivalence of the 'Ou-boum' of the Marabar Caves (to take an example from Bhabha) 'displaces those dualities in which the colonial space is traditionally divided: nature/culture, chaos/civility', thus pushing the specific experience of encountering 'colonial nonsense' beyond all possibility of discursive reconstruction (Bhabha 1994a: 177). In discourse, these moments are registered only as 'inscriptions of an uncertain colonial silence that mocks the social performance of language with their non-sense [and] [. . .] baffles the communicable verities of culture with their refusal to translate' (ibid.: 177).

What does Bhabha mean? To answer that, let me dwell on the text Bhabha chooses to discuss in his essay—*A Passage to India* (1924) by E. M. Forster— and on Forster's literary descriptions of the Marabar caves. In writing about the caves, Forster appears to consciously emphasize the inexplicable, primaeval force of a beyond. We are told at the very outset that the caves are something more than words can describe or minds fully comprehend. The 'extraordinary' caves stand agape at the edge of the city of Chandrapore opening a passage into a reality that is beyond both the 'general outline of the [native] town' that persists 'like some low but indestructible form of life' and the 'tropical pleas- aunce' of the British 'city' inland (Forster 1924: 7–8). In this land, already fis- sured by race, class and religion, the caves pose a very different threat—that of a rugged dismissal of the flat plains and of leopards and snakes—of another existence that survives outside of the human and outside of civilization. The caves are like 'small black hole[s]' that gape and suck men in 'like water down a drain' only to belch and return them to humanity (ibid.: 21; 146–7). Describ- ing the primitive otherness of these caves, Forster writes: 'Nothing, nothing attaches to them, [. . .] Nothing is inside [. . .] if mankind grew curious and ex- cavated, nothing, nothing would be *added* to the sum of good or evil' (ibid.: 124–5, my emphasis). The caves as such are beyond human imagination and do not 'depend upon human speech' (ibid.). Outside of language and reality, they are best appreciated at a distance—they only look 'romantic in *certain lights* and at suitable distances' (ibid.: 126, my emphasis). The Marabar caves metaphorically represent the impossibility of *knowing*, *embracing* or *controlling* India—'Nothing embraces the whole of India, nothing, nothing' (ibid.: 145). And to add to the confusion, the caves produce an eerie echo from time to time, 'bou-oum' or 'ou-boum', 'entirely devoid of [any] distinction', the 'sound as far as the human alphabet can express' (ibid.: 147). Indeed, as Forster's novel suggests, the mysterious inexplicability of these caves challenge reason and human fellow feeling, opening up between the self and the Other a for- bidding unbridgeable chasm.

A similar situation of inexplicability is illustrated in 'By Bread Alone' where Bhabha discusses the anxious moment of the Indian Mutiny. He discusses how a known material object—the chapatti—ruptured the established imperial systems of knowledge and authority by their sheer nonsensical itineraries during the mutiny. The rumour of these organic missives, Bhabha shows, opened up a grim anxious space between the colonizer and the colonized and between the colonial military and native civil lines. Nothing remained certain, no one reliable, as every gesture and each new day brought newer anxieties to the British camp. The Mutiny is an uncivilized, regressive, irrational moment within colonialism; a moment beyond signification (was it a sepoy war, a mutiny or a war of national independence?).

In this sense, the inexplicable echo of the Marabar caves and the mysterious chapattis of 1857 share a common ground. Both unravel the empty core of an already fragile colonial order held together by bridge parties and an affective family romance between European officers and their subordinate native sepoys. The ominous echo and the seditious bread announce the impossibility of containing the colony through discourse. These moments *stage* the limits of the colonial symbolic system. The impact of the *non-sense* dismounts the fantasy of the white man's Word and knowledge, representing moments when 'the sign of identity and reality found in the work of empire is slowly undone' (Bhabha 1994a: 176–7). For what echoes through the Marabar caves or what transpires through the uncanny circulation of the chapattis remains a complete enigma to the authority. They produce questions that remain unanswered, only eliciting responses outside of language—in Adela's case, hallucinations and scarring of the body; and in the case of the infamous chapattis, an inability to form judgment about its origin or aim. If anything, imperial experiences of such encounters strip off the power and the will to knowledge and representation, creating a state of desperation similar to that of psychosis (Bhabha 1994b: 294).

Confrontations with the beyond are too momentous for words. These experiences can be felt and registered only at the level of the body and they end with the death of the subject. Is it not an end for Adela too at the culmination of the trial? In fact, would it be wrong to say that Adela as the 'subject supposed to know' or as the 'subject who wants to know (India)', dies even before the trial begins. For she fails to figure out what *really* happened in the caves—did she imagine it or was it real? Adela's failure to testify at the trial represents her as a stain that denudes the imaginary of the imperial master in the eyes of the colonized. Similarly, in the context of the chapattis, Kaye's failure to arrive at a conclusion on a matter of such great importance to the empire can only be read as the death of the imperial historian's power to rationally investigate, understand and communicate the idiosyncrasies of the colonized. These signal the death of all those ideals that constitute the self of the colonizer as the master. The effect of these phenomena can be stated only thus: 'Cultural difference, as Adela experienced it, in the nonsense of the Marabar caves, is not the acquisition or accumulation of additional cultural knowledge: it is the momentous, if momentary, extinction of the recognizable object of culture in the disturbed artifice of its signification, at the edge of experience' (Bhabha 1994a: 179–80). This 'extinction' of the object shreds the imaginary masks of imperial identity and authority, and the subject is left stripped, negated and looking back at his abject self. It is in this looking back that the anxiety of the real is situated.

References

ENGLISH SOURCES

BHABHA, Homi. 1994a. 'Articulating the Archaic: Cultural Difference and Colonial Nonsense' in *The Location of Culture*. New York and London: Routledge, pp. 175–98.

———. 1994b. 'By Bread Alone: Signs of Violence in the Mid-nineteenth Century' in *The Location of Culture*. New York and London: Routledge, pp. 283–302.

———. 1994c. 'The Other Question: Stereotype, Discrimination and the Discourse of Colonialism' in *The Location of Culture*. New York and London: Routledge, pp. 94–120.

CHATTERJEE, Partha. 1989. 'Caste and Subaltern Consciousness'. *Subaltern Studies* 6: 169–209.

CROOKE, William. 1906. *Things Indian: Being Discursive Notes on Various Subjects Connected with India*. London: John Murray.

DEVI, Mahasweta. 1990. 'Strange Children' in *Of Women, Outcastes, Peasants, and Rebels* (Kalpana Bardhan trans.). Berkeley, LA and Oxford: University of California Press, pp. 229–41.

FANON, Frantz. 2004. *The Wretched of the Earth* (Richard Philcox trans.). New York: Grove Press.

FINK, Bruce. 1996. *The Lacanian Subject: Between Language and Jouissance*. New Jersey: Princeton University Press.

FORSTER, E. M. 1924. *A Passage to India*. New York: Harcourt, Brace and Company.

FREUD, Sigmund. 1955. 'Notes upon a Case of Obsessional Neurosis' in *The Standard Edition of the Complete Psychological Works of Sigmund Freud*, VOL. 10 (James Strachey ed., trans.). London: Hogarth Press and the Institute of Psycho-Analysis, pp. 151–318.

———. 1959. 'Inhibitions, Symptoms and Anxiety' in *The Standard Edition of the Complete Psychological Works of Sigmund Freud*, VOL. 20 (James Strachey ed., trans.). London: Hogarth Press and the Institute of Psycho-Analysis, pp. 77–175.

———. 1964. 'Analysis Terminable and Interminable' in *The Standard Edition of the Complete Psychological Works of Sigmund Freud*, VOL. 23 (James Strachey ed., trans.). London: Hogarth Press and the Institute of Psycho-Analysis, pp. 209–54.

GAIT, Edward Albert (Indian Census Commissioner). 1902. *Census of India, 1901*, VOL. 15. Allahabad: Office of the Superintendent of Government of Printing, India.

GREEN, Garth L. 2002. 'The Turn to History'. *Anthropological Quarterly* 75(4): 807–16.

HARARI, Roberto. 2001. *Lacan's Seminar on Anxiety: An Introduction* (Jane C. Lamb-Ruiz trans.). New York: Other Press.

KAYE, John William. 1865. *A History of the Sepoy War in India, 1857–58*, VOL. 1. London: W. H. Allen.

LACAN, Jacques. 1962–63. The Seminar of Jacques Lacan. Book X. Anxiety, 1962–63. Unofficially translated by Cormac Gallagher from the unedited French typescripts of the seminar officially published in 2004. Available at http://www.valas.fr/IMG/pdf/THE-SEMINAR-OF-JACQUES-LACAN-X_l_angoisse.pdf (Last accessed on 21 August 2012.)

———. 1981. *The Seminar of Jacques Lacan. Book XI. The Four Fundamental Concepts of Psychoanalysis, 1964* (Jacques-Alain Miller ed., Alan Sheridan trans.). New York and London: W. W. Norton.

———. 2006. 'The Mirror Stage as Formative of the *I* Function as Revealed in Psychoanalytic Experience' in *Écrits: The First Complete Edition in English* (Bruce Fink trans.). New York and London: W. W. Norton, pp. 75–81.

———. 2007. *The Seminar of Jacques Lacan. Book XVII. The Other Side of Psychoanalysis, 1969–70* (Jacques-Alain Miller ed., Russell Grigg trans.). New York and London: W. W. Norton.

LOOMBA, Ania. 2005. *Colonialism/Postcolonialism* (2nd edn). New York: Routledge.

MANNONI, Octave. 1990. *Prospero and Caliban: The Psychology of Colonization*. Ann Arbor: University of Michigan Press.

MILLER, Jacques-Alain. 2005. 'Introduction to Reading Jacques Lacan's Seminar on Anxiety (Part I)' (Barbara P. Fulks trans.). *Lacanian Ink* 26: 8–67.

———. 2006. 'Introduction to Reading Jacques Lacan's Seminar on Anxiety (Part II)' (Barbara P. Fulks trans.). *Lacanian Ink* 27: 8–63.

MOORE-GILBERT, Bart. 1997. *Postcolonial Theory: Contexts, Practices, Politics*. London and New York: Verso.

RAGLAND-SULLIVAN, Ellie. 1986. *Jacques Lacan and the Philosophy of Psychoanalysis*. Urbana and Chicago: The University of Illinois Press;

SAID, Edward. 1979. *Orientalism*. New York: Vintage.

SHEPHERDSON, Charles. 2001. 'Foreword' to Roberto Harari, *Lacan's Seminar on Anxiety: An Introduction* (Jane C. Lamb-Ruiz trans.). New York: Other Press, pp. ix–lxxix.

SHORE, Frederick John. 1837. *Notes on Indian Affairs*. 2 VOLS. London: John W. Parker.

WHITWORTH, George Clifford. 1885. *An Anglo-Indian Dictionary: A Glossary of Indian Terms Used in English, and of Such English Or Other Non-Indian Terms as Have Obtained Special Meanings in India*. London: K. Paul, Trench.

YULE, Henry, Burnell, Arthur Coke and Crooke, William. 1903. *Hobson-Jobson: A Glossary of Colloquial Anglo-Indian Words and Phrases, and of Kindred Terms, Etymological, Historical, Geographical and Discursive*. London: John Murray.

FRENCH SOURCES

LACAN, Jacques. 1949. 'Le stade du miroir comme formateur de la fonction du Je telle quelle nous est revelee dans l'experience psychanalytique'. *Revue Française de Psychanalyse* 13(4): 449–55. Subsequently published in *Écrits* (1966).

———. 1966. *Écrits*. Paris: Éditions du Seuil.

———. 1973. *Le Séminaire. Livre XI. Les quatre concepts fondamentaux de la psychanalyse, 1964* (Jacques-Alain Miller ed.). Paris: Éditions du Seuil.

———. 1991. *Le Séminaire. Livre XVII. L'envers de la psychanalyse, 1969–70* (Jacques-Alain Miller ed.). Paris: Éditions du Seuil.

———. 2004. *Le Séminaire. Livre X. L'angoisse, 1962–63* (Jacques-Alain Miller ed.). Paris: Éditions du Seuil.

The Transsexual Body Written: Writing as Sinthome[1]
PATRICIA GHEROVICI

'Why do so many transsexuals write memoirs?'—Jay Prosser tackles this question by noting that for transsexuals, even long before any book is published, there is always a founding autobiographical act:

> [I]n the clinician's office where in order to be diagnosed as transsexual s/he must recount a transsexual autobiography. The story of a strong, early, and persistent transgendered identification is required by the clinical authorities, the psychiatrists, psychologists, and psychotherapists who traditionally function as gatekeepers to the means of transsexual 'conversion.' Whether s/he publishes an autobiography or not, then, every transsexual, as transsexual, is originally an autobiographer. Narrative is also a kind of second skin: the story the transsexual must weave around the body in order that his body may be read (Prosser 1998: 101).

Perhaps this quote ends on a wrong choice of verb. Given that most transsexuals use the verb 'to read' as saying 'to guess somebody's anatomical identity' which often entails not 'to pass', one might be tempted to say that transsexuals write but in order not to be read.

Deirdre N. McCloskey, a renowned economist and historian, who transitioned from male to female in her mid-50s, offers in her memoir *Crossing* (1999) not only a good example of this peculiar use of 'to read' but also of the pathos involved in being 'read':

---

1 Excerpts of a different version of this essay have been published in the author's 2010 book *Please Select Your Gender: From the Invention of Hysteria to the Democratizing of Transgenderism* (New York and Oxford: Routledge).—Ed.

Kate invited Deirdre to her house [. . .]. The two women took her husband and her husband's father to a Thai restaurant for Father's Day, a feminine duty, Deirdre observed, with Kate wrapping presents and organizing ceremonies for her men. Deirdre couldn't tell if the men read her, which merely showed that they were courteous, because they must have. Kate's father-in-law asked Deirdre how it felt to be such a tall woman.

[. . .] At the airport that evening [. . .]. It was late and her makeup was slipping. The clerk laughed at her and called her sir [. . .]. The flight was fourteen hours [. . .]. The young Australian woman in her row was pleasant and didn't seem to read her, despite Deirdre's croaks and stuttering from tiredness (1999: 194–5).

[. . .] After a week of unusual amount of being read, which I cannot understand, I had one of my rare middle-of-the-night anxiety attacks. Nothing pathological, just waking up too early and being unable to go back to sleep while thoughts tumbled. Is the genital surgery healing right? Am I just too tall? Will the facelift work? Can I ever get the voice right?

[. . .] In time, in time. The facial operations and slow effects of hormones, and morning and evening applications of Estée Lauder products by the half gallon, finally left her unread. Two years later she had stopped testing for passing. Almost (ibid.: 204–5).

Max Wolf Valerio, a Native American/Latino poet, writer and performer who transitioned from a feminist lesbian to a heterosexual man, chronicled in detail the first five years of his hormonal and social transformation. In *The Testosterone Files* (2006) he notices, to his chagrin, that taking testosterone has left him with an incipient receding hairline. He, however, welcomes this change as a potential cue for people to 'read' him as male (2006: 324). Helen Boyd, who lost her husband to another woman when he became the other woman (her husband, a cross-dressing heterosexual man, decided to consider sex-reassignment surgery), as she puts it in *She's Not the Man I Married: My Life with a Transgender Husband* (2007), writes: 'It is almost impossible for [her husband] Betty to present [himself] as a feminine male because her femininity means that she is often just read as a woman' (2007: 85). Both Valerio and Boyd use 'read' differently from McCloskey, perhaps to convey that gender is a matter of interpretation, that gender is always a representation to be decoded. These two diverging uses of 'reading' for gender presentation, one as not passing and the other as a call for interpretation, will find their key in Jacques Lacan's concept of the letter, writing and nomination, all converging in later developments on the notion of the *sinthome*.

As we know, Lacan gave a new clinical meaning to the term symptom, when he rewrote it as *sinthome*, using an old French word that he had re-coined in course of his reading of Joyce. His seminar on Joyce asserts that a *sinthome* is a creative knotting together of the registers of real, symbolic and imaginary. The word *sinthome* describes the function of Joyce's art and provides a more comprehensive interpretation of the function of the father in the Borromean knot.[2] By the time of the *sinthome*, the knot took on one specific characteristic: in the Borromean pattern, if one ring is unknotted, the other three come loose. The *sinthome* is identified as the fourth ring knotting the tripartite registers, which, as Lacan argued, are not knotted in psychosis. In *Le Séminaire. Livre XXIII. Le Sinthome, 1975–76* (2005), his innovation was to contend that the father could be a fourth ring keeping the other three knotted: 'the father is after all nothing else than a symptom, a *sinthome*' (2005: 19; my translation). With the knot of the Name-of-the-Father, Lacan developed a concept of active nomination identical to writing, in a process of naming as writing or vice versa. We shall see that this later contribution proves extremely illuminating in transgender clinical issues.

Lacan defines the *sinthome* as an artifice, emphasizing art and the creative aspect of the knot—thus, the *sinthome* is a creation, an invention. One cannot discuss sex-change memoirs without referring to the medical ideology that brought about sex-change development. Prosser, a trans man himself, disagrees with a constructivist view that has been put forward by Bernice Hausman, who

---

2 One can trace back a non-clinical use of the term symptom to the fourth session of *Le Séminaire. Livre XIX. . . . Ou Pire, 1971–72* (. . . Or worse; 2011). There, Lacan implicitly refers to Louis Althusser's notion of symptomatic reading by engaging in a discussion of the symptom and necessity in the context of the reading of Karl Marx.

sees transsexual memoir as entirely shaped by medical technology (see Hausman 1995). Prosser remarks that in most sex-change narratives, the relation of authorship and authorization between clinicians and transsexuals is mobile, dynamic and therefore, highly complex (1998: 9). If published sex-change memoirs are second versions of the first transsexual autobiography told in the doctor's office, it does not necessarily mean that they have been constructed by medical discourse. This, however, does not contradict the fact that autobiographical reports to clinical experts have to conform to the constraints of a genre. And published or unpublished transsexual autobiographers follow the formal constraints of the genre systematically.

Like Prosser, Hausman has observed that the transsexual population is well read, for strategic reasons (1995: 143). In order to successfully obtain the medical treatments requested, the story of transsexuality has to match the officially sanctioned aetiology, and thereby perpetuates it. The account has to be convincing because the 'right' story can confer legitimacy to the sex-change demand. Autobiographical narratives of successful transsexuals include detailed inside information, written by those who have managed to manoeuvre adroitly the complicated and strict guidelines of sex-change protocols. Memoirs become self-help or 'how-to' manuals. Some autobiographies are so aware of this function that they include ample lists of useful information: telephone numbers of plastic surgeons, endocrinologists, support networks, advocacy groups and so on.

Hausman points out that while the autobiographies offer the transsexual reader an authorizing membership in a group and a sense of identity, the clinical autobiographical narrative also teaches them to conform to pre-established parameters defining the 'official' transsexual narrative (ibid.: 144). Hausman is not the first to expose the limitations that this tendency imposes on the construction of transsexual subjectivity. Sandy Stone argues that the installation of an 'official transsexual history' in order to successfully obtain surgical and hormonal sex-change treatment has produced a situation in which the potential for the 'intertextuality' of transsexual subjectivity is erased: '[t]he highest purpose of the transsexual is to erase him/herself, to fade into the "normal" population as soon as possible. Part of this process is known as *constructing a plausible story*—learning to lie effectively about one's past. [. . .] authentic experience is replaced by a particular kind of story, one that supports the old constructed positions' (1991: 295). The transsexual who erases the ambiguities and complexities of lived experience for the sake of normality is, thus, not very different from the patient who comes to see an analyst because the plausible story told no longer lies about the past efficiently. In both cases, we have a symptom with the potential to begin the analytic process and create artificial neurosis. And yet, even when the transsexual narrative may follow every cliché, I want to highlight the tremendous impact that the discovery of a memoir has on many transsexuals. Often revelatory, the encounter with this type of text is a defining moment with an anchoring function in the realization of identity.

LIVES ALTERED BY THE PRINTED WORD

Memoirs of sex change are not only numerous, they often have an impressive, life-transforming effect on future transsexual readers—the experience of reading other people's memoirs becomes a turning point in their own evolution. For example, Mario Martino writes in *Emergence* (1977)—which the blurb advertises as 'the only complete autobiography of a woman who has become a man'—that, as Marie, in 1967, she was the first in her town to buy a copy of Christine Jorgensen's 1967 memoir (Martino 1977: 40). In her autobiography *Conundrum* (1974), Jan Morris recounts with poignant detail the charged emotions felt upon the discovery of a dusty volume of *Man into Woman: An Authentic Record of a Change of Sex* (1933) in a bookstore in the Welsh town of Ludlow (1974: 57–9). And another famous transsexual author, the tennis champion Renée Richards, recalls that reading *Man into Woman* had more propitiatory effect on her previous life as Dr Richard Raskind than her earlier discovery in her mother's bookshelves of the 'expert' Richard von Krafft-Ebing's 1886 *Psychopathia Sexualis* (here 1894) (Richards 1983: 54–5). Raskind found very little identificatory comfort in what she dismissed as mere stories of 'lunatics'. Furthermore, the book made her fear that she was crazy. Discovering the story of Einar Wegener two years later was a lucky breakthrough: 'I had hit the jackpot' (ibid.: 55). Nancy Hunt, a male-to-female transsexual and award-winning journalist, describes the life-transforming effect that reading a first-person account of sex reassignment had on her. She writes in *Mirror Image: The Odyssey of a Male-to-Female Transsexual* (1978): 'I can remember only once when my life has been altered by the printed word. That was upon reading an article in the *New York Times Magazine* on March 17, 1974 [. . .]. It described the transition from man into woman of an English journalist now known as Jan Morris' (1978: 137). Similarly, after 28 years of living as a woman, Dhillon Khosla discovered the truth of his gender when reading several interviews of female-to-male transsexuals in an article that appeared in 1994 in *The New Yorker*: 'And as I read the things these men said [. . .] [f]lashes of recognition went off in my mind, arranging themselves like the pieces of a puzzle [. . .]. The relief, however, was short-lived. Next came the tough question: Now that I knew the truth, what was I going to do about it?' (2006: 4–5) In a similar way for Wayne/Jayne County, a rock 'n' roll female impersonator in New York and the author of her sex-change memoir, *Man Enough to Be a Woman* (1995), it was reading the autobiography of the transsexual Canary Conn that revealed to her the truth of her gender and gave her a new sense of identity and purpose: 'I decided that I had a transsexual identity.' County concluded that she was already female, and chose to 'go the whole way and have a sex-change' (County and Smith 1995: 99).

Since an individual's private encounter with the printed word has such illuminating effect, this potential of the letter has not been neglected by organizations such as the Foundation for Gender Education which sells books about transsexualism and transvestism, and uses transsexual autobiographies as the mainstay of their educative outreach. While autobiographical texts indeed institute a certain discursive hegemony with their mimicked formulaic schemata, I want to stress that such formulaic narratives still have a transformative effect upon the readers, who feel 'saved' by the printed word. The importance of 'reading' is taken up by Stone in what she claims is 'the essence of transsexualism':

> I could not ask a transsexual for anything more unconceivable than to forgo passing, to be consciously 'read,' to read oneself aloud, and by this troubling and productive reading to begin to write oneself into the discourses by which one has been written—in effect, then to become a (look out—dare I say it again?) a post-transsexual (1991: 299).

NARRATIVE TRANSITIONS

There are several unavoidable tensions in transsexual autobiographies. If the aim of the autobiography is to document the transition, for example, how a man becomes a woman, it is in contradiction with the claim 'I was woman all along, but happened to be in the wrong body.' Prosser contends that this tension between transformation and continuity of self falls within the autobiographical genre itself (1998: 119). Often the motivation for the transition is to accomplish a sex change that will not leave markers of the former sex on the body since the transsexual wants to 'pass' as a 'normal' member of the new sex. The autobiography defeats this purpose; it blows the transsexual's cover by making public the account of the steps of the transition, very often documenting the transformation through photographs and thus making the transsexual publicly recognized as one. Prosser emphasizes this paradox and highlights the fact that while there may be a sex change accomplished by surgery and hormones, the somatic transformation is not sufficient; writing autobiographies of sex change generates 'its own transitional moments (more symbolic, more in keeping with the flow of the story) to cohere the transsexual subject. Narrative enacts its own transitions' (ibid.: 123).

In his 2005 anthology of transsexual memoirs, Jonathan Ames aptly sums up the structure of sex-change autobiographies as a three-act saga: 'first act: gender-dysphoria childhood; second act: the move to the big city and the transformation [. . .] [and the third act:] the sex change' (2005: xii). My own experience confirms that this is a universal pattern. For Ames, this is the basic outline of all transsexual memoirs: 'A boy or a girl very early on in life feels terribly uncomfortable in his or her gender role, and there is a sense that some terrible mistake has occurred, that he or she was meant to be the other sex' (ibid.).

I have developed elsewhere the idea of the 'mistake' or 'error of nature' at the core of transsexualism—the 'error' of nature is a way of rephrasing the sexuation formulae according to the phallic premise (see Gherovici 2007). By addressing the organ, the aporia of sexual signification is exposed: that of taking the phallus for a signifier of sexual difference (see Lacan 2011: Session 1). I want to emphasize here that Ames finds that transsexual autobiographies follow the structure of a classic literary genre, the *Bildungsroman*, which he describes as 'the coming-of-age-novel' (2005: xii). He notes that following its blueprint in transsexual memoirs, we have a progression in which the main characters, now aware of the 'error of nature', see family and society as trying to reform them. Often, the protagonists also struggle internally, taking great pains to repress their drive to become the opposite sex. Eventually, our heroes leave their hometown and venture into the outside world, often ending up in a big city. Once in the new context, they begin to masquerade as the other sex, perhaps only privately, and eventually more publicly. With time, the disguise and perfected ability to 'pass' becomes more and more permanent and successful, particularly in the second half of the twentieth century with the increased availability of hormone treatments and of surgical technologies to manipulate the body. Ablations and implants as well as the climactic sex-reassignment surgery will finally help the memoir's protagonist reclaim a place of self-acceptance and peace. Ames emphasizes the literary and sociological significance of these memoirs whose appeal is universal since they deal with questions that haunt everyone such as 'Who am I? And What am I?' (ibid.: xii–xiv)

Ames' description of transsexual memoirs as *Bildungsroman* or a novel of formation is slightly misleading. In fact, transsexual memoirs could be described more appropriately as *Künstlerroman*, 'a novel of the artist'. Though there may not be such a huge difference between the two genres, this nuance is important for psychoanalytically influenced ears. On the one hand, one would have a 'formation' (*bildungen*) of the unconscious, which means that unconscious phenomena are made visible in transsexual symptoms, and on the other hand, one comes close to Lacan's analysis of James Joyce when he presents art as a *sinthome*.

Following the path of strict 'formations', Catherine Millot (1990) and others, like Moustafa Safouan (1974), have argued that all transsexuals are psychotic. Millot was the first to introduce the idea that the transsexual symptom can have a structural function analogous to what Lacan sees in writing when he reads Joyce. Importantly, I would disagree with a generalized diagnosis of psychosis. In the same way that one should not talk about psychosis but only of a psychotic structure in Joyce, one should use caution when talking of psychosis in transsexuality. In my clinical practice, I prefer to talk of transsexual symptoms which one can locate in neurosis, perversion or psychosis.

Since transgenderism cannot be systematically defined as pathology, sex change should not be considered either as treatment or as cure. Some transsexual discourses and practices acquire more sense today in so far as they try to inscribe sexual difference without a direct reference to the phallus. In that 'not-all' sense, they are close to psychoanalysis. In order to unleash the potential of the questions brought about by transgender discourses and practices, the questions need to remain open.

THE LOGIC OF THE *SINTHOME*

In his theoretical itinerary, Lacan moves from the phallus to the lack, from the logic of sexuation to topology and knot theory, from the Borromean knot to the *sinthome*. This evolution allows him to speak of sex without a direct relation to the difference of the sexes or to the phallus in the classic sense. Lacan began his career working on paranoia and concluded with a new theory of madness with the invention of the *sinthome*. One may assess the transsexual phenomenon according to three stages in Lacanian thinking: the first corresponds to the notion of the paternal metaphor; the second corresponds to the formulae of sexuation and the third, to the Borromean knot (*sinthome*) (Millot 1990: 31).

The theory of the *sinthome* offers an alternative to Lacan's version of the Freudian Oedipal father which in the 1950s became the Name-of-the-Father. The *sinthome* pluralizes the function of the Name-of-the-Father and generalizes its effect of separation. As Geneviève Morel points out, the *sinthome* allows the child to separate from the law of the mother by relying on something contingent (the father, his law, a trait modelled on him, an element borrowed from society) (2006: 69). Lacan's theory of the *sinthome* is very useful clinically in cases of transgenderism because it offers a novel way to think about sexual difference. The quadruplicity articulated by the *sinthome* (real, imaginary, symbolic and the Σ of the *sinthome*) allows us to rethink sexual difference and the relations man/woman and parent/child without relying exclusively on the phallus or the Name-of-the-Father.

I will argue that sex-change memoirs are a narrative form with a specific function for the subjectivity of their authors—they help embody sexual difference and in some cases, function as a process of self-invention for their authors.

Moreover, they provide an excellent testing ground for Lacan's theory of the *sinthome*. Even though sexual difference may appear like an outdated topic today, since the psychoanalytic perspective that sexual difference is not a question of anatomy but rather of its consequences, may sound already like a cliché, we can note that a majority of transsexuals struggle to conform rigidly to the normative demands of a sexual identity in contradiction with their anatomical sex. While they engage in technologically assisted manipulations of their bodies, their torment seems to be the result of the limits imposed by an anatomy that is experienced as a tragic destiny.

Sex-change requests literalize in the flesh what psychoanalysis calls castration. This is illustrated in a gripping passage from Martino's *Emergence*, a memoir of a 'painful life to live, a painful life to write' (1977: 11). Martino, a nurse, played the dual role of subject of study and clinical authority, to use psychoanalytic jargon, which generates some humorous self-awareness. He describes a second phalloplasty that seems to fail (the first one was unsuccessful and the neopenis had to be surgically excised). As the tip of his new penis becomes black, rots away and is necrotized, he has to sit in water every night, to 'very slowly, cut away the dead tissue. Talk about castration complex! Psychologically this cutting was almost impossible for me, yet it had to be done' (ibid.: 262). Mario breaks away from the increasing distress about the inadequate results of the surgery when he realizes that though he wanted 'a perfect phallus', he has to accept its impossibility. 'So today I'm happy with what I have: a respectable phallus—three fourths perfect' (ibid.: 263).

The notorious error made by Sigmund Freud himself when calling 'castration' a procedure that should more appropriately be called 'eviration' (as any cattle raiser or veterinarian knows, castration only refers to the ablation of testicles, this is why any medical dictionary defines castration as 'bilateral orchidectomy') explains that his very invention of the castration complex was affected by the castration complex—that it cannot be reduced to anatomical reality and is marked by the error of taking an organ for a signifier of sexual difference. In the same way that nothing is missing in the real of the mother's body, the phallus is characterized by its ability to be embodied as a detachable and transformable object. Freud's confusion between the operation of gelding or castration with the potential amputation of the penis can be found in everyone's unconscious.

The transsexual struggle illustrates what psychoanalysis has shown: that the phallus, which has no relation to anatomy, is a signifier used by both men and women to signify their sex and help them embody their sexuality. At times, the signifier and the organ are confused with one another. The phallus is 'no signifier of sexual difference' but of 'sex unity' (there is only one signifier to signify two diverging positions). 'In psychoanalysis, as well as in the unconscious, man knows nothing of woman, and woman nothing of man. The phallus epitomizes the point in myth where the sexual becomes the passion of the signifier' (Lacan 1970: 64; my translation). The phallus renders testimony to the fact that sexual identity is always precarious. The human infant *becomes sexed* without fully symbolizing unconsciously a normal, finished sexual positioning.

A RED HERRING

For Lacan, the phallus is the mean and ratio by which sexual difference is introduced. Regardless of the anatomical differences of the sexes, both boys and girls have to renounce the fantasy of being the mother's phallus. The phallus, which is a notion that Lacan reworks over the years, expresses the profound dissymmetry that defines both sexes. This is a trajectory already marked by Freud. In 1919, expressing his divergence with Wilhelm Fliess, Freud gave this explanation of bisexuality in 'A Child is Being Beaten' (here 1955): 'The dominant sex of the person, which is the more strongly developed, has repressed the mental representation of the subordinated sex into the unconscious. Therefore the nucleus of the unconscious (that is to say, the repressed) is in each human being that side of him which belongs to the opposite sex' (1955: 200–1). Here, one needs to understand that the repressed opposite sex is the Other sex, 'this sex which is not one' to use Luce Irigaray's words, the woman's side (see Irigaray 1985). In 'Analysis Terminable and Interminable' (1937; here 1964) Freud refers more explicitly to 'the repudiation of femininity' as a 'biological fact, a part of the great riddle of sex' (1964: 252). The great riddle of sex is what the analyst struggles with and that which cannot be reached through the usual processes of analysis. Although Freud's description of the 'wish for a penis' and the 'masculine protest' as a biological bedrock relies on a language paradoxically close to that of Fliess (Pontalis 2000: 26), the idea of a sexual dissymmetry persists but will be mediated by the Oedipal structure. In both sexes, castration is violently opposed, but men experience castration as an impending danger whereas women come into contact with it as something that has already happened. The Freudian concept of bisexuality can thus be understood as a precursor to Lacan's formulae of sexuation—even when both men and women experience castration anxiety, there is no equivalence between their sexualities (Freud 1964: 252–3).

This may throw new light on Lacan's aphorism 'there is not such a thing as a sexual relation,' since there is no unconscious representation or symbol of the opposition masculine–feminine. Lacan contends in *The Seminar of Jacques Lacan. Book XI. The Four Fundamental Concepts of Psychoanalysis, 1964* (1973; here 1981a): 'In the psyche, there is nothing by which the subject may situate himself as a male or female being [. . .] the human being has always to learn from scratch from the Other what he has to do, as man or woman' (1981a: 204). Quite ill-equipped, speaking subjects have to find a role in the field of the Other, oriented only by the representatives in the psyche of the consequences of sexuality, because sexuality for humans is represented in the psyche by the relation of the subject to something other than sexuality itself. Sexual reproduction relates to the fact that the living being subjected to sex falls under the blow of individual death. A sexed living being is no longer immortal. Sex represents a portion of death for the living being (ibid.: 205).

Feminist and deconstructive critiques of the Lacanian concept of the phallus neglected Lacan's main innovation on the question of sexuality. This is an aspect that Tim Dean emphasizes when he calls our attention to Lacan's logic of the *objet petit a* as a breakthrough that offers an understanding of sexuality that is non-normative. As Dean observes, 'it is not so important that the phallus may be a penis, or in Judith Butler's reading, a dildo, as it is a giant red herring' (Dean 2000: 14 and Butler 1993: 57–91). The phallus is clearly a misleading clue comparable to the use of smoked herrings to mislead hounds following a trail. To pun somewhat on the phrase, I would like to suggest that the phallus is less a red herring than a read herring—in fact, like gender, it is subject to interpretation and it is always read, like a text.

Two different logics seem to be at work in Lacan's theses: one can be aligned with phallocentric discourse, while another derives from his concept of the object. I have been persuaded by Dean's approach to Lacan's concept of the *objet petit a* as an alternative, counter-heterosexist understanding of the plurality of sexuality and the diversity of forms desire may take (Dean 2000: 214–68). The *objet petit a* is an object that commemorates a loss and a lack and defines human sexuality as asexual. According to Lacan, desire has no proper object.[3] Then we can define the human economy of desire as mediated by the *objet petit a* qua cause of desire that demarcates a sexuality that is in fact asexual. The *objet petit a* takes as its usual form something that may or may not be gendered. Faeces, the voice and the gaze are not exclusive to one sex.[4] The *objet petit a* is defined by Lacan also as the object of partial drives. For Freud, the sexual drive is essentially partial.[5] This is the same for Lacan who notes that 'sexuality comes into play only in the form of partial drives' (1981a: 176). As Phillipe Van Haute observes, 'according to Freud there is no genital drive that would direct us, of itself and naturally, to the opposite sex. Certainly in the unconscious there is no representation of "masculinity" or "femininity"' (2002: 141).

The biological definition of sex dependent on reproductive functions is narrow and easily challenged by transsexualism. The notion of gender puts forward a masculine–feminine bipolarity that is similar to that of language, when we classify words. This may look like the Aristotelian logic of class and attribute. This bipolar system seems to be predicated on complementarity. But this relation of complementarity is 'imaginary' because it pairs a trait that confirms the presence of the attribute and thus membership in a class, granting thereby an imaginary identification with a sex. Lacan formalizes his theory of sexual difference by using symbolic logic and modal logic. Here, let us insist on Lacan's concept of the *sinthome*, which he calls the singularity of a creation compensating for a defect in the body image and its knotting with the main elements of a subject's structure. I will argue that, if for the unconscious 'there

---

3 Lacan states in 'The Subversion of the Subject and the Dialectic of Desire in the Freudian Unconscious' (1966b; here 2006c): '[M]an's desire is the Other's desire' (p. 690).

4 Lacan refers to drives that originate in a relevant erogenous zone whose objects are partial (that is, anal drive, zone: anus, *objet petit a*: faeces) (ibid.: 692–3).

5 In *Three Essays on the Theory of Sexuality* (1905; here 1953), Freud posits human sexuality as essentially polymorphous and perverse.

is not such a thing as a sexual relation,' there will always be the symptom-*sinthome* as a way of tinkering with the body.

It is obvious that sex-change narratives describe painful stages the narrator goes through, manipulating a body that is experienced as foreign. Transsexuals feel a discrepancy between their anatomical sex and ascribed gender. Sufferers claim that they are members of the opposite sex: 'a female spirit trapped in a male body', for example. In many memoirs of sex change, the body has a very specific status of a rigid constraint, an exterior that oppresses the interior in which the real being, the true self, is trapped, locked. Tamsin Wilton notes that the image of the body as a cage or prison is recurrent in such narratives (2000: 237–54). Sex change appears as the only possible escape from the confines of excessive jouissance: 'I was trapped inside a living chamber of horrors' (Griggs 1998: 88). Lewins generalizes: 'In the case of transsexuals locked inside a prison of flesh and blood, there is a constant ache for emancipation' (1995: 14) while Morris reiterates the same idea: '[I]f I were trapped in that cage again nothing would keep me from my goal' (1974: 186). In such narratives, that people can have a self which stands in opposition to their body is taken for granted. Wilton observes that it is perplexing because those in the medical profession would often assume that if the problem 'is in your mind', then an intervention at the level of the body would be ruled out. In sex-change transformations, the Cartesian dualism on which medical practice is sustained is abolished.

INCORPORATIONS

Transsexuals have a peculiar, truncated relation to their bodies, and I will claim that in transsexual artificiality one may find, on certain occasions, a creative *sinthome*, in the form of an answer that may help reclaim the body and regulate jouissance. Let us explore this contention with Deirdre McCloskey's *Crossing*. Deirdre was born male and was called Donald. Donald cross-dressed since the age of 11 and at 52, after 30 years of marriage with two grown-up children, realized that he not only wanted to become a woman, but that he had been a woman all along. McCloskey calls this 'an epiphany': 'On the twentieth day of August 1995 a little after noon the dam broke and the water of his life swirled out onto the plain. He knew himself. Herself. That's it, she said: I am a woman' (1999: 51). At 54, he became Deirdre.

The memory of the event of Donald's first cross-dressing at 11 is clear. He was in bed, sick. His mother was downstairs in the kitchen taking care of his new baby sister:

[Donald] was having the first wet dream of maleness. Oddly his dreams were of femaleness, of having it, of being. Upstairs in the bathroom he took a pair of his mother's panties from the laundry basket, put them on, and found a rush of sexual pleasure—not joyous, or satisfying, merely There. It was a mild ache, pleasant and alluring, mixing memory and desire: the women half dressed in Filene's [store], the little ballerinas, his mother. There was nothing of male lust in it except the outcome. It was not curiosity about what lay underneath women's clothing. It was curiosity about being (ibid.: 5–6).

Donald's description calls up the dissymmetry in the phallic function, which creates the opposition that Freud summed up as 'having' and 'not having', and which becomes in the Lacanian reading 'having' and 'being'—man has the phallus and woman does not, but because of this, she can embody it and thus be the phallus. Donald was grappling with the relation of the subject to the phallus that, as Lacan states in 'The Signification of the Phallus' (1966a; here 2006b), 'forms without regard to the anatomical distinction between the sexes and that is thus especially difficult to interpret in the case of women and with respect to women' (2006b: 576). In the Freudian Oedipal model, we have a binary of having and not having it, of presence and absence: boys have it, girls do not. For Freud, castration is a loss that women think they have suffered, and men fear to suffer; hence it organizes the sexual imaginary. For Lacan, castration is a more fundamental loss affecting both sexes, since both are castrated: nobody has the phallus or can be it. Since the phallus is essentially the mother's missing penis, we can see that from a Lacanian perspective, it is the object that appears in the place of a symbolic lack in order to veil it.

The phallus is a signifier without a signified, and it works through absence (see Lacan 1998: 75). But let us see the sequence of events: Donald 'was having the first wet dream of maleness' when he cross-dressed for the first time. We can attribute this to some difficulty in symbolizing his erection, or was it a confusion between the organ and the signifier? Or was it the pleasure of imagining that he would find the turgescent penis in his mother's underwear? If we follow Lacan's 1958 discussion of Daniel Paul Schreber's transsexualism, we can conclude that in Schreber's case, the Name-of-the-Father was foreclosed, and that the real was summoned in place of the symbolic.[6] Could it be that for Donald, the penis was seen as a phallus and that the body itself became a foreign body? Is Donald's sex change an illustration that sexual difference needs to be embodied imaginarily and symbolically? Or was his request for a physical transformation a way to escape sexual difference altogether? Is his femininity a natural, innate one copied from the mother, as Robert J. Stoller proposes is the case in male-to-female transsexualism?[7] Or is it a phallic femininity as masquerade, as one may find in hysteria? And can this phallic femininity be found in cross-dressing practices, considering the position vis-à-vis castration that grants the transvestite the jouissance of his organ veiled in feminine clothes? Or is it femininity related to a 'jouissance beyond the phallus', like the one Lacan attributed to the mystic?[8]

A longer detour through the case of Schreber will be necessary since his 1903 *Memoirs of My Nervous Illness* (here 2000) is prototypical of the genre. Here one might say that Schreber is to Freud what Joyce is to Lacan: both are writers

---

6 See Hubert (2001): 206.

7 For Stoller, 'protofemininity' is an innate predisposition in both females and males. Stoller writes:

> Though it is true that the boy's first love is heterosexual, and though fathers are too-powerful rivals, there is an earlier stage in gender identity development wherein the boy is merged with [the] mother. Only after months does she gradually become a clearly separate object. Sensing oneself a part of mother—a primeval and thus profound part of character structure (core gender identity)—lays the groundwork for an infant's sense of femininity. This sets the girl firmly on the path to femininity in adulthood but puts the boy in danger of building into his core gender identity a sense of oneness with mother (a sense of femaleness). Depending on how and at what pace a mother allows her son to separate, this phase of merging with her will leave residual effects that may be expressed as disturbances of masculinity (1985: 16).

8 Morel 1994–96. 'Le pousse-à-la-femme: problématique' in *Figures de pousse-à-la-femme*: Cercle Franco-Hellenique de Paris de L'École Européenne de Psychanalyse, Seminar 1994–96, p. 6, quoted in Mahieu 2004: 28.

who deposit in a text a truth about the experience of jouissance that crosses all limits. Jouissance underpins the creation of a *sinthome* by which text and body are held together. Lacan's claim that Joyce is saved from psychosis by writing is well known. Similarly, Schreber is freed from seclusion by his memoirs. Let us note that for Lacan, Joyce's entire oeuvre is to be treated as a memoir. But Lacan's questionable biographical reading, nevertheless, is not on the side of psychobiography. I will argue that he approaches Joyce's work as a memoir to emphasize its function as *sinthome*.

Let us retrace our steps. Freud noted that Schreber's 'idea of being trans-formed into a woman was the salient feature and the earliest germ of the delu-sional system. It also proved to be the one part of it that persisted after his cure, and the one part that was able to retain a place in his behavior in real life after he had recovered' (1958: 20). Lacan follows the path shown by Freud by highlighting the core function of Schreber's transformation into a woman, and wonders whether this is a 'properly psychotic mechanism, one that would be imaginary and that would extend from the first hint of identification with and capture by the feminine image, to the blossoming of a world system in which the subject is completely absorbed in his imagination by a feminine iden-tification' (1993: 63). Here, Lacan presents the imaginary aspects of what he will systematize later under the name of the 'thrust-towards-the-Woman'.

THE PRESSURE TO CHANGE INTO A WOMAN

Krafft-Ebing writes in *Psychopathia Sexualis*: 'But who could describe my fright when, on the next morning, I awoke and found myself feeling as if completely changed into a woman; and when, on standing and walking, I felt vulva and *mamae*!' (1894: 203)

Lacan gave new meaning to a phenomenon often observed in psychotic patients: feminization by replacing a literal interpretation of Freud's 'rejection of homosexuality' with what later became a new theory of psychotic transsex-ualism under the tag 'thrust-towards-the-Woman'. This is a tricky phrase, '*pousse-à-la-femme*', which would be better rendered in English as 'driving one to become a woman' if the term 'drive' were not already a technical concept translating Freud's *Trieb*.

Renée Richards, 72, was asked recently about the motivations for her sex change more than 30 years ago. By a striking coincidence, she described her decision to change sex as the result of an unyielding 'pressure to change into a woman', which sounds like a good translation of Lacan's expression '*pousse-à-la-femme*'. She also talked about wishing for something that could have stopped that 'pressure' and prevented the surgery: 'What I said was if there were a drug, some voodoo, any kind of mind-altering magic remedy to keep the man intact, that would have been preferable, but there wasn't.' She seemed to have regrets about something that she felt was inevitable: 'Better to be an intact man functioning with 100 percent capacity for everything than to be a transsexual woman who is an imperfect woman.' However, the imperative to turn into a woman became a way to ward off suicide: 'The pressure to change into a woman was so strong that if I had not been able to do it, I might have been a suicide' (see Wadler 2007). Was that a psychotic moment, or an acting-out? How does the 'pressure to change into a woman' entail a performative femininity?

Millot refers to the feminization often observed in psychosis and notes that primary transsexuality may not involve psychotic symptoms, which may make us question whether the 'pressure-to-change-into-the-Woman' is specific to psychosis or whether it could be considered a more generalized phenomenon (1990: 42). Franz Kaltenbeck proposes the application of the '*pousse-à-la-femme*' to all clinical structures, always keeping in mind a differential diagnosis. He considers the 'pressure-to-change-into-the-Woman' in psychosis to be the opposite of the attraction towards a woman one may find in neurosis and perversion. He notes that the attraction that the Other woman possesses for the hysteric woman shows that the Other woman is not an exclusive element specific to the genital drive of men. He calls the '*pousse-à-la-femme*' a 'clinical belvedere', a vantage viewpoint for both sexes and for all structures (neurosis, perversion and psychosis) (1992: 9–10).

As we have seen, for the unconscious, regardless of one's sex, the opposite sex is always female. The 'thrust-towards-the-Woman' can be a way of writing what does not cease not being written. Freud discovered that the fantasy of feminization he heard in his neurotic patients displayed a structural character. On the one hand, it represented a feminine attitude: 'There can be no doubt that the original fantasy in the case of the girl, "I am being beaten (that is I am loved) by my father", represents a feminine attitude' (1955: 201). He anticipated that this neurotic fantasy which implied an underlying feminine attitude was also to be found in psychosis: 'I should not be surprised if it were one day possible to prove that the same fantasy is the basis of the delusional litigiousness of paranoia' (ibid.: 194).

Éric Laurent, like Kaltenbeck, applies the 'pressure-to-change-into-the-Woman' to both men and women. He sees it not as a phenomenological category but as a logical concept related to the drive (1992: 12). For him, this thrust is how the drive functions in psychosis, aiming at the Woman that all men lack (1989: 31). This would be the urge to find 'the woman that does not exist' (Lacan 1990: 60). Morel observes: 'The woman only exists in psychosis as a vanishing point of convergence in a delusional perspective, as a point placed in the infinite' (2002: 226; my translation).

In Lacan's sexuation formulae, the symbolic phallus requires the correlate of a barred Woman. If the Name-of-the-Father is foreclosed, the Woman exists as a delusional substitute, equivalent to the exception of the primal father $\exists x\text{-}\Phi x$. The Woman functions as an ideal image of the body and as an empty envelope that produces jouissance, a jouissance beyond the phallus, the jouissance of the Other.[9] The Woman becomes a solution to the problem of the real of jouissance. Thus Lacan writes in 'On a Question Preliminary to any Possible Treatment of Psychosis' (1959; here 2006a) that, for Schreber, 'unable to

---

9 Jean-Claude Maleval, exploring what he calls the psychotic 'dislocation of jouissance', clearly distinguishes phallic jouissance from jouissance of the Other:

> The jouissance of the Other is not regulated by the law of the signifier, in a manner that it finds its satisfaction in objects that are not separated from the subject. In Freudian terms, this would be a pre-genital jouissance, this is to say that it is not subjected to the primacy of the phallus. This jouissance is crazy, enigmatic, outside the symbolic; it is centred in the subject's body and on its organs [. . .]. The foreclosure of the Name-of-the-Father implies the absence of a limit regarding jouissance, a limit established by the loss of a primal object. The psychotic subject finds himself invaded by the jouissance of the Other, his body becomes the site of various diverse phenomena, pleasant and painful, voluptuous and anxiety provoking (1997: 119–20; my translation).

be the phallus the mother is missing, there remained the solution of being the woman that men are missing' (2006a: 472).

American drag queen Ru Paul is very aware of the difference between impersonating a woman and Woman. Reportedly, he once said: 'I do not impersonate females! How many women do you know who wear seven-inch heels, four-foot wigs, and skintight dresses?' He added: 'I don't dress like a woman; I dress like a drag queen!' The crucial role played by 'the' Woman for some transsexuals calls to mind a case that I supervised of a male pre-surgical transvestite who was transitioning to female, whom I will call Victoria. Tall, attractive and seductive, she insisted that she knew how to give sexual pleasure to any man—she had what it took for that. She could guarantee that no man could be dissatisfied with her, that she could offer pleasure to every man in the world.

For Victoria, access to universal jouissance was only a problem of time— in the end, she would give pleasure to all men. She not only felt superior to biological women, she often felt observed enviously by other women because she was much better looking and 'more woman than them', which she felt was because of her ability to provide jouissance to men. She was positioned as the woman with a W but focused on inscribing the All (she was Woman, $\exists x\text{-}\Phi x$, and she could give pleasure to All men, 'x'). Assuming the position of the exception, it was as if Victoria rewrote with Schreber the phrase: 'There is no woman that can be more woman than me as far as jouissance is concerned.' In that feminizing metamorphosis, she tried to prove that the Woman existed by becoming one.

Victoria's case evinces a particular relation to the body: as an eight-year-old boy, she was raped by a relative. This violent attack against her body was experienced with extreme detachment. It was as if her body was an envelope divested of libidinal value. In the transsexual artificiality of the embodiment of the Woman, Victoria remade and reclaimed her body in all its imaginary narcissistic value. With proficient make-up, carefully chosen clothes and silicone implants, she made of her becoming the Woman, her creative *sinthome*. She would quip: 'Women envy my body. But I made it. I worked on it.'

Millot's thesis is that Woman as a founding exception ($\exists x\text{-}\Phi x$) can function as a sort of Name-of-the-Father (Millot 1990: 36–46). It amounts to a myth similar to that of the father of the primal horde, and appears as both the limit and a substitute for the paternal function. Both the father of the primal horde and Woman are mythical starting points of unbridled fullness whose 'primordial repression' constitutes the symbolic order.

I will not explore any further the important function of the 'pressure-to-change-into-the-Woman' in McCloskey's memoir to avoid the treacherous waters of applied psychoanalysis, nor will I discuss how in *Crossing* the author is obstinately defining what a woman is, with overtones that are not only essentialist but that give a description of femininity in all the glory of full make-up, high heels, good manners, sense and sensibility, as if every woman should become the Woman (that one that Lacan has taught us, does not exist). I will prefer to focus on the function of writing in sex-change autobiographies. I will argue that memoirs of sex change offer for their authors the effect of reparation, an effect Lacan explained when he talked about Joyce's ego.

A PORTRAIT OF A WOMAN AS A YOUNG MAN

Some 20 years after a seminar that dealt with Schreber's transsexual psychosis, Lacan turned his attention to Joyce in *Le Sinthome*. He observed that Joyce's body could fall, slip away, like an envelope letting go of its contents. He focused on a passage in *A Portrait of the Artist as a Young Man* (1916; here 1992), where Stephen remembers a moment of rage at his schoolmates that suddenly faded away: he had felt his anger falling from him 'as easily as a fruit is divested of its soft ripe peel' (Joyce 1992: 87). Lacan remarks that this transformation of anger is suspect and concludes that Stephen has a particular body, one that could fall from one's self, like a wrapping that does not fully hold the contents (2005: Session 10, p. 149). For writing can 'hold' the body. When we talk of an important writer, art is hidden in artificiality. Taking into account the complex relationship that transsexuals have with their bodies—they often say their souls are trapped in a body of the wrong (opposite) sex—I will claim that an art similar to Joyce's (with all due proportion observed) can be found in transsexual artificiality; it gives birth to an art which, I will argue, is tantamount to a creative *sinthome*.

Here, it is important to stress the function of writing as modifying the materiality of the body and therefore impacting a point of view. To use another example, we have seen how painful it was for Deirdre to be 'read' as a transsexual; a nose job, a face lift, make-up classes, a voice operation, a collection of wigs—all these are aimed at transforming herself in a way that would make her 'unreadable'. Similarly, Lacan described Joyce's work as 'unreadable' because the signifier stuffs the signified (1998: 37). When a transsexual body is read, is it a body that is reduced to a letter? Is Deirdre's desire to pass, not to be read, a way of rejecting the letter as an effect of discourse? Or when Deirdre is read, has her distraught feeling of inadequacy something to do with readability, as if a sexual relation that can neither be written nor be read had become legible?

This sex-change memoir faithfully follows the requirements of the genre: the boy was already a girl. That transsexual narrative already plotted in the body, however, acquires coherence in it through the narrative. The autobiographical narrative changes the subject of the narrative, boy becomes girl, or vice versa, its narrative composes the 'I'. It is noteworthy that *Crossing* is written in the third person when narrating the stories of Donald and Deirdre, with an intermediate stage as a cross-dressing Dee, all along punctuated by occasional comments in bold type and in the first person singular for the voice of Deirdre. This voice-over progressively inscribes Deirdre as our hero, finally allowing her to 'hear the good news of forgiveness, the duty to offer, and the grace to receive' (McCloskey 1999: 16). McCloskey goes from fearing to 'be read like a book, detected in the wrong gender', aware that 'testing for being read is [a] paranoid style of life' (ibid.: 29) to writing a book in order to 'live as a woman, without notice or comment' (ibid.: 254). Although McCloskey's memoir renders her another mode of credibility, the effect of her writing lacks the opacity, the enigmatic quality that one finds in Joyce's and that makes of his work a *sinthome*. Deirdre McCloskey is no longer torn and thrilled by crossing (deciphering, inventing, undoing meaning) because she is finally passing.

What can one say about the transformation via the written narrative that occurs in Morris' *Conundrum*? Morris saw her 'escape from maleness into womanhood' (1974: 10) as a journey with 'some higher origin or meaning. I equate it with the idea of soul, or self, and I think of it not just as a sexual enigma, but as a quest for unity' (ibid.: 9). In 'unity' Morris could realize the truth of her sexuality:

I have had no doubt about my gender since that moment of self-re-alization beneath the piano [when she realized that she was born in the wrong body]. Nothing in the world would make me abandon my gender concealed from everyone though it remained; but my body, my organs, my paraphernalia, seemed to me much less sacrosanct, and far less interesting too (ibid.: 25–6).

Trapped as she was in a 'sexual incongruity' (ibid.: 172), for Morris 'gender' is opposed to 'body', 'organs', 'paraphernalia': 'I was born with the wrong body, being feminine my gender but male my sex, and I could achieve completeness only when the one was adjusted to the other' (ibid.: 26). She separates feeling like a woman from having the body of a woman: 'Male and female are sex, masculine and feminine are gender, and though the conceptions overlap, they are far from synonymous' (ibid.: 25). Kenneth Paradis points out the political implications of Morris' carefully constructed argument: 'By locating the truth of sex in the experiencing self rather than in the reproductive anatomy, the body becomes an object of subjective agency that can legitimately be altered' (2008: 157). With this strategy, Morris anticipates a trend: 'Could it be that I am merely a symptom of the times, a forerunner perhaps of a race in which sexes would be blended amoeba-like into one? The world was contracting fast [. . .] might not mankind discard its sexual divisions too?' (1974: 42).

Morris explains that she was not simply looking for a sex change but for the realization of her self: 'That my inchoate yearnings, both born from wind and sunshine, music and imagination—that my conundrum might simply be a matter of penis or vagina, testicle or womb, seems to me still a contradiction in terms, for it concerned not my apparatus, but my self' (ibid.: 21–2). Her quest was for a state of unity that was experienced as completion, making her body whole. 'I had myself long seen in my quest some veiled spiritual purpose, as though I was pursuing a Grail or grasping Oneness' (ibid.: 105). Trapped between a mythically and essentially female self/spirit and a constraining male anatomy, she longs for the One. This brings to mind Lacan's mirror stage, as if for Morris something had failed during the stage that leads the child to make its body image correspond to its mirror image and therefore conceive an image of itself. To make sense of how her feminine self, alienated in her male body, eventually manages to achieve unity via a genital ablation, hormones and transsexual autobiography, one needs to explore the idiosyncrasies of her peculiar relationship to her body.

Morris writes that in her previous life as a man, 'though I resented my body, I did not dislike it. I rather admired it, as it happened. It might not be the body beautiful, but it was lean and sinewy, never ran to fat and worked like a machine of quality, responding exuberantly to a touch of the throttle or the long haul home' (ibid.: 79); it was 'a marvelous thing to inhabit' (ibid.: 82). But by her mid-30s, after the birth of her daughter Virginia, she developed a bitter self-repugnance: 'I began to detest the body that had served me so loyally' (ibid.: 89). She became exiled from her body, experienced as an exterior One to which she tried to reconcile herself. 'And so I asked myself, in mercy, or in common sense, if I cannot alter the conviction to fit the body, should we not in certain circumstances, alter the body to fit the conviction? [. . .] 'To alter the body! To match my sex to my gender at last and make a whole of me' (ibid.: 49). 'All I wanted was liberation, or reconciliation—to live as myself, to clothe myself in a more proper body, and achieve Identity at last' and her solution to the dilemma was 'to adapt my body from a male conformation to a female, and I would shift my public role altogether, from the role of a man to the role of a woman' (ibid.: 104). In Casablanca, Morris underwent sex reassignment surgery with Dr B. 'I had a new body. Now when I looked down at myself I no longer seemed a hybrid or a chimera: I was all of a piece [. . .] I felt above all deliciously *clean* [. . .]. I was made, by my own lights, normal' (ibid.: 141).

The sex-change operation triggers an effect of normalization that affects the body and the spirit, as Morris attests: 'My body seemed to be growing more complex, more quivering in its responses, but my spirit felt simpler' (ibid.: 107). Of her previous life as James she says: 'I was a writer. Full as I was of more recondite certainties, I have always been sure of that too. I never for a moment doubted my vocation' (ibid.: 67). In writing about her writing, she describes her style as if it were already revealing an essential, traditional femininity, 'the quick emotionalism, the hovering tear, the heart-on-sleeve, the touch of schmaltz' (ibid.: 133); 'I often detected in myself a taste for the flamboyant [. . .] often a compensation for uncertainty' (ibid.: 132). She admits that 'creating to please my senses was certainly my own literary method' (ibid.: 95). I would argue that writing was an attempt to make body and spirit cohere, not so much to please her senses but as a strategy to regulate excess jouissance. This is achieved by way of an artifice, of a supplement (a sex change and writing about it) which allows for an incarnation of what was before only experienced in the real. This real is what is enacted in mystical phenomena or realized in psychosis. The real is the impossibility of sexual equivalence or rapport, the 'sexual incongruity' experienced by Morris. Since sexuality is linked to the death of the body, to reproduction, one can say that the body goes towards jouissance, to death, and that art, beautiful writing, touches on something of the beauty that glorifies the body while it regulates its jouissance.[10]

When Prosser talks about 'transsexual mirror stages', he quotes Morris' mirror scene in *Conundrum*, which describes her, minutes before going to the operating room for a sex change. Already anaesthetized, pubes shaven and disinfected, she staggers while going 'to say good bye to myself in the mirror. We would never meet again, and I wanted to give the other self a long last look in the eye, and a wink for luck' (ibid.: 140). The 'I' who writes will emerge 'alive, well, and sex-changed in Casablanca. [. . .] I had a new body' (ibid.: 140–1). Prosser describes this scene not only as a transitional moment in Morris' transsexual trajectory but as a crucial point in the transsexual narrative. This is when the 'me' written about in the biography and the 'I' that writes, 'so far separated by sex—are fused into a singly sexed autobiographical subject, an integral "I"' (Prosser 1998: 100). Morris' writing of the memoir allows her to embody her body. The sex-reassignment surgery re-knots the imaginary. She writes that as she reawakes from the surgery, despite the pain, 'I found myself, in fact, astonishingly happy' (1974: 140). The Moroccan surgeon who performs her sex change, seems aware of the stakes in her ordeal; during the post-operatory examination, Dr B. comments in a mix of French and heavily accented English: ' "*Trés, trés bon*, you could nevair get surgery like this in England—you see, now you would be able to *write*" ' (ibid.: 142).

And Morris writes, constructing with *Conundrum* a text that gives credibility to her being a woman. The memoir comes full circle. It opens with 'I was

---

10 See Lacan (1973–74: Session 9).

three years old when I realized that I have been born in the wrong body and should really be a girl. I remember the moment well, it is the earliest memory of my life' (ibid.: 3). Given that 'It is only in writing this book that I have delved so deeply into my emotions' (ibid.: 169), it is fair to say that Morris completes the evolution towards a solution to the conundrum of her existence through writing. The book closes with:

> [I]f I stand back and look at myself dispassionately, as I looked at my-self that night in the mirror in Casablanca—If I consider my story in detachment I sometimes seem, a figure of a fable or allegory [. . .] I see myself not as a man or woman, self or other, fragment or whole, but only as a wondering child with the cat beneath the Bluthner [piano] (ibid.: 174).

This is the vignette that begins the autobiography and ends it, which acquires new meaning through writing. The letter may be the same, but it reads differently. Now, being-able-to-do-with, Morris has acquired *savoir-faire*, know-how. Finally, a One has been achieved through her singular sinthomatic iden-tification, and it testifies to the power of transformation contained in writing.

I will conclude by saying that sex-change memoirs are meant to be read, to be interpreted. They beg for deciphering. They may be symptoms or *sinthome*.They may not be great literature but they aspire to the most essential function of literature. They are letters that somehow inscribe sexual difference. Writing a sex-change memoir aims not merely at 'passing', but in fact, has to deal with castration and to negotiate the real.

In some cases, writing one's transsexual transformation may be of the order of the *sinthome* when it achieves a re-knotting of the three registers. Then, the *sinthome* will pay attention to the singularity of the quasi-artistic production that aims at re-knotting a body whose consistency is never given once and for all.

Morris describes her trajectory as inevitable:

> I do not for a moment regret the act of change. I could see no other way, and it has made me happy [. . .] Sex has its reasons too, but I suspect the only transsexuals who can achieve happiness are those [. . .] to whom it is not primarily a sexual dilemma at all—who offer

no rational purpose to their compulsions, even to themselves, but are simply driven blindly and helplessly [. . .] we are the most resolute. Nothing will stop us, no fear of ridicule or poverty, no threat of isolation, not even the prospect of death itself (ibid.: 168–9).

One can see how her *sinthome* is necessary. Lacan adapts the classic philosophical definition of 'necessary as that which cannot cease being', and changes it for 'necessary as that which does not cease being written'. The *sinthome* is what does not cease to be written, it turns and returns. Written again and again, in Morris' case, her *sinthome* has produced less a 'woman' than a 'woman of letters'.

References

AMES, Jonathan (ed.). 2005. 'Introduction' to Jonathan Ames (ed.), *Sexual Metamorphosis: An Anthology of Transsexual Memoirs*. New York: Vintage, pp. ix–xvi.

BOYD, Helen. 2007. *She's Not the Man I Married: My Life with a Transgender Husband*. Emeryville, CA: Seal Press.

BUTLER, Judith. 1993. 'The Lesbian Phallus and the Morphological Imaginary' in *Bodies That Matter: On the Discursive Limits of 'Sex'*. New York and London: Routledge, 57–91; 257–65.

COUNTY, Jayne and Rupert Smith. 1995. *Man Enough to be a Woman*. New York and London: Serpent's Tail.

DEAN, Tim. 2000. *Beyond Sexuality*. Chicago and London: The University of Chicago Press.

FREUD, Sigmund. 1953. *Three Essays on the Theory of Sexuality* in *The Standard Edition of the Complete Psychological Works of Sigmund Freud*, VOL. 7 (James Strachey ed., and trans.). London: Hogarth Press and the Institute of Psycho-analysis, pp. 123–246.

————. 1955. '"A Child is Being Beaten": A Contribution to the Study of the Origin of Sexual Perversions' in *The Standard Edition of the Complete Psychological Works of Sigmund Freud*, VOL. 17 (James Strachey ed., and trans.). London: Hogarth Press and the Institute of Psycho-analysis, pp. 175–204.

————. 1958. 'Psycho-Analytic Notes on an Autobiographical Account of a Case of Paranoia' in *The Standard Edition of the Complete Psychological Works of Sigmund Freud*, VOL. 12 (James Strachey ed., and trans.). London: Hogarth Press and the Institute of Psycho-analysis, pp. 1–82.

————. 1964. 'Analysis Terminable and Interminable' in *The Standard Edition of the Complete Psychological Works of Sigmund Freud*, VOL. 23 (James Strachey ed., and trans.). London: Hogarth Press and the Institute of Psycho-analysis, pp. 209–54.

GHEROVICI, Patricia. 2007. 'Is Sexuality Nature's Joke?'. Seminar given at Après-Coup Psychoanalytic Association, New York, 2 June.

————. 2010. *Please Select Your Gender: From the Invention of Hysteria to the Democratizing of Transgenderism*. New York and Oxford: Routledge.

GRIGGS, Claudine. 1998. *S/HE: Changing Sex and Changing Clothes (Dress, Body, Culture)*. Oxford and New York: Berg.

HAUSMAN, Bernice L. 1995. *Changing Sex: Transsexualism, Technology, and the Idea of Gender*. Durham, NC and London: Duke University Press.

HUNT, Nancy. 1978. *Mirror Image: The Odyssey of a Male-to-Female Transsexual*. New York: Holt, Rinehart and Winston.

IRIGARAY, Luce. 1985. *This Sex Which is Not One* (Catherine Porter trans). Ithaca, NY: Cornell University Press.

JORGENSEN, Christine. 1967. *Christine Jorgensen: A Personal Autobiography*. New York: Paul Eriksson.

JOYCE, James. 1992 [1916]. *A Portrait of the Artist as a Young Man* (Seamus Deane ed.). New York: Penguin.

KHOSLA, Dhillon. 2006. *Both Sides Now: One Man's Journey through Womanhood*. New York: Penguin.

KRAFFT-EBING, Richard Von. 1894. *Psychopathia Sexualis: With Special Attention to Contrary Sexual Instinct* (Charles Gilbert Chaddock trans.). Philadelphia: The F. A. Davis Company.

LACAN, Jacques. 1981a. *The Seminar of Jacques Lacan. Book XI. The Four Fundamental Concepts of Psychoanalysis, 1964* (Jacques-Alain Miller ed. and Alan Sheridan trans.). New York and London: W. W. Norton.

———. 1990. *Television: A Challenge to the Psychoanalytic Establishment* (Joan Copjec ed. and Denis Hollier, Rosalind Krauss and Annette Michelson trans). New York and London: W. W. Norton.

———. 1993. *The Seminar of Jacques Lacan. Book III. The Psychoses, 1955–56* (Jacques-Alain Miller ed. and Russell Grigg trans.). New York: W. W. Norton; London: Routledge.

———. 1998. *The Seminar of Jacques Lacan. Book XX. Encore: On Feminine Sexuality, The Limits of Love and Knowledge, 1972–73* (Jacques-Alain Miller ed. and Bruce Fink trans.). New York and London: W. W. Norton.

———. 2006a. 'On a Question Preliminary to any Possible Treatment of Psychosis' in *Écrits: The First Complete Edition in English* (Bruce Fink trans.). New York and London: W. W. Norton, pp. 445–88.

———. 2006b. 'The Signification of the Phallus' in *Écrits: The First Complete Edition in English* (Bruce Fink trans.). New York and London: W. W. Norton, pp. 575–84.

———. 2006c. 'The Subversion of the Subject and the Dialectic of Desire in the Freudian Unconscious' in *Écrits: The First Complete Edition in English* (Bruce Fink trans.). New York and London: W. W. Norton, pp. 671–702.

LAURENT, Éric. 1989. 'Límites en las Psicosis' in Éric Laurent (ed.), *Estabilizaciones en las Psicosis*. Buenos Aires: Manantial, pp. 21–35.

LEWINS, Frank. 1995. *Transsexualism in Transsexuals*. Melbourne: Macmillan.

MAHIEU, Eduardo Tomas. 2004. *El empuje a la mujer: Formas, transformaciones y estructura*. Cordoba: El espejo Ediciones.

MARTINO, Mario. 1977. *Emergence: A Transsexual Autobiography*. New York: Crown Publishers.

MCCLOSKEY, Deirdre N. 1999. *Crossing: A Memoir*. Chicago and London: The University of Chicago Press.

MILLOT, Catherine. 1990. *Horsexe: Essay on Transsexuality* (Kenneth Hylton trans.). New York: Autonomedia.

MOREL, Geneviève. 2002. *Ambigüedades sexuales: sexuación y psicosis*. Buenos Aires and Paris: Manantial.

———. 2006. 'The Sexual *Sinthome*'. *Umbr(a): A Journal of the Unconscious* 1: 65–83.

MORRIS, Jan. 1974. *Conundrum—An Extraordinary Personal Narrative of Transsexualism*. New York: Harcourt Brace Jovanovich.

PARADIS, Kenneth. 2008. *Sex, Paranoia, and Modern Masculinity*. New York: State University of New York Press.

PROSSER, Jay. 1998. *Second Skins: The Body Narratives of Transsexuality*. New York: Columbia University Press.

RICHARDS, Renée. 1983. *Second Serve: The Renée Richards Story*. New York: Stein and Day.

SHAPIRO, Judith. 1991. 'Transsexualism: Reflections on the Persistence of Gender and the Mutability of Sex' in Julia Epstein and Kristina Straub (eds), *Body Guards: The Cultural Politics of Gender Ambiguity*. New York and London: Routledge, pp. 248–79.

SCHREBER, Daniel Paul. 2000. *Memoirs of My Nervous Illness* (Ida Macalpine and Richard A. Hunter eds and trans). New York: New York Review of Books.

STOLLER, Robert J. 1985. *Presentations of Gender*. New Haven, CT: Yale University Press.

STONE, Sandy. 1991. 'The Empire Strikes Back: A Posttransexual Manifesto' in Julia Epstein and Kristina Straub (eds), *Body Guards: The Cultural Politics of Gender Ambiguity*. New York and London: Routledge, pp. 280–304.

VALERIO, Max Wolf. 2006. *The Testosterone Files: My Hormonal and Social Transformation from Female to Male*. Emeryville, CA: Seal Press.

VAN HAUTE, Philippe. 2002. *Against Adaptation: Lacan's 'Subversion' of the Subject* (Paul Crowe and Miranda Vankerk trans). New York: Other Press.

WADLER, Joyce. 2007. 'The Lady Regrets: At Home with Renée Richards'. *The New York Times*. 1 February 2007. Available at http://www.nytimes.-com/2007/02/01/garden/01renee.html. Accessed on 26 January 2011.

WILTON, Tamsin. 2000. 'Out/Performing Our Selves: Sex, Gender and Cartesian Dualism'. *Sexualities* 3(2): 237–54.

FRENCH SOURCES

HUBERT, H. 2001. 'L'enigme transsexuelle' in François Sauvagnat (ed.), *Divisions subjectives et personnalités multiples*. Paris: Presses Universitaires de Rennes, pp. 201–238.

KALTENBECK, Franz. 1992. 'Le "pousse-à-la-femme", un belvédère clinique'. *La Lettre Mensuelle* 112 (September–October): 9–10.

LACAN, Jacques. 1959. 'D'une question préliminaire à tout traitement possible de la psychose'. *La Psychanalyse* 4: 1–50. Subsequently published in *Écrits* (1966).

———. 1966a. 'La Signification du phallus' in *Écrits*. Paris: Éditions du Seuil.

———. 1966b. 'Subversion du sujet et dialectique du désir l'inconscient Freudienne' in *Écrits*. Paris: Éditions du Seuil.

———. 1970. 'Radiophonie'. *Scilicet* 2/3: 55–99.

———. 1973. *Le Séminaire. Livre XI. Les quatre concepts fondamentaux de la psychanalyse, 1964* (Jacques-Alain Miller ed.). Paris: Éditions du Seuil.

———. 1973–74. Le Séminaire. Livre XXI. Les non-dupes errent/ Les noms-du-pére. Unpublished manuscripts.

———. 1974. *Télévision*. Paris: Éditions du Seuil.

———. 1975. *Le Séminaire. Livre XX. Encore, 1972–73*. Paris: Éditions du Seuil.

———. 1981b. *Le Séminaire. Livre III. Les Psychoses, 1955–56* (Jacques-Alain Miller ed.). Paris: Éditions du Seuil.

———. 2005. *Le Séminaire. Livre XXIII. Le Sinthome, 1975–76* (Jacques-Alain Miller ed.). Paris: Éditions du Seuil.

———. 2011. *Le Séminaire. Livre XIX. . . . Ou Pire, 1971–72* (Jacques-Alain Miller ed.). Paris: Éditions du Seuil.

LAURENT, Éric. 1992. 'Lettre à la "Lettre mensuelle"'. *La Lettre Mensuelle* 114: 12–13.

MALEVAL, Jean-Claude. 1997. *Logique du délire*. Paris: Masson.

PONTALIS, J. B. (ed.). 2000. *Bisexualité et Différence des Sexes*. Paris: Éditions Gallimard.

SAFOUAN, Moustafa. 1974. 'Contribution à la psychanalyse du transsexualisme'. *Scilicet* 4: 137–59.

Afterword:
The Enigma of Jouissance
Russell Grigg

Novelists often declare that characters in their novels tend to take on a life of their own, so that the author can never say in advance what twists and turns the plot may take or what the characters might do. I have found that much the same thing happens when I write a theoretical essay. I begin with an idea, formulate a thesis and map out the general argument. And then, once it is written, I find that I have ended up in some place different from where I intended to go. This essay is no exception.

My original idea was that the traumatic nature of jouissance is not due to its intensity or strength or power, but rather to the fact that it is enigmatic. I was taking my cue from a remark in the 1975 'Geneva Lecture on the Symptom' that Jacques Lacan made in relation to Little Hans: 'The enjoyment [jouissance] that resulted from [Little Hans'] *Wiwimacher* is alien to him—so much so that it is at the root of his phobia. "Phobia" means he has got the wind up' (1989: 16). That is to say, the jouissance is traumatic for Little Hans because he has no way of understanding its source and origin, or in less psychological terms, because it is not inscribed in a signifying chain. Thus, it is traumatic, not because of its intensity but because it is enigmatic. So my thesis initially was that jouissance is traumatic precisely in so far as it is meaningless, in so far as it escapes or exceeds the symbolic network within which it is inscribed. And, I would have argued, we can see this in the case of Little Hans, in the case of Daniel Paul Schreber and in many cases of ordinary psychosis.

However, the more I looked into the issue, the more it seemed to me that my title had a second meaning, as relevant as the first: the very *concept* of jouissance itself is enigmatic, in that it is not well understood and leaves us with a number of puzzles, though it might seem odd to say so, since it seems rather clear, these days, with all that has been written on it, that jouissance is the special type of satisfaction which lies beyond the pleasure/pain dialectic; that is, beyond the pleasure principle. It is related to the drive and Sigmund Freud's concept of satisfaction, *Genuss*, of the drive, and to the *objet petit a* or *object a*. However, I see several obscurities with the concept and wish to clarify some of the issues that it raises. But before I turn to them I would like to comment on what jouissance is.

My focus in this essay is on the use to which Lacan puts this specialized concept. While there is quite a lot of discussion about this concept in the literature, most of these commentaries focus on the ways in which Lacan's thinking about jouissance changes and evolves.[1] While this discussion is important, since it brings out some substantive theses and some reflections on the reasons for the concept's evolution, there is nevertheless a prior issue to be addressed which is at risk of being confused with this: the issue of the meaning of the concept and whether it has more than one meaning. It is important because, strictly speaking, not all the changes in Lacan's use of the concept are in the concept of jouissance; at least some of the changes are in the ways in which Lacan thinks about the sources and the consequences of jouissance. If, indeed, there is more than one sense of the term, as I believe there is, there is the further issue of what, if anything, the different meanings have in common. It would be odd if they had nothing in common, but we should not dismiss this possibility out of hand.

We might thus wonder not only whether jouissance is only produced through transgression, or whether there is mystical jouissance in mystical experience, or what its connection is with the satisfaction produced by a symptom, but also whether the concept is being used in different ways in each of these contexts and whether these different uses have anything in common. This is a necessary step, without which we will be prone to the confusion expressed, for instance, in Dylan Evans' comment that 'jouissance does not retain a stable meaning' across Lacan's work and that its 'resonances and articulations

---

1 The three most detailed discussions I am aware of are by Miller (1999), which has been translated into English (see Miller 2000) but it is best to read it in the original, Braunstein (1992) and Evans (1998).

shift dramatically over the course of his teaching' (Evans 1998: 2), which may confuse the distinction between changes in what the term refers to and questions about what Lacan thinks the conditions and consequences of jouissance are, that is, the distinction between what the concept means and what Lacan thinks is true of it.

The broadest possible definition of jouissance, as Lacan understands it, is that it is synonymous with the drive's satisfaction; it is not necessarily sexual, nor is it necessarily unpleasurable, though it can be both. At different stages of his work, Lacan states that this satisfaction can arise from imaginary, real or symbolic sources—for instance, the narcissistic jouissance obtained from the imaginary dyad of ego and alter-ego; the symbolic jouissance obtained from the *Witz* [wit], as analyzed by Lacan in *Le Séminaire. Livre V. Les formations de l'inconscient, 1957–58* (The Formations of the Unconscious; 1998b); or the jouissance that arises from a symptom and whose origin is ultimately 'the real' of one's drive. In this most general definition of the term, despite its having been elaborated by Lacan at different times, these cases combine to show the different possible ways—imaginary, symbolic and real—in which human beings enjoy.

Jouissance also refers to satisfaction that, though satisfying a desire, can be experienced as unpleasurable. This is not an original observation with Lacan. Freud drew attention to it as early as *The Interpretation of Dreams* (1899; here 1953), where he pointed out that the satisfaction of an unconscious wish is capable of producing anxiety. Two of the implications of the Freudian discovery of a division at the heart of human subjectivity are that the subject will repudiate and prohibit the satisfaction of his most fundamental desires, and that these can only be satisfied in a disguised form if distress and anxiety are to be avoided.

For Freud, the satisfaction of a desire—or the fulfilment of a wish—will be perceived as unpleasurable when the desire is repressed ('repudiated', 'prohibited') and when there is not sufficient disguise. It would be possible to restrict the use of 'jouissance', then, to refer to the illicit satisfaction of a repressed desire where there is no pleasure. It would, however, not only be unnecessary but also unfortunate because it would, for no good reason, cut the link between the satisfaction of desires that are repressed and those that are not. Moreover, jouissance cannot be merely the (un)pleasure obtained from the satisfaction of a repressed desire, and its relationship to transgression is a little more complex than that. We get an idea of this greater complexity by considering the detailed treatment the concept of jouissance is given in *The Seminar of Jacques Lacan. Book VII. The Ethics of Psychoanalysis, 1959–60* (1986; here 1992) where it is important to appreciate that his analysis is developed out of two phenomena: the special sort of satisfaction obtained from the re-nunciation of desire, especially in the name of the moral law, and the special kind of satisfaction arising from acts of transgression. These two phenomena would appear to be opposite—and there is no answer to the enigma of jouis-sance unless one recognizes this opposition and resolves it. This is the under-lying and fundamental issue concerning Lacan's concept of jouissance and it is the central enigma that I address here. There are three general obscurities with the concept on which I should comment.

The first concerns the source and origin of jouissance, which is absolutely not the body because, firstly, there is jouissance even where the body is not at stake—there is jouissance in thinking, for instance. The jouissance in the men-tal life of obsessionals, at the root of their ruminations, is not *bodily*. Secondly, as Lacan tells us, there is *jouis-sens*, enjoy-meant, an enjoyment of meaning, which we derive from the blah-blah-blah of language, just as—as Lacan demon-strates with his study of Joyce—there is the jouissance of the letter. It is because its source is not the body that Lacan describes jouissance as 'of the real'—in the sense of belonging to the real and sharing its features or characteristics—whereas the body is located largely in the imaginary. But how clear is the idea that the source of jouissance is not the body but the real?

The second obscurity with the concept of jouissance is: why does Lacan draw a profound distinction between jouissance and language? This distinction runs so deep as to be a form of 'dualism', a true ontological dualism that re-places and rivals the mind/body dualism of René Descartes; it is a jouissance/sig-nifier dualism.

What, to my mind, is profoundly obscure about this dualism, whereby the signifier and jouissance belong to two incommensurate and opposite registers—the symbolic and the real respectively—is that it is very difficult to see how one can maintain the opposition for long. The concept of jouissance cannot be understood without reference to the register of meaning or be defined without the concept of meaning; and since meaning is what signifiers produce, the dualism collapses.

But why does the concept of jouissance always invoke the realm of meaning? It is because, first, when Lacan refers to jouissance, the question of meaning is never far away. In *The Seminar of Jacques Lacan. Book XX. Encore: On Feminine Sexuality, The Limits of Love and Knowledge, 1972–73* (1998a) for example, he famously refers to the 'jouissance of the idiot' (1998a: 81, 94), which locates jouissance in the realm of meaning—albeit in the form of the absence of meaning. Second, considering the enigma of jouissance concerning Little Hans' *Wiwimacher*, where, the fact that it is an enigma implies that it is located in the field of meaning—an enigma is an enigma because we expect it to have a meaning and we then worry because we fail to decipher the meaning. This is roughly how Lacan defines an enigma, though his definition is narrower, when he claims that an enigma is an utterance whose statement we do not understand. Third, by thinking of jouissance as a concept that makes no sense without reference to meaning we can throw light on the differences between what Lacan calls phallic jouissance, *jouissance phallique* or the idiot's jouissance and jouissance of the Other, *jouissance de l'Autre*. On the one hand, we think of phallic jouissance as regulated by a network of signifiers and thus imbued with meaning and, on the other, we think of the Other's jouissance as lying outside the field of signifiers altogether and thus inaccessible to meaning. This relationship between the two types is important, and I will return to discuss it at greater length, after a brief mention of a further complication with the concept of jouissance.

JOUISSANCE AND SYMPTOM

Lacan's thinking about jouissance evolves especially in relation to the nature of symptoms. There is, nevertheless, one constant throughout his teaching, which is that a symptom is a source of enjoyment, even if his views about the rest change. In an excellent article, 'Paradigms of *Jouissance*', Miller discerns six uses of the term at different moments of Lacan's teaching (see Miller 2000).

One might not agree with the entire classification, but we can agree that the basic point—that Lacan's use of the term evolves—is undeniable. I want to mention three ways in which Lacan uses the term.

In the first instance, jouissance is fixated and regulated by signifiers that encode—'encipher'—the unconscious in the form of symptoms. Thus, a symptom is both a body of signifiers and a source of enjoyment. A symptom embodies jouissance—though 'embodies' is not quite the right word since a symptom is not invariably inscribed on the body but can affect thought as well, for example, in the form of procrastination or doubt or compulsive ideas, as I have already observed. It might be more accurate to say that a symptom *insignifies* jouissance. It is because a symptom is a product of repression that its jouissance is experienced as unpleasure.

In the first conception of jouissance, then, there is a close relation between meaning and jouissance. That symptoms both have meaning and are a source of satisfaction was Freud's discovery, which Lacan formulates by stating that a symptom is a source of jouissance whose meaning is closed off to the subject. It is a question of meaning, even if the meaning is opaque.

This observation is important clinically. People visit a psychoanalyst because they are miserable or anxious or lonely or in the midst of a personal crisis or disturbed by a compulsion to harm themselves and they also want to know what is going on, why they feel, think and act as they do. Each of these phenomena is a problem because its meaning is opaque, not only because it makes them miserable. Or, rather, the opacity of the phenomenon is integral to the misery. It is not a question of quantity or strength or degree of jouissance. That there is 'too much' or 'too little' jouissance cannot be said in any absolute sense, since its 'amount' is necessarily relative to its 'meaning', the reason for its occurrence and its motivation. The significance of deciphering a symptom's meaning is that, by unpacking the hidden reasons that motivate it, it makes the jouissance understandable. Of course, what I have put in psychological terms of 'understanding', etc. can also be expressed in a different way, by talking about the regulation of jouissance, in terms of a phallic economy, and so on.

Thinking in terms of the *regulation* of jouissance is particularly relevant when we turn our attention to psychosis, since here, the *failure* of the regulation of jouissance in the absence of the signifier, the Name-of-the-Father, has devastating consequences. Schreber, for instance, is invaded by jouissance, which finds expression in psychotic phenomena such as the destruction of body parts and organs, the manifestation of a persecutory other and Schreber's transformation into a woman, or into The woman who will become the partner of God. Again, as discussed by Jonathan Redmond, in more 'ordinary' cases of psychosis, we see more subtle signs that the regulation of jouissance has failed, leading to accounts of 'partial foreclosure' or some alternative way of explaining why in many cases with an evidently psychotic structure, the classic symptoms of psychosis never develop or appear (see Redmond 2009).

When we speak of the regulation of jouissance in each of these contexts, we use a quantitative metaphor and are at least implicitly appealing to something that can be measured. But this language is pure metaphor, since there is no real suggestion that we can ever quantify jouissance. 'Regulation' is a metaphor of exchange, of the market that can be regulated, deregulated or unregulated. In neurosis, jouissance is 'regulated', whereas in psychosis, it is 'deregulated' or 'unregulated'. In either case, it is only a metaphor and to speak of the regulation of jouissance is to say that it is structured by signifiers; and to structure something by signifiers is to make it meaningful.

One of the subsequent ways Lacan thinks about jouissance, one that has enjoyed a huge degree of success, dates from *The Ethics of Psychoanalysis*, where jouissance is construed as impossible, or, in Lacan's terms, as real. This is what Lacan means by Freud's concept of *das Ding* (the Thing): satisfaction of the drive occurs neither in the symbolic nor in the imaginary but in the real. One does not repress jouissance, since it is in the real and since repression is a phenomenon of signifiers and therefore implies deciphering or decoding; rather, one *defends against* jouissance, which is henceforth neither a product of the symbolic nor related to it but exists even before the conditions that make repression possible arise.

It would seem that if jouissance lies outside the symbolic and the imaginary it is fundamentally inaccessible—except in the one exceptional way described in this seminar, which is by forcing a break through the symbolic by challenging the fundamentals of the symbolic universe in a procedure, or better, an act, that Lacan calls 'transgression'. Taking Antigone's refusal to comply with the edicts of her ruler, Creon, as the prime example, this transgression readily takes on a heroic dimension and we thus acquire a tendency to indulge in praise of the hero who fearlessly and uncompromisingly advances into the horrific destruction of the symbolic world. This understanding of jouissance is most famously advocated by Slavoj Žižek, who has treated Antigone's actions as definitive of the mode of access to jouissance and as inaugurating a new—and in my view, romanticized—ethics of the real. Žižek is right to point to the ethical character of Antigone's act, for the strange thing is that there is no transgression in Antigone in anything but the most superficial of senses. Of course, she breaks the law, but it is Creon's law, and she breaks it 'as a matter of principle' and for the sake of a higher law that, she believes, overrides Creon's law. Apart from the ethical conclusions that Žižek draws from his reading of *The Ethics of Psychoanalysis*, which I have discussed elsewhere (Grigg 2008: 119–31), Lacan's redefinition of jouissance is problematic for several reasons.

First, by locating jouissance in the real Lacan makes a radical break with his initial teaching, which is not a problem in itself. However, he thereby introduces a fundamental distinction and an unbridgeable gap between the signifier and jouissance, to the point where one has to wonder how psychoanalytic praxis, the talking cure, can ever possibly operate and have any effect upon a subject's jouissance. And this is a problem because if the only means of access to jouissance is through transgression, if it lies in the real, outside and untouched by the symbolic, then how can a procedure that operates by deploying signifiers have any impact upon the sources of a subject's enjoyment? If we aim to effect some alteration in a subject's modes of enjoyment, then there must be something commensurate between the manner of our intervention, which of course is through language, and the outcome of this intervention, which is to modify jouissance.

Second, the thesis here is that the only means of access to jouissance is through transgression. The idea has encountered considerable success, particularly in the academy. But how true is it? Symptoms are a form of jouissance. But are we therefore to conclude that symptoms are a form of transgression? Is not a symptom rather the opposite of a transgression? A symptom is the result of repression, and do we not repress desires instead of transgressing? Moreover, we also know that enjoyment is permanent and, effectively, inescapable for speaking beings. So, where is the relationship between jouissance and transgression?

Lacan himself rather discreetly abandons this thesis about the relationship between transgression and jouissance in *The Seminar of Jacques Lacan. Book XVII. The Other Side of Psychoanalysis, 1969–70* (1991; here 2007) where he introduces the four discourses, by remarking: 'What analysis shows, if it shows anything at all [. . .] is very precisely the fact that we don't ever transgress' (2007: 19). I think that he abandons the thesis that transgression is the sole route to jouissance because it faces too many difficulties to be correct.

However, what should not be lost in all of this is the really important distinction that emerges in *The Ethics of Psychoanalysis* between jouissance and *desire*, which marks a difference between what lies on the side of the pleasure principle and what lies beyond pleasure. Yet, while jouissance and desire are distinct, they are not completely independent. As the texts of Marquis de Sade illustrate very well, one of the characteristic features of pleasure is that it can act as a sort of obstacle to jouissance. As Miller contends, an opposition becomes established between the homeostasis of pleasure and the constitutive excesses of jouissance; between what is of the order of the Good, well-being, the side of pleasure on the one hand and, on the other, the excess of jouissance, the component of bad or evil that jouissance conveys; between what is of the order of the lure, of attraction, of pleasure, of the signifier, of the imaginary and of the semblant, and, on the other side, what is of the order of the real. We need to hold to this distinction because it marks a breakthrough.

The third moment I want to discuss occurs in Lacan's *Encore*, and the associated text, 'L'Etourdit' (1973), for here Lacan gives the concept of jouissance quite a different meaning from that which he had given it at the two earlier moments I have described. It is well known, notorious even, that in this seminar he introduces the idea of a specifically feminine jouissance. Since this concept has arguably produced the greatest amount of misunderstanding and ill-informed commentary on any of Lacan's views, I will clarify a point about it. This involves making some very specific and precise comments on some details of *Encore*, which can be encapsulated in two of Lacan's statements.

The first of these statements is not an incidental aside. Rather, it is significant enough for Lacan to write it up in large letters on the blackboard at the very first session of his seminar on 'Encore' on November 21, 1972: 'Jouissance of the Other, of the Other's body that symbolizes it, is not a sign of love' (1975: 11; my translation).[2] However, shortly afterwards in the same session, he adds that 'phallic enjoyment is the obstacle preventing a man from enjoying a woman's body because what he enjoys is enjoyment of the organ' (ibid.: 13).[3]

The contradiction is clear: the first proposition states that there is jouissance of the Other, even though it is not a sign of love and the second says that no man ever enjoys a woman's body because he only ever gets enjoyment from his organ.

The apparent contradiction, and hence a lot of the confusion, arises because of a failure to recognize the ambiguity that exists in French with the term *la jouissance de l'Autre*, where, specifically, the genitive *de* has a subjective and an objective sense. In the subjective sense, the jouissance is 'the Other's jouissance', its jouissance—or more appropriately, her jouissance, since this is the famous feminine jouissance that Lacan introduces—or, as it is sometimes translated by Bruce Fink, 'Other jouissance'. On the other hand, the genitive use of *de* in the objective sense means that there is a subject who enjoys the Other and has *la jouissance de l'Autre*, enjoyment of the Other. In this second, objective sense, one's jouissance of the Other is phallic jouissance.

And we now get, in a nutshell, Lacan's thesis that there is no sexual relationship. On the side of the objective genitive, we have phallic jouissance, which is introduced by castration and regulated by language, is subordinate to the symbolic order and is an obstacle that prevents access to jouissance of the Other. From this side, there is no possible access to jouissance of the Other; one is left with nothing but one's jouissance of the idiot, as Lacan puts it. The other side, which is that of the subjective genitive, is that of the Other's jouissance. The

---

2 The original French expression is '*La jouissance de l'Autre, du corps de l'Autre qui le symbolise, n'est pas le signe de l'amour*' (Lacan 1975: 11).

3 The original French expression is '*La jouissance phallique est l'obstacle par quoi l'homme n'arrive pas, dirai-je, à jouir du corps de la femme, précisément parce que ce dont il jouit, c'est de la jouissance de l'organe*' (ibid.: 13).

French have become accustomed to calling this meaning of '*la jouissance de l'Autre*' '*la jouissance Autre*', which translates as Other jouissance, but this is because in French, there is no obvious way of resolving the ambiguity of '*la jouissance de l'Autre*'. It can be resolved in English by calling it the Other's jouissance.

So, then, what can we say about this question of the Other's jouissance? To begin with, I think that the French term *jouissance Autre*, Other jouissance, is misleading because it suggests that Lacan is referring to a form of jouissance that lies beyond, somewhere else . . . follow my gaze, my son, my daughter. The reference to Saint Teresa suggests this too, with the notion of an Other jouissance that reaches out to a beyond.

But I believe this is an incorrect conception. For Lacan—and he is explicit about this—the Other's jouissance remains nevertheless jouissance of the body; it is always and everywhere *jouissance du corps de l'Autre*, jouissance of the Other's body, or, to make it even more explicit, the Other body's jouissance. Lacan's intention is not to refer to some '*Other* jouissance', as if it were an experience from the Other side, which would have the effect of making it religious and mystical. The Other's jouissance is the Other's bodily jouissance, and it is, by definition, inaccessible to anyone whose jouissance is solely phallic.

So, the Other's jouissance is in a sense the mystic's jouissance—but the ambiguity lies in the fact that the latter can be seen as lying in a beyond and occurring out of the body. Or it can be seen, and I think correctly so, as a form of bodily jouissance that escapes the phallic economy. The reference to the mystic's jouissance has to be seen in this context and it is intended to entail that feminine jouissance is not the exclusive property of women but, since there are male mystics, is also known to men. It goes beyond the logical closure of the phallic economy regulated by the symbolic. It goes beyond language and lies outside discourse even as it finds expression within the body.

As has often been pointed out, the formulae of sexuation are about the ways in which the sexual relationship fails.[4] These two forms of jouissance are two forms of the impossible, and hence failed, relationship between the signifier

---

4 One of the best discussions of this is to be found in Copjec (1994). See also Shepherdson (1994).

and the real. The phallic form is this impossibility that is experienced as a failure. The form of the Other's jouissance is this impossibility that is experienced as a beyond. There is, then, no sexual relationship because the juxtaposition of these two kinds of jouissance does not result in any kind of correspondence between man on one side and woman on the other.

To return to my theme, there is enigma in both phallic jouissance and the Other's jouissance. Indeed, the Other's jouissance *is only* an enigma, since it is defined by being enigmatic and, as such, calls incessantly to be rendered and regulated. Phallic jouissance, although in principle regulated, is susceptible to find expression in forms that escape regulation. The psychotic experience is a case in point. And, to make one last point, a speculative one, if in Schreber there is a thrust-towards-the-woman, *une pousse-à-la-femme*, then he can be compared with mystics—an idea that would no doubt have appealed to him.

The relationship between jouissance, meaning, pleasure and desire is complex and a fuller analysis than I am able to give here is called for. Nevertheless, a few broad conclusions can be drawn. The opposition between jouissance and signifier is situated within the semantic field. The opposition between jouissance and desire is making the wrong contrast because they are not alternatives—one of the meanings of jouissance is that it is synonymous with the satisfaction of desire. Even the opposition between jouissance and pleasure is not a hard and fast one, since it only applies where repression is concerned. And finally, jouissance cannot be equated with transgression without further comment, since, as the case of Antigone shows, it is precisely by cleaving to the moral law itself that jouissance arises. These are, I acknowledge, mainly negative conclusions, even if prompted by discussions of jouissance in the literature. They do show the complexity of the concept, even its polysemy. I am inclined to think that the multiple meanings of the concept are a significant factor in thinking about Lacan's claims, but this range of meanings has its limits and we must also acknowledge that the substantive claims Lacan makes about jouissance change, which means there is an internal criticism of his views, not simply an attribution of a different meaning to the term on different occasions.

References

ENGLISH SOURCES

COPJEC, Joan. 1994. 'Sex and the Euthanasia of Reason' in Joan Copjec (ed.), *Supposing the Subject*. London: Verso, pp. 16–44.

EVANS, Dylan. 1998. 'From Kantian Ethics to Mystical Experience: An Exploration of Jouissance' in Dany Nobus (ed.), *Key Concepts of Lacanian Psychoanalysis*. London: Rebus Press, pp. 1–28.

FREUD, Sigmund. 1953. *The Interpretation of Dreams* in *The Standard Edition of the Complete Psychological Works of Sigmund Freud*, VOLS 4 and 5 (James Strachey ed., and trans.). London: Hogarth Press and the Institute of Psycho-Analysis, pp. ix–630.

GRIGG, Russell. 2008. *Lacan, Language and Philosophy*. Albany: State University of New York Press.

LACAN, Jacques. 1989. 'Geneva Lecture on the Symptom' (Russell Grigg trans.). *Analysis* 1 (Australia): 7–26.

———. 1992. *The Seminar of Jacques Lacan. Book VII. The Ethics of Psychoanalysis, 1959–60* (Jacques-Alain Miller ed., Dennis Porter trans.). New York and London: W. W. Norton.

———. 1998a. *The Seminar of Jacques Lacan. Book XX. Encore: On Feminine Sexuality, The Limits of Love and Knowledge, 1972–73* (Jacques-Alain Miller ed., Bruce Fink trans.). New York and London: W. W. Norton.

———. 2007. *The Seminar of Jacques Lacan. Book XVII. The Other Side of Psychoanalysis, 1969–70* (Jacques-Alain Miller ed., Russell Grigg trans.). New York and London: W. W. Norton.

MILLER, Jacques-Alain. 2000. 'Paradigms of Jouissance' (Jorge Jauregui trans.). *Lacanian Ink* 17: 8–47.

REDMOND, Jonathan. 2009. 'Body events and ordinary psychosis'. Presentation at '"Anything but the symptom": Jouissance and the Body'. Joint workshop of the Australian Centre for Psychoanalysis and the Lacan Circle of Melbourne, Saturday 21 March.

SHEPHERDSON, Charles. 1994. 'The Role of Gender and the Imperative of Sex' in Joan Copjec (ed.), *Supposing the Subject*. London: Verso, pp. 158–84.

FRENCH SOURCES

BRAUNSTEIN, Néstor. 1992. *La jouissance: un concept lacanien*. Paris: Point Hors Ligne.

LACAN, Jacques. 1973. 'L'Etourdit'. *Scilicet* 4: 5–52.

———. 1975. *Le Séminaire. Livre XX. Encore, 1972–73* (Jacques-Alain Miller ed.). Paris: Éditions du Seuil.

———. 1985. 'Conférence à Genéve sur le symptôme'. *Le bloc-notes de la psychanalyse* 5: 5–23.

———. 1986. *Le Séminaire. Livre VII. L'éthique de la psychanalyse, 1959–60* (Jacques-Alain Miller ed.). Paris: Éditions du Seuil.

———. 1991. *Le Séminaire. Livre XVII. L'envers de la psychanalyse, 1969–70* (Jacques-Alain Miller ed.). Paris: Éditions du Seuil.

———. 1998b. *Le Séminaire. Livre V. Les formations de l'inconscient, 1957–58* (Jacques-Alain Miller ed.). Paris: Éditions du Seuil.

MILLER, Jacques-Alain. 1999. 'Les six paradigmes de la jouissance'. *La Cause freudienne: Revue de psychanalyse* 43: 7–29.

Notes on Contributors

GAUTAM BASU THAKUR is Assistant Professor of English at Boise State University, USA, where he teaches literature, literary theory, postcolonial studies and psychoanalysis. He has taught at Motilal Nehru College under the University of Delhi, India, and at the University of Mississippi, USA. He has published several articles on literature, postcolonial theory, psychoanalysis and culture studies in India and USA, and is currently working on a book tentatively titled *Indian Mutiny and the Rearrangement of Sovereign Desire*.

SANTANU BISWAS is Associate Professor of English at Jadavpur University, Calcutta, India, where he teaches literature and psychoanalysis. He is currently Visiting Research Fellow at Deakin University, Melbourne, Australia. He has written several articles on literature and psychoanalysis and has delivered numerous lectures on Lacan and literature in India and abroad. He directed the first national conference on Lacan in India in 2001 and the first international conference on Lacan in India in 2007. He is the founder of the Lacan Study Circle of Calcutta, and is an honorary member of the Lacan Circle of Melbourne. He is a member of the editorial board of *(Re)-Turn: A Journal of Lacanian Studies* (USA) and joint editor of *Clinic/Culture* (France and USA).

NANCY BLAKE is Professor of Comparative and World Literature at the University of Illinois, Urbana-Champaign, USA, where she teaches literature, psychoanalysis, translation and feminism. She is the author of several books on literature, psychoanalysis and literary theory, including *Ezra Pound et l'imagisme* (Université Paul Valéry, 1979), *Henry James: Écriture et absence* (Cistre, 1985), *Gertrude Stein* (Université Paul Valéry, 1980), *John Barth* (Université Paul Valéry, 1985) and *Robert Steiner: Une Rhétorique de la passion* (Belin, 2001). She has also written about 80 articles on literature and Lacanian theory .

GEOFF BOUCHER is Senior Lecturer in the School of Communication and Creative Arts at Deakin University, Melbourne, Australia, where he teaches literature and psychoanalysis. He is the author of *The Charmed Circle of Ideology* (re.press, 2009), co-author of *The Times Will Suit Them: Postmodern Conservatism in Australia* (Allen and Unwin, 2008) and *Žižek and Politics: A Critical Introduction* (Edinburgh University Press, 2010), co-editor of a collection of critical essays on Slavoj Žižek entitled *Traversing the Fantasy* (Ashgate, 2006), and author of several articles on Slavoj Žižek, Judith Butler and Jacques Lacan.

PATRICIA GHEROVICI is a practicing psychoanalyst at Philadelphia, USA. She is a senior member, analyst and supervisor at the Après-Coup Psychoanalytic Association, New York, USA. She is a founding member and director of the Philadelphia Lacan Study Group and Seminar. She was the clinical director of the Cumberland Life Center, a bilingual mental health outpatient clinic in the Latino ghetto in Philadelphia. She is the author of *Please Select Your Gender: From the Invention of Hysteria to the Democratizing of Transgenderism* (Taylor & Francis, 2010), as well as of numerous articles on the Lacanian clinic. She is the winner of the Gradiva Award in Historical Cultural and Literary Analysis and of the 2004 Boyer Prize for Contributions to Psychoanalytic Anthropology for her book *The Puerto Rican Syndrome* (Other Press, 2003).

RUSSELL GRIGG is Associate Professor of Philosophy, Deakin University, Melbourne, Australia, where he teaches philosophy and psychoanalysis. He is the English translator of *The Seminar of Jacques Lacan. Book III. The Psychoses, 1955–56* (Routledge, 1993) and *The Seminar of Jacques Lacan. Book XVII. The Other Side of Psychoanalysis, 1969–70* (W. W. Norton, 2007) and of numerous short pieces by Lacan, as well as the co-translator of the complete English edition of the *Écrits* (W. W. Norton, 2006). He is the author of *Lacan, Language and Philosophy* (State University of New York Press, 2008), co-editor of *The Other Side of Psychoanalysis: Reflections on Seminar XVII* (Duke University Press, 2006), and author of numerous articles on psychoanalysis and philosophy. He is the founder President of the Lacan Circle of Melbourne. He is a practicing psychoanalyst at Melbourne and a Member of the École de la cause Freudienne and the New Lacanian School, Paris, France.

JEAN-PIERRE KLOTZ is a practicing psychiatrist and psychoanalyst in Bordeaux and Paris, France. He is an analyst member of the École de la cause Freudienne and the New Lacanian School, Paris. He has extensively lectured on Lacan in different parts of the world and is the author of numerous articles on the Lacanian clinic.

CHRISTOPHER LANE is the Pearce Miller Research Chair of Literature at Northwestern University, USA, where he teaches literature and psychoanalysis. He is the author and editor of numerous books on literature and psychoanalysis, including *The Ruling Passion*: *British Colonial Allegory and the Paradox of Homosexual Desire* (Duke University Press, 1995), *The Burdens of Intimacy*: *Psychoanalysis and Victorian Masculinity* (University of Chicago Press, 1998), *The Psychoanalysis of Race* (Columbia University Press, 1998), *Homosexuality and Psychoanalysis* (University of Chicago Press, 2001), *Hatred and Civility*: *The Antisocial Life in Victorian England* (Columbia University Press, 2004) and *The Age of Doubt*: *Tracing the Roots of Our Religious Uncertainty* (Yale University Press, 2011). He has also written numerous articles on literature and psychoanalysis. He is the winner of the 2010 Prix Prescrire Prize for Medical Writing (France) for his book *Shyness*: *How Normal Behavior Became a Sickness* (Yale University Press, 2010).

JACQUES-ALAIN MILLER met Jacques Lacan in 1964 as a student of the École Normale Supérieure where Lacan began to give his seminar following his excommunication by the IPA in 1963. He founded the journal *Cahiers pour l'- Analyse* in 1966 whose editorial board included Alain Badiou, François Regnault and Jean-Claude Milner. In the same year he married Lacan's daughter, Judith Lacan. He became the Director of the Department of Psychoanalysis at the University of Vincennes, then St Denis (Paris VIII), a few years after its foundation by Lacan. He launched the journal *Ornicar? Bulletin périodique du champ freudien* in 1975 and was its editor in 1980 when Lacan dissolved L'École Freudienne de Paris and founded L'École de la Cause Freudienne. He is also the editor-in-chief of *Ornicar? Digital*. In 1964, he received Lacan's permission to establish texts out of the transcripts and recordings of his seminars. Since then he has established the texts out of all the seminars of Lacan, though not all of them have been published yet. Quite appropriately, he was chosen by Lacan as the sole editor of his seminars and other works. He has also been the supervisor of the English translations of Lacan's works. He began his own weekly course on Lacan in 1981 called 'L'Orientation lacanienne'; and since the early 90s his work began to be translated into English and published in the USA in the journal *Lacanian Ink* edited by Josefina Ayerza. In 1992, he set up the World Association of Psychoanalysis (WAP) in order to advance Lacan's teachings, transmit psychoanalysis, ensure the formation of analysts and guarantee their qualification and the quality of their practice. He is responsible for the massive expansion of Lacanian psychoanalysis in Spain, Great Britain, Italy, Argentina and Brazil. The WAP now has 1636 members across Europe, USA, Israel and Australia. Since 2001, he has moreover been working to secure the independence of psychoanalysis from government control in France. He is the director of the Département de Psychanalyse at the Université de Paris VIII, where he also teaches. He is widely recognized as the most eminent Lacanian psychoanalyst in France.

JEAN-MICHEL RABATÉ is the Vartan Gregorian Professor in the Humanities at the University of Pennsylvania, USA, where he teaches English, comparative literature, literary theory and psychoanalysis. He is also a Senior Curator at Slought Foundation based in Philadelphia, USA. He is the author of more than 20 seminal books and edited volumes on literature, psychoanalysis and literary theory, including *James Joyce: Authorized Reader* (Johns Hopkins University Press, 1991), *Joyce Upon the Void: The Genesis of Doubt* (Macmillan, 1991), *Lacan in America* (Other Press, 2000), *Jacques Lacan: Psychoanalysis and the Subject of Literature* (Palgrave, 2001), *James Joyce and the Politics of Egoism* (Cambridge University Press, 2001), *The Cambridge Companion to Lacan* (Cambridge University Press, 2003), *The Palgrave Advances to James Joyce Studies* (Palgrave Macmillan, 2004), *1913: The Cradle of Modernism* (Wiley-Blackwell, 2007), *The Ethics of the Lie* (Other Press, 2008), *The Future of Theory* (Wiley, 2008) and an introduction to a special issue of *Interfaces* called 'Architecture Against Death'. He has also written numerous articles on literature and psychoanalysis.

ELLIE RAGLAND is Professor of Literature at the University of Missouri-Columbia, USA, where she teaches psychoanalytic theory, critical theory, comparative literature and world literature. She is the editor of the journal *(Re)-turn: A Journal of Lacanian Studies*. She is the author of over 100 articles on literature and psychoanalysis, as well as of several important books and edited volumes on literature, philosophy and psychoanalysis that include *Lacan and the Subject of Language* (Routledge, 1991), *Essays on the Pleasures of Death: From Freud to Lacan* (Routledge, 1994), *Lacan and the Philosophy of Psychoanalysis* (Routledge, 1996), *Critical Essays on Jacques Lacan* (G. K. Hall, 1999), *The Logic of Sexuation: From Aristotle to Lacan* (State University of New York Press, 2004) and *Lacan: Topologically Speaking* (Other Press, 2004). She is a practicing psychoanalyst at Missouri-Columbia and an analyst member of the New Lacanian School and the World Association of Psychoanalysis.

MATTHEW SHARPE is Lecturer in the School of International and Political Studies at Deakin University, Melbourne, Australia, where he teaches philosophy and psychoanalysis. He is the author of *Slavoj Žižek: A Little Piece of the Real* (Ashgate, 2004), co-author of *The Times Will Suit Them: Postmodern Conservatism in Australia* (Allen and Unwin, 2008), *Understanding Psychoanalysis* (Acumen, 2008) and *Žižek and Politics: A Critical Introduction* (Edinburgh University Press, 2010), and author of numerous articles on psychoanalysis and philosophy. He is a founding member of the Melbourne School of Continental Philosophy.

SLAVOJ ŽIŽEK is a senior researcher at the Department of Philosophy, University of Ljubljana, Slovenia; professor at the European Graduate School, Saas-Fee, Switzerland; research project coordinator at the Kulturwissenschaftliches Institut, Essen, Germany; International Director, Birkbeck Institute for the Humanities at Birkbeck, University of London; and President of the Society for Theoretical Psychoanalysis, Ljubljana. He has been a visiting professor at, among others, the University of Chicago, Columbia University, London Consortium, Princeton University, New York University, The New School, University of Minnesota, University of California, Irvine, and University of Michigan. He is the author of numerous articles and about 60 books on Lacan, politics, philosophy and film. Some of his books are *The Sublime Object of Ideology* (Verso, 1989), *Looking Awry* (Massachusetts Institute of Technology Press, 1992), *Everything You Always Wanted to Know About Lacan But Were Afraid to Ask Hitchcock* (Verso, 1992), *Metastases of Enjoyment: Six Essays on Woman and Causality* (Verso, 1994), *The Plague of Fantasies* (Verso, 1997), *The Ticklish Subject* (Verso, 1999), *The Fright of Real Tears* (British Film Institute, 2001), *The Puppet and the Dwarf*:

The Perverse Core of Christianity (Masachusetts Institute of Technology Press, 2003), *Enjoy Your Symptom: Jacques Lacan in Hollywood and Out* (Taylor & Francis, 2007), *First As Tragedy, Then As Farce* (Verso, 2009), *How to Read Lacan* (Granta, 2011), *Living in the End Times* (Verso, 2011) and *Hegel and the Infinite: Religion, Politics, and Dialectic* (Columbia University Press, 2011).

Index